Praise for *First Ladies*

"A wonderful read for anyone who loves American history, and especially the genuinely 'inside story' of the various presidencies."
—Hugh Hewitt

"Fascinating, rarefied insights into each first lady."
—*Philadelphia Inquirer*

"This chronological account engages pairs of historians—including the exceptional Carl Sferrazza Anthony—in discussing the personality, marriage, passions, and legacy of each first lady, resulting in a fluid, conversational style. . . . This accessible account replaces stodgy depictions of stuffy, untouchable first ladies with the relatable, often tragic stories of the determined women who made it up as they went along, to the benefit of their husbands and country."
—*Publishers Weekly*

"An appropriate and valuable examination of the lives and roles played by the 45 women most closely identified with the U.S. presidency. . . . In this time when the role of all women in our society is undergoing a long-overdue sea change, the collection is especially valuable as an illustration of how these women adapted to, and contributed to, the presidents whose lives they shared."
—*The Washington Times*

"The book is a budding history buff's dream (and will likely make its readers the star of good party conversation at Mother's Day brunch)."
—*The Hill*

"Offers a rich trove of insights and anecdotes—some trivial, some profound—about the women who have occupied what is arguably the highest unelected political position in American society. . . . *First Ladies* is useful as a wide-ranging, rough-draft introduction to 'all the presidents' women.'"
—*Weekly Standard*

"Revealing while also riveting. . . . Susan Swain's carefully edited insights should carry a warning that reading one interview can lead to reading all of the others nonstop."
—*New York Journal of Books*

"An absolutely fascinating read."
—*The Erudite Lit-ite*

FIRST LADIES

ALSO FROM C-SPAN:

First Ladies

*Presidential Historians
on the Lives of 45 Iconic
American Women*

SUSAN SWAIN *and* C-SPAN

PUBLICAFFAIRS
New York

Hardcover first published in the United States in 2015 by PublicAffairs™,
an imprint of Perseus Books, LLC., a subsidiary of Hachette Book Group, Inc.

Paperback first published in 2016 by PublicAffairs

Extensive searches of copyright registration were conducted for all images
reproduced in this book. Every effort was made to obtain necessary permissions and
clearances. The editor and publisher apologize for any inadvertent oversights. If made
aware, acknowledgements will be updated in all future printings.

PublicAffairs books are available at special discounts for bulk purchases in the U.S.
by corporations, institutions, and other organizations. For more information, please
contact the Special Markets Department at the Perseus Books Group, 2300 Chestnut
Street, Suite 200, Philadelphia, PA 19103, call (800) 810-4145, ext. 5000, or e-mail
special.markets@perseusbooks.com.

Book design by BackStory Design

The Library of Congress has cataloged the hardcover as follows:
Swain, Susan.
First ladies : leading presidential historians on the lives of 45 iconic American women
/ Susan Swain and C-SPAN.—First edition.
    pages cm
  Includes bibliographical references and index.
  ISBN 978-1-61039-566-3 (hardcover)—ISBN 978-1-61039-567-0 (electronic)
1. Presidents' spouses—United States—Biography. I. C-SPAN (Television network)
II. Title. III. Title: Leading presidential historians on the lives of 45 iconic American
women.

ISBN 978-1-61039-717-9 (paperback)

E176.2.S84 2015
973.09'9—dc23
                                                                              2014047710
LSC-C

10 9 8 7 6 5 4 3 2

I get by with a little help from my friends...

C-SPAN is directing any royalties from the sale of this book to the non-profit C-SPAN Education Foundation, which creates history and civics teaching materials for middle and high school teachers and students.

CONTENTS

Contents

A NOTE TO READERS ON STYLE

This book is an outgrowth of C-SPAN's special yearlong history series, *First Ladies: Influence and Image* produced by our network between February 2013 and 2014.

During this series, each first lady had her own ninety-minute program (although certain early first ladies had only a segment within a program), generally featuring two historians/biographers as guests, with video and photographs from places associated with her life. Each chapter in this book has been crafted from the interviews with these programs' featured guests. Our goal with this book is to present a collection of expert opinions in those experts' own words. To achieve this, our interviews have been transcribed and then excerpted in a style consistent with many prior C-SPAN books. Questions have been omitted to achieve a conversational essay style. The transcripts were minimally edited in an attempt to preserve the individual voices and perspectives of our interviewees. As we edited, we took care to remain faithful to each contributor's original meaning. Brackets and ellipses were used where words or phrases were, respectively, added or deleted within paragraphs. An extra space between paragraphs in an essay signals that we pieced together non-sequential portions of the program in order to more cohesively tell the first lady's story.

The chapters presented here are long excerpts from our programs about the first ladies, but we did have to make choices about what to include. In keeping with C-SPAN's public affairs mission and our commitment to providing the public with the entirety of the programs we produce, the complete videos and transcripts of every *First Ladies* program in our series are available online at www.c-span.org/firstladies.

INTRODUCTION

From Martha Washington to Michelle Obama, most of the forty-five women you will read about in this book are famous because of the men they married. Nonetheless, many of the significant moments of our American presidents' lives were affected in no small measure by the contributions of their wives.

Martha Washington's tending to her husband's Continental Army troops and her skills at diplomacy helped George Washington's effort to successfully fight the British, setting the stage for his presidency. Abraham Lincoln's frontier style was polished by well-bred Kentuckian Mary Todd, who encouraged Mr. Lincoln's political aspirations even after his initial electoral defeats. In the early days of the twentieth century, Helen Taft actively lobbied President Theodore Roosevelt for her husband Will's advancement to the White House, even though it's commonly held that he preferred his eventual position as chief justice. By agreeing to marry him, widower Edith Galt lifted the spirits of the deeply grieving widowed president, Woodrow Wilson, as a world war loomed. And more recently, in the Johnson household, Lyndon's political aspirations were greatly supported by Lady Bird's business prowess. All of these presidential couples are framed in the public consciousness as partners, yet the life stories of the presidents tend to become the stuff of legends, while their wives' stories, and their contributions to American history, are much less well-known.

This is the reason why, for the better part of a year, from Presidents' Day 2013 through February 2014, C-SPAN took on the task of adding greater dimension to the biographies of the first ladies with a special series called *First Ladies: Influence and Image*, which I was privileged to host. This book is an outgrowth of the television series and both are unique in offering this wonderful collection of insights by fifty-six of the country's top contemporary authorities on first ladies.

A word on what you are about to read: the chapters in this book are not capsule biographies of the first ladies. Drawn from edited transcripts of our television interviews with our first lady experts, the chapters use the narratives of our contributors to add humanity and color to the basic facts of the first ladies' lives.

You will discover in this book several big themes that cross the generations of women who have occupied the White House. One is the frequent loss of presidential children, tragedies which struck first ladies Martha Washington, Mary Lincoln, Jane Pierce, Ida McKinley, Grace Coolidge, Jacqueline Kennedy, Barbara Bush, and others, reminding us that even those who live lives of relative privilege cannot escape the limitations of contemporary medical knowledge.

Through the lives of the first ladies, you will also be able to trace the evolution of the role of women in American society. Abigail Adams and Dolley Madison were of a generation imbued with revolutionary fervor; these women had a genuine sense they were building a new nation. This era was soon followed by tough-minded frontier wives like Rachel Jackson and Margaret Taylor who maintained family lives even as they confronted harsh new environs. Lucy Hayes is emblematic of Civil War women who went to the battlefields to tend to grievously wounded soldiers. She is also an example of Gilded Age wives who had no vote, few personal property rights, and who followed prescribed roles in society; these women had to maneuver within those norms to get things accomplished. Interestingly, in a bow to the notion of women's proper place in society, a number of first ladies of this era did not support the burgeoning women's suffrage movement.

The twentieth century, with its world wars and industrial revolution, brought enormous changes to society as a whole, and to women in particular. You will read about first ladies of that era, including Florence Harding and Lou Hoover, who broke new ground in their own accomplishments and in their early use of mass media to support their husbands' presidencies. In the 1930s and '40s, Eleanor Roosevelt's long and active tenure provides an obvious stepping-stone to our modern age of first ladies who are public figures in their own right, pursuing causes that are aided by their celebrity status.

In his foreword to this book, presidential historian Richard Norton Smith describes first ladies as being "closer to the unscripted dramas of personal struggle and family travail." And indeed, across the decades, you will read tales of ambition and sacrifice; of joy and loss; of concerns for privacy coupled with a political need for public exposure; of risks to personal security offset by a desire to connect with the public. Pay note to the first ladies' quotes highlighted in each chapter. It's impressive to see how often these women lament the loss of privacy and loss of self that accompanies this unelected, uncompensated role. Across centuries, first ladies' personal sacrifices, and those of their families, have often been a price paid for their husbands' political ambitions.

The *First Ladies* project was initially proposed to us by Mr. Smith. As C-SPAN's historical advisor, Richard cheerfully lobbied us for months to take on a series that would give every first lady, even those who have long slipped from modern consciousness, their due. As we mapped out our approach, he was joined by three other well-known first lady scholars to form the series' academic advisory team: William Seale, the White House Historical Association's historian, whose brain seems to brim with intimate details about presidential families; Edith Mayo, the curator who created the much-visited First Ladies exhibit for the Smithsonian Institution's Museum of American History; and Rosalyn Terborg-Penn, an expert on African American women and mid-nineteenth century history.

Our major partner for the television series was the White House Historical Association, which since its founding in 1961 with the support of Jacqueline Kennedy, has been the keeper of the history of the presidential manse and its occupants. WHHA's assistance was essential; they provided research help, ongoing promotional assistance, and, importantly, access to their vast image archives that enriched both our series and this book.

Terry Murphy, C-SPAN's vice president of programming, tasked Mark Farkas, our longtime executive producer of special series, with leading a small editorial team for the project. Video journalist Andy Och was dispatched to historic sites around the country, toting a small camera and a laptop for editing video. Andy dubbed himself "First Ladies Man" on Twitter, tweeting historical facts as he traveled. (Clearly, Andy had caught the first ladies bug.) We can't say enough nice things about the staff and volunteers we worked with along the way who support the various presidential homes, museums, and archives across the country. While these organizations vary greatly in size and funding, from the internationally recognized facilities at Mount Vernon, to the many sites preserved by the National Park Service, to small, independent homes like the Tylers' Sherwood Forest, they all share a dedication to preserving and interpreting the lives of our first families. These folks were of enormous assistance in our effort to bring the first ladies' lives to C-SPAN viewers.

Working on the *First Ladies* series was a real joy for all of us at C-SPAN. Particularly energizing was the community of series watchers who connected with us, and each other, via calls to our live programs and through social media. We heard about small viewing groups gathering in living rooms to watch each week's installment and of cross-generational family members who would make plans to watch the programs together and discuss what they learned. Particularly delightful were the on-air calls we received from viewers as young as eight who were watching the series with their families and learning about our first ladies.

Working on this book over the past several months created an opportunity for our small editorial team to reacquaint ourselves with this thoroughly enjoyable project. Our goal was to capture the very best of the television series for you in these pages. We hope our book will inform and entertain you and, most of all, entice you into learning even more about these intriguing women.

Susan Swain
Washington, D.C.

FOREWORD
Richard Norton Smith

"The study of history is useful to the historian by teaching him his ignorance of women."—HENRY ADAMS

Nineteen fourteen was a momentous year for American women in all their diversity. In May, President Wilson issued a proclamation establishing Mother's Day as a holiday along decidedly traditional lines. That summer, Margaret Sanger challenged tradition by promoting birth control in her newly founded journal, *The Woman Rebel*. Two thousand women tramped Fifth Avenue protesting Germany's invasion of neutral Belgium. The so-called "war to end war," though failing spectacularly in its stated justification, was to significantly redefine the role of American women in the workplace and the political arena, supplying the final impetus to amend the Constitution and extend to voteless women the same rights of self-determination for which their president would contend at the peace conference.

Woodrow Wilson, cherishing "exactly the right sort of wife," and the father of three daughters, did not lack for the woman's viewpoint. Both traditionalist and activist, exercising an influence all the more potent for its discretion, Ellen Wilson personified the Modern Woman, circa 1914. A preacher's daughter from Rome, Georgia, whose disdain for Sabbath entertainments recalled nothing so much as Sarah Polk's ban on dancing and Lucy Hayes's strictures against intoxicating drink, Mrs. Wilson was also a professionally schooled landscape painter. Her passionate attachment to Woodrow and their three daughters had not dulled her talents nor diminished her individuality. True, she looked askance at women's suffrage. And there were those who, recalling her Southern origins, believed her campaign to rid Washington of despairing neighborhoods with names like Slop Bucket Row and Constitution

Alley more a forerunner of Lady Bird Johnson's beautification campaign than the revolutionary civil rights laws passed by Mrs. Johnson's husband. Never mind: one-fifth of the capital's eighty thousand black residents called these back alleys home, and Ellen Wilson was the first first lady—or president, for that matter—to insist that attention must be paid.

In the nineteenth century, bachelor James Buchanan and his charismatic niece, Harriet Lane, had retreated to a cottage on the elevated grounds around the Soldier's Home, two miles north of the White House. Setting out from the same refuge one steamy morning in July 1863, Mary Lincoln was seriously injured when her coach turned over and she dashed her head against a rock. Ironically, the demands of her husband's job—the shared ambition to which the Lincolns had dedicated their energies since their earliest courtship—had prevented her husband from giving Mary the attention she craved. Abraham Lincoln was more likely to be found that week at the war department telegraph office, monitoring fresh intelligence from besieged Vicksburg and the savagely contested cornfields of South Central Pennsylvania.

It costs to be America's first lady. Half a century after Gettysburg, Woodrow and Ellen Wilson sought their own escape from the clammy embrace of a Potomac summer. The Wilsons had spent the summer of 1913 at a rented estate in Cornish, New Hampshire. Home to famed sculptor Augustus Saint-Gaudens and painter Maxfield Parrish, the verdant region bordering the Connecticut River held special attraction for Ellen Wilson. But Ellen did not return to Cornish in 1914. Bedridden with a kidney condition known as Bright's disease, her health deteriorated as July melted into August. By then, not even the prospect of a European war touched off by the murder of the Hapsburg heir to the throne of Austria-Hungary could distract Ellen's husband from the private tragedy unfolding in her second-floor bedroom overlooking the rose garden that was to be her chief embellishment to the White House.

On the morning of August 6, in deference to the dying first lady, Congress passed her slum clearance bill. (Like so many Progressive-era reforms, it, too, would fall victim to the European war, leaving another wartime president's wife, Eleanor Roosevelt, to take up the cause of Washington's slum dwellers.) Around five in the afternoon, Ellen Wilson's labored breathing ceased. An emotionally devastated Woodrow expressed the wish that someone might assassinate him. Amidst the public grief, a few paused to remember the more flamboyant heroism of another first lady. August 1914 marked one hundred years exactly since Dolley Madison rescued George Washington's portrait before British invaders could torch the president's house.

It may have been no coincidence that 1914 also marked the first attempt by the Smithsonian Institution to interpret America's first ladies. All but ignoring these women in either their public or private capacities, it presented them instead as "The Wives of the Presidents," their place in history largely defined by the clothes they wore, starting with Helen Taft's donated inaugural gown of white silk chiffon. There was irony here as well as ignorance, for Mrs. Taft hardly conformed to the demure domesticity of her era. In the Philippines, where her husband distinguished himself as America's first viceroy, Nellie did not hesitate to overturn racial barriers at social events, much as she would later welcome divorced persons to her White House entertainments. As befitting the co-founder and president of the Cincinnati Symphony Orchestra, Mrs. Taft sponsored regular Marine Band concerts for the public. Forget the Japanese cherry blossoms—and remember that it was Nellie Taft, an unlikely feminist, who employed her own bully pulpit to advocate for better working conditions for immigrant factory employees no less than for the clerks and typists who comprised the bulk of the federal workforce.

It costs to be first lady. Within weeks of her husband's 1909 inauguration, Nellie suffered a crippling stroke. It took years for her to regain the power of speech, yet she never lost her voice. In 1914, she was a former first lady, her spouse swept out of office in the Progressive-era tide that relegated him to third place behind Woodrow Wilson and Theodore Roosevelt. Bored with her new life in the college town of New Haven, Connecticut, Nellie blazed another trail by becoming the first first lady to publish her memoirs (*Recollections of Full Years*). Elsewhere that year, Edith Roosevelt nearly became a widow as her aging husband navigated Brazil's brutally hostile River of Doubt. Across the Atlantic, a mining engineer's wife named Lou Henry Hoover, the first American of her gender to earn a geology degree, assisted her husband, Bert, in organizing a campaign to feed ten million Belgians and residents of German-occupied France. Among those the Hoovers helped repatriate to America were the widow and teenage daughter of former President Benjamin Harrison.

In Marion, Ohio, Florence Harding encouraged her gregarious husband to run for the United States Senate, even as he carried on a long-running affair with a neighbor's wife. Simultaneously, Grace Coolidge, Vermont-born and college educated, was raising two young boys in a modest duplex in Northampton, Massachusetts. The monthly rent of $27 appealed to her thrifty spouse, recently elected president of the state Senate. Two years had passed since Grace chaperoned a local high school class on a trip to Washington, D.C. Little could she imagine returning there one day to live, or the terrible price she would pay for her years as first lady.

For everyone associated with C-SPAN's series on first ladies, this was a rare opportunity to personalize the past. Because we were interested in individuals more than institutions, we did not limit our narrative to the years each of these remarkable women lived at 1600 Pennsylvania Avenue. The best history wears a human face. Only by examining the full sweep of their lives against the backdrop of their times, its cultural context, and the evolution of their domestic relationships could we free America's first ladies from the lifeless textbook and popular mythology alike.

It is no accident that first ladies often outstrip their husbands in popular appeal, emotional access, and book sales. Closer to the unscripted dramas of personal struggle and family travail, they deal with the universal and the timeless. "I should not blame my own heart if it lost all faith in you. I hope it may not…but I shall not forever be telling you I love you when there is evidently no more desire for it on your part than present manifestations indicate." So Lucretia Garfield wrote her dashing congressman husband early in their marriage, when his wandering eye threatened to reduce future relations between the couple to a mere "business correspondence." Ultimately, James and Lucretia were bonded by a series of family tragedies—the loss of multiple children, and an assassin's bullet that forged a heartbreaking intimacy as the country looked on.

Historical patterns are elusive. For both Jane Pierce and Grace Coolidge, the sudden death of a child undercut an already strained marriage. For Jacqueline Kennedy, it seems to have had the opposite effect. Who knew that Mamie Eisenhower desegregated the White House Easter Egg Roll, or that Florence Harding anticipated People for the Ethical Treatment of Animals in her advocacy of animal rights? Who could imagine Lucy Hayes sending flowers to the funeral of Peggy Eaton, the woman at the center of an ancient scandal that nearly brought down Andrew Jackson's presidency? If they didn't know it before, C-SPAN viewers know now that Robert Kennedy credited Lady Bird Johnson with carrying Texas for the Kennedy-Johnson ticket; that Pat Nixon advised her embattled husband to burn his White House tapes; and that three first ladies in the twentieth century—Ellen Wilson, Bess Truman, and Betty Ford—struggled with the emotional legacy of a suicidal father.

Along with the new history, the series introduced viewers to new historians, perceptive interpreters like biographer Kristie Miller on Ellen and Edith Wilson; Annette Dunlap explaining the origins of "keyhole journalism" in a press corps besotted with young Frances Cleveland; and Catherine Allgor revealing "Queen Dolley" Madison's addiction to snuff. Bill Seale, without question the world's foremost authority on life in the White House, took us inside Julia Grant's kitchen and a controversy involving her husband's Army cook, whose most elaborate concoction was apple pie and cheese. And the incomparable Edith Mayo, more responsible than anyone for humanizing the women inside the Smithsonian's dress collection, gave definition to this more undefined of jobs. "As the most visible women in America," she writes, "the first ladies have evolved from the president's social and ceremonial partners to advocates of social causes and political allies in [their] own right." Edith Roosevelt put it even more succinctly, describing the first lady as "the perfection of invisible government."

History can be habit-forming; of this, I have been reassured by countless viewers of *First Ladies: Influence and Image.* "What am I going to do on Monday?" they ask, now that C-SPAN has completed its series. Of course, you can watch it all over again online, a useful exercise if only to more closely observe and admire moderator Susan Swain's amazingly deft juggling of phone calls, tweets, talkative as well as non-talkative guests, and her own prodigious homework. Or you can relive the series in the pages of this book, which preserves the most illuminating insights enhanced by an assortment of images, many provided by our series partners at the White House Historical Association. Here, you can experience vicariously over two hundred years of a history we are only now coming to appreciate for the sacrifice, courage under stress, personal style, and public grace that make America's first ladies a perennial, and deserved, subject of fascination.

FIRST LADIES

Martha Dandridge Washington

"I never goe to the publick place—indeed I think I am more like a state prisoner than anything else, there is certain bounds set for me which I must not depart from—and as I can not doe as I like I am obstinate and stay at home a great deal."

Martha Washington,
c1876

Born: June 2, 1731, Chestnut Grove, Virginia
Married: 1750–57, to Daniel Parke Custis (widowed); 1759, to George
    Washington (1732–99)
Children: Daniel Custis (1751–56); Frances Custis (1753–57); John (Jacky)
    Custis (1755–81); Martha (Patsy) Custis (1757–73)
Died: May 22, 1802, Mount Vernon, Virginia

Contributors:

PATRICIA BRADY, social and cultural historian specializing in first ladies and, in particular, the Washington family; author of several books, including *Martha Washington: An American Life*

RICHARD NORTON SMITH, presidential historian, executive director at five presidential libraries, author of several books, including *Patriarch;* history consultant for C-SPAN; academic advisor for C-SPAN's *First Ladies* series

PATRICIA BRADY: The opinion the public had of [the Washingtons] had begun with the Revolution. At that point, when Martha Washington would join her husband, as she did every year, at the Army's winter camps, people would just line up, be on every tree, on every fence post to look at her. She said, "I felt as though I were a very great somebody."

And she was somebody, for the first time, as his wife. The newspapers reported on how important it was for Washington to have her. So, when they came back as president and his lady, the public already had an opinion of them. They were singular characters. Other politicians were not in the same ballpark at all.

Martha went every winter to join him in the camps and to make a home, not just for him but for all the young officers who were on his staff, to encourage other officers to bring their wives and daughters to come and visit and make it a social time. Out of the actual eight years of the Revolution, she spent, overall, five years at the front.

RICHARD NORTON SMITH: Indeed, one of the things that fostered an emotional bond between Mrs. Washington and what would be the American people was the perception that she had sacrificed every bit as much as her husband during the war. This is another chapter in her training, in a sense, for being first lady. He was, in effect, for eight years, the closest thing to an executive the country had, and she was a first lady, of sorts. One touching story: they had one room on the second floor of the Potts House at Valley Forge, and they had an hour every morning that was sacred, one hour when they were absolutely not to be disturbed. Wouldn't you love to be a fly on the wall for those conversations, because undoubtedly, Washington unloaded a lot.

BRADY: Martha Washington wasn't just entertaining the Americans, she was entertaining officers from France, from Germany, and she was able to charm them. One particular French officer said it was so wonderful to be there drinking tea, singing, and just chatting. At the end of the evening, one would go home feeling better. Can you imagine feeling better at Valley Forge? She had charm beyond belief.

One thing that is really important from that time, and I know it sounds weird, is the change in her sewing habits. All American women sewed. Well-to-do women sewed embroidery, tapestry, and fancy work. When she was there and the local ladies came to call, she was not doing fancy work. She had the knitting needles out, and she was knitting socks for the soldiers. These were infantrymen and they marched on those feet, and they got holes in their socks. She must have knitted thousands of socks, and encouraged others to knit them, as well as raising the money to make linen shirts, which served as uniform shirts for them. She really, physically, in terms of her work, and emotionally, in terms of her leadership, helped support the troops themselves.

SMITH: There's a wonderful story where a group of women knew they were going to be calling upon the general's lady, expected this very grand figure, and to their astonishment, they found her knitting and wearing a speckled apron. So she clearly was not someone to stand on her position or on her title.

The decisions about what a republic was, what a president was, were inseparable from many of those that we would perhaps almost condescendingly today attribute to the East Wing of the White House. For instance, would the president and first lady accept private dinner invitations? Would the president and first lady go to private funerals? What do you call the president? What do you call his consort? The reason why these questions, which seem trivial to us today, matter is because each one of them in their own way defines the nature of this new government, which was a spinoff from its royal antecedents. Yet the country was split right down the middle, certainly between those who feared that it was in any way aping the British king, George III. Then, and two hundred years later, we have this dichotomy about what a president is. How close do a president and his wife get to us? The fact that Mrs. Washington had, every week, a Friday night reception that anyone could walk into as long as they were decently dressed, you certainly wouldn't find that in London. It helped to define not only her role, but in a larger sense, the access the Americans would have to their presidents.

BRADY: [The Washingtons made their decisions about how to comport themselves by] talking it out. People today see Washington always as this strong leader, cast in marble; but he was more than a statue. He always liked to talk to his associates. That's one reason he was criticized as a general, because he liked to talk to his staff before making a decision. In government, he thought that all the best minds of the country would get together, talk things through, and make the right decision, because we were the first modern republic. So, whatever they did mattered. It was important.

SMITH: One of the things that Martha Washington, frankly, found not altogether to her liking was the fact that she was uprooted from the agricultural, rural life at Mount Vernon that she'd been born into, that she had mastered and relished. And this is only the latest chapter of her sacrifice, which, in its own way, you could argue, matches anything that her husband sacrificed.

BRADY: That's true. She did not want to go to a city. She did not want to live in the North. She wanted to be home at Mount Vernon, but she had to be there with her husband to do what her husband wanted to do, so she gave it up. But the thing that made her so very unhappy was to discover, once she got [to the capital city], that Washington had consulted with John Jay, James Madison, and John Adams, and they had all decided that presidents could have no personal lives; that any entertainment, any going to visit people, any having people in, was, in fact, a public act....That was just for one year, but that first year was terrible for her. At the same time, it was pretty good for him, because Jefferson hadn't come back from Paris yet. That was probably Washington's honeymoon with the presidency.

SMITH: Offsetting that, there's a line that someone should carve over the entrance to the White House, because it goes to the heart of who this woman was, and why she was the ideal first first lady.... She talked about how the experience of her life had taught her that "our happiness or misery depends upon our disposition and not our circumstances." That is a remarkably wise observation, but it's an observation distilled from a life full of tragedy. She'd lost a husband, she lost all four of her children, she lost countless nieces and nephews, and then she found herself repeatedly uprooted from the life she expected, to follow George either on the battlefield, or on a different kind of battlefield.

BRADY: When they married, the Washingtons both felt the same way [about slavery]. They had grown up in Virginia. A good part of the wealth of Virginia was built on the labor... of enslaved black people, and so they agreed with it. At that time, Washington was rather strict with his slaves, but as time went on, his views started to change. He was the only one of the Founding Fathers who freed his slaves; the rest kept them until they died. Martha Washington's opinions didn't change. It was very unfortunate. I wanted it to be different, and so I looked for and read every word I could find, and the one slave she actually owned personally, she did not free. She left [the slave] to her grandson.

The truth is, Martha felt that [slave-holding] was the way society was supposed to be, and that [an escaped slave named] Oney Judge had let her down, because she'd always been kind to her. Martha didn't understand that Oney wanted to be free, that she wanted to learn to read and write, and that she wanted to find Christ in her own way.

Martha had three granddaughters, and the eldest one, Eliza, was fairly bad-tempered and was capricious, and nobody would have wanted to work for her, much less belong to her. When Oney Judge was told that...she would be going to be sent to live with Eliza when she got married, she decided enough was enough and took off.

SMITH: To round out the Oney Judge story, friends of hers smuggled her to Portsmouth, New Hampshire, and then there was this conundrum because Mrs. Washington wanted her back, and wanted the president to advertise for her return. It put Washington in a very awkward situation. [Intermediaries for the Washingtons urged Oney Judge to return, but she refused and lived out her life as a fugitive slave in New Hampshire.]

In a lot of ways, it can be said of Washington, as later on of Lincoln, that he outgrew the racist culture that produced him. One major reason was because during the Revolution, after having initially turned thumbs down to the idea of recruiting free blacks, the fact of the matter is that African Americans played a vital role in the winning of the Revolution. Washington saw firsthand what these people were capable of doing. He saw the courage. He saw the sacrifice. They were humanized in a way that, quite frankly, on the plantation was not possible. Life taught him a lesson, in some ways, very different from Martha.

BRADY: [George Washington's second term was a torment.] Yellow fever was killing people [in Philadelphia], right and left. Alexander Hamilton had a very bad case, but survived. But the real torment for Washington was to see that his friends and the men he respected, instead of all coming together to make a new form of government, were falling apart into two parties. He would never have believed that Jefferson and Madison and Hamilton would become enemies of one another, and that they would be doing everything that they could to keep each other out of office instead of working together.

[Abigail Adams was an important help to Martha Washington through all this.] They really had a lot in common. They were both wives who were partners; they were not wives who were stuck to the side and left out of everything, and both were deeply committed to the idea of this new republic. They were very political in that way. They also helped each other socially. Abigail was extremely tickled by the fact that her place [at the Friday levees] was to the right of Martha Washington, and if another lady came up and took her place before she arrived, the president himself would ask her to leave so that Abigail could sit there. She almost had a crush on Martha Washington. She said she was a wonderful person, which she was.

SMITH: Abigail, being an Adams, has left us some delightfully waspish accounts of life in Philadelphia, including the Washingtons' Friday night receptions. But the one person who escapes her occasionally harsh tongue invariably is Martha. She said of Martha Washington, there was "not the tincture of hauteur about her," which is a wonderful phrase. Even now, it does evoke the sense of this woman who could have been queen and George Washington, who could have been king, and not the least of their accomplishments is that each refused the crown.

BRADY: Martha Washington loved to read [the newspapers]. She read a lot, and when she didn't actually read the papers herself, Washington would frequently spend an evening reading aloud to her and whoever else was there. He would read a story and they would all talk about it.

SMITH: That doesn't mean she liked what she read. She came in for some criticism, but not personal criticism. Certainly one of the fissures from a very early day, even in New York, was this democratic with a small "d," Jeffersonian element, who were always on the lookout for anything that seemed monarchical. There were those who thought the president's weekly levee on Tuesday afternoon, and Martha's dinner every Thursday, and her Friday night receptions, and the fact that he rode in a carriage to Federal Hall...[indicated] aristocratic, if not royalist, inclinations, and [they] were always on the lookout for that. [So, the criticism] was not so much directed at the first lady, per se, as at the administration that she represented.

…Martha was a teenager when she became the fiancée of Daniel Parke Custis. He was twenty years older and was a bachelor because his dad never let him marry—nobody was good enough. Not only did she overcome this elite prejudice on the part of his father, but she helped bring Daniel into a real life in his late thirties with the children and everything else. But he was so much richer than the other people around them. She came from a lower-gentry family. She learned how to manage property and to manage money, things that would serve her really well for the rest of her life. She was smart as far as money went.

BRADY: [At age twenty-five, Martha became a very wealthy widow, perhaps the wealthiest in the Virginia colony, so she was quite a catch when she met Colonel George Washington.] He was such a hunk. He was six-foot-two in a time when most men were five-foot-eight, or five-foot-nine, a wonderful horseman, a wonderful athlete, fabulous dancer, very charming. He loved to talk to women his whole life long. He had begun to show the kind of leadership that he would later show more of. But in the estimation of those days, he was the lucky one: she was the catch, rather than he.

SMITH: But he would also be a real catch. Remember that she had four children by Daniel Custis, two of whom died quite young, and two of whom survived for now, and she had all that property, so George Washington would also fulfill vital roles as a partner.

BRADY: She could trust him because he was so clearly, from the time he was really young, a person of such integrity. As a widow, she was in fine shape because her husband did not leave any kind of trustee. She could do what she wanted to. It was much more common to leave your estate to male trustees; Custis just didn't get around to writing his will in time. But once women married, then they became *feme covert*, which meant that they were covered women and that all of their financial and any other kind of dealings were covered by their husbands.

SMITH: Martha had a dower portion of the Custis estate, which was a third that she had a lifetime interest in, and that included, in her case, about eighty-five slaves. The rest had to be managed for her children.

Washington said later on, famously, that in effect, he had adopted all her children. Washington loved children. Washington was rather sensitive to the fact that he had no children of his own.... He treated her children very much as if they were his own. It's interesting, by one estimate, she brought twenty thousand pounds to their marriage, and he spent a good deal of that immediately, sending away orders for toys, for wax dolls for Patsy, the daughter, and he spent quality time with them. And they lost both of them. It was a shattering experience. Patsy, who died, it's believed, of epilepsy one day at dinner in the Verdigris dining room at Mount Vernon, and then Jacky [died]. He had not participated in the Revolution until the very end, and joined his stepfather's staff, then came down with some kind of camp fever and died a few days later.

BRADY: From the time Martha first gave birth at eighteen or nineteen, she was a really wonderful mother. She doted on her children, her grandchildren, her nieces, her nephews. During the war with the young officers, young aides-de-camp, she was more or less like a housemother at a fraternity; she looked after these young men.... Forever afterward, the young men of those days remembered her as their foster mother.

The Marquis de Lafayette was another of the young men whom she became a mother to. When he came here, although he was the richest man in France, he was one of the most unhappy. He was escaping from persecution by his in-laws and by the court..... He was eighteen years old when she finally met him, and she saw him as another son. Lafayette saw part of that as what America was like, a place where people could be made over, and he could be made over.

SMITH: Lafayette is also one of the better observers who give us a window on the relationship between the Washingtons. He writes in a letter, "People ask, why did Martha spend every winter of the Revolution with Washington?" Lafayette said it was simple: "She loved her husband madly."

Mount Vernon was their North Star, the place they always wanted to return to, the place they were happiest. You know, it's remarkable... that after the president died, maybe the greatest sacrifice of all that Martha was asked to make, and yet the last ultimate [one], she was willing to have his remains removed from Mount Vernon and moved to the new Capitol building in Washington, D.C. Fortunately, that never happened. Bureaucracy took over.

The Marquis de Lafayette had a special relationship with the Washingtons, as depicted in this c1859 painting of Lafayette's 1784 visit to Mount Vernon.

Running Mount Vernon offered Martha an apprenticeship. If there was an ad for first lady in 1789, Martha Washington's prior experience really qualified her uniquely. If you go to Mount Vernon today, you notice there are two wings that were added during the Revolution, for which she oversaw the construction. There's the dining room, which is a very public space, and then there is a very private wing, which contains their bedroom and his study. They had six hundred different people a year, strangers, who showed up just because they wanted to see the most famous man on earth. They were all welcomed. They were all greeted. Most of them were fed. They were given a bed overnight. But even Washington got sick of the demands, so he would disappear in the evening. He'd go to his study and work, leaving Martha to converse with the visitors.

The fact that she burned all their correspondence is in some ways a metaphor. That's where they could be themselves. That's where they could say to each other what they didn't say anywhere else. One reason why she burned those letters is because that was the unvarnished George Washington. It wasn't simply the uniquely intimate relationship that existed between them. She was the only person on earth who could hear his doubts, his fears, and his opinions of his colleagues.

BRADY: Martha Washington was very careful with his papers, as was he. They were always kept in a big trunk. When they seemed they might be in danger, the trunk was removed. That building of his image, but a truthful image, having the letters showing him as a military man and as a political man, was important, but as far as she was concerned, their private life was just that...and she had not enough privacy in her life.

[Two Washington letters were found hidden in her desk after she died.] They were fabulous. They were both from him to her and they were written in 1775, in Philadelphia, when he has just accepted command of the Continental Army, which doesn't exist yet, of a nation which doesn't exist yet—without asking her. He's writing and saying, "My Dearest, I had to accept this. My honor required it. But please, my dear Patsy, don't be angry with me." He goes on and on about why it's important, and why she needs to support him. And before he goes off to become the leader of the war, he makes time to go out and buy some of the nicest new muslin in town so that she can make some nice dresses out of it. Now, that's a husband worth having.

SMITH: I don't think anyone reading those letters would subscribe to the still widely held view that their relationship was in some ways a businesslike one. This was a love match.

[George Washington was reputed to have had a special relationship with Sally Fairfax.] Here's a classic example of where Martha Washington did her cause no good by burning all of those letters. In the late 1950s, two letters were discovered, which the then-reigning biographer, James Thomas Flexner, made a great deal out of.

Sally Fairfax was the wife of George William Fairfax, who was a neighbor and close friend; some would describe him as Washington's best friend. They lived at Belvoir, just down the river. Clearly, there was an infatuation. Sally was slightly older and very sophisticated to someone like George, who wanted as a young man very much to be part of the colonial aristocracy and to advance in the British military. And so someone like Sally, who was even then unattainable, nevertheless held a special allure. Exactly what was the nature of that relationship is still being debated. We talked earlier about George Washington's integrity. It was something even then, so I don't think the relationship went beyond a lovesick young man.

BRADY: We don't disagree. There's no doubt when those two letters surfaced, you can't read them any other way but that he was a lovesick puppy.... I, too, don't think it went further than infatuation because he did care too much about his friend.... Those couples visited all the time. Sally Fairfax and her husband were there when Patsy Custis dropped dead after getting up from the dining room table, and were at her funeral. Then, in 1773, as it's becoming clear that a revolution is coming about, the Fairfaxes go back to England, never to return, so there's no continuing relationship beyond friendship.

SMITH: [Once the presidency ended], they were just glad to be home. Washington had very much wanted to leave after his first term, but allowed himself to be persuaded against his instincts that it was his patriotic duty [to stand for reelection]. It's safe to say Martha was not happy. Martha wasn't particularly happy that he took the first term. She recognized that it was unavoidable, and her life, too, had been caught up in that of her country. I'm not sure she would have divorced him if there had been a third term, but a third term was not in the cards from either one of those standpoints.

BRADY: George Washington twice had ailments that almost killed him during the time that he was president, and she was terrified that the presidency would literally kill him. When you think about every president we know, and you look at the pictures of when they start and eight years later, they [look] more than eight years older, for sure. It's a very aging job.

SMITH: Remember, Washington's success as president depended on his persuading everyone that he was not a political partisan. He didn't call it a federalist government; he called it a national government. He went out of his way to include all the sections of the country. Of course, Hamilton and Jefferson had their cockfight in the cabinet, much to his displeasure. He kept those people around him long after they wanted to leave. He made that sacrifice. He was willing to see himself pilloried in the press as a dupe of King George and someone who'd betrayed the Revolution, and Martha had to suffer all of this, in effect, vicariously. It's always been harder, in some ways, for a first lady or a presidential child to put up with the criticism than for the president, who accepts it as part of the job.

BRADY: She was involved [emotionally in the in-fighting], and she took Madison and Jefferson into hatred. She hated Thomas Jefferson once he started his newspaper campaigns against Washington. The reason Jefferson brought Washington into it, of course, was to defeat Hamilton. He said, "Oh, it's a shame how much the president suffers from these sorts of attacks, but it's necessary to build our party so, oh well." She never forgave him, never. Jefferson never realized that she was smart enough to see what he was doing, but she thought Jefferson was horrible, and the fact that he was elected president was shocking to her.

SMITH: Jefferson made the mistake of underestimating Martha Washington. The flip side of that is that Martha grew even closer personally, and finally politically, to the Adamses. And she was certainly glad that it was John Adams and not Thomas Jefferson who won the presidency to succeed her husband.

BRADY: Washington lived two years [after the presidency] and Martha lived two and a half beyond that. They had a great time. The house again had broken down, and things in the fields weren't being done the way he wanted them to be. He was experimenting with a million crops, and dealing with the grist mill, and the distillery, and all of the things he pioneered. She had to reorganize the housekeeping. But what's so interesting is that Mount Vernon became the symbol of the nation after they retired. There is no White House; that's not built yet. Washington, D.C., is building up, but it doesn't really exist as a large place. When foreigners and [other] important visitors come, what do they want to see? There's no building worth seeing in D.C. They want to see Mount Vernon, and they want to see Washington, and after Washington dies, they want to see Martha Washington and talk to her about what it was like. They see her as the living remnant of that history. So, they continue to have their posts until they die, both of them.

[After George Washington died, Martha left their bedroom and moved to a garret in the mansion.] When he died, she said, "It's over. My life is just waiting now." She really and truly did not want to be in that room, where they had been so happy. '

SMITH: She became, if anything, more secluded, certainly emotionally secluded. Her devotions became even more central to her day. Every day, she would walk down the path to the tomb, what's called the "old tomb," and pray. Basically, she was literally counting the days until she could be reunited with the love of her life.

Martha Washington's legacy:

BRADY: Martha Washington was the first, and she was one of the best. Those things always count. She was able to help George Washington make it through the American Revolution, and then two awful terms as president. She was his helpmate—always.

It's important to know how smart and how powerful she was, and how dependent he was on her. His achievements were his achievements, but having her there with him made them more possible.

SMITH: She defines influence in a way that perhaps contemporary Americans might have difficulty understanding. But the fact of the matter is, she was the most influential person on the face of the earth with the president of the United States.

Abigail Smith Adams

Abigail Adams, c1812

"In the new code of laws which I suppose it will be necessary for you to make, I desire you would remember the ladies and be more generous and favorable to them than your ancestors. Do not put such unlimited power into the hands of the husbands. Remember, all men would be tyrants if they could. If particular care and attention is not paid to the ladies, we are determined to foment a rebellion, and will not hold ourselves bound by any laws in which we have no voice or representation."

Born: November 11, 1744, Weymouth, Massachusetts
Married: 1764, to John Adams (1735–1826)
Children: Abigail Amelia (Nabby) (1765–1813); John Quincy (1767–1848); Susanna (1768–70); Charles (1770–1800); Thomas Boylston (1772–1832)
Died: October 28, 1818, Quincy, Massachusetts

Contributors:

EDITH GELLES, senior scholar, Clayman Institute for Gender Research, Stanford University; author of several books, including *Abigail and John* and *Abigail Adams*

C. JAMES TAYLOR, former editor-in-chief, *Adams Papers,* Massachusetts Historical Society

EDITH GELLES: [Abigail Adams is a historical figure in her own right] primarily because she left us letters, and we have a record of her life. But her letters are not ordinary, they're extraordinary. They're wonderfully written, and there are many of them. Abigail was a letter writer at a time when women couldn't write for publication. Her letters became her outlet. They are the best record we have of women's roles in the American Revolution and the period of the early national government of the United States.

C. JAMES TAYLOR: The Adams family gave the Massachusetts Historical Society a collection; we probably have seventy thousand-plus documents over several generations, and probably about three hundred thousand pages. For Abigail and John, which is the most important part of the collection, there are about 1,170 letters that they exchanged over the years. [How frequently they would write to one another] would depend.... For example, we don't have any letters after 1801 because after John leaves the White House, they are together almost all the time. But for periods when there's fairly regular mail delivery between Massachusetts and Philadelphia or later to Washington, D.C., they wrote at least once a week and sometimes twice a week....

GELLES: Abigail's letters have been in print and read since 1840, when her grandson first published an edition of her letters, which went through four editions in the 1840s. She was a bestseller through the nineteenth century. People knew her. She's always been famous.

TAYLOR: As early as 1776, John is telling her to put the letters up, to keep them. At a certain point, there's almost a consciousness in some of the letters, particularly his letters; they know, and I don't know when they cross that threshold, that they are important. This is one of the reasons that the family saves the letters.... Their letters extend from 1762 to 1801, almost forty years, and they are the most important forty years in American history. [The Adamses understood that they were players in history and were writing for the ages.]

GELLES: One of the important things to understand about Abigail is she started out as a naive young woman, whose expectations were to have a normal life, like her mother did. The Revolution disrupted that, and her whole life shifted. One of the reasons she has become so great a model for us as women is that she used the opportunity of this disruption in her life to grow as a person. She begins as a naive young woman, and she does become a very sophisticated, worldly, opinionated woman.

TAYLOR: This is one of the things that makes her most attractive. A good character in a novel develops over time, and Abigail is like a good character in a novel. She develops.

GELLES: She was the daughter of a minister, Reverend William Smith.... If there was nobility in the clergy and the political world of the Massachusetts Bay Colony, [this was it]. Her mother's family were Nortons and Quincys. She grew up in a household that was quite middle class for that time, and had two sisters and one brother. She was, by all reports, sickly as a child and therefore didn't go to any kind of public schooling, of which there were a few, but was educated at home by her mother, and she read at random in her father's library.

TAYLOR: [Abigail and John] met at her father's house. He went as a dinner guest with a lifelong friend named Richard Cranch, who then married [Abigail's] elder sister. Abigail was not yet fifteen at that time. John, at least in his diary, was not particularly enthusiastic about Abigail at first, but apparently things changed over the years. He was nine years older than her, twenty-three or twenty-four years old.

GELLES: [John Adams was a lawyer.] The family lore suggests that it wasn't [so happy about John's profession]. When Charles Francis Adams wrote about it, he suggests that her family disapproved of her marrying a lawyer. But she was also very young when she met him; they were being protective of her as well.

TAYLOR: [John's early interests were] very local. His trajectory was to be a great lawyer in Massachusetts. That's what he saw. He was following that line—and probably would have been one.

[Abigail became political] very early on. When John is active at the Continental Congress, she craves news and she wants the newspapers from Philadelphia. She wants pamphlets when they're published, so one of the things we know is that she's consuming the news at that time, all the news that was printed.... I would say that, by the middle 1770s, she's on board; she was an ardent revolutionary. She was very supportive not only of the Revolution, but of the fact that John was participating. They were partners in everything that he did. As a matter of fact, at some point he writes to her thanking her for being a partner in the activities. Later on, she is perhaps more conservative than John, in some ways, when it came to national politics.

GELLES: In one particular letter, Abigail was ruminating about conditions in her life and what was going on in her world, and she says, "I long to hear that you have declared an independency...." She knew John was on this [congressional] committee. "...And, by the way, in the new Code of Laws which I suppose it will be necessary for you to make, I desire you would remember the ladies and be more generous and favorable to them than your ancestors." This is a bold and remarkable statement for a woman to have made in that era.

My sense of Abigail is that she wrote at night, and she would enter a kind of reverie in which she just followed her thought pattern wherever it went. She changes topics in her letters very many times. [This particular letter] starts out with a political statement about why the Southerners can favor slavery and still be doing a rebellion against a tyranny, and she questions that. Then she moves on and in the middle of a paragraph, makes this "remember the ladies" statement.... John was actually in a position to do something, to make change, because he was on the committee that was drafting the Declaration of Independence. So he actually could have made a move for women's rights at that time. It's remarkable that she did suggest that.

TAYLOR: I am sure that before John rode off to Philadelphia, she filled his ear with a lot of ideas along the way. But John, in his response, notes that there are several groups of people, servants, slaves, etc., who are also moved during this time to think about their rights and independence.

...Probably in the Adams household, there were a lot of kitchen table discussions between John and Abigail. Abigail may not have been most obvious in making the decisions, but she influenced John a lot. We know that, much later, after the Revolution, when he has his political career, that she's very influential in helping him formulate some of his ideas.

GELLES: .... In this one letter, she brings out so many ideas that her threat to foment a revolution is indicative of one of the ways the Adamses related to each other. They teased each other. His response to her was a tease also. He writes, "It sounds to me as if 'every group, any tribe is going to make a revolution.'" Jokes are a way people have of de-escalating an argument and bringing it down to normal; it's really one of the ways in which they related.

This is one of the most appealing things about John and Abigail, and some of the other Adamses. They have a life that you can follow because of the documents. You see them in good times and in bad. You see death in the family. You see triumph.... It's a wonderful story and the reason [we know this] is because we have these documents; there's texture there that you don't have with the other founders.

TAYLOR: [In America in the late seventeen and early 1800s] ...there is an expansion going on. This is one of the things that is very difficult for the Adamses because politics are changing. They are New Englanders, they are Federalists. As time goes by, and as the population moves south and westward, it makes it more difficult for the politics that they believe in. Abigail was opposed to slavery. She had a black servant who had been a slave of her father's. Abigail cared for the woman, Phoebe Abdee, for the rest of her life after her parents died. In fact, Phoebe lived in the Adamses' house when they went to Europe.

GELLES: Abigail was a very religious woman. In times of turbulence, when things went wrong in her life, she thought it was a case of punishment. When there was an epidemic during the war years when John was away and people were dying, and her servants were sick, she said, "It's a scourge sent upon us." She truly believed that life was providential. Her letters continually referenced the Bible. When things got bad in her life, she became more religious and more conservatively religious.... She was probably more conservative in her religion than John Adams.

For the first decade of their marriage, Abigail and John lived together. It was during this decade that events happened that escalated towards war. This was a simultaneous parallel occurrence at the personal level and at the more global political level....There was danger once Lexington and Concord had happened, once there was fighting in the Massachusetts Bay area. More than that, they didn't know if there would be danger. They never knew where the next troop deployment was going to happen, so she was ready at any minute to move away from the house, to move inland, to take her children and bring them to safety.

From 1774 until 1784, they were apart most of the time. He came home a couple of times for a couple of months, but during that time, she was mostly alone on the farm, by herself, bringing up the children.

[John wrote to Abigail: "We live, my dear soul, in an age of trial. What will be the consequence, I know not."] This is a wonderful quote because they had no idea that there would be war, although they suspected there would be. They did not know its duration. They did not know it would separate the colonies from the mother country, all of the things that we now take for granted.... He is saying, "We don't know what is going to happen."

TAYLOR: John Adams was very concerned [about his family when he was away]. There's one heart-wrenching period where she's pregnant and she's writing right up until the time when she begins labor. Because of the time and distance, which is something that is so hard for us to understand now with our instant communication, he's writing back, hoping that's she's going to have a daughter and that everything will be fine. In the meantime, the infant is born dead. Abigail had a premonition that this was going to happen. So while he's writing happily, joyfully, she has buried this child. John knows that Abigail is capable of doing almost anything that a woman or a man could do during that time, but there's still a certain helplessness on his part. He's so consumed by what he's doing in Philadelphia, but then reflects and sends letters saying, "Kiss little Tommy and Johnny." A lot of it is very, very emotional.

GELLES: At the end of her life, when her daughter-in-law, Louisa Catherine, lost a child, and the daughter-in-law was in St. Petersburg, Russia, Abigail wrote to her and for the first time that I've seen in her correspondence, made a reference to having lost a baby daughter. It was a closed topic.

Charles, [one of the Adamses' sons, died of alcoholism]. People did not know about alcoholism in those days, and it was considered sinful. It was not considered a disease. Charles is, throughout the correspondence, treated as a person who was sensitive. He went to Europe with his father and John Quincy in 1779, and he had to come back because he was homesick. Thereafter, every reference that one sees about him is that he was a sweet child, a very pleasant child, but also fragile. He may have gotten into some trouble when he was in Harvard, so his life was irregular.

TAYLOR: You know from the correspondence between Abigail and her sister, for example, that they kept an eye on Charles, that there was a problem, and it's never fully discussed. One of the things that was difficult for young Abigail was that her brother was an alcoholic and had left his family.

GELLES: John Adams was vice president for eight years. Abigail moved to New York for one year, because New York was the capital for the first year. She loved it. She had a beautiful house on the Hudson, overlooking New Jersey. She was also happy because her daughter lived nearby. Then she moved to Philadelphia, and she spent the entire year ill. It was not a good climate for her, and her health was always precarious. They decided after that year in Philadelphia together, that she would stay at home. There wasn't really a precedent for the second lady, the vice president's wife, to be living with the men. It was by choice. So, Abigail had the liberty to choose to go home, and she did for the next six years.

TAYLOR: Abigail was not at all [a national figure at that time]. She was known because she had been the wife of the minister to Great Britain. One of the problems that they had was that people thought that they were monarchical, that they had been tainted by their time in Europe. This is one of the interesting things about Abigail. She grows up a minister's daughter, and at some point she's at Versailles and the Court of St. James, so she's an extraordinarily sophisticated person by that time, much more so than Martha Washington. Martha Washington was American elite; Abigail was international.

GELLES: Abigail loved Martha Washington. Abigail met Martha when she was the wife of the vice president. Whenever they had social events, they were very close. Whenever she wrote about Martha, which wasn't much, but when she did, it was in the most glowing terms.

TAYLOR: One of the things she did just after she knew John was going to be elected president, she wrote to Martha Washington asking her about how to be the first lady, about etiquette, and how she would carry it out.

GELLES: We know that Martha wrote back and said, "You know inside yourself how to behave."

When Abigail referred to the presidency as "a splendid misery," it meant…splendid in that they were at the pinnacle of his political career and her career. They had risen to the top, but it was nothing but trouble, agonizing trouble from the very beginning. At very first, John was enthusiastic about becoming president, and Abigail said, "I'm going to stay here in Quincy because I've got things to do." She was taking care of John's mother and said, "I won't be there until October." He said, "That's fine, you don't have to come until October." Once he was in the presidency, he discovered that it was the loneliest place in the world. He started writing letters saying, "Drop everything you are doing. Come here, I need you immediately." And she did.

TAYLOR: One of the interesting things, one of the reasons she was hesitant about [coming to the capital city] is, she said, "I like to be outspoken, I like to speak my piece." She knew in that context she couldn't, but when she was in Quincy, she could.

GELLES: Abigail became ill in 1798 and went home again, and had to stay in Quincy for an extended time. John followed her, and he stayed there for too long, according to his cabinet members, who finally urged him to come back to Philadelphia, which was then the capital…. She was quite ill for close to a year, and possibly close to death during that time.

TAYLOR: The major problems were international. There were also internal political rifts, and you have the creation of political parties in America, the two-party system. We had problems with the British; particularly, we had problems with the French. American political parties were divided between pro-French and pro-British, and one of the things that John was troubled with during this time was keeping the country out of war. He was successful, and that is probably the thing he should be most recognized for during those years.

GELLES: This also subverted his career, because the politicians of the time were, maybe like politicians forever, enjoying the exercise of making war. They were very close to war; the population, in general, was outraged by the piracy that was going on. American ships were being taken on the seas, and American diplomats were being badly treated, in France, especially. The French Revolution had happened. John Adams kept us out of war.

TAYLOR: The Alien and Sedition Acts were a reaction to some of the international problems of that time. There was a belief on the part of some people that we were about to be overrun by French revolutionaries and that they were influencing people in America. There were rumors that our cities were going to be burned; it was terrorism that they were anticipating.

The opposition party, the Democratic-Republican Party, and Jefferson, in particular, was very enthusiastic about the French and the ideals of the French Revolution. This is where [Jefferson and Adams] begin to go in different directions. Also, some of the press was very vehement in their criticisms of the administration. So, they muzzled the press, and this is the thing that John Adams is probably most criticized for.... The act came out of Congress and Adams signed that legislation. Abigail was even more vehement, even more conservative, than John was at that time.

GELLES: Historian Page Smith has said that the press was the most scurrilous at this time in American history.... They made up stories that were not true, and the Adamses were seriously worried about this. It should be said that Jefferson also supported the Alien and Sedition Acts, except that he believed that the states should be passing sedition laws, not the national government. He was in favor of states' rights, which was part of what separated [Adams and Jefferson]. Also, at that time, people didn't have the same horror about suppressing the press that we have today.

TAYLOR: Abigail probably took [newspaper criticism] as part of politics, but she was much more defensive about her husband. Abigail didn't have great ambition for herself, but she had great ambition for John and she had great ambition for her boys, particularly John Quincy. She was very defensive of him. This is one of the reasons why the relationship with Jefferson is so difficult, because she had really loved Thomas Jefferson as a friend, and Jefferson turned on her husband.

GELLES: [In 1800, the Adamses became the first presidential couple to inhabit the White House.] It was pretty miserable. They did not have

The Adamses were the first presidential family to live in the White House, which was woefully unready for comfortable living, as this 1966 painting of laundry being hung in the East Room depicts. *Credit: White House Historical Association*

heat. They had to gather wood, such as it was in that area, and stoke fires in the fireplaces. The mansion was not finished when they moved in. Abigail describes Georgetown as "a swamp"; the city was not yet built. It affected the way she entertained. It affected her entire role as first lady in that she was limited by what she could do in that drafty, cold, uncompleted house. They had one stairway they could use to go to the second floor.

TAYLOR: In 1800, by the time the electoral vote was counted, they pretty well knew that John was not going to be reelected. They were disappointed. One of the things that John said throughout his public life was that he was always going to go back to the farm and retire. He loved the farm, so, in that sense, it wasn't so bad. It was the defeat of his ideas in what some people referred to as the "Revolution of 1800" [that was most painful]. John did not attend the Jefferson inauguration. Some people say it was because he was being spiteful. Those of us who defend Adams say he had to catch an early stage[coach] to get back. The truth might be somewhere in between. [Probably the hardest thing] was that a man who, in a sense he felt had betrayed him, had defeated him.

GELLES: Abigail lived until 1818, and so they lived together for another eighteen years. They were idyllic years in some ways, and very difficult in other ways. It was not an easy retirement. They were very happy to be together. Abigail refused to go visit her daughter because she said, "I can't leave John. I'm not going to leave John." Her daughter had a mastectomy without anesthesia, and came from New York state to her parents' home, to die. So, it was a time of satisfaction and peace and also, very great disruptions in their lives. They had problems with grandchildren and children. There was constant drama going on. One grandson went off and fought in a revolution in Venezuela and John refused to bail him out.

[After Abigail died at age seventy-four,] John was surrounded by family. He was not isolated. He had always, as his house hostess and care-taker, a niece who lived with him and had lived with them for most of her life. Grandchildren came and children came, so there was always traffic through the house; people came and the militia came from Boston. There was a lot going on during those years. He was quite palsied and he couldn't write his own letters, so he had someone write for him, but he carried on this incredible correspondence with Jefferson during those years. [Their letter writing culminated with these two bitter enemies coming to peace with one another, and both dying on the same day, the fiftieth anniversary of the Declaration of Independence.]

Abigail Adams's legacy:

GELLES: Abigail Adams was influential. As we think back to the American Revolution, she's the only woman. Her record of letters provides the only insights we have at a sustained level during that entire period of the Revolution and the early national period. So, she's historically significant. She is also an exemplary person who tells us about women's lives in that time and what it was like to be, not just first lady, or not just the wife of the American minister, but to be a wife and a mother and a sister and a daughter.

TAYLOR: The thing that I always think about with Abigail is the relationship, the partnership. Without Abigail, there's no John; without John, there's no Abigail. With the kind of support she provided to him in Europe, in the presidency and the vice presidency...he could go off and be this great public person, which is exactly what she wanted.

Martha Wayles Jefferson

Martha Jefferson Randolph, c1830, namesake of her deceased mother, and the official hostess of the Jefferson Administration. *Courtesy Monticello/Thomas Jefferson Foundation; by Thomas Sully*

Born: October 19, 1748, Charles City County, Virginia
Married: 1766–68, to Bathurst Skelton (widowed); 1772, to Thomas Jefferson (1743–1826)
Children: Martha (Patsy) (1772–1836); Jane Randolph (1774–75); unnamed son (1777); Maria (Polly) (1778–1804); Lucy Elizabeth (1780–1781); Lucy Elizabeth (1782–1785)
Died: September 6, 1782, Monticello, Virginia (twelve years before the Jefferson presidency)

Contributors:

CATHERINE ALLGOR, professor of history, University of California Riverside, specializing in Early America and political women; author of numerous books, including *Parlor Politics*

WILLIAM SEALE, White House historian; author of many books, including *The President's House;* editor, *White House History;* academic advisor for C-SPAN's *First Ladies* series

WILLIAM SEALE: Martha Wayles Jefferson was from a well-to-do planter's family, the Wayleses. She had slaves and land. [Thomas Jefferson] basically married minor wealth in Virginia, which he did not come from. Jefferson was no businessman at all...he acquired plantations, but he didn't know how to run them very well, and a lot of what he had came through her. His father was a surveyor and acquired a tremendous amount of land out west in Charlottesville. Martha was from closer to the coast.

They were very happy together. Thomas was very much in love with her, and Martha's death was devastating to him. It was unexpected and happened very quickly, and he was a grieving widower despite what popular fancy may say. He never really got over the loss of his wife.

Of their six children, there was only daughter Martha (known as "Patsy") left. Patsy's husband, Randolph, was later governor of Virginia, but he wasn't much of a son-in-law. He had, I wouldn't say it was a drinking problem; he was just a drunk. The household was not harmonious because of that; it was very much dominated by Jefferson and a worshipful Patsy.

Monticello was an unfinished house because Jefferson never had the money to furnish it, so I don't think it was an altogether happy situation. Jefferson used to step into his study and lock the door and spend all of his hours there. Patsy's husband straightened out when Jefferson died, and did okay. There was always some sort of tension there with the three of them together.

Martha "Patsy" Jefferson Randolph was tall and pretty with golden hair and, according to Margaret Bayard Smith, who wrote many memoirs at the time, she handled herself beautifully. She made a great thing of her father. There's a description of her going to a dinner in later years and she passed a room and said, "Oh, that's where my father died," for all of the crowd [to hear]. She definitely pumped up the fact that she was Jefferson's daughter. Altogether, she was a woman who handled things very well. Yet, when Jefferson died, Monticello just fell apart, and all the contents were auctioned off and they lost the place. The continuity wasn't there, as it was in some other families.

[Patsy served as Jefferson's White House hostess] very briefly. Dolley Madison is often said to have been the pinch-hit hostess, but scholarship has proven that Jefferson really had no one there. Jefferson looked on the [presidency] as a work experience…. He really only wanted to be in one place, and that was Monticello. At the White House, he constantly had dinners, not big ones, in what is now the Green Room. It was usually all men, and it was all business…. Now and then there were big dinners and Dolley Madison did pinch-hit. She was the wife

Thomas Jefferson (standing) and family at breakfast at the president's beloved Virginia home, Monticello, with James and Dolley Madison. *Credit: Thomas Jefferson Foundation at Monticello; watercolor by G.B. McIntosh*

of the secretary of state. She was very much in the background, though. Then, toward the end of his administration, his daughter would come. I don't know how much help she was, but he was just tickled to have her.

Jefferson lived in the White House as a house. He lived in one section of the first floor with his bedroom upstairs. There is a famous encounter of him with the British minister who came to call at the White House. Jefferson was in undress, which doesn't necessarily mean he was in his pajamas; it means he was in everyday clothes. He had worn overshoes and had no wig because he didn't wear a wig, normally, and he wasn't powdered. A great to-do was made out of it, but the greatest to-do was made by the minister's wife, who wasn't even there. Mrs. Elizabeth Merry was very obnoxious about it; Minister Anthony Merry understood. His letters home to the foreign office in England said he understood what Jefferson was doing; he was illustrating this republican simplicity idea. So the real issue was Mrs. Merry; finally, Jefferson said, "She will either conform, or eat her soup alone." He did not tolerate her.

In Europe, the White House would not have been a palace by any means. It was what Washington had wanted: a suitable house for the first gentleman of the land. Jefferson simplified it in the sense that the state dining room, or the levee room, became his office. When you read his inventory at the end, it wasn't all that simple. Where he bought all this stuff, or acquired it, I do not know, because the receipts were not in the government records. It could have been that these records were burned in 1814, but it became quite elaborate. He wanted people to come in and he opened the White House to the public in the spring of 1801. When the expeditions came back, Lewis and Clark and Pike, they all brought things and he made a sort of museum in the entrance hall with Indian headdresses and the skins of huge bears that no one could imagine, and horns and peace pipes. There were even two real little bears which were brought back in saddle bags from the Rocky Mountains. Jefferson fell quite in love with the little bears, and when [portrait artist] Charles Wilson Peale took them to his museum in Baltimore and killed them and mounted them, Jefferson was quite disappointed. He said they had known no friend but man.

Jefferson's big presidential receptions would have been for Fourth of July, where he announced the Louisiana Purchase in 1803, and New Year's. He honored those traditions, but he didn't have other big receptions. That was to come later, even later than the Madisons. The White House wasn't finished, the East Room wasn't finished; there really wasn't a big room to use. Jefferson had his big dinners in the White House entrance hall with all his peace pipes and other things. Patsy was his hostess because she was the lady of the house. The enslaved African Americans that came from the farm, the house servants from Monticello, would have been there, too. In fact, Jefferson complained about them because there were too many personal associations, and he couldn't fire them and send them home. He said it would work much better with employees because he could fire them, and so there was that difficulty. Patsy must have assumed some management because she was a capable individual.

Jefferson believed in Republican simplicity. The Federalists had imitated royalty, not to a great extent, but to an extent in the demeanor of the presidency with their ceremonies, their formalities. In part, it was to please the diplomatic community who were needed to support this country. Jefferson had been in France during the [French] Revolution when equality of man was very symbolic...and he came back to the United States and was horrified [by what he was seeing in the new capital]. He said, "There is everything but crowns here." He provided one of the best descriptions of one of George Washington's receptions. It was a reception for Jefferson, and Jefferson clearly didn't approve of it. When Jefferson got to the White House, he just cut it all off. He had no ceremonies, and people dined at a round table...where all were supposedly equal; however, Jefferson did all the talking.

CATHERINE ALLGOR: Jefferson's social program, if you will, is not an accident. He was not interested in power sharing. He was interested in securing his own political power. He had dinner parties with men of one party or the other. He would sit with his group, the Republicans, as they were called, and he would keep *au courant* and rally his supporters. Then there would be a dinner party with the opposition, the Federalists, and that was all about keeping an eye on the enemy.

Dolley Madison's role in the Jefferson Administration is not the big story of that time. Jefferson had been to France, and he had seen women at social events. He was horrified and shocked, especially about their political power, because it fell outside the [framework of] official power. So he cut off all these events and the White House was open only for Fourth of July and New Year's Day. That was partly because he wanted to curtail the power of women.

However, there was something else going on at the [Madisons'] house on F Street: Dolley Madison setting up the connections and networks she would bring to the White House. So during the first years of Jefferson's administration, the center of social and political life was not the White House, or the President's Mansion as it was called, but Dolley Madison's house on F Street.

What's significant is that Thomas Jefferson seemed to love Dolley even though she is conducting this social circle under his nose. He is a great hater; nobody hated like Thomas Jefferson. So, the fact that he seemed to really adore Dolley speaks volumes about her.

Hostess Martha Jefferson Randolph's legacy:

SEALE: [Martha] "Patsy" Jefferson...took her place at the head of society, and she was very popular in Washington, very liked as the president's daughter, but her main role was to be there with Jefferson. She lived in the White House, was with him, and had breakfast with him and was what was left of his family.

Dolley Payne Madison

"And now, dear sister, I must leave this house or the retreating party will make me a prisoner in it by filling up the road I am directed to take. When I shall again write to you or where I shall be tomorrow, I cannot tell."

Dolley Madison, c1873

Born: May 20, 1768, New Garden Quaker Settlement, North Carolina
Married: 1790–93, to John Todd (widowed); 1794, to James Madison (1751–1836)
Children: John Payne Todd (1792–1852); William Temple Todd (1793)
Died: July 12, 1849, Washington, D.C.

Contributors:

CATHERINE ALLGOR, professor of history, University of California Riverside, focus on Early America and political women; author of numerous books, including *A Perfect Union: Dolley Madison and the Creation of the American Nation*

EDITH MAYO, curator emerita, First Ladies exhibit, Smithsonian National Museum of American History; academic advisor for C-SPAN's *First Ladies* series

CATHERINE ALLGOR: The paradox of Dolley Madison [is that] you understand her as an eighteenth century woman, raised in a certain culture, but when she becomes first lady, she starts adapting the past in a way that paves the way for modernity, and she also creates the first lady role that we have come to know. Every modern first lady, everybody all the way up, looks to her; so, in some ways, she's definitely a product of her time, but she opens the door for a lot of women.

There were two big stories about this era and the first one is disunion…. The Early Republic—this is what we call this time period—was a time of great anxiety. Nobody was sure that this union was going to hold. In fact, people at the time would refer to the United States in the plural. They would say, "The United States of America are," which signaled that it's not quite holding together. There is a real fear that it's going to fall apart. One of the sources of this disunion might be what they called regionalism; later, they're going to call it sectionalism as they head toward the Civil War. James Madison's primary political goal is unity. If we keep that in mind…Dolley Madison's work is going to become understandable.

Madison was the idea guy. He was very theoretical, and he and other members of the founding generation understood unity as a concept and that it was their number one job. But how do you bring forth unity? What Dolley Madison did, along with other women of the time, is take these abstract concepts and translate them into action, so she's enacting unity on this national stage…. She brought people together. She launches her drawing rooms: Every Wednesday night, it doesn't matter if your vice president has died; there will be a drawing room. She put people in that room together. That sounds nice, but this is about more than just nice. For the Early Republic, it's a time of survival. This feeling of disunion is exacerbated in Washington because all of these regionalisms come together with the most fractious Congress that we've ever had. These are people who didn't just disagree with each other, they dueled and fought each other, not just in the streets, but on the floors of Congress. That's why bringing people together and having them see each other as humans is not just lovely, but crucial.

EDITH MAYO: Dolley Madison's drawing rooms were very different from what [her predecessors] had done. Theirs were extremely formal. Dolley's was much more open. You had everybody at Dolley's drawing rooms able to have access to the chief executive and his lady, and that's very important for forging a unity in the United States. Dolley starts out as the wife of [Jefferson's] secretary of state. What she is doing is forging networks—social networks—on which politics and diplomacy can be conducted in a civilized manner through the ceremonial forms of dinners, receptions, and parties so that some of these tensions and animosities that play themselves out in the halls of Congress have a way of being resolved at parties in an amicable way. She really is forging new networks that will work for both politics and society.

ALLGOR: The founders understood that this American Revolution that they had was more than just a political revolution. They were going to—and this is a phrase they loved—"build the world anew." That meant everything was under consideration; this was going to be the new world and they were going to scorn everything of the old world—absolute kings and monarchies and courts. And so, they turned to the women. This is actually a political theory called the Scottish Enlightenment, which says that in a culture, laws can come and go, but what they call "manners," stay. Manners are not just teacups, but the way people treat each other, how they regard each other, and how they behave. This is very appealing to these new Americans; for one thing they are inventing a whole bunch of laws they are not sure people are going to buy and they really need people to behave. So the phrase they use is "republican virtue." That meant that people would put the interests of their country before themselves. How do you get people to do that? They look to the women of this class to start enforcing what they call the "national manners." This is a very important part, and these women, these elite white women of the cities, were very conscious of that.

MAYO: Washington, D.C., was a very muddy place. Abigail Adams had written home that it was the very dirtiest hole of a place that she'd ever been in her life. The roads were rutted; the houses were separated far apart. It's very rudimentary. Part of what Dolley is doing is building a social network among the women so that a lot of this is overlooked. Politics and diplomacy and fashion can carry people over the fact that they are not living in some fantastic capital of the world.

ALLGOR: ....We have one of [Abigail Adams's] letters, about 1816, quite far into Abigail's life. She writes asking for a favor of Dolley Madison, and says, "Even though we have never had the pleasure of an acquaintance," so we know they probably didn't meet. But what's so interesting is that Abigail is asking Dolley Madison for patronage, that is, to give a job to a relative. Sometimes you ask why we study women's history, why we study first ladies, and the big answer for me is that we learn things you just wouldn't know otherwise. If you look at Dolley Madison, you understand there's a huge patronage network. Men will not touch patronage. It's too royal, it's too courtly, it's too corrupt. But their wives and daughters are playing patronage the whole time. And so, we have this one moment where we have a former first lady asking another for patronage.

Henry Clay is a famous one of Dolley's congressional allies. The reason we know about him…gives you a glimpse behind the curtain into how politics worked. Leading up to the War of 1812, James Madison really wasn't sure he wanted to go to war. In fact, he was so secretive about it that scholars disagree: some think he was dying to go to war, some people, not. But he surely had to walk a fine line, and if he decided he did want to go to war, he needed to have allies. He couldn't ally himself with Henry Clay and the war hawks, but he had Dolley do it. And so, we have several famous stories about Dolley and Henry Clay sharing a snuff box together.

We have to look at these stories not as celebrity mentions, but as a form of political analysis. When people at the time were looking at them, they weren't just saying, "Look at Dolley Madison with Henry Clay." They're trying to read the energy and read the wind. She courted people on both sides of the aisle—that was the good thing about her—but when she singled somebody out for special attention, people knew there was something up in the air. [As for her use of snuff itself,] she was addicted, I'm afraid.

MAYO: These women were very aware of their place in history. Particularly, if you are a first lady, even early on you know that you are centrally positioned to influence aspects of politics…. They knew exactly what they were doing and they enjoyed wielding the power that was given to them.

ALLGOR: Dolley was a good Congress-goer…from the start. One of the things she did for other women is that she would go to the debates and she would go watch the Supreme Court argue, and that allowed other women to do that as well.

MAYO: This was Dolley's way of bringing the women into the knowledge of what was going on politically, so that while they were part of this social network that she was setting up in Washington, they could also be part of the political networks as well. She would get the women together and they would go up to Capitol Hill. She called them "Dove

Parties," which was part of educating the women's side to what was going on in politics at the time.

ALLGOR: This is a time when it was part of the deal of going into public service [to personally finance presidential entertaining]. This is why rich white men were supposed to take on the burden of public service, because a lot of it comes out of their own pockets. The Madisons were not the first presidential couple to leave [the presidency] much poorer than when they had come in. What Congress did do, though, was give her quite a hefty amount to redo the executive mansion, which she did very well.

MAYO: [Dolley Madison was given] a furnishing budget because the previous occupants had brought their own furniture, and then, when they left the presidency, they took it home with them. Decorating was a thing that Dolley wanted to do because she felt that the mansion needed to have a stately, elegant look for the new nation. She took the decorating very seriously. She wanted to make it look as if we could be on somewhat equal terms with the powers of Europe so that they could conduct diplomatic negotiations in a proper setting.

ALLGOR: This is one of those reasons we look at women as well: it gets resolved with women. So you have a revolution and you fight against everything Britain stands for, but now you're stuck with the nation. How are you going to express legitimacy and authority? These former British colonists, the only vocabulary of power they have is royalty, and so we have these strange moments. All of a sudden John Adams is arguing for titles for the presidency, and they go back and forth. The women of these families took it on, so George Washington is "Mr. President." Martha Washington is "Lady Washington." James Madison is "Mr. President." Dolley is "Queen Dolley."

The men have to tread this very strict line, but the women get to express the aristocratic longings, and that's one of the messages Dolley is sending out. It's only when we look at the women of that time do we understand that a lot of that beginning of the American nationhood is predicated on royalty....

MAYO: "She dressed a queen" was what you see in a lot of the reports or in a lot of the letters. Dolley looked every inch a queen.... She bought a lot of her materials in Paris, so she's very elegantly dressed and she looks to American eyes as a queen, and that's fine because she's not the head of state. She's walking a very fine line where she expresses the finer things to which the nation aspires, but she is not royalty. She's always walking this very fine line down the middle.

ALLGOR: [Dolley dressed consciously to get attention.] We have to look at the context here. This is a new nation. We all know it's very fragile and there's not a lot of bureaucracy or structure, and that was deliberate. We don't want that royal court, remember? So the people at the time focused on personalities and on the figure of the person.... It always seemed like George Washington was posing for statues. In the Early Republic, it's going to become Dolley and, interestingly, descriptions of her are about her being on the move. We have to understand this is not just a fashion report, but rather a form of political analysis. She is deliberately creating this. She's not wearing what an actual queen would wear or real court dresses. She was wearing an adaptation; what she imagines Americans would imagine as queen, and she put plumes on her turbans to make herself even taller.

A lot of the Madisons' resources went toward creating these outfits, these ensembles. At one point she got the bills, and she [said], "Don't even tell my husband," because between buying the stuff from France and paying the duties on it, it was quite a lot.

[Dolley and James Madison's personal differences] became politicized. A lot of the criticism toward the Madisons focused on James Madison, who was so tiny and pygmy-like. Somebody called him an anchovy.... Thomas Jefferson was big and tall. Washington was described as a hunk. And then, you have this little tiny guy...with a big brain. This is why we have his press secretary coming out—Edward Coles, Dolley's cousin—saying he's five-feet-six, and he's not. But why do we have a press secretary coming out to say this? It's because size mattered.

Dolley's height and her good health led to all kinds of scurrilous rumors about her sexuality, that she was overly sexual, that she was too, in their phrase, "hot," and the reason that the Madisons never had children was because she was literally burning up his essence. When you read the newspapers at the time, you realize that [these kinds of conversations] were quite serious for these people.

MAYO: The public was mostly proud [of what Dolley did]. The Federalists were a little put off by this; they thought it was too regal, a little too queenly, and a little too court-like. But there was a lot of discussion about creating a republican court with a small "r," and so that's part of what she was doing. One of the things that is ingenious about Dolley is that she takes European influences and filters them through a democratic lens. They give you something to aspire to as a new nation, how elegant and wonderful it can be, but you don't offend people who dislike the courts and the royalty of Europe.

ALLGOR: ...People will tell me, "Dolley Madison invented ice cream." Well, she didn't, but what happened is, almost immediately while she was living and after her death, she becomes closely associated as a symbol of American womanhood. Her name and her image get co-opted by everything to do with ice cream, hairpins; there's even a sexy Dolley brand of cigars. She becomes a "brand" so quickly that this association of Dolley Madison with ice cream becomes one of those things where people think she invented. It really goes to show how important she was and how large she loomed in the American imagination.

MAYO: People wanted to attach whatever their product was to her name so that this would recommend it. She foreshadows what Frances Cleveland does in the late nineteenth century where Frances' face and name are plastered on all kinds of products for sale.

ALLGOR: The War of 1812 had been going on for a couple of years and there have been various rumors going around the city that the capital was the target. Washington City from the beginning has an inferiority complex, and so the men in charge would say, "No, they're never coming to Washington. Baltimore is the place. It is of so much more consequence." When the British do march on Washington City, it is not prepared.

James Madison is in the field overseeing the troops and Dolley is alone in the White House. She begins a letter [to her sister] on the day before what was going to be the last day of the [original] White House, August 24, 1814. She's waiting for her husband to come home while preparing for the worst, so she's writing this letter to her sister and she's running up to the roof with a telescope looking for her husband. She is observing how badly the battles are going and she's also packing things. She's packing silver, she's packing what she considers the people's pos-

In 1814, Dolley Madison won the public's hearts by saving the White House's George Washington portrait and many valuable documents as the British Army advanced. *William Woodward, artist. 2009. Courtesy Montpelier Foundation*

sessions, and she's sending them away. Finally, the word comes, it's time to go.

MAYO: The British are indeed coming. If she waited any longer she might have been captured, and that would have been a huge prize of war, so she knew that she had to leave. She wanted to wait for her husband to come home, but that did not take place. She had to leave before he got back. They reunited a couple of days later in Virginia. Apparently, she had the table set for dinner and the British came in [to the White House] and thought that was wonderful. She did save the Gilbert Stuart portrait of Washington, which was one of the things that endeared her to the entire nation. Dolley knew exactly what she was doing.

ALLGOR: She sensed that all of the cabinet papers including, by the way, James Madison's notes on the Constitutional Convention [had to be saved]. She took them and she sent them away in carts. At the last minute, she decides on this painting. There's some evidence that it might even be a copy, but it didn't matter; she understood the psychological import. She got her servant and her slave, Paul Jennings, to wrestle it off the wall and break it out of the frame, and she gave it to two gentlemen from New York who put it in a cart and took it away. All of this is getting scattered to the four winds hoping something will survive. And then she herself is taken away by carriage.

We only have this letter [to her sister, about the approaching troops] in her fair hand. In the 1830s, when we think she's beginning to think about her legacy, her friend Margaret Bayard Smith, the journalist, wants to write about her…. On the one hand, Dolley's thrilled with being the topic of history, but she's also cautious. She mentions this letter, but we don't actually have the original of this letter. We have a fair copy, which Margaret Bayard Smith reproduces. At *Washington History*, that great magazine that William Seale has, there's a terrific article by David Mattern that suggested Dolley may have altered that letter for history's sake.

When you are trying to find out whether someone was really as symbolic as we say, sometimes it's very instructive to look at their enemies. [British] Admiral Cockburn framed all of his threats toward Washington at Mrs. Madison: He was going to come and dine at Mrs. Madison's table. He was going to make his bow at her drawing room. He was going to parade her through the streets. He's not attacking James Madison in rhetoric, he's attacking her, so we know Dolley really was a public figure. In fact, when he got to the White House and she wasn't there, he took things of hers, including her cushion because he said he wished to "warmly recall Mrs. Madison's seat." Her planned dinner party is interesting, too. It seems odd to be having a dinner party when Washington is in exodus. But she's really doing what she'd always done: trying to hold the capital together even as it was falling apart. So, she had fully intended to have a dinner party that day.

MAYO: [The destruction of the White House was] pretty complete inside. It had to be almost totally rebuilt. The Madisons did not move back in. It wasn't until the Monroe Administration that [a presidential family was] able to move back in the White House….

There are places in the basement where you can still see burnt timbers. When they did the restoration of the White House under the Trumans, they found a lot of charred wood and charred bricks that were taken out and saved as remnants from the fire.

After the British had burned Washington, there was a great deal of conversation even in Congress about whether the capital should remain in Washington, which was now destroyed, or should they move the capital back to Philadelphia. James and Dolley leased the Octagon House, which was only a few blocks away, and immediately began to entertain in a grand style. This really sent a signal to the diplomats in

Washington, to the Congress, to the people, that they were not going to turn tail and run. They were going to stay in the capital.

ALLGOR: The Quaker part [of Dolley's story] is irresistible. We just don't know enough about her childhood, but my theory on this is that one of the central tenets of Quakerism is to regard people as inner lights, as God.... Dolley goes on to become famous for being incredibly empathic and sympathetic and warm. People said, "When you talk to her, it was like you were the only person in the room." I think that comes from her Quakerness.

MAYO: The fact that she was able to take on this role and do so well was because Quakers believe men and women were equal and so you don't get any sense with her of being "lesser than." She fits right in and does her thing. That comes from her Quaker background as well.

ALLGOR: [As to where Dolley was born,] that's a little bit of a family scandal. She wants very much to be considered a Virginian, born and bred. Her mother's folks are indeed from Virginia and probably her father as well. But what happens is that John Payne converts to Quakerism; Mary Coles, her mother, is Quaker. They go off and they live in the frontier, which is in North Carolina, in a Quaker community...and Dolley is born in North Carolina. So she is North Carolina's only first lady. What's sad about that is she spends most of her life denying it. Something went bad on the North Carolina frontier—we think it has to do with her father's rather shady business practices—and they moved back to Virginia. And so, she is raised in that loving circle of kith and kin in the gentry world of chattel slaveholding.

...Her father frees his slaves and they go to Philadelphia for about ten years. Things are terrible for the Paynes in Philadelphia—children die, her father gets drummed out of the Quakers, her mother has to open a boardinghouse. Dolley is pushed into marrying John Todd. She has two children and one of them dies [of yellow fever as an infant, on the same day that her husband also dies of the disease]. It's all horrible. And then, she is this beautiful twenty-five-year-old widow. You could argue that in...the capital of the United States, she could have had her pick of any man, but she picks James Madison. It turns out to be a great pick. But why did she do that? It's one of those moments where she said, "I could go back to the world that I lived in, the world of [plantations]."

James Madison immediately fell in love with her. The family lore is that he saw her on the street and, like a lot of men, just fell for her and was very romantic. He was almost [in his] mid-forties and had never married, which is very odd. Marriage is a very pragmatic business in this age, and romantic love isn't necessarily a part of it. So Dolley's approach to the marriage was rather pragmatic: He was a good person. He would be a tender protector for her [surviving] son. As the marriage went on, she fell deeply in love with James, and James got over his infatuation to love her deeply as well....

One of the stories her niece [relayed is] that when James Madison was courting Dolley, First Lady Martha Washington cornered her and said, "Is it true what they say about you and James Madison?" Dolley blushed and stammered and Martha Washington apparently said, "The general and I think it's wonderful, even that he is much older than you."

We don't have anything from Dolley at that time [about her views on slavery]. What we do know is by the time she's a woman in middle age and older, she has exactly the same kind of weird attitude towards enslaved Americans that Southerners had, which is a kind of inability to understand them as humans. When James Madison dies and he doesn't free slaves, which everybody thought he would, everybody begins to blame Dolley. Part of that blame is fine because she does start selling slaves as soon as she can; but some of that is a reflection of people's disappointment with James Madison.

MAYO: [The Madisons returned to the Montpelier plantation after his presidency ended.] There, they were besieged by people who wanted to associate themselves with the Madisons. They had many political visitors in addition to family and friends; just as with the Washingtons and the Jeffersons, everybody wanted to meet the great personages. They always had people in the house with them, not only their relatives, but also many political visitors as well.

ALLGOR: [Dolley was happy being at Montpelier] because, at that point, she loved her husband very much and Montpelier was where he wanted to stay. He didn't want to go [back to Washington,] and so she stayed as well. It's interesting that the descriptions of her at this time aren't those same politically fraught descriptions. She's described as happy, contented, Adam and Eve in paradise. But, she definitely missed Washington and would write to her friends in Washington and say, "Tell me all the news." She would sometimes complain a little bit, "I haven't been out," and "Keep me up to date and just let me know what's happening." For her own self, she probably would have wanted to go back to Washington for a visit, but James Madison was going to stay put.

MAYO: What they had [financially] was what they lived on when they retired. The supposition was that if you were wealthy enough to get into politics in the first place, you'd be able to support yourself afterwards. But Dolley had this ne'er-do-well son, Payne Todd, from her first marriage, and he ran through their estate. He ran up enormous debts. He ended up in debtors' prison twice and each time James and Dolley would bail him out. After Madison died, Dolley unwisely put her son in charge of Montpelier. That was a disaster, so she ended up losing Montpelier and living in poverty.

[After the death of her beloved James in 1836, Dolley returns to Washington and] becomes the grand dame of Washington society once again. Because people know about her poverty but don't want to actually confront her with it, the couples in the White House, the Polks and the Tylers, invite her to come to dinner on many occasions.

The younger first ladies always ask her advice on entertaining and handling large crowds of people, so she becomes an ex-officio first lady adviser. That's how she happened to do the matchmaking between Angelica Singleton and Abraham Van Buren, the president's son. She's very much in the social mix again and very much a behind-the-scenes player again.

ALLGOR: You have to remember, Washington is her town. She worked for sixteen years to build this town and the President's Mansion as a symbol for Washingtonians. It was under her tenure that the President's Mansion got a nickname: they called it the White House. All this comes to a head when they burned Washington and the White House, and so she can be credited with a kind of nationalism around the end of the War of 1812. So, when she comes back to Washington, it is like the past has come to light. She wore many of the same clothes. I'm sure she would have loved to have new ones, but she was poor. It had this effect of making her seem like truly a relic from [the Revolutionary] era and everybody wanted to use her.

[Dolley Madison remained in Washington until her death, in 1849, at the age of eighty-one.] I call this her iconic phase where she's not just a person, but she begins to become a symbol. There's a bust made of her, there's a medal cast, and she's awarded a seat on the floor of Congress with escorts, which is unheard of to do, and for a woman to do it. There's a lot of attention being paid to her and she starts to become a symbol even while she is living.

Dolley Madison's legacy:

ALLGOR: Dolley Madison is important for several reasons. She does set a role of first lady. Historians look at her because she lets us know, among many other things, the role of aristocracy in this first, great democracy. But, in the end, the question is really, why does this matter? For Dolley Madison, what she has offered us is a model for governance that stresses civility and empathy. Dolley Madison is modeling this for us, but she's not going to win, right? But we look to our founding generations because we need examples, we need role models, and her way of conducting politics, of stressing the building of bridges and not bunkers, is a model that she has bequeathed us and one we can use for the future.

MAYO: Martha Washington...perfected the aspect of the role, which was the social partner to the president and a hostess for the nation. When you get to Abigail Adams, she becomes a political partner with her husband and pioneers that role. Dolley is the one who brings the two roles together, so that she becomes both the social partner and the political partner for her husband. That sets all kinds of precedents for the future first ladies, and she is still held up as a standard by which others measure themselves today.

Elizabeth Kortright Monroe

"...it was improbable for any female to have fulfilled all the duties of the partner of such cares, and of a wife and parent, with more attention, delicacy and propriety than she has done."
—James Monroe

Elizabeth Monroe,
date unknown

Born: June 30, 1768, New York City
Married: February 16, 1786, to James Monroe (1758–1831)
Children: Eliza (1786–1840); James Spence (1799–1801); Maria Hester (1803–50)
Died: September 23, 1830, Loudon County, Virginia

Contributors:

DANIEL PRESTON, editor, *The Papers of James Monroe, James Monroe Museum and Memorial Library,* University of Mary Washington

RICHARD NORTON SMITH, presidential historian; executive director at five presidential libraries; author of several books, including *Patriarch*; history consultant for C-SPAN; academic advisor for C-SPAN's *First Ladies* series

RICHARD NORTON SMITH: The Monroe years are popularly known as "The Era of Good Feeling." You could probably take issue with that, particularly in the second term. What had happened was, by that point we were as close to being a one-party state as at any time in American history. The old Federalist Party had basically died off; the War of 1812 had been concluded at a standoff that most Americans were willing to consider a victory. We had established once and for all our independence. It was a period of great boom in the country, and physical expansion. A number of states came into the Union during Monroe's day, and yet Washington City remained this very raw, incomplete place with dirt roads.

Elizabeth Monroe, like Louisa Adams, suffers for her straits. They were both seen as somehow alien. Elizabeth was born in this country but she had her blossoming overseas, in France especially. The Monroes became famous for the Frenchness in the way they approached life in the White House. You can see it in the furniture of that period that they bought; you can see it in the food that they served. Then, as now, there was also a nativist element that took exception to a first lady who somehow didn't seem quite American enough.

DANIEL PRESTON: Elizabeth Monroe did not like the public parts [of her role as first lady]. She married James Monroe when he was a member of the Continental Congress, so through their entire adult life, he was in one public office or another. She was very much used to him being a public figure, being in the U.S. Senate, being governor of Virginia, being abroad as a minister of the United States, serving as secretary of state—this was her life. To go to the White House was not anything that unusual. It wasn't anything unexpected. People had talked about Monroe being president for years…. When Monroe was president, he did two tours around the country, and they were phenomenal because no one ever saw the president. No one ever heard the president talk…. James Madison gave three speeches when he was president; Thomas Jefferson did two. People never saw the president. They never heard the president, let alone the first ladies. So there really isn't a public perception. It was just simply a different time.

[James Monroe met Elizabeth "Eliza" Kortright in New York City when she was just a teenager, seventeen years of age. His home in Virginia became an important part of their lives in between their various political postings.] Monroe made a joke later in life [that]…"Mrs. Monroe was a little uneasy about leaving New York but she has become a good Virginian." So, she seemed to have fit into the life very easily.

Something…that really says a lot about her character from a very young age is [her move to Virginia]. When she married Monroe, he was twenty-eight. In October of 1786, he finished his term in Congress and they went to Virginia. She left her family with whom she was very close, and all of her friends, and went to Fredericksburg, Virginia. She went from New York City to little, dinky Fredericksburg, which was a river port in Virginia. She didn't know anybody. She bounced along the bad roads not knowing where she was going, or what was going to happen when she got there. She was just shy of eighteen and she was seven months pregnant, so it must've been a grueling trip. It really indicates the stamina, the strength she had that she was willing to make that sort of trip, and that she could do it.

The Monroes were in France in the mid-1790s. James had been appointed U.S. minister to France. They arrived in Paris a week after Robespierre had been guillotined, so it was at the height of the Reign of Terror. The Marquis de Lafayette had been forced to flee France for not supporting the more radical elements of the revolution. His wife was not able to leave. She and her mother and other family members were arrested, imprisoned; her mother had been executed. Gouverneur Morris, who had been minister before Monroe, had worked to try to get her out of prison, but Morris was not popular with the French government at all since he had pretty much condemned revolution and said he supported the monarchy.

When the Monroes came, they picked up this effort to try to get a release and they staged a very dramatic event to draw attention to Madame Lafayette. They hired a very expensive carriage. Elizabeth Monroe dressed herself in her best and went to the prison where Madame Lafayette was being held and asked to see her. The governor of the prison didn't know what to do. There was this crowd gathering because everyone wanted to see who this person was, coming in this carriage. Word spread that it was the wife of the American minister. She met with Madame Lafayette and made her case a public one.

Some stories say that the next day, Madame Lafayette was released. It was actually a couple of months, but [the Monroes' efforts] pretty much kept Madame Lafayette from going to the guillotine and officially did lead to her release. The Monroes became the conduit for money from the United States to her to enable her to go to Austria and join her husband....

The Monroes were absolutely devoted; they were apart for [only] a couple of months here and there throughout their forty-four year marriage. Congressman Samuel Mitchell from New York...wrote to his wife that he had been at a dinner at the president's house when Jefferson was president. It was right before Monroe left to go to France to negotiate what became the Louisiana Purchase. Mitchell wrote, saying, "Monroe has a fine conjugal feeling. He can't stand to be separated from his wife so he's taking her with him to go to Europe." That was pretty much their attitude. Monroe was devoted to family as well.... If they had their choice of how they would spend time, it would be with their family.

SMITH: [The White House had been burned by the British in the War of 1812 and the Monroes were the first to move back in after its reconstruction.] This was hugely important symbolically, because, even by then, the White House had become, in effect, America's house. One of the reasons why, then and since, its occupants have been often targeted for criticism, much of it unfair, is because we all think that it's our house.

PRESTON: The White House was not ready in March of 1817, when Monroe became president, and they lived in another house for several months. In June, Monroe left Washington and went on that four-month tour around the country. His family went back to Virginia. He returns to the president's house in September of 1817 and at that point, it was ready for occupancy. They began moving furniture, but the furniture they ordered wasn't ready. He used his own personal furniture. They borrowed furniture from elsewhere. It was really a haphazard system of furnishing the house. Some of the rooms were still empty. It wasn't like it was when the Adamses had moved in, where the plaster was still wet and the rooms were simply not usable. There just wasn't any furniture for it.

[Buying French furniture and speaking French was as controversial for politicians then as it would be today.] It goes really back to the beginning, to Washington and the first presidency, of trying to balance the new republican standards of simplicity and openness, but at the same time, somehow maintaining a dignity and majesty for the national gov-

These Blue Room chairs are part of the original collection the Monroes ordered from France to furnish their White House. *Bruce White for the White House Historical Association*

ernment. How do you be open, but at the same time present the country as being something special, particularly for visitors? For the Monroes, [as] for other presidents, the White House became the tool for doing that. Monroe was praised, people who met him always commented on what a plain, straightforward, unostentatious person he was. But when you look at how he and Mrs. Monroe furnished the White House, it's very different. He much understood the importance of symbolism and for him, the White House was a symbol of the United States. It was [their goal] to present it in a fashion for which "majesty" is really the best word.

SMITH: Not only majestic but Napoleonic. The Monroes had actually befriended Napoleon when they lived in Paris. Ironically, the president originally had ordered fifty-six pieces of mahogany furniture from France but he was told by the French that mahogany was not appropriate in a gentleman's house. What is preserved today in the White House's Blue Room is what Monroe got in its place.

PRESTON: It was President Monroe who set out this order [for the White House furniture]. He didn't stipulate specific pieces of furniture. He wrote to merchants that he dealt with in France, and said, "We need chandeliers, we need chairs," it was not real specific design although he did want American symbols; he wanted eagles and these sorts of things. But the two Monroes undoubtedly talked about this because when they were abroad in Europe and friends would write and ask for them to buy things for them, it was usually Elizabeth Monroe who did the purchasing.

SMITH: Mrs. Monroe was also the first in a long line of first ladies who would be criticized for an alleged obsession with fashion. It was known that she paid up to $1,500 for her gowns. It was alleged that she had picked up the French habit of painting her face and applying rouge. Silly as all this sounds now, to this rough-hewn, rawboned Yankee republic, it takes them back to the debates at the very beginning of the republic about what kind of nation we were going to be.

PRESTON: Elizabeth Monroe and Dolley Madison were great friends for years and years, but they have very different temperaments. Dolley Madison was very social by nature. She loved large receptions, she loved dinners, was perfectly happy to get in her carriage to go visiting all day long.

Elizabeth Monroe wanted to stay home with her family. She was devoted to her daughters, to her grandchildren. At the White House, that's what she really enjoyed, what she wanted to do. She did not like large crowds. She was very uncomfortable at the large receptions...but was very charming in smaller groups, at small dinners when there was a small circle of friends together, or a small group of visitors. Everyone praised her charm, her affability, her conversation and said she sparkled. She was just a very different type of person than Dolley Madison.

...Elizabeth Monroe was an almost invisible first lady during a lot of those eight years. She had serious health problems. She had excruciating headaches. It was thought she suffered from rheumatism, arthritis, and there are a number of people who believe that she may have had late-onset epilepsy, which was known as the "falling disease" at that point. That's something that would've certainly been kept a secret from the public. One of the byproducts of her ill health is that she often had stand in her place her daughter, Eliza. It is Eliza, quite frankly, who's responsible for a number of the actions that had been blamed on her mother that gave off an aura of snobbery and exclusivity. For example, the first White House wedding of a president's daughter [Maria Hester

Monroe] took place, and Eliza took over the preparations. It was Eliza who said, "This is a family affair, the diplomatic corps is not going to be invited."

When you talk about those five hundred or six hundred [influential Washingtonians], a disproportionate number of them thought they should have been invited to the Monroe wedding and they wrote down their thoughts. Unfortunately for Elizabeth Monroe's historical reputation, we have access to [their complaints,] but we don't have her side of the story.

Unfortunately, there's not a lot [of documentary evidence about Elizabeth Monroe]. Family lore based upon what Monroe's elder daughter reported was that at some point after he left the presidency, Monroe burned all personal correspondence. There is one letter that survives that is written by Elizabeth and there is one letter from James to her that survives. What baffles me is that there's only one letter that she wrote to somebody else. She had an extensive correspondence with her sisters and with her friends, and these letters don't seem to be anywhere. It seems like somebody would have kept some of these. Consequently, firsthand evidence of what she actually thought about things, we don't have. There's a lot of filtered evidence of what people wrote about her. There are letters that Monroe wrote to his daughters and to his two sons-in-law who were political advisors that talk about family matters. A congressman wrote letters home talking about meeting Mrs. Monroe. Other women in Washington recorded in their diaries meeting her. There's a fair amount about her, but we don't have really anything from her point of view, which is very maddening.

SMITH: Monroe did say in this one letter [we have] where he refers to Elizabeth Monroe as his partner in all things. There's some consensus, although there's an unfortunate lack of documentation, that this would include sharing his political secrets with her. But don't think of Elizabeth, certainly in a modern sense, as a political figure.

PRESTON: She was certainly aware of what the president was doing. We do only have that one letter she wrote, but there are letters in her handwriting that she copied for him, he either made copies to send to others or to keep. She was certainly aware of what was happening in the political world and they were together for so long and they were so close that it's inconceivable that they did not discuss public matters.

Elizabeth Monroe's legacy:

PRESTON: [Elizabeth Monroe should be known] for her elegance. She brought a sense of style. She was known for her beauty, for her sense of fashion, but mostly for her elegance, bringing a sense of real style. If I was going to compare her to a modern first lady...I would think of Jacqueline Kennedy, with that sense of fashion and style and elegance that she brought to the White House.

Louisa Catherine Johnson Adams

"There is something in this great unsocial house which depresses me beyond expression."

Louisa Catherine Adams,
c1821

Born: February 12, 1775, London, England (to American parents)
Married: July 26, 1797, to John Quincy Adams (1767–1848)
Children: George Washington (1801–29); John II (1803–34); Charles Francis (1807–86); Louisa Catherine (1811–12)
Died: May 15, 1852, Washington, D.C.

Contributors:

AMANDA MATHEWS, assistant editor, *Adams Papers*, Massachusetts Historical Society

RICHARD NORTON SMITH, presidential historian; executive director at five presidential libraries; author of several books, including *Patriarch;* history consultant for C-SPAN; academic advisor for C-SPAN's *First Ladies* series

AMANDA MATHEWS: John Quincy Adams was born in 1767 and Louisa in 1775. They met in London. John Quincy Adams was the resident minister to The Hague in the Netherlands and he was sent from there to London to exchange the ratifications for the Jay Treaty. By the time he got to London, the business had already been concluded. He didn't really have a lot to do, so what he spent his time doing was visiting the house of the Johnsons. Joshua Johnson, Louisa's father, was the U.S. consul at London and he entertained all the Americans who came through London…. Americans would come and socialize and enjoy evenings of entertainment with his many daughters, who were all talented.

John Quincy would come and enjoy their company and after a little bit of time, made his intentions known that it was Louisa and not her older sister, better known as Nancy, that he was interested in, and they began their courtship and engagement.

[After they married,] John Quincy was appointed from the Netherlands as the minister to Prussia in Berlin, so they go straight to Berlin. They spend the first four years of their marriage in Berlin. She doesn't actually see the United States until 1801.

The first four years of marriage were somewhat difficult. Louisa Catherine experienced four miscarriages in that time before finally giving birth to her first son, George Washington Adams. That caused a bit of controversy, naming the oldest son after George Washington, and not after John Adams.

RICHARD NORTON SMITH: Even people who admire John Quincy Adams, and I'm certainly including myself among them, would not suggest that he was a modern figure in terms of outreach to people, generally, but…he would not have been an easy man to be married to. This is a stormy relationship. The Adamses argued over the same things that married couples have been arguing over since there was marriage. They argued over money, they argued over their children. One of the small tragedies in Louisa Catherine's life, a life that was filled with tragedy where her children were concerned, is this: her husband had been appointed minister to Russia, and she learned at the last minute that her elder sons, George Washington Adams and John Adams II, are going to stay behind. She can't take her children with her to Russia. They're going stay behind with John and Abigail to be raised as Americans on American soil.

You often get this sense of a woman who is powerless within her marriage to be making fundamental parental decisions; that they were reserved, as most decisions were, for John Quincy.

MATHEWS: Their years in Saint Petersburg were difficult in some ways. Saint Petersburg was a hardship outpost. It's cold. It's forbidding. There weren't a lot of other women there; most of the diplomats' wives didn't travel with their husbands when they got sent to Saint Petersburg. They had a baby girl, Louisa Catherine Adams, and the little child died just after about a year and that really devastated her mother, Louisa. It was very painful, and for John Quincy, he is also very much torn apart by this.

The War of 1812 in the U.S. had broken out. John Quincy was sent to Paris to negotiate a treaty and he left Louisa with their youngest son, Charles Francis, in Saint Petersburg. Eventually, when peace was resolved and he was sure that he'd either be returning home or be sent to London, he asked her to join him. She made this arduous and perilous journey from Saint Petersburg in the winter to Paris, with her son, who was only about seven at the time, and a couple of servants that she basically met that day. She didn't know if she could trust them. As she was crossing Europe, she encountered dangerous travel conditions, but also, Napoleon has escaped from Elba and was coming back to France, and she encountered resurgent armies there to greet him. She was crossing some very perilous territory in Europe.

SMITH: Her life was in danger throughout this trip. She went through the Alps in a carriage in the wintertime with a seven-year-old. The resourcefulness of this woman is just extraordinary.

MATHEWS: When they got back in 1817 to Washington, they'd been gone from Washington for quite awhile. John Quincy had served in both Saint Petersburg and London, and a lot of people in Washington don't know him. The way the etiquette situation worked in Washington, it favored people who had been there for awhile. The Adamses wanted to shake things up,... "We are going to have these parties and you can come even if we haven't connected in formal visits." That put them in a position of power as a social leader. They were making the rules now, trying to take back a little bit of power that Congress had. Louisa said that Congress makes and unmakes presidents at their whim; they wanted to pull a little bit of that power back to the executive. She has her "sociables" starting in 1819; some seasons they are weekly and other seasons every two weeks, where hundreds of people would come. They became the center of entertainment in Washington.

SMITH: [One of the balls Louisa threw was for her husband's chief rival for the White House, Andrew Jackson.] It was very simple: The

Adamses hoped to talk Jackson out of running; they flattered him about running. So many people came to the house on F Street that night that they had to shore up the floors. It was something like nine hundred people who attended.

I would have loved to [have been] a fly on the wall. Louisa must have been a remarkable hostess. She had attracted attention; she had been a favorite in the Russian court when her husband was U.S. envoy there. Czar Alexander of Russia made her one of his favorite dancing partners. There clearly was a charisma about this woman that had set her apart in the courts of Europe. Tragically, it very rarely comes through in the American setting.

MATHEWS: Her charisma certainly does [come through] in these "sociables." She complains that even though she has no political power, everybody seems to want to know her and force her to spend time with them. She claims to be quite put out by the imposition. But the same charm that she exhibits in Europe is still exhibited in the United States.... She must have been very affable and that must have made people feel very comfortable in her presence.

Because campaigning is not allowed, John Quincy can't come out and say, "I would like you to vote for me for president." Candidates can't do that; you can't ask for office directly. You have to use these subtle back channels, and women were a good conduit for that. People come to Louisa to spread their gossip and to ask for favors. She knows that she can't trust these people; she's not naive. A lot of them are spreading false information, they're misleading, they all have their own agendas. She's aware of the political game that's going on, she's not a fan of it.

SMITH: [Here's a sample diary entry from Louisa Adams: "I have the happiness of meeting with a variety of these misleaders who are either not gifted with common sense or have a sort of mind which I have often met with, utterly incapable of comprehending anything in a plain way. Whether this proceeds from an error in their education or from a natural defect in the formation of the brain, I will leave philosophers and metaphysicians to decide."] You read that quote and you realize why there was an instant bond formed between Louisa and her father-in-law, old John Adams. John Adams was a man of strong opinions and little reluctance to share them with anyone who would listen. He had a stern

New England conscience, a profound sense of right and wrong. He and his exotic European [born] daughter-in-law seemed to have hit it off from the first; Abigail [Adams] was a little bit [of a] harder sell.

[The presidency was won in the 1820s through a very different system than we have today.] Everyone in Monroe's cabinet, among others, had wanted to succeed him, and that included John Quincy Adams, the secretary of state. The great popular hero was Andrew Jackson, the hero of the Battle of New Orleans, then a somewhat controversial figure in his own right. There was a multi-candidate field and no one got a majority either of the popular or electoral votes. In both cases, Jackson came in first; Adams came in second. So the election went to the House of Representatives. The man eliminated by the Constitution, fourth place finisher Henry Clay, ultimately threw his support to Adams. That was enough to win him the presidency, which turned out, in many ways, to be a poisoned chalice because, from day one, there were charges of a corrupt bargain. A [cloud] hung over the Adams presidency, it's safe to say. Adams himself sounded almost apologetic in his inaugural address, and it was as if the election of 1828 began almost before he took the oath of office.

MATHEWS: The White House years are very unpleasant years for the Adamses and it was readily apparent to everyone in the family. Charles Francis Adams, their son, talks about it in his own diary, about how sad the household seems at the time.

The cloud under which the presidency began never lifts, and because the campaigning for 1828 begins almost instantly, Louisa feels very personally the attacks on her husband, on his character, some attacks on her character;...they finally reached the pinnacle and it's not a happy pinnacle. It's a very stormy four years for them and the White House is not a very comfortable place to live.

SMITH: John Quincy Adams was one hundred years ahead of his time, which makes him look better to historians than he did to his contemporaries. This was a man whose legitimacy had been questioned and yet famously, in his first message to Congress, he introduces breathtaking programs that in some ways anticipate the New Deal by a century, saying that the federal government should be in the road building business, there should be a national university here in Washington. He even proposed a national astronomical observatory, what he called a White House of the sky. For this, he was ridiculed by the Jeffersonian-Jacksonian small government crowd. It did nothing to enhance his popularity at the time. It may have contributed to his defeat for reelection. But one hundred years later, he looks somewhat prophetic.

MATHEWS: Abigail Adams has passed by the time John Quincy attains the presidency, so Louisa can't ask her mother-in-law about handling the first lady role, and the role has somewhat shifted. Louisa generally follows the precedents that Monroe set, with a more formal, reserved White House, and not attending the public functions. But it did help [having had a mother-in-law who had been first lady]. She was familiar with her mother-in-law's opinions and the way she had carried herself, and she wanted in some ways to keep that in mind and honor that.

[Louisa Catherine didn't continue her "sociables" once they got to the White House.] The "sociables" were informal, there was music, there was often dancing. Once they get to the White House, the entertainments are much more restricted, they're open to a lot of people, especially the "drawing rooms," but there's not that kind of dancing until the end of their term. As they're on their way out, for the last great "drawing room" she holds, they have music and dancing. People stay until two o'clock in the morning talking about how gracious the Adamses are, knowing that they have failed in their reelection. It's probably one of the greatest entertainments that they have in their four years there.

SMITH: Louisa was accused, bizarrely, of extravagance in furnishing that great unsocial house. One of the controversies that marred the Adams years concerned a billiard table which supposedly the first lady had purchased using the tax dollars of honest working men; somehow this [demonstrated a] very un-American quality that people wanted to read into her.

On the other hand, there are these wonderful, bizarre letters confirming her addiction to chocolate. Louisa Catherine Adams was a chocoholic. I often say, being married to the sourest man in Washington, she took her sweets where she could find them. Apparently, she had her sons and others buy chocolate shells by the barrelful. She writes about the medicinal qualities of fudge. It was as if she took her pleasures where she could find them. That's pretty pathetic.

MATHEWS: I wouldn't go too far on John Quincy's sourness. There is very much an affection between the two of them and a great love; otherwise, she could have stayed behind in Quincy.

Louisa is not speaking out politically the way perhaps Abigail [Adams] did with her husband; she's not a public political figure.... She has her own private views of them, although her views on politics are more about how people behave. She's much more interested in everyone conducting themselves properly. She doesn't like when people who are supporting the policies that her husband supports have crossed the line in terms of decorum.

SMITH: Adams did seek reelection in 1828. A lot of people think to this day it was the most scurrilous campaign in American history.... Andrew Jackson, denied the presidency four years earlier, overwhelmed John Quincy Adams. Like his father, John Quincy didn't stick around to see his successor's inauguration. But he did come back to Washington just a couple of years later in a unique role, the only American president to this day who came back as a member of the House of Representatives.

History repeated itself in one other tragic way. John and Abigail had lost a son during the interregnum between his defeat and the inauguration of Thomas Jefferson and George Washington Adams almost definitely committed suicide [just around the time his father, John Quincy, was losing the election].

MATHEWS: It was May 1829, so the power had already shifted to Andrew Jackson. They had asked George back to Washington to escort the family to Quincy. It was on that trip that he either fell or jumped off the boat, a devastating family and personal tragedy.

SMITH: Then, in 1834, his brother John died of alcoholism.

MATHEWS: [After losing,] the Adamses don't come back to F Street initially, because that house had been rented out during their presidency. They don't get back there until the end of the 1830s, but their years there are much better after about 1834. The first few years are just so much tragedy; [then] things really improved. They're able to socialize and entertain and have these dinner parties, and there's no more striving. They've already [achieved] all that can happen.

And so, these are years more of peace, but there's certainly still a lot of political struggle and Louisa talks about that. Between her and John Quincy, there is somewhat of an understanding. She always knew that he needed politics in order to live. Even though she had been very angry at his insistence on going back to Washington...eventually, she cooled off and decided she would follow him.

SMITH: [It was a fifty-year marriage and] there was some mellowing on both their parts. They had been through the worst. The White House was a thing of the past. She was more politically aligned with him in his congressional career because the old charges about the corrupt deal had, in some ways, come between them, and that was in the past. Some may say they grew closer in the last years.

There is a touching coda to the story in her later years just as John Quincy became more and more outspoken in his opposition to slavery and famously played a role in the 1840 Amistad [slavery] case. There is this wonderful correspondence between Louisa Catherine and the Grimke sisters, Angelina and Sarah, who were pioneering feminists, abolitionists, and activists of their day. Louisa came probably as close there as anywhere else to spelling out her evolving sense on women's roles.

MATHEWS: Toward the end of Louisa's life, when she is corresponding with Sarah Grimke, there's the sense that she seeks an equality of the mind for women, but not so that women can run for office; it's not that kind of feminism. It's not so that women can play the front role, it's so that women can better fulfill their primary functions as mother, wife, and daughter. This is where her religion comes in again: God had created men and women equal in this way and in their minds, they could be equals and partners, but complementary partners. It was not for women to become more like men.

SMITH: One reason why life was better for them at the end was that the public attitude towards John Quincy had changed. Admirers called

The Adamses are the only presidential couple to return to Washington for service in the U.S. House, where John Quincy Adams died after nearly 17 years as a congressman.

him "Old Man Eloquent." South Carolinians called him "The Madman from Massachusetts." His career in Congress was in so many ways an expression of that dogged commitment to principle, even at the risk of unpopularity. In the end, he won some of his battles. He won, for example, the repeal of the gag rule that slavery forces had imposed on Congress. He became an immensely respected elder statesman.

In February 1848, on the floor of the House, one member of Congress looked over in his direction and said, "Look to Mr. Adams. Mr. Adams is dying." His forehead had flushed a very mottled color and he tried to stand and he fell over. He was carried to the speaker's office just off the floor of the House. Henry Clay came to visit him. Of course, Louisa came, and he didn't recognize her. Supposedly, his last words were, "This is the last of Earth but I am content," which I never believed. I don't think John Quincy Adams was ever contented for a moment, but he died in the Capitol, in effect, doing his duty. He was eighty-one.

MATHEWS: Louisa lives another four years. She stays in Washington, cared for by John Adams II's wife, Mary Catherine Helen Adams. She lives quietly. Her health is fading and she has a stroke the following year and is somewhat invalided for the rest of her life. Charles Francis Adams meets with her about a year before she dies and records in his diary how content she seems. Not that she was looking forward to death, but that she had truly resigned herself and could face the end with great courage and faith.

[She is not better known among first ladies, and] that's partly because John Quincy's presidency has been so obscured for so long that it diminished interest in her. What makes John Quincy interesting to historians today is his post-White House years, which people did not seem to think that Louisa was really a part of, somewhat mistakenly. That's really kept her from being more prominent. Plus, Abigail outshines, when you're talking about the Adamses. It has kept Louisa from getting her due....

Louisa Catherine Adams's legacy:

MATHEWS: In some ways, [Louisa Catherine is the first modern first lady]. She works with the Washington Female Orphan Asylum, so, in that sense, that's somewhat modern, having this cause that she was involved in. She does work politics in her parlor in such a way as to help win the presidency for her husband in her own way.

She's a fascinating figure. The interest in her should be every bit as much as for her mother-in-law, Abigail. She's a woman who saw more of the governments of the world than most women of that day in London, in Berlin, in Saint Petersburg, in Washington, and she truly experiences and reflects on these experiences through her letters and her diaries and her memoirs in a way that really bring a richness to our understanding of the world in the period she lived in.

SMITH: Partly, Louisa's is a life of tragedy and that's what sticks with me. This is a woman who lived through extraordinary events and crossed paths with these remarkable historical figures, but it was in the domestic life where she suffered loss after loss after loss. Even the apparent triumph of their lives together, the presidency, turned out to be, in many ways, disappointing. And yet, that's not the note on which the story ends. There's real inspiration there for all of us.

Rachel Donelson Jackson

"I had rather be a doorkeeper in the house of God than live in that palace in Washington."

Rachel Jackson, c1831

Born: June 15, 1767, Halifax County, Virginia
Married: c1785, to Lewis Robards; 1791, to Andrew Jackson (1767–1845)
Children: Andrew Jackson Donelson, her nephew (adopted 1809); Lyncoya, Creek Indian child (adopted 1813)
Died: December 22, 1828, Nashville, Tennessee (between Andrew Jackson's election and inauguration)

Contributors:

PATRICIA BRADY, social and cultural historian specializing in first ladies; author of several books including *A Being So Gentle: The Frontier Love Story of Rachel and Andrew Jackson*

MICHAEL HENDERSON, former superintendent, Martin Van Buren National Historic Site; museum consultant

MICHAEL HENDERSON: Andrew Jackson is the first Westerner. We'd had Virginia presidents from the Old South before that. Jackson is someone completely different; he grew up in the frontier. Socially, the change is enormous. Even though he's a planter, he's not of the old planter class of the South that the previous presidents had been from, and nor was he like a New Englander either. This is a Westerner, and he brings very different values and very different ambitions to the White House.

PATRICIA BRADY: In 1824, Andrew Jackson wasn't quite sure that he was ready to be president, he wasn't quite sure he was the right man. However, when he won the vote and it was stolen from him, then he knew he was meant to be president; that election, he thought, had stolen the "people's presidency." When he came out [as a candidate] in 1828, he came out fighting.

HENDERSON: [Increasing numbers of voters participated in 1828.] A lot of it was the growing development of an actual national party that Martin Van Buren had been working on in Albany and... with people in the South, particularly in Virginia. This is also a period of great technological change. We have railroads and we have newspapers and we have all kinds of new communication methods that are coming to bear, as well as a much larger electorate. There is almost general white male suffrage in all of the states. There are more people voting, there's more interest in voting, and there's more opportunity to hear about it.

BRADY: [Rachel Jackson became a major issue in the 1828 campaign, a first for electoral politics,] to the extent that it happened. Abigail Adams had taken some hard hits from the press as well, being referred to as "Madam Presidentress,"...but this was the first time that someone actually went out attempting to find dirt, found what they thought was dirt, and publicized it widely.

    Charles Hammond was in Cincinnati and he hated Jackson and wanted to see Jackson go down, and he didn't care what it took. When he found out that Rachel had been divorced, he really despised her. He was very rigorously fundamentalist. It was a moral issue for him. He really thought that she would disgrace the White House.... To call a lady who'd been married for thirty-six years a whore, and adulteress, a bigamist, that was unprecedented. She was accused of being married before she met Jackson, and she was, in fact. She was married very unhappily to a man who treated her and her family very badly. Her whole family hated him, and, out West, they didn't believe that you had to stick by your man for fifty years if he was horrible. They believed in dissolving an unhappy marriage. And so, they did.

[Rachel was also criticized during the campaign because] she smoked a pipe and she had a Tennessee accent; she did not have an East Coast accent.

HENDERSON: It's difficult to talk about it in a country that supposedly doesn't have [societal] classes, but there's certainly a strong class issue to [the campaign against Rachel Jackson. Its subtext was]: Would this person be virtuous enough and... genteel enough to represent the United States?

BRADY: [When Jackson was victorious after this contentious campaign, Rachel] at first thought she wouldn't go to Washington. She thought the situation was too volatile and that people might be rude to her, they might snub her...and then they decided that that would be like admitting that they were wrong, which they did not believe they were. And so, she decided to go.

Then, on December 22, Rachel died of heart attack. [She was buried in the] white satin gown that she planned to wear to the inaugural ball. She was buried two days after she died.... All the local dignitaries, all the businesses in town, all the church bells tolled, everything closed down and there was a huge attendance at her funeral.

Rachel Donelson Jackson was the daughter of one of the first families of Tennessee. She and her whole family came to Tennessee via a thousand-mile river trip in which many people on the trip died. They were on a flat boat and they survived. They were some of the earliest white settlers and her family was quite prominent in the area. She was part of the gentry of Tennessee.

[Near present-day Chatham, Virginia, was] where she was born and lived until she was twelve, when they decided to go over the mountains into the new territory. We know nothing about her girlhood; we just extrapolate that it was like the girlhood of other children on the western edges of settled territory.

[Her first husband was ten or eleven years her senior.] His name was Lewis Robards. Her family left the area of Nashville because the war between the whites and the Indians was so ferocious. The whites wanted to stay there; the Indians did not want them there, and so it was a battle for territory. The Donelsons left and went to Kentucky where things were safer. That's where they met Lewis Robards. [The marriage lasted] just three or four years. He was too mean.

It took courage [for Rachel to leave Robards,] but it took more than that. It took the support of her family. She would never have left him if her family had not supported her because you couldn't live without a family out West. She adored her family and they adored her, so they pretty much were part of the whole decision to elope with Andrew Jackson. [At the time she met him, Jackson] was a nobody.

Jackson was one of the boarders at her mother's...palisade; they had a sort of fort where they lived, and he was in one of the cottages with another bachelor lawyer who was there. Why is one of the gentry renting out cottages? Well, first of all, it's nice to have some hard money. But, second of all, in terms of this being a long-going war, to have extra guns on hand is always a good thing.

HENDERSON: This is the Far West at this point, recently settled. Most of the settlers from Tennessee either came by river, the long way, or they came over the mountains. But, this was still really rough country that was not even as settled as Kentucky.

BRADY: ...All his life, Jackson...couldn't bear to see women mistreated or badly treated in any way, so his gallantry was involved with what he saw as abuse of [Rachel by her husband Robards]. Then, when they fell in love, they decided to elope to Natchez, which was Spanish territory at that time.

They stayed there for close to a year, and when they came back, they simply said, "We're married now." And her whole family, including her mother, said, "Yes. This is our son-in-law, Andrew Jackson." Who's going to tell them no? Who's going to say, "Oh, no. What about that other husband?" People just accepted it because the family, neighbors, and friends accepted it.

HENDERSON: It was tricky because their divorce was filed in Virginia by Robards, but there were stipulations in that settlement that it had had to be posted a certain amount of time and in different places, and

Robards didn't go through with posting all of it right away. He was really playing games with the whole divorce.

BRADY: Robards had to take it to court in Kentucky before a jury, and by that time, Rachel and Andrew had been living together as a married couple for two years. So, when Robards accused her of adultery, she was, in fact, living with Andrew Jackson. If she had fought it, then she'd still be married to this person she hated. That made no sense. So, Rachel and Andrew just ignored it and then quietly were remarried.

Rachel, despite her deep wish for them, had no children. She was one of eleven, and those of her brothers and sisters who married had very large families as well. [Rachel and Andrew] adopted one of the twin sons that belonged to her brother and sister-in-law when they were middle-aged, so there was an Andrew Jackson, Jr. who was actually her nephew.

HENDERSON: There was also another son. Jackson had been in battle and had slaughtered many people, women and children, found an infant and tried to give it back to a Creek woman who was alive. She said, "You'd best kill him, you've killed all of his family anyway." Jackson takes the baby home and raises him as a son. Here's Jackson, the Indian killer, and yet he's adopted this boy and raises him as his own.

BRADY: Jackson writes an awful lot of letters to Rachel saying, "He's something special. He's an orphan; I was an orphan. There's some reason I found him and he is not to be in the servant's quarters. He's to be in the house and he's to be educated." He wanted to send him to West Point, but John Quincy Adams was president by then, so [the appointment] was impossible.

The Hermitage became the Jacksons' home early in the nineteenth century. They started in that area, at a bigger place, and then he got into some financial troubles and they moved to the Hermitage, which, at that time, was a log house.

[Eventually,] they had some three hundred slaves; it was a rather large plantation.... They would bring perhaps a couple of personal servants to Washington. Things had become iffier as abolitionist sentiment grew in the North, and it became less and less possible to bring slaves to free territories.

HENDERSON: [Andrew Jackson comes to Washington as a new widower.] He has the inauguration [and afterward] he rides on horseback back to the president's house and the public is invited in. There were about twenty thousand people who had attended the inauguration. The house is opened to the public, and this is the democratic republic—the people of the West—and they crash the house and dance on the tables, they drink all the wine. There were sixteen hundred pounds of cheese that been sent as a gift to the new president and it was completely devoured.

The White House was really beaten up pretty badly. Even Jackson himself had to be escorted out because they were afraid for his safety.

BRADY: He left the party early. He went back to his hotel to go to bed. [Washington, D.C., reacted to these events with the new administration] with horror.

The White House wasn't social very much at all for the first year. First of all, they have to refinish it and replace all the drapes and the chair seats where muddy boots have been trampling and put things back together. Even after that, to the disappointment of Washington society, [the Jackson Administration] said, "We are in deep mourning. We will not be giving parties."

Rachel's niece and nephew were with [President Jackson] all of this time. They were so close, all these nieces and nephews…. Andrew Donelson had been one of their wards and became the president's secretary. He had married his first cousin, Emily Donelson. They had planned all along to come with the Jacksons to Washington, and [after Rachel died,] they went ahead and accompanied him.

[Emily Donelson served in the role of first lady as official hostess for the administration.] She was a very pretty girl, she was young, in her early twenties. She had very good manners. She'd been trained at a ladies' academy in Nashville.

Washington society loved her. One of the main reasons they loved her was because she was young and malleable and the old grand dames of Washington could run all over her as they could not someone like Rachel. They always liked the innocent young nieces.

Emily Donelson, c1830, Rachel Jackson's niece, who served as official hostess during the early years of Jackson's administration.

HENDERSON: Jackson believed in democracy with small "d," and he was very concerned about moneyed interests and about elites controlling the country. That is the core of the democracy that he was trying to create. He really believed in people being part of this democracy, but it didn't preclude him being cultivated and having manners and becoming a lawyer and learning how to interact in society.

BRADY: Jackson always wanted to be a gentleman. That was one of his goals, to prove that he was a gentleman, and if you look at some of his controversies, they're because, in the early days, other men did not treat him as equal.

Peggy Eaton was the daughter of a Washington, D.C., hotel keeper and tavern owner. Many politicians stayed in his hotel and the family got to know the politicians well. Peggy was beautiful, she was well-educated, she liked to sing and perform. She actually sometimes appeared in public, which, God forbid, any lady should do, and so, she was seen as not quite quiet.

HENDERSON: I call her "Margaret" because that's what she liked to be called; I think "Peggy" is a bit of an insult because she didn't like to be called that. She really was somebody who was going up against a different class and was going at it in a very difficult way. She was out-spoken and bold and that was not a woman's role.

She was beautiful, she was vivacious, and she didn't really know her place. She really interfered and went into situations that were part of the men's realm. This is a period in American history when domesticity and the rise of domesticity is becoming very specific, and there is a woman's sphere and there is a men's sphere. The woman's sphere is to guard the household and to guard the morals of society, while the men go out and fight in this new capitalist world.

BRADY: Peggy's husband...was a purser on a naval vessel. He killed himself, and then she was a widow. The one person who had consistently lived at the O'Neill's hotel was John Henry Eaton, who was one of Jackson's closest friends and...a supporter of Rachel Jackson's throughout all those bad times. Eaton was worried, at Margaret's suggestion, that he might have ruined her reputation. There was a lot of talk that the two had had an affair, and that's why her husband killed himself. Eaton asked Jackson, "Should I marry her?" Jackson said, "Certainly." He was always one for love and romance, helping others to elope.

HENDERSON: Jackson was familiar with Margaret, too. Jackson had stayed in the same boardinghouse and knew her when she was a young girl, so he thought that she was perfectly respectable and that this marriage was a good thing.

[The Eaton marriage rose to the level of a cabinet issue because] Margaret Eaton broke another rule: she married too soon. She should have been in mourning for at least a year and she married John Henry Eaton well before that. And that was a problem.

BRADY: Once the Jackson cabinet was named and it included Eaton and his new wife, whose social bona fides are not so good, Peggy presses right ahead and calls on one of the haughtiest of the wives of the other cabinet members, Floride Calhoun. Floride refuses to return her call.... In those days, that was akin to slapping someone in the face.

HENDERSON: The protocol of society was very structured. The first person that you would see when you came into town was the vice president, and you would leave your card. So, Margaret Eaton started in on this process, but she did it incorrectly, and Floride Calhoun was not about to return the call to this woman.

BRADY: All of the cabinet wives except one refused to call on Peggy Eaton. When the president gave a big party, and she was an honored guest often at his side attempting to force these women to recognize her, it was a "hello," and then they would walk on. Everything was so cold and so ugly and Margaret was totally mortified. Worst of all, among those who gave the cut to Margaret was Emily Donelson, Jackson's niece [and official White House hostess].

HENDERSON: Unfortunately, it was Jackson's gallant defending of Margaret Eaton that really turns it from a social crisis into a political crisis. He couldn't leave it alone. He spent enormous amounts of time trying to defend her honor, getting affidavits about where she was, tracking down the people who made these terrible comments. Finally, it becomes in Jackson's mind that... it's not just [about] Margaret, it's an attack against him.

BRADY: That's when Jackson grows to hate [John C.] Calhoun, [whom he sees as the instigator of the attacks against Eaton]. Emily Donelson was so influenced by the ladies that she joined in the ostracism of Margaret Eaton. She did receive her at the White House, but the president demanded that she treat her as a friend, and she would not. And so Jackson sent Emily Donelson home.

HENDERSON: Secretary of State Martin Van Buren had the unfortunate benefit of being a widower himself, so he didn't have to have this social political push from a wife as the other cabinet members did. He was free to go and see Margaret Eaton, which he did. He called on her frequently; he treated her well and he gained tremendous respect from Jackson for that.

There is this very interesting nineteenth century historian who says that the whole political history of the thirty years...[prior to] the Civil War, can be attributed to the moment when the "soft hand of Martin Van Buren touched Mrs. Eaton's knocker." Although there's a double entendre there, it really points out the fact that Martin Van Buren undercuts Calhoun, steps in, and places himself in position to be the next one to run for president where once Calhoun had been the natural choice.

Rachel Jackson's legacy:

BRADY: Rachel Donelson Jackson was the woman of Andrew Jackson's life. He loved her. She was his touchstone. When she died just a few months before he was inaugurated, he was bereft, he really was. He spent all of his time thinking about her and her memory, and having her portraits in his bedroom so he could think of her. It really changed the way his first administration went.

Jackson was not just devastated [by Rachel's death], he was embittered. That's why this whole first term really didn't accomplish anything, because he was either in mourning or he was attempting to help out Peggy Eaton. He was fighting with his favorite niece and nephew. He actually asked his cabinet to resign. It was a huge thing that involved him because he saw Peggy Eaton as a surrogate for Rachel. If they could treat Peggy Eaton this way, they might have treated his wife that way and he could not let it go.

[Had Rachel Jackson lived, it would have been different.] She did not like extensive entertaining. She was very religious, and what she liked to do was to go and hear the leading preachers of the day. She would have had family and friends alike around her in the White House. I think it would have been a very domesticated White House.

Hannah Hoes Van Buren

"...a tender mother and a most affectionate wife."—Hannah Van Buren Obituary, Albany *Argus*, February 9, 1819

Hannah Van Buren, likeness created c1886

Born: March 8, 1783, Kinderhook, New York
Married: February 21, 1807, to Martin Van Buren (1782–1862)
Children: Abraham (1807–1873); John (1810–1866); Martin, Jr. (1812–1855); Winfield Scott (1814–1814); Smith Thompson (1817–1876)
Died: February 5, 1819, Albany, New York (eighteen years before the Van Buren presidency)

Contributors:

PATRICIA BRADY, social and cultural historian specializing in first ladies; author of several books including *A Being So Gentle*

MICHAEL HENDERSON, former superintendent, Martin Van Buren National Historic Site; museum consultant

MICHAEL HENDERSON: Martin Van Buren talks very little about Hannah Hoes. They were first cousins; they knew each other growing up. In Van Buren's case, he was a Dutch speaker, and so he married into the Dutch community in the Hudson River Valley that were Dutch speakers. These were their own people.

Hannah was his wife; [she died at age thirty-four]. They had all of these children together. He had her re-interred in Kinderhook, New

York, later in his life…. We don't have too many stories of him having romantic dalliances with other women or even possibly proposing. He has friendships with women, but he never seems to have another romantic connection.

Martin did not mention Hannah in his autobiography. It's a rambling autobiography, but it's eight hundred pages long and you would think that he might have [mentioned her]. His son, John, when he had his first child, wanted to name the girl after his mother, and he wrote to his father, "Was her name Hannah or Anna?" So, he probably didn't even talk to his sons very much about his wife. He always kept a locket with a painting of her with him and that's all we know.

PATRICIA BRADY: Van Buren was not so odd in not mentioning his wife. Many nineteenth century political leaders or scientific leaders would talk about their lives without mentioning wives or children. That was just so personal. It had nothing to do with their success.

HENDERSON: During the election of 1840, supporters of Van Buren started to refer to him as "Old Kinderhook." The phrase "OK" had just hit the streets in Boston. It was picked up by the campaign as a way to talk about "Old Kinderhook." It stuck, and "OK" became the universal expression that we use all the time.

BRADY: [In office,] Van Buren was facing a tremendous political crisis because of the Panic of 1837, which he inherited from Jackson's policies.

HENDERSON: He was a Depression president and this was the first huge economic depression that the United States had had….We already had an interconnected global economy and there were calls out on banks from London; there were calls out to American banks, but they didn't have the money and they collapsed. As the banking crisis started to go on—we don't have a national currency at this point, so state banks started to collapse and everything rises up…. By that May, there were riots over food in New York City. It was really serious.

[Even with the bad economy, Martin Van Buren] was a very social person; that was one of his great skill sets. He had charming little dinner parties; he was very personable. He, like Jackson, always liked women and had lots of women friends, so, there was still a social side to the White House because a lot of his politicking was done socially.

BRADY: Van Buren was not a backward country clod. Van Buren loved society, he was known as "the Little Magician" because he was always pulling off little plans. Men who disliked him, like Calhoun, would say, "Oh, he just appeals to the ladies," meaning that he worked through the ladies, through the backdoor. He had become very social and so had his sons.

In terms of large-scale entertaining, the New Year's Day party, which was traditional at the White House, was pretty much his big party until his eldest son married Angelica Singleton. Dolley Madison had a beautiful cousin, Angelica Singleton. Martin Van Buren had four single sons including [one who served as] his secretary and chief aide. Dolley introduced them all at a dinner party.

HENDERSON: Van Buren spent the first year in the White House without a hostess. Angelica Singleton and Abraham Van Buren married in November of the next year, so she was hostess for the '38-'39 season, at which she was wildly successful. Everyone thought she was beautiful and glamorous and did a fabulous job. Then, they went on an extended honeymoon through Europe, where she met the Queen of England and was presented at the court of [French King] Louis Philippe and she really took to it.... Louis Philippe really thought that she was incredible. They really took Europe by storm.

BRADY: European courts were fascinated and really relieved that they turned out to be "civilized." They weren't backwoods barbarians, which was what they expected of Americans.

HENDERSON: When Angelica came back [to Washington] for the next season is when she had a problem; that's when she tried creating [a court-like] tableau at the New Year's open house. This is a country that's interested in democracy, this is just the beginning of the next presidential election season, and here is Angelica acting in a queenly manner. That didn't go over well.

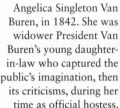

Angelica Singleton Van Buren, in 1842. She was widower President Van Buren's young daughter-in-law who captured the public's imagination, then its criticisms, during her time as official hostess.

BRADY: Angelica was dying to [serve as first lady]. She was twenty-two. She was excited. It was all glamour and wonderment and she wanted a bigger stage for herself, too.

HENDERSON: [Van Buren lost the 1840 election and returned to Lindenwald, the house in Kinderhook, New York,] that Van Buren bought while he was president. He bought it in case the White House didn't work out…. This is a period in the American history when farming was something you could make money at. Van Buren did put a lot of effort into running Lindenwald as a working farm, and made money doing it. He also had his family there. He had cousins come, as well as nieces and nephews from his wife's brothers and sisters. He had the Singleton family stay there. John Van Buren and his wife, Elizabeth Vanderpoel, stayed there, so it was a house full of family.

He left the White House and although he never claimed to run again, he certainly made it clear that if the country called for him, he would do his duty and step forward. In 1844, he really thought he was going to get the Democratic nomination in Baltimore, and he didn't—and it was a big deal. It was yet again another major crack in this National Party between North and South.

Then… Martin Van Buren comes up to 1848 and makes a pretty substantial decision that he is going to go against what he spent his life working for—a unified national Democratic Party; he will run a third-party campaign with his son, John.

Van Buren runs on this Free Soil ticket, which is a very interesting third party, a forerunner of the Republican Party. They believed in free soil, free labor, and free men, no slavery.

BRADY: What's so important about this period is that it's the time when steamboats have changed the whole situation about selling from the South; slave power is growing. The South is the most profitable part of the country and abolition sentiment is growing like crazy in the North. That's why we have somebody like Van Buren running on the Free Soil ticket, which is, in fact, an abolitionist party.

HENDERSON: There's this great elephant in the middle of the room, slavery, which really comes into focus. [And, by 1848,] we have set the stage for the coming of the most horrific test of democracy that we have had, the Civil War.

Hostess Angelica Singleton Van Buren's legacy:

BRADY: At first, public opinion of Angelica was very positive.... It was the trip to Europe that did her in and did a great deal of harm to the Van Buren administration. She was too naive to realize that she had gone overboard. She was shocked when public opinion lashed out at her because we were in a depression and she was posing with ostrich feathers on a dais as though she were a queen.

She did actually recover. They tore out the dais and she stopped doing the posing. But by then, the administration was almost over anyway. And Angelica was part of what sank it.

HENDERSON: Angelica wasn't going to sink this administration. [In addition to] this terrible depression, there were some serious issues that the United States was just coming to talk about, slavery being a huge one; Indian removal being a huge one. These are really big, difficult issues. The sides, the North and the South, are quickly pulling apart from each other. The room for negotiation is rapidly evaporating and the center isn't going to hold.

Anna Symmes Harrison

"I wish my husband's friends had left him where he is; happy and contented in retirement."

Anna Harrison, in a
twentieth century portrait.

Born: July 25, 1775, Flatbrook, New Jersey
Married: November 22, 1795, to William Henry Harrison (1773–1841)
Children: Elizabeth Bassett (1796–1846); John Cleves Symmes (1798–
   1830); Lucy Singleton (1800–1826); William Henry, Jr. (1802–1838);
   John Scott (1804–1878); Benjamin (1806–1840); Mary Symmes (1809–
   1842); Carter Bassett (1811–1839); Anna Tuthill (1813–1845); James
   Findlay (1814–1817)
Died: January 25, 1864, North Bend, Ohio

Contributors:

EDITH MAYO, curator emerita, First Ladies exhibit, Smithsonian Museum of American History; academic advisor for C-SPAN's *First Ladies* series

EDNA GREENE MEDFORD, professor and chair, department of history, Howard University; focus on Jacksonian, Civil War, and Reconstruction-era history

EDITH MAYO: Almost no one has ever heard of Anna Harrison. We know she was born in New Jersey, and she was very well-educated, with an Eastern elite education. She married William Henry Harrison, who went on to become a great military hero both in battles with the Indians and the British in the War of 1812. He distinguished himself on the battlefield and was declared this great military hero.

EDNA GREENE MEDFORD: He had actually studied medicine for a short period of time and decided to join the military shortly thereafter, and moved to Ohio. He became the territorial governor of Indiana and before that, was a noted Indian fighter.

[School children] have grown up hearing the phrase, "Tippecanoe and Tyler Too," from William Henry Harrison's 1840 campaign. He was elected at the age of sixty-eight, [a record no president broke until Ronald Reagan].

The term Tippecanoe comes from the battle of Tippecanoe, where he fought against the Shawnee leader Tecumseh and his brother. The two Native Americans were attempting to establish a pan-Indian movement. As territorial governor, Harrison was instrumental in securing land for white settlers, and, of course, that clashed with Native American interests, and so at that battle Harrison was considered the victor. We're not so certain about that, but he became important enough in that battle that it carried him into public office.

MAYO: Meanwhile, Anna has ten children and is raising them on the American frontier in a series of out-of-the-way forts, making sure they all get an excellent education. Just the physical hardships were difficult and it was not an easy task to corral ten children without a lot of help...or to educate them on the frontier. She was an exemplary person, having met all those challenges very successfully.

She was knowledgeable behind the scenes, but she wasn't keen to be involved in a political life.... She was reluctant, even though she had been the wife of the territorial governor of Indiana, and she acted there as his first lady. She had doubts of whether her training and her experience would allow her to be a good hostess in the White House fishbowl.

Anna was not very happy that her husband had been elected president.... She had a series of illnesses that had left her in ill health, so when he made the journey to Washington, D.C., for the inauguration, she did not come. The decision was made for them to wait until the spring weather arrived so that the journey to Washington, which must have been very difficult in 1841, ...got better, and she would make the trip. The problem was, of course, that he died only one month into his presidency and she never made it to Washington.

MEDFORD: We don't know an awful lot about Anna Harrison. We know that she was a very religious woman. We know that she was a

First Lady Anna Harrison didn't make it to Washington for her husband's March 1841 inaugural. The president was dead just one month later.

reluctant first lady.... Ironically enough, the day that she was all packed up and ready to join President Harrison in Washington was the day that she had notification that he had died.

...The argument has always been that Harrison died because he was not prudent enough to wear a top hat and coat at his inauguration, and he spoke too long, and so he was exposed to very cold weather, and he caught a cold and died. It's a little bit more complex than that. He was an older gentleman; he was sixty-eight. He was exhausted by all of the office seekers in the first month of his presidency. All of that compromised his health, and so he did eventually catch a very bad cold that turned into pneumonia, and as a consequence of that, he did die.

[Anna Harrison was the first first lady to have a public education and she was an avid reader of political journals throughout her life.] ...Even though she didn't come to the White House, she did use what influence she had to get appointments for her nephews and for her sons and grandsons....

Because Anna was not [in the White House for the month of Harrison's presidency], there were two other women who carried out her duties; one was Jane Irwin Harrison, who was a widow. She was married to one of the Harrison men, but he had died. When Harrison apparently asked her to serve in that capacity, she was assisted by one of her aunts by the same name, Jane Irwin Findlay, who was an older woman and gave her some guidance.... And Dolley Madison offered advice whenever she got away with it.

Anna Harrison's legacy:

MAYO: Anna Harrison is one of these first ladies who is first lady by virtue of being married to the president, but she never carried out any first lady duties.

MEDFORD: [Anna Harrison's husband became president; her son was a congressman; her grandson, Benjamin, was also elected president.] They were considered one of the first families of Virginia. You would have had Harrisons that were very much involved in the American Revolution, you have one signing the Declaration of Independence, so they have this long history of political involvement.

Anna did live with the family of [President Benjamin Harrison] in her later years. Her home burned and she went to live with one of her sons, the father of Benjamin. What influence she had on the future president, we really don't know, but we assume that, as grandmothers are wont to do, they do have influence.

She was the first presidential widow that was able to get a pension for her service. Her husband had died in office and she needed the assistance, and so Congress did appropriate $25,000 for her.

Letitia Christian Tyler

"Mother attends to and regulates all the household affairs so quickly that you can't tell she does it."—Daughter-in-law Priscilla Tyler

Letitia Tyler. *Courtesy White House Historical Association*

Born: November 12, 1790, near Richmond, Virginia
Married: March 29, 1813, to John Tyler (1790–1862)
Children: Mary (1815–47); Robert (1816–77); John, Jr. (1819–96); Letitia (1821–1907); Elizabeth (1820–70); Anne Contesse (1825); Alice (1827–54); Tazewell (1830–74)
Died: September 10, 1842, at the White House, Washington, D.C.

Julia Gardiner Tyler

"The President says I am the best of diplomatists...I have commenced my auspicious reign, and am in quiet possession of the Presidential Mansion."

Julia Tyler, 1844. *Credit: Sherwood Forest Plantation*

Born: May 4, 1820, Gardiner's Island, New York
Married: June 26, 1844, to John Tyler (1790–1862)
Children: David Gardiner (1846–1927); John Alexander (1848–83); Julia (1849–71); Lachlan (1851–1902); Lyon Gardiner (1853–1935); Robert Fitzwalter (1856–1927); Pearl (1860–1947)
Died: July 10, 1889, Richmond, Virginia

Contributors:

EDNA GREENE MEDFORD, professor and chair, department of history, Howard University; specialist in Jacksonian, Civil War, and Reconstruction-era history

TAYLOR STOERMER, Graduate School of Arts and Sciences fellow and instructor of public history, Harvard University, focusing on the American Revolution and its modern relevance

EDNA GREENE MEDFORD: [William Henry Harrison's death just one month into the presidency created a constitutional crisis.] John Tyler decided that he was not going to let Congress think too long about that, and so he declared himself the president and...Congress agreed to pass resolutions declaring him president. Not everyone agreed with that, however, and so occasionally mail came to the White House, addressed to the "acting president" or to the "vice president," and Tyler had those documents returned unopened.

...Tyler was an interesting president because although he was elected on the Whig ticket with William Henry Harrison, he actually had been a Jacksonian Democrat earlier in his political career, [then] clashed with Jackson and the Democrats, and had joined the Whig party. Once he became president, he abandoned the Whig platform and angered them and they expelled him from the party.

TAYLOR STOERMER: Letitia and John Tyler met where almost everybody in the Virginia Tidewater met—in Williamsburg. They actually lived not that far from one another. John Tyler is from Charles City County in a place called Greenway, and Letitia Tyler is from New Kent County, which is really just a stone's throw away.... We don't know exactly where they met, but we know that they met in about 1811, 1812. John Tyler went to William and Mary with Letitia's brother, and so their families certainly became involved with one another and they met at a very young age. They were both the exact same age, so they were twenty-one, twenty-two when they met, and they fell in love very quickly.

They had a lot of children. One of the things that really kept them apart for a great chunk of their married life [was that] John Tyler was constitutionally incapable of being out of public office. He was addicted to it, to a certain extent. He left Letitia at home to run the family, to run the business, and to continue to manage this incredible brood of children that they had almost from the very start.

We have evidence that Letitia counseled John in one very important way: in earlier elections, she told him to "get out of politics, come home, stay out of it, I want you here." He couldn't stay out of politics, so by the time he was in the Senate in the 1830s, she gave up....

The Tylers had a number of different plantations. One of the issues with John Tyler and with his family is that they are always on the very edge of solvency, and so they never lived in one place for longer than ten years.... They own probably no more than between thirty and thirty-five slaves at a particular time and they're growing mainly wheat and corn over about six hundred to nine hundred acres. They owned several plantations in Charles City County. They then moved to Gloucester County on the other side of the York River in Virginia. They are continuing to try to figure out a way, during these very striking economic challenges to the country that follow the Panic of 1819, or what's going on in 1837, to keep their heads economically above water. With John Tyler gone for so long and for so often—six months out of every year while he is in public office—this leaves a lot of that burden resting on Letitia's shoulders.

MEDFORD: [Letitia was a pretty tough woman. She had a stroke and was partially paralyzed, yet continued to handle the operations.] That's indicative of the kind of life that women lived during that time, even wealthy women. It's rural living, and life was tough for them, but life was made easier for them by their enslaved laborers and they certainly did use those to great advantage.

STOERMER: John Tyler is one of the staunchest supporters of slavery that ever inhabited the White House. He was vocal about it throughout most of his career. He believed firmly that "slavery is the greatest property that a Southerner can own." He believes this is the backbone of the society. Letitia's views, we know a little bit less about....

[The Tylers learn one month after the 1840 election that Harrison has died and they will inherit the White House.] It gets us into a very interesting conversation about what is a first lady: Is it just someone who happens to be married to the president, or do they fulfill these very particular roles? With Letitia, she is by nature a retiring person; she prefers to stay at home, she prefers a quiet life. She does not like the kind of public activities that we would normally associate with the first lady, so even without her illness, even without the stroke, it would have been a fairly quiet White House. However, that just...means that she has to have other people do it for them. It's a big family and it is a closely-knit family. A lot of their daughters were living in the White House, they have a son and daughter-in-law living in the White House, so she really turns all of that extraordinary social energy over to them, in particular, their daughter-in-law Priscilla Cooper Tyler.

MEDFORD: Priscilla Cooper Tyler is serving as unofficial hostess, along with the Tyler daughter Letitia, the namesake. Priscilla is an interesting person because she was an actress at a time when it was not a good thing for a woman to be doing that; it was not considered respectable. But the Tylers accepted her and, more importantly, Letitia accepted her. She was very close to her and so she would have been performing most of the functions that Mrs. Tyler would have been performing had she been able to do so. It's not so much that Letitia is not doing anything; even though she is disabled because of the stroke, she is still giving orders from her bedroom, so to speak....

Congress did not appropriate money for the Tylers, at least not to fix up the White House. The White House was an absolute mess at that time, just really in very poor repair, so Tyler must have used some of his own funds to entertain people, and they did entertain lavishly.

STOERMER: They are on a shoestring, so you assume that a lot of this [entertaining] is coming out of his salary as president. One of the people who is the most extravagant in that entire White House is John Tyler himself. He spends most of his life in one sort of complicated debt after another and having his family, particularly people like Letitia, trying to keep them outside of it....So Priscilla probably was taking a page out of Louisa Catherine Adams's book. During the congressional session, she will hold two formal dinner parties every week. Every other week, she will do public receptions in the evenings. She will hold public parties every month that would have as many as a thousand people. She opened up the White House on New Year's. She opened up the White House on July Fourth, and she started the tradition of having the [United States] Marine Band perform on the South Lawn. They are finding ways to do all that, but they might be doing it with mirrors because Congress, given their battles with John Tyler, doesn't appropriate a cent for the upkeep of the White House during his entire presidency.

Letitia Tyler died on September 10 in 1842; she had another massive stroke. There is no evidence that there is any kind of lingering; she dies fairly quickly. It hits the family like a ton of bricks.

[There was no White House memorial service] that we know of. They kept things very private. She was buried at her home, in New Kent County, Virginia...so it was a very quiet event, but it was mostly manifested in the impact that it had on her children. They were devastated.

From his letters, we know that President Tyler was obviously emotionally attached to Letitia, who was a huge part of his life for a very long time, and he loved her dearly. However, we also have evidence that he is seeing Julia Gardiner probably about four months after Letitia's death.

Julia Gardiner is a young woman from Long Island, New York, from East Hampton, where, in fact, Anna Harrison had gone to school. She is from a very well-known, long-standing New York family with ties deep into the seventeenth century....The family still owns Gardiner's Island. Her father was a New York state senator. They were in Washington frequently for the social seasons and she was well known at the White House and to the daughters of the Tylers. She was even known to come over not just for the levees and for the parties, but to also do things like [play] quiet games of whist. She was quite beautiful and quite rambunctious and was very well-educated both here and in Europe, so it made her quite a charming woman to be around.

She quickly caught the widowed president's eye. This [relationship] moved shockingly quickly. Julia Gardiner was thirty years younger than John Tyler and when they got married, she was twenty-four and he was fifty-four.

[They married in secret on] June 26, 1844. It was only four months after the disaster of the USS *Princeton* [when Julia's father was killed before her eyes in an accident]. There is still a period of mourning that should be publicly and appropriately observed, but John Tyler has secured, even in that rough period of time, the permission of her mother for them to get married.

Her mother was worried about Tyler's financial situation and whether he would be able to continue her life in the manner that she was accustomed. When he was able [to convince her of] that sufficiently, she gave her permission. They had a very small, private, secret wedding at an Episcopal church in New York City. There were only a handful of people there: one of his sons, a couple of his political friends, and a few members of her family. The public didn't know about it until the next day.

It shows up in the newspaper that he is going off...to take a little bit of vacation, and he pops up in New York City. Then it's in the newspaper the next day, "Oh, by the way, the president has just gotten married into one of New York's most prominent social families."

MEDFORD: People gossiped about it: it was "so soon" after his wife's death, although it really was not so soon after her death. But they were very much concerned about the age difference, with many people feeling that it was unfair to Julia that she was married to this man who was so much older than she was. A lot of people didn't like it; his daughters certainly did not. They were very loyal to their mother, understandably. There was one daughter [Letitia] who never got over it. The other daughters made their peace and the sons never seemed to have a problem with it, but that one daughter never reconciled with her stepmother.

Julia Tyler sees herself as queen of the land. She had spent some time in Europe.... She admired how the queen received her guests, seated on a bit of a pedestal. Julia decided to do the same thing for a time. She saw it very much as she was the first lady of the land and she was going to make the most of it.

STOERMER: It seems that what she did was develop her own court.... She had these young women who were joining her they would call the "vestal virgins".... She really believed that she was representing something much bigger than just being the wife of the president, and to do that requires display. It requires a very conscious shaping of image as an element of political communication.

MEDFORD: She received her guests surrounded by these women all dressed in white. But, she seemed to be able to do no wrong. She had her critics, but a lot of people loved her, especially men.

STOERMER: [Julia Tyler loved publicity;] the more notorious the better. She made a point of cultivating the friendship of a reporter. She would report what was happening in the White House in terms of the social events, and he gave her a lot of personal attention in the articles that he wrote. So, she was out there in a way that respectable women were not. But this is a new era;...this is the time when the women's movement is under way and interestingly enough, someone like Julia Tyler fits in to a certain extent. She is very conservative in some ways, but in terms of breaking through the traditional way that a woman should behave, she is doing it in a way that other women are not at that time.

She also brought dancing to the White House. She brought the waltz, the polka. She brought a number of things to the White House, but...it does work both ways. The abolitionist press starts to see these kinds of things that Julia is doing in the White House, this level of extravagance, as being yet another example of the corruption of the slave party. Particularly with it being a distressed economic period, ...the only way they could be doing that is because they're gathering all of their wealth and benefits from the fact that they owned other people....

The abolitionists sent people [to Washington] just to keep an eye on the Tyler White House and report back on things like this....

MEDFORD: To a certain extent, Julia redeems herself when she responds to the Duchess of Sutherland, who had criticized slavery in America. She writes a letter back and says, "You need to take care of business at home; you've got people from the lower classes there who are starving." She doesn't say slavery is right, but she does imply that slavery is not as bad as what's happening elsewhere.

[John Tyler was castigated by the Whigs, essentially thrown out of his party, for some of his positions. When the next election came around, in 1844, there was no chance of him being nominated,] especially since he had also alienated the other party. There was no one there to really support him.

[During the vote on the annexation of Texas, which was a key final event in the Tyler presidency,] Julia was keeping tabs of where people stand. She was going to Congress, listening to the debates. She is trying to twist a few arms, but I don't think she is that important to [its final outcome].

STOERMER: Julia certainly believes she has a lot of influence, but... there are much more complicated balls in the political air over the Texas annexation issue than anything that Julia Gardiner Tyler is going to solve, especially in those months after the election... but she firmly believes that she is responsible. John Tyler [also] believes that she is responsible and when, on March 1, 1845, he signs the joint resolution that annexes Texas, he gives her the gold pen that he signed it with and she puts it around her neck and wears it as a trophy.

Especially when you're talking about a main matter of public legislation and public policy, it's tough to find another first lady who is so overtly engaged in this kind of effort. Whether that level of influence is successful, or is meaningful or not, she is certainly out there actively supporting her husband's position on annexation. She is talking to everybody she can about it; she is writing a great deal about it; she is holding all of the social events at the White House in order to influence that piece of legislation. So if we're talking about a first lady who's involved in a matter of national public policy, and being involved explicitly, you can peg that to Julia Tyler.

MEDFORD: ...She is perhaps the first first lady who really wants to get involved in that way. The other women are willing to simply play the traditional role; although you have some women who may be saying all kinds of things to their husbands, they're not making it public....

STOERMER: In the last two weeks of the Tyler presidency, it is really nothing but Julia Gardiner Tyler at her absolute, extravagant best. They start off with a party for three thousand people; two weeks later, they have a party to celebrate James Knox Polk and the annexation of Texas. John Tyler then says, "You can no longer say that I am a man without a party."

[The Tylers returned home to Sherwood Forest.] They really became a very big, fairly close-knit family, all gathered there for the most part, at Sherwood Forest. The Civil War does a lot in bringing them more closely together. The members of the family that are cast in other parts...all have to come back to Sherwood Forest. They do start to see Julia not necessarily as a stepmother—some of them refer to her as a sister—and they certainly come to love her and appreciate her and accept her into the family, as such. Her children and Letitia's children, although they are of considerable age difference, do end up more than reconciling; they become very, very close.

Sherwood Forest got its name because during one of John Tyler's breaks with the Whigs, he was referred to as Robin Hood. He embraced that and called their home Sherwood Forest, and Julia embraced it, too. When she got there, she got uniforms and developed new liveries for the enslaved men who rowed their riverboat, and she had bows and arrows sewn on their collars as part of their uniforms.

MEDFORD: In 1861, there was an attempt to stay secession, and John Tyler was very instrumental in that last-ditch effort. To do that, there was a peace conference held in Washington in February of 1861.... Once that failed, he decided to back the Confederacy, to back secession. He had been elected to the Confederate Congress. He was very much a secessionist, and when he died, his coffin was covered with the Confederate flag. The North, the Union, did not acknowledge his having passed.

STOERMER: John Tyler was seventy-one [when he died]. He was never sworn in as a member of the Confederate Congress. It was just about to meet, so he was in Richmond for that session. From what we know, Tyler caught a cold and died. The last child that he and Julia had together was when he was sixty-eight; she was two years old when he died.

MEDFORD: [After John Tyler died in 1862,] Julia leaves and goes to Staten Island to live with her mother and she spends the entire [Civil War] there. She actually goes to Bermuda for a short period of time, so she is not at Sherwood Forest [for the war]. Of course, she is impacted financially by the war because she loses her enslaved laborers. She returns there [after the war] to try to get it into some kind of order, but doesn't live there again. She spends the remaining years in Richmond.

Sherwood Forest, the Tylers' plantation, still remains in family hands and is open to the public.

STOERMER: In the South, [the perception of Julia Tyler after the war is] quite good; in the North, not quite so good. She is still referred to in the South as "the ex-presidentress," something that she insists upon. John Tyler's memory is still revered in the South after the war as being somebody who was able to legitimize the cause of the Confederacy. Julia Gardiner Tyler certainly is contributing to this lost cause notion, something that she refers to as the "holy Southern cause." There really isn't any rehabilitation of her husband because in the South she does not feel like he needs to be rehabilitated except when it comes to getting her pension, which is something she desperately needs. They have two homes: Sherwood Forest and they also have a summer home near Hampton, Virginia, which actually goes through the same kind of war damage that Sherwood Forest goes through. She has to sell that property just to maintain Sherwood Forest, which is mostly for her family to live in. She spends a lot of the time fighting for her pension, which she doesn't get until 1881 when she is awarded $1,200 a year. The main argument against it is, "Yes, you may have been first lady, but your husband became a traitor to the United States, so there's no reason why we should ever honor that."

She died in 1889. Obviously, there are a lot of other things going on in the country by then. She had been largely focusing on her family, focusing on maybe a personal legacy in that sense and on maintaining what the family could hold on to, something like Sherwood Forest, so they can pass that on.... Later on in her life, so much of her energy was devoted to the pension fight and to other things that [her own public image] was far from her mind by then.

Julia Tyler's legacy:

STOERMER: Honestly, the jury is still out [about Julia Tyler]. Here, you can see the possibilities of a woman in [the first lady's] position. But on the other hand, you can also see perhaps some of the limitations, as with Letitia and with some of the other first ladies [who served in this role].

MEDFORD: [Julia Tyler is remembered] as the vivacious person she was; quite ambitious. Her story conveys the possibilities for first ladies. Not all of them pursued her path, but she was able to do some things that were significant.

[As for John Tyler,] oh my God, I cannot change my opinion of him. He is a person who turns his back on his own party; that's one thing. He supported a cause that was creating serious issues for a whole race of people. He was more than willing to perpetuate slavery, forever if possible. I can't separate his legacy from that.

Sarah Childress Polk

"If I should be so fortunate as to reach the White House, I expect to live on $25,000 a year and I will neither keep house nor make butter."

Sarah Polk, 1846. *Courtesy White House Historical Association*

Born: September 4, 1803, Murfreesboro, Tennessee
Married: January 1, 1824, to James Knox Polk (1795–1849)
Children: none
Died: August 4, 1891, Nashville, Tennessee

Contributors:

PAUL FINKELMAN, professor of American history, constitutional law, and race and the law, Albany Law School; and author or editor of several books, including *Congress and the Crisis of the 1850s*

CONOVER HUNT, consultant for museums and historical organizations; author of several books including co-author, *Remember the Ladies: Women in America, 1750–1815*

CONOVER HUNT: [Sarah Polk is frequently in the top tier of modern historians' surveys of most influential first ladies.] She was truly a political partner with her husband. They did not have children at a time when women were expected to be mothers, be hearth and home, the keepers of the faith. She was very much her husband's political equal and his partner. She never went too far within the boundaries of what a proper early Victorian lady should be in the nineteenth century, but everyone knew that they shared an office in the private apartments. She was active in discussions at the many state dinners they had.

James would ask her to mark newspapers and articles for him to read. She was his sounding board. Franklin Pierce, before he became president, told her husband that he would much rather talk politics with Sarah Polk than with James Polk, and yet the women of the time accepted her. She was very pious, very religious, a very strict Presbyterian. She did not allow dancing in the White House. She got rid of hard liquor, but they had wines and brandies with the frequent dinners they had.

She was not a prude; she was very much a woman who knew what she wanted and set her rules out and everyone had to play according to those rules. And she was respected for it. She was very, very popular.

PAUL FINKELMAN: President James K. Polk is certainly not very well-known, and he's certainly important. When he was nominated for president, he held no public office. he had been a one-term governor [who twice lost his bid for reelection]. And before that, he had been a member of Congress [and House speaker]. He was a lawyer practicing law in Tennessee, and he was what is known as the first dark-horse candidate.

He had hoped to get the vice presidential nomination; that's what he was pushing for. Suddenly, in a deadlocked convention, out of nowhere, Polk is the presidential nominee.... Polk runs against Henry Clay of Kentucky; Clay had run for president twice before this. Clay believes it's his turn to become president. He expects it will be a cakewalk to the presidency because no one's heard of Polk. But Clay makes a number of mistakes during the campaign, and in the end, in a very close vote, Clay loses to Polk....

HUNT: There was no stumping at all during the 1848 campaign. Sarah was her husband's campaign manager for his congressional campaigns and his gubernatorial campaigns, but during the presidential campaign, there was no active campaigning.

Historian William Seale calls the Polk presidency an imperial presidency, meaning that the couple thought the office of the presidency, and the White House as the official executive residence, needed to be highly respected, and so there was more formal protocol. It was a very liberal approach. You could come with an introduction to any of their receptions, because Polk was a Democrat. But at the same time, people were well-dressed. There were more formal dinners. There were multiple courses. It was considered an honor to be at the White House....

Sarah Polk reorganized the staffing at the White House. She was a very well-organized woman. She hired a steward. They brought in their own servants and got rid of some of the paid staff. She then got her steward to cut deals with the various vendors and grocers in the Washington area: if they gave them significant discounts, [the White House] would give them the American version of the royal seal. It was kept rather quiet, but [the message was:] if you want us to buy your rolls for our White House dinners...you're going to have to give us a discount. And it worked. They were very frugal in that way, always, during the entire time they were married.

FINKELMAN: She owned those servants and that's important to understand. The Polks come from very wealthy circumstances and they are slave owners and they bring a lot of assets with them. Polk can afford to be president just as John Tyler could afford to be president.

HUNT: Dolley Madison has come back to Washington at this point, and Sarah Polk and Dolley became very close. Dolley mentored Sarah, and Sarah fed Dolley, which was very important [because Dolley was broke]. The Polks treated her as a grande dame and honored her in all of their entertainments. Sarah and Dolley were the two war first ladies, the War of 1812 and, thirty years later, the Mexican War. There are many parallels between Dolley Madison and Sarah Polk—the sense of self, the sense of fashion, the understanding the role of the first lady in conveying the indirect help that would support her husband's presidency. It's not easy to be a first lady during war. There were many detractors as the war went on....

FINKELMAN: Photography makes its debut at this time, but they're just beginning to figure it out.... It is almost a novelty in the 1840s, and it's not all that terrific. First of all, you have to sit for a long time. It's not a single shot, click, and your picture is there. You have to sit rigidly and not move while the photograph is being taken. What's much more important than photography is the very sophisticated linotype and art in newspapers. You get wonderful campaign posters being done when Polk runs. Currier, who later becomes half of Currier and Ives, does a campaign poster for Polk's opponent, Henry Clay.

HUNT: Central heating and gas lights arrived at this time, too. Sarah did hold out when they put in the gas lights and insisted that the Oval Room at the White House be lit with candlelight. When they shut down the gas for the night, the whole White House went dark during a reception and yet the Oval Room was still lit with beautiful candle lighting. These were experiments, but it ultimately saved the presidential family a lot of money because they had to heat the White House out of their $25,000 salary.

FINKELMAN: What we are getting at, which is always true for the White House and for every presidency, is that technology is going to change the way presidents campaign, the way presidents portray themselves, and the way presidential families live.

HUNT: Sarah Polk had one of the most advanced educations for a woman of her day. Her father was a great believer in educating women. She and her older sister were educated at academies in Murfreesboro and Nashville, and then he sent them to the Salem Academy in Winston-Salem, the famous Moravian school that is Salem College today. It was five hundred miles away. It took them a month to get there and they were there for two years. That atmosphere encouraged her to speak her mind and participate in discussions.

Sarah had a well-established sense of style from her childhood. She grew up with silks and satins. During the White House years, she dressed elegantly for evenings and receptions. In the summer of 1847, they sent an order to Paris for some gowns for the first lady which were not in the usual style. All of the invoices survived, and so do the gowns, which is amazing. The top designers in Paris were asked to make some gowns.... This order for clothes with lots of accessories cost about $450. Dolley Madison's order in 1811 cost $2,000. [Sarah Polk was searching for the sweet spot between frugality and her public image,] but she did it so well. Everyone said that she was beautifully dressed. She had beautiful deportment. She carried herself like a lady, acted like a lady, and was very gracious.

FINKELMAN: It's important to have some perspective on what is happening to women at this time. For most American women, not much is changing and not much change is being asked for. The most important

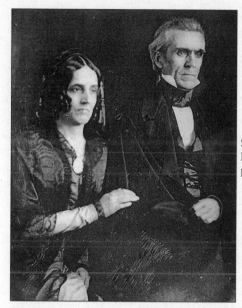

Sarah Polk was President James K. Polk's genuine political partner, unusual for this era.

changes for women, the cutting edge of women in politics, is actually coming out of the anti-slavery movement, so that in the North, you have thousands and thousands of women who are politically active for the first time in American history.

Starting in the 1830s, there's something which is known as the "great petition campaign." Literally hundreds of thousands of petitions show up in Washington asking Congress to do things like not annex Texas because it was seen as a great slave conspiracy, which it was, and to repeal the Fugitive Slave Law, or to end slavery in the District of Columbia. Many of these petitions were gathered by women and many women signed these petitions, so what you get is women actively participating in politics to change America for the better.

The other great women's movement is the temperance movement. Women are also active in movements to prevent prostitution. These are things that are close to what would be considered domesticity for women, but it's outside the house; it's out in the public space. What's fascinating is that someone like Sarah Polk, probably with the exception of temperance, would have been appalled at what most of these activist women were asking for.

Eventually, about 1848, some of the abolitionist women along with a few men such as Frederick Douglass, who's at the 1848 political convention, are asking for the right to vote for women. It was a long time coming, but its beginning is at this time.

HUNT: The Polks [met because they] ran in the same circles, probably through either Andrew Jackson or through her own father's family. Polk graduated from the University of North Carolina and then went into law and studied in Nashville and became clerk of the legislature. They met there or they met at Andrew Jackson's home because the Polk girls were often there.

We think that Andrew Jackson advised Polk to marry Sarah. "This is who you need as a wife," he would say. It is commonly said that she told Polk she wouldn't marry him unless he ran for office. He did, and he won, and they were married in 1824.

Andrew Jackson and his wife, Rachel, did not have any children of their own and had many different young people that they took in. Jackson would write to Sarah and call her "my daughter."

Sarah and James K. Polk also had no children…. They spent a lot of time with nieces and nephews. Sarah, as first lady, brought her nieces into the White House to help her with entertaining and returning calls because she did not return calls, which was a change in tradition.

FINKELMAN: Had they had children, Sarah would have had slaves who would have raised the children, who would have done all of the diapers. She might have slaves who would have been wet nurses when the children were infants. The notion of the burden of families for someone like Sarah Polk would be very different than, say, when we talk about Abigail Fillmore, a woman of very modest means who, in fact, has to raise her own children without the help of a house full of slaves to do the work for her.

HUNT: Sarah was very actively involved [in James's life in Washington]. He went to D.C. without her for his first term in Congress and never tried that again, because she didn't like being left at home at all. At that time the congressmen lived in a boardinghouse and established what they called a "mess," several different elected officials living together and sharing meals and a parlor. They did that for years, until he became speaker and then they had to have a larger apartment.

She attended the sessions of Congress. She was very attentive to the issues of the day, and the elected members of Congress who were in the mess with her knew that she was a very tuned-in congressional wife.

James K. Polk, in his will expressed that he hoped that when she died, she would manumit their slaves. As it turned out, she sold their plantation before the Civil War. But the issue of slavery was not really brought to the forefront either during their marriage or during his administration. It became much more critical with the two administrations that follow Polk.

FINKELMAN: In some ways, that's not true. The politics of America from the 1830s to the 1860s is swirling around slavery, all the time. The opposition to the Mexican War which Polk starts, and which we didn't have to wage, in part comes from the Northerners. They see it as a vast conspiracy to steal Mexico so that slave owners could have someplace to go. Southerners say as much. They say, "We want Mexico because we want a place for slavery to spread to." Slavery is on the table.

The reality is the Polks were slave owners. They are not opposed to slavery. They liked being slave owners. Being a slave owner is very good for the Polks, and I suspect that she treated her slaves as kindly or unkindly as was necessary to get the labor and the support from the slaves that she wanted. That's what slavery was about.

HUNT: James K. Polk voluntarily served one term and lived just three months [after leaving the White House]. Sarah wore widow's weeds for the next forty-two years until she died at the age of eighty-eight. The house they had purchased that had been fixed up for their retirement became a shrine to her husband. She was very reclusive, only went to church, but she did receive people. During the Civil War, Sarah did not take sides.... The Confederates and the Union troops respected her. She was completely neutral and she isolated herself in that period prior to the Civil War. People put their artifacts in storage at Polk Place to preserve them and she just went right on. She earned a great deal of respect for that from both sides.

Sarah Polk's legacy:

FINKELMAN: Polk chose to be a one-term president, which probably was good because he probably would not have gotten a nomination again and he probably would have been defeated. He was not very well-liked when he left office. It is true that he started a war which was successfully won, but when it was over, he didn't want to have peace.... Polk was forced to bring a treaty to Congress that he did not actually want to sign or have Congress ratify.

HUNT: James K. Polk might not have been able to achieve his ambitious one-term agenda without Sarah's help. She certainly kept the White House running because he literally worked himself to death. She handled his legacy well after his unfortunate early death. Most of the legacy is his: the first postage stamp, the permanent Treasury Department, the almost doubling the size of the United States, and we have many things to be thankful for.

The first ladies themselves are not so much innovators. Sometimes they embrace those aspects of the American character that the public needs, and Sarah did that very, very well.

The Taylor Administration, 1849–1850

Margaret Smith Taylor

Margaret Taylor,
date unknown

"My wife was as much
a soldier as I was."
—Zachary Taylor

Born: September 21, 1788, Calvert County, Maryland
Married: June 21, 1810, to Zachary Taylor (1784–1850)
Children: Ann Margaret (1811–75); Sarah Knox (1814–35); Octavia
Pannel (1816–20); Margaret Smith (1819–20); Mary Elizabeth
(1824–1909); Richard (1826–79)
Died: August 14, 1852, Pascagoula, Mississippi

Contributors:

PAUL FINKELMAN, professor of American history, constitutional law, and
race and the law, Albany Law School; and author or editor of several books,
including *Congress and the Crisis of the 1850s*

CONOVER HUNT, consultant for museums and historical organizations; author of several books and co-author, *Remember the Ladies: Women in America, 1750–1815*

PAUL FINKELMAN: Zachary Taylor [was the last Southerner elected for sixty-four years until Woodrow Wilson, and the last president to hold slaves while he was in office]. He had never done anything political. He had been a career military officer for his entire life. His wife, Margaret Smith Taylor, or Peggy Taylor, as she's known, had traveled with her husband to some of the most remote military bases in the country. She had been a military wife, the wife of a man who started as lieutenant and ended up as a major general. Taylor's politics were almost unknown other than that he said over and over again that he supported Henry Clay.

Henry Clay had lost to Polk, and Henry Clay believed that it was his time to win [in] 1848. It was going to be a Whig year. Clay's party is the Whig Party. And then, out of nowhere, Taylor gets the nomination and Clay is absolutely devastated that he doesn't get to be nominated. In addition to Taylor getting the nomination, a completely obscure, almost unheard-of person, Millard Fillmore, gets the vice presidential nomination.

We had this strange axis of Taylor, who was a Louisiana sugar planter, running with Fillmore, who was the comptroller of the state of New York.

CONOVER HUNT: I don't think Margaret Taylor realized that when her husband came back from the war, she was going to end up being first lady.

FINKELMAN: There is a story that apparently Taylor was on a steamboat when the movement to make him the nominee arose and somebody asked him who he was going to vote for. Taylor said, "I'm not sure." The man said, "Well, I am voting for Taylor. Why won't you vote for Taylor?" ...And Taylor says, "Well, I wouldn't vote for Taylor because I personally know his wife doesn't want him to run for president." That certainly could have been the truth.

HUNT: Peggy Taylor was not particularly keen on being first lady. She had gone around to all of his postings with him and had innumerable children. It's very interesting that their daughter Sarah Knox married the young Jefferson Davis, who fought with Taylor in Mexico. Unfortunately, their daughter died after only three months of marriage. Later, when they were in the White House, the Taylors became quite close with Jefferson Davis and his second wife, Varina, and Varina was very close to the first lady.

The first lady let her daughter do a lot of the entertaining, but it was such a brief amount of time that they were in office.

FINKELMAN: She basically retreats to the upstairs of the White House. Oddly enough, like her predecessor, she came from a political family. One of her aunts was married to a three-term governor of

Maryland, and one of her cousins was married to Senator Reverdy Johnson of Maryland. She came from a very wealthy family of Maryland planters although she spent most of her early years in the Washington, D.C., and Northern Virginia area. Among other things, one of her playmates was Nelly Custis, the granddaughter of Martha Washington. This is somebody who has been around politics. But she is the opposite of Sarah Polk, she doesn't want to be involved in politics....

The Taylors were very wealthy. They had lots of slaves. They had a plantation in Louisiana. Some of the slaves would travel with them when they went to bases. She was not a high society woman. She was not a woman who wanted to be around a crowd, and this was not a world that she felt at all comfortable with. When she got to Washington and dealt with the gossip and the parties, she simply felt that this is not where she was comfortable; she didn't know how to compete and she didn't know how to operate. [The gossip about Peggy Taylor was much like Rachel Jackson, that she was a pipe-smoker.] The pipe-smoking is utter nonsense. In fact, all of the people who were close to her say that she was allergic to smoke and nobody smoked around her....

Zachary Taylor went to a July Fourth parade and he watched the parade on a very hot day. Zachary Taylor was a teetotaler and he either spent the day eating cherries and milk, or cucumber and milk, depending on who you talk to. One imagines what a bowl of milk would look like after a hot July day in Washington, D.C., without ice to keep it cold; he got some kind of intestinal disease. He was a very tough man. He had survived winters in Michigan and Minnesota. He had survived Florida. He had survived the deserts of Mexico. He was rough and ready. The one thing he could not survive was mid-nineteenth century medicine. When he got sick, he was bled, and they did all sorts of other things including giving him mercury, which would have killed him if they gave him enough. He may have died from an intestinal virus. He may have died from a bacterial infection. He may have died because his doctors killed him. What we do know is that he died very suddenly, to the great shock of the nation.

When Fillmore becomes president, he gets letters from people saying that Taylor was poisoned. Americans love conspiracy theories, and this was a conspiracy theory.

Perhaps Taylor was the last president who could have managed to somehow change the sectional conflict because he was a Southern

President Zachary Taylor's death in July 1850 was sudden, stunning the nation and First Lady Margaret Taylor.

slaveholder who did not believe in spreading slavery to the West. He thought that all of the territories that had been taken from Mexico ought to be free. He was a man who was willing to stare down and, if necessary, lead an army to suppress Southern anti-nationals, Southern suggestions of secession at one point. The Texans were planning to march into Santa Fe and seize all of what is today New Mexico.

[After Taylor dies,] Millard Fillmore very graciously asks Margaret Taylor to stay on in the White House as long as she wishes. She moves out two days later. She's had enough.... Peggy Taylor dies two years later, in 1853. She was born in 1788, so that makes her about sixty-five when she dies.

Margaret Taylor's legacy:

FINKELMAN: Taylor was elected in November of 1848, but didn't take office until March 1849, and Taylor dies in July of 1850. There is essentially a fifteen-month period when they're in the White House and Margaret Taylor doesn't want to be there.

The Fillmore Administration, 1850–1853

Abigail Powers Fillmore

> "...I am already beset by office seekers."

Abigail Fillmore, circa late 19th century

Born: March 13, 1798, Saratoga County, New York
Married: February 5, 1826, to Millard Fillmore (1800–74)
Children: Millard Powers (1828–89); Mary Abigail (1832–54)
Died: March 30, 1853, Washington, D.C.

Contributors:

PAUL FINKELMAN, professor of American history, constitutional law, and race and the law, Albany Law School; and author or editor of several books, including *Congress and the Crisis of the 1850s*

CONOVER HUNT, consultant for museums and historical organizations; author of several books and co-author, *Remember the Ladies: Women in America, 1750–1815*

PAUL FINKELMAN: Millard Fillmore, [who became president when Zachary Taylor died in office just fifteen months into his term,] grows up in abject poverty, as had Andrew Jackson. Millard Fillmore's family does not own their land in an area where all farmers own their land. Abigail Powers's father dies when she is two. They don't have very much money. She becomes a schoolteacher. She is the first first lady to have worked outside the home. Significantly, she not only works outside the home before she's married, but after she's married for the first few years, she works as a schoolteacher when Millard is starting his law career. These are people who have experienced poverty and who have not at all achieved anything that would be considered other than middle class status....

Abigail Powers was twenty-one years old and she was teaching in a private academy [when they met]. Millard Fillmore had been apprenticed to a textile factory to learn how to run cloth-making machinery. This was during the 1830s, in the middle of the depression, after the Panic of 1837. The factory laid off everybody for a while. Fillmore used this time to go back to school and fell in love with his teacher, and she fell in love with him.

It is hard to tell from the pictures we see today, but both of them are described at the time as being very attractive people. Queen Victoria would later say when she meets Fillmore, after he wins the presidency, that he was the handsomest man she ever met. Here you have these two young, handsome people. Fillmore is over six feet tall at a time when most men don't grow to be that tall. He must have been a striking figure. Abigail gloms onto him. Millard gloms onto her, but they have a very long courtship because her family doesn't want her to marry.

They ultimately don't marry until about five or six years later. For two years, their courtship is only by letters. He moves to East Aurora, New York, and then goes to Buffalo, where he becomes a lawyer.

It's important to understand [the role of religion in their lives]. Abigail is the daughter of a Baptist minister and she's raised in a Baptist community in rural upstate in New York...in a very poor part of the state. Millard has various religious training growing up, but when they get married, they are married by an Episcopal priest because in the town that Abigail lives in by this time, the most prestigious church is the Episcopal church.

They then move to Buffalo and they become Unitarians because all of the smart people, all of the successful people, are becoming Unitarians. So, religion for the Fillmores reflects their journey from poverty to middle class status to, ultimately, a secure position in society, and they change churches as they go up the social ladder.

[About the Fillmores' views on slavery:] what's odd about both Millard and Abigail is they come from a part of New York known as the "burned-over district." It's called that because it is said that the fires of revivalism burned over it so often. It was the most anti-slavery part of the United States, the center of the anti-slavery movement. Just south of where Fillmore is growing up, William Seward, one of the most anti-slavery senators in the Senate, is starting his political career. Just down the road, Frederick Douglass will live in Rochester, New York. And yet, with all this anti-slavery activity going on, neither of the Fillmores ever lifts a finger to fight slavery. They never show any hostility to slavery at all, and they show no sympathy whatsoever to free blacks. It's really quite shocking that they are completely clueless about this. When he's running for vice president, somebody accuses him of helping fugitive slaves escape. In a letter that is so shocking that I wouldn't say it [out loud], he says incredibly horrible things about black people, and says, "Why would I ever lift my finger to help them?"

The Compromise of 1850 is introduced by Henry Clay, the disappointed guy who didn't get to be president. The goal is to solve the nation's problems. As it emerges in the Congress, the Compromise of 1850 is a series of separate bills. It will, among other things, organize the New Mexico territory, which would include Arizona, and the Utah territory, which includes Nevada and Utah and parts of Colorado and Wyoming. It would admit California into the Union as a free state. It also would prevent the open auction of slaves in Washington, D.C. It would also give millions of dollars to Texas. Most importantly, it created the Fugitive Slave Law of 1850, which creates the first federal law enforcement bureaucracy in the United States.

It's an outrageously unfair law, in which alleged fugitive slaves are not even allowed to testify at hearings on their own behalf. If a free black is seized in New York and someone says, "This is my fugitive slave," the man can't say, "No, you've got the wrong person." It created draconian punishments for anyone who interfered with the law. Fillmore pushes the Fugitive Slave Law, signs it almost immediately after it is passed by Congress, and then very aggressively enforces it wherever he can.

There is no documentary evidence whatsoever that Abigail advised Fillmore not to sign the Fugitive Slave Law. This is the sort of apocryphal thing that people like to claim because they want to enhance people's reputations without any evidence whatsoever.

Abigail Fillmore established the first White House library in a room that today is called the Yellow Oval Room. *Peter Vitale for the White House Historical Association*

HUNT: [Abigail Fillmore successfully lobbied key committee members to bring a library to the White House.] She was there at those dinner parties, talking to congressmen; it was the standing that she couldn't do [because of an injured ankle]. She obviously convinced them, and here comes $2,000 to set up a White House library, which was a lot of money.... Apparently, she did a very good job of selecting a broad category of volumes for the library.

[The room in the White House that the Fillmores established as their library is today called the Yellow Oval Room. During the Fillmores' time, it was filled with bookcases and musical instruments and became something of a salon in Washington.] She participated in the formal dinners downstairs, and there was always receiving going on. The White House had very little privacy [for the first family].

FINKELMAN: I don't think [Abigail used her salon to advance her husband's policy goals]. For one thing, few congressmen in those days were interested in talking to a novelist or talking to a cultural figure. She brought the woman known as the "Swedish Nightingale," Jenny Lind, to the White House. Lind would have been a celebrity, and so perhaps the members of Congress would have wanted to come to see the celebrity. In a sense, there's a bifurcation here between Abigail Fillmore creating a cultural setting where the former schoolteacher really wants them to [learn the members' cultural tastes]....

[The library she created had] a lot of Shakespeare. Probably lots of histories. We know there were a lot of geography books. They were very interested in foreign countries, as President Fillmore sends Commodore Perry to open up Japan. This is, in part, because Fillmore has this personal interest in things foreign and things exotic.

HUNT: [Abigail Fillmore died in the Willard Hotel very shortly after the inauguration of their successor, Franklin Pierce. Her life story is one of] books, love of learning, and literacy and, yes, careers for women.

Abigail Fillmore's legacy:

HUNT: To my knowledge, [the Fillmores' library and Abigail Fillmore herself were not instruments of social change]. But you have to look for the long term. What we're beginning to see as we go into the second half of the nineteenth century is more and more work for middle class women teaching. Obviously, the public would be aware that they had a first lady who was a teacher, an honorable profession. Also, having that library certainly was known.

Jane Appleton Pierce

> "My precious child, I must write to you, although you are never to see it or know it."

Jane Pierce, c1886

Born: March 12, 1806, Hampton, New Hampshire
Married: November 19, 1834, to Franklin Pierce (1804–69)
Children: Franklin, Jr. (1836); Frank Robert (1839–43); Benjamin (1841–53)
Died: December 2, 1863, Andover, New Hampshire

Contributor:

ANN COVELL, writer and author, *Remembering the Ladies: A Century of U.S. First Ladies*

ANN COVELL: The political situation was dire at the time Franklin Pierce was elected. Everything was in turmoil. There were problems between the North and the South on the slavery issues. The Democratic Party to which Pierce belonged was split and...they were having to find a nominee for the presidential election, but they didn't want anybody from the South because of the slavery situation.

Franklin Pierce appeared to be the best bet as a nominee at that time, mainly because of his reputation as a marvelous raconteur. He had remained popular with the South, and it was felt that there was a good chance that he would be able to win that nomination. There was a great deal of politicking, but eventually, he was nominated on the forty-eighth ballot [and he won the White House in a landslide against Whig candidate Winfield Scott].

Jane Pierce [became] deeply depressed by the death of her last surviving son, especially under the terrible circumstances in which he died. [Eleven-year-old Bennie died before his parents' eyes in a train wreck.] She didn't come to the White House for at least a fortnight after the inauguration. She didn't even attend the inauguration. When she came, she immediately said, "I will have mourning bunting surround the house." Such was her influence with her husband that he agreed to it. He accepted that it would only last for a year. In fact, the mourning period lasted for over two years.

Pierce did manage to influence the powers that be that Jane needed a new luxurious bathroom on the second floor of the White House where the family lived. So, yes, she influenced that. But as far as any other influences are concerned, they were all negative. The Pierces made the White House a morbid place.

Jane thought that God was punishing them for some misdemeanor. She did tend to blame Franklin in the first instance because he had not kept her aware of the circumstances of his nomination. When he did eventually inform her, he reassured her that he wouldn't get elected. He said, "I'm a dark horse nominee. I won't get elected." She felt that he was being punished through the death of Bennie, and drew away from him, and that made things completely worse. If both of them had come together during that time and talked it through, they would have saved themselves a lot of unhappiness.

Franklin appeared to have great difficulty in forming his cabinet. Perhaps it was the attitude within the White House at that time and the fact that he didn't have Jane around him to comfort him as she had done with previous problems they'd had together. Also, he was mourning, grieving deeply for Bennie himself. The feeling is that he could not put his whole heart and soul into the job of being president of the United States, and a lot of people feel that this delayed the establishment of his cabinet. Once he did establish the cabinet, it ran for the whole term, which was the first time that a cabinet had run for the whole of the four years. So, he did work well in the end by getting the best team together.

[Jane was deeply fundamentalist. Her father, the president of Bowdoin College, was a well known preacher.] I don't really know [what attracted Jane and Franklin Pierce]. I think they just fell for each other. Opposites attract, I suppose, and they were opposite, completely and utterly.

[Franklin Pierce was a big drinker.] At one time, after he'd left the Senate and came back to live in Concord, [New Hampshire,] he gave up alcohol, but when he went down to [fight in] the Mexican War, we hear that he probably took up alcohol again. It wasn't a new thing for Franklin. He had always drunk. His father had been a tavern keeper, and he had spent a lot of time with his father, so that was probably where he took up the drinking habit.

After the Mexican War, he didn't let Jane see him drink, but he kept on drinking. It got heavier at his most unhappy times, but I don't think that it was as a result, particularly, of those circumstances. He would have been drinking anyway.

Jane Pierce cast aside her responsibilities as first lady, really. Fortunately, Franklin had a good secretary, Sidney Webster, and Jane also had a mentor who was her aunt, Abigail Kent, who took over her official duties.

[Jane Pierce spent her White House days cloistered on the second floor of the White House, where she would compose letters to her dead son and connect with spiritualists.] The letters that she wrote to Bennie were not in any way mystical or spiritual or under the influence of these spiritualists. They were really a way for her to express her great grief. Modern psychologists would agree with that action because they do say nowadays if you are grieving, or you've got some terrible trouble, write it down and it helps. Increasingly, her writing became worse and worse, and her letters were hardly legible in the end, but she was a prolific letter writer, particularly to her mother.

[Her letters reveal] that she was very selfish. She seemed hooked on being ill, but they were never serious illnesses; they were usually colds. She would have a cold at the drop of a hat. If she didn't want to do

Jane Pierce spent her time in the White House consumed with grief over the death of her young son Bennie, killed before her eyes in a train accident. *Courtesy Pierce Brigade, Concord New Hampshire*

something, she would say, "I'm sorry, I've got a cold coming on." She didn't like to mix with people, and she used her supposed ill health [as an excuse].

Jane was very fond of her mother and of her sister, Mary, but she didn't seem to write very much to her sister, Frances, for some reason. Neither did Frances write to her.... She controlled her family in almost every family letter, and, indeed, in letters to friends. There was always a concern about Jane: "How is dear Jane? Is her cold any better?"

She was very fortunate in that her whole family rallied, and much to her husband's pleasure, they did come and see Jane and spent time with her, particularly her sister Mary's children, of whom they were both very fond. But Franklin hardly went to see her. He was grateful that the family visited so he didn't have that torment of having to go into a morbid environment. He had enough to think about [as president].

Although she had treatments like bloodletting, which was a favorite treatment in those days, there was never any diagnosis made, and she lived to quite a good age, in her sixties. It was at that stage when she was diagnosed as a consumptive.... So the impression I have of Jane is that she used the illness to get her own way, and she was going to have it her own way, whatever happened.

...In spite of what people have said, Jane participated in some of the events within the White House during the first two years. For instance, she did attend most of the meetings that first ladies generally had, Friday afternoon teas, when people could come in and see her and speak with her. When the mourning period finished, perhaps it was a relief to her; she did attend more and more events, and she even attended the president's levees, which he had on Thursday afternoons.

[Despite her distaste for politics, Jane Pierce became very involved in the slavery issue and got very vocal in advising her husband about the Kansas-Nebraska Act.] Nancy Mason, her aunt...had a relative, Dr. Robinson, who was the leader of the anti-slavery movement in the Kansas area. He had been hauled in front of a court because this was a very pro-slavery area.... If found guilty, which was likely in that state at that time, he would be hanged. Nancy had written to Jane to make a plea to try and save Dr. Robinson from this fate.

By then, Jane was beginning to see Franklin a little bit more. They met two or three times a day by then and she had an opportunity to speak to Franklin about it. He listened very carefully and then he telegraphed the appropriate person, and Dr. Robinson was freed. I don't know of any other incident where she might have been useful and persuasive with regard to slavery. They were both anti-slavery, but he saw the sense of having slaves in the South. That was the difference between them.

Franklin Pierce lost his bid for reelection in 1856 because he signed the Kansas-Nebraska Act, and that was a very unpopular thing to do. Stephen A. Douglas drew it up, but Franklin signed it. If he hadn't signed it, I don't think he would have lost his popularity because he was still deemed to be a very good politician.

As a result, James Buchanan and Stephen A. Douglas put their names forward as nominees...which meant that Franklin wouldn't have had the two-thirds majority that he needed to be re-nominated. On the seventeenth ballot, James Buchanan won the nomination and then the election for president.

The first six months after the White House, the Pierces stayed with their former secretary of state. Then, James Buchanan, who liked Franklin Pierce, although he didn't like his politics, felt very sorry for their situation of Jane's deteriorating health and illness, and said, "Would you like to take a trip over to Madeira? If so, you can go for six months and you can go on the cutter *Powhatan*." Jane hemmed and hawed, and she wasn't going to go, but her aunt, Mary, decided that she must go. So off they went to Madeira on *Powhatan*. Unknown to her, Franklin had also organized a European trip which happened to take two years, but they first went to Madeira and loved it. Jane improved dramatically and even went horse riding and hardly ever had a cold. She went from being eighty-five pounds in weight to one hundred pounds. She loved every minute of it and wrote a letter to her sister during that time to say, "I can't believe who I was when I was in the White House. I'm a completely different person."

Franklin's health [improved in Madeira, too,] because he didn't have the worries of state. Then they set off on their wonderful European tour. Towards the end of that tour, she started being ill again, and she was disappointed about that, after such a long time of being well.

When they eventually got back to Concord, Franklin bought a farm, but she became so ill that she went to live with her sister in Andover, where Bennie had been taken after the accident, and she died there at sixty-three. She is buried in the Pierce family gravesite.

Jane Pierce's legacy:

Jane Pierce was very reluctant about being first lady. If she had any influences [on the administration], they were negative. She came into the White House as a forty-seven-year-old lady who, it is well-known, hated politics.

Harriet Lane

"Uncle places so much confidence on me that he gives himself no uneasiness."

Harriet Lane, c1855, President Buchanan's niece and official hostess

Born: May 9, 1830, Mercersberg, Pennsylvania
Married: January 11, 1866, to Henry Elliot Johnston
Children: James Buchanan Johnston (1868–81); Henry Elliott Johnston (1869–82)
Died: July 3, 1903, Narragansett, Rhode Island

Contributors:

ANN COVELL, writer and author, *Remembering the Ladies: A Century of U.S. First Ladies*

FEATHER SCHWARTZ FOSTER, history lecturer; author, *First Ladies: An Intimate Portrait of the Women Who Shaped America*

FEATHER SCHWARTZ FOSTER: The political atmosphere in 1858 was just terrible. Buchanan...had been a contender for about twelve years. He was very well-known. He'd been in politics for forty years. He was an old man by the time he got to be president, about sixty-five. He got elected president because he had been out of the country for four years during the Pierce Administration, so he didn't get tainted with a lot of the politicking and the ugliness and the divisiveness that had been going on.

They were looking for somebody who was, they used the word "available" a lot. That did not mean that he had nothing better to do; it meant that he would be acceptable all the way around.

The best way to put it is that, politically, he was a dud. He ranks down at the very bottom of the barrel. Socially, Buchanan was brilliant. The whole atmosphere in the White House was brilliant. There hadn't been anything like it since Dolley Madison. You had a little flurry with Julia Tyler, but she was only around for eight months and past that, the White House didn't really sparkle. Under Buchanan, it sparkled.

Buchanan was from Mercersburg, Pennsylvania. He chose Lancaster for his adult home. [Wheatland, the estate he built there,] was a lovely home on a nice piece of property. They were very social and he invited many people to come to Wheatland [which served as a launching pad for his several bids for the presidency].

When James was a young man, he was engaged to a woman and it didn't work out too well.... The engagement was broken and not all that much later, she died, and some suspect that she committed suicide. The relationship between Buchanan and his former intended's family really was very bad. They wouldn't let him come to the funeral. Just how much he loved her, how much was true, how much was embellished, we probably will never know.

ANN COVELL: She was called Anne Coleman. Buchanan had apparently been thrown out of college for some misdemeanor, and my understanding is that her father discovered the reason for James being thrown out of college and talked to him about it and then told his daughter, Anne. Anne had a few words with Buchanan about it. We can only guess what the secret was. They split up, and it upset her so much that she apparently did commit suicide.

[Buchanan never married; he became our only bachelor president. He asked his niece, Harriet Lane, to serve as official hostess of his White House.] Harriet had been orphaned at an early age. He took her under his wing. When her father died, Buchanan was made her guardian.

FOSTER: Both her parents had died by the time she was about nine or ten. James took care of a bunch of his nieces and nephews [and] took very good care of Harriet Lane. He had a very affectionate relationship with her. He loved her dearly. She loved him dearly. He was like a father figure to her and he sent her to the best schools. She had the best of everything. Buchanan did very well for himself.... Money was not an object. She could have just about anything that she wanted, and he saw to it that she was trained to be exactly what she was: a brilliant social success.

COVELL: [One of the influences on Harriet Lane's education was when her uncle was appointed ambassador to Great Britain, and Harriet met the Queen of England.] It's unusual that somebody should charm Queen Victoria in such a way, but she certainly did. It was her youth and her effervescence. She was such a change for this rather stiff royal court. She was a very happy girl, a delightful girl. Even the Prince of Wales, and he was only eighteen years old, fell under her spell. Harriet was about twenty-eight by then. Queen Victoria...gave her an official title, which wouldn't normally be given to a niece; it would only be given to the wife of an ambassador.

   ...Harriet enjoyed her time on the continent a lot. She learned a lot. She really grew over there.

FOSTER: The first three first ladies, Martha, Abigail, and Dolley, were far harder-working and more actively involved in their husbands' lives and in their careers [than ladies of this generation]. When we stopped being colonies and started being a country, by the 1800s or so, that generation was growing to more prominence. They were very prosperous. Men wanted their wives to have all sorts of lovely things, and they catered to them a lot more. Women didn't have to work quite as hard, and ladies at that time started being frailer, probably, until after the Civil War.

COVELL: As first lady, [Harriet Lane was a trendsetter. The advent of] photography helped because her image was able to be reproduced rather than just depicted in a portrait, but she was a fashion trendsetter. She looked good in clothes. She had a nice figure. She was buxom but she wasn't fat. She made a lovely appearance. The only detrimental thing I ever read about Harriet Lane is that some people thought she was a little stiff or maybe a little too formal. But with the political situation being what it was during those times, she needed to be.

Previously, first ladies were never mentioned in the press because it wasn't protocol to write about ladies and report their names. Many first ladies remain unknown to this day simply because...the press didn't feature them in any way.

FOSTER: [The press began to focus on Harriet Lane and] she was good copy. She liked to dance. She gave a lot of parties. She was an elegant hostess. She dressed well and had a lot of friends.

This White House liked to entertain, but did not get a budget for entertainment, and like most early presidents, Buchanan supplemented the costs himself. [A goal of their entertaining was to attempt to bridge the country's huge political divides, but] I don't think anything was successful in those days. The tensions were so high that it was very difficult. He used it as effectively and as efficiently as just about anybody else could. The White House really glittered.

They had two dinners a week for forty people at each dinner. Since tensions were at a tremendous all-time high, Harriet wore another hat.... She also was very actively involved in the protocol. She would spend hours working on the seating plans.... Fortunately, she knew all the players. She knew all of these different senators and cabinet members and congressmen...and where to put them, and worked very hard at it.

Was Harriet a political adviser to the president in the sense of Abigail Adams? No. She was more in the Dolley Madison vein of being socially helpful to him. She was observant. He trained her to listen well and to observe and to take note of what was going on and to form opinions. However, she was usually quite quiet about expressing her opinions, which was one of the reasons that she was very popular; she didn't do anything wrong.

As first lady, Harriet Lane did develop an interest and empathy for Native Americans. Before she got to the White House, she didn't show any particular interest, but there were some Indian chieftains who came to the White House to visit. They made a great impression on her and she became interested in Indian welfare…. The Indians thought of her as their great white mother.

One huge success of the Buchanan Administration was the visit by the Prince of Wales, the son of the reigning monarch. He was the highest ranking foreign person that ever came here. Everybody knew Queen Victoria and they all knew about the Prince of Wales. He was going to Canada, and Buchanan [said to] Queen Victoria, "Listen, as long as he's in the neighborhood, have him come on down." He did and they invited him to stay at the White House.

[In a mark of how popular Harriet Lane was, a Coast Guard cutter was named after her, an honor given to only two other first ladies.] She invited some friends of hers to have a party on the ship. "Nunc," as she called her uncle the president, got wind of this and hollered at her, but not for having a party. He was perfectly happy that she had a party, but the ship was public property. He felt that she should not abuse public property. He was very straightlaced about her not accepting gifts other than flowers or a box of candy.

[In 1860, James Buchanan's divided Democratic party lost the White House to Abraham Lincoln.] Harriet went back to Wheatland with her uncle for about five years or so, and then married Henry Johnston. They moved to Baltimore, where he was a banker and was quite prominent and well-to-do.

Harriet Lane was thirty-five years old when she got married…. She had known Johnston for years and they always seemed to like each other. Maybe by that time, it was time for her to get married. Buchanan was very happy about it. He died a year and a half later. He probably knew that he was getting on in life, and this way Harriet would be settled.

She had about fifteen happy years. Then, both of her sons died within a year of one another. They were twelve or thirteen—young boys. She's another first lady who lost both of her children.

About a year and a half after the boys died, her husband died. Harriet is now around fifty-ish and she is a widow on her own. She moves back to Washington, D.C., and she gets to be a little bit like Dolley Madison.

The USS *Harriet Lane*, a Coast Guard cutter. Only two other first ladies have had a ship named after them.

She gets invited to the White House just about every time they're going to have a big [event]. No party is a party unless she's there. And she does a lot of good. [She and her husband founded the Harriet Lane Home for Invalid Children, one of the first such institutions and still part of Johns Hopkins Hospital. Her art collection was donated to the Smithsonian, becoming the foundation for the National Gallery. She helped create the St. Albans School and the James Buchanan Memorial in Washington, D.C.]

Harriet Lane's legacy:

FOSTER: If she were Mrs. Buchanan instead of the niece of Buchanan, she would be second to Dolley Madison in the nineteenth century.

COVELL: She should be second even though she is Miss Lane and not Mrs. Buchanan, because of the influence she had on people. Everybody loved her. Harriet Lane brought tranquility, is the word I think of, to the role of first lady after the previous three presidencies. She was just a great girl and everybody loved her.

The Lincoln Administration, 1861–1865

Mary Todd Lincoln

"The people scrutinize every article that I wear with critical curiosity. The very fact of having grown up in the West subjects me to more searching observation. To keep up appearances, I must have money, more than Mr. Lincoln can spare for me."

Mary Lincoln, c1860

Born: December 13, 1818, Lexington, Kentucky
Married: November 4, 1842, to Abraham Lincoln (1809–65)
Children: Robert Todd (1843–1926); Edward Baker (1846–50); William Wallace (1850–62); Thomas (Tad) (1853–71)
Died: July 16, 1882, Springfield, Illinois

Contributors:

RICHARD NORTON SMITH, presidential historian; executive director at five presidential libraries; author of several books, including *Patriarch*; history consultant for C-SPAN; academic advisor for C-SPAN's *First Ladies* series

ROSALYN TERBORG-PENN, professor emerita, Morgan State University, focus on nineteenth and twentieth century America and slavery; academic advisor for C-SPAN's *First Ladies* series

RICHARD NORTON SMITH: [Today, she's generally referred to as Mary Todd Lincoln, but she called herself simply "Mary Lincoln."] Abraham Lincoln famously said, mocking the pretensions of his wife's family, that God only needed one "d" and the Todds of Kentucky needed two. She probably laughed the first thousand times she heard that joke. You can just imagine these two: He's six-foot-four. She's five-foot-two, if that. He had a habit of introducing themselves as "the long and the short of it," another joke she probably endured more than enjoyed.

What brought them together, this very unlikely couple, was a shared love of politics, which was unusual for a young, well-bred lady of that era. Henry Clay, a neighbor of the Todds who was a good friend, and who was Lincoln's political hero, was the political matchmaker behind this unlikely union.

Mary Todd left her native Lexington, Kentucky; it's been speculated that a relationship with her stepmother may have been a factor. In 1839, she went to Springfield, Illinois. Her sister was married to a man named Ninian Edwards, Jr. His father had been governor of territorial Illinois, and Mary was immediately thrown into the social set. Springfield was a tiny town, maybe twenty five hundred people, but it was very hierarchical. Mary was wealthy and well-educated. This is something that people tend to overlook, and why Lincoln was attracted to her in the first place, classic opposites attracting. This was a young woman who could have had her choice. No fewer than four future United States senators expressed interest in Mary.

[Still, Abraham Lincoln wasn't certain, and he broke off their engagement for a year and a half.] The local newspaper editor, a man named Simeon Francis, and his wife, stepped in and said, "Well, this is ridiculous. You care for each other," and reignited the friendship. By November of 1842, without really telling anyone, they announced to the Edwardses that they were marrying that night.

One of the things that Mary did that she doesn't get a lot of credit for was to add some polish to her unpolished husband. She was his advocate. She imagined, after he'd lost two races for the United States Senate, that his political career wasn't over. She imagined him in the White House long before he ever did, and her famous strawberry socials in the parlor on the first floor were just one tangible way in which she conducted a campaign for him.

[When the Lincolns arrived at the White House in 1861,] the political process had broken down. There were four parties that ran in 1861, [and] Lincoln won with just under 40 percent of the vote. The sheer news of his election led seven Southern states almost immediately to secede.

ROSALYN TERBORG-PENN: [The capital city was not welcoming of these Westerners, the Lincolns.] Historian Catherine Clinton, one of Mary Lincoln's biographers, says that she broke the elite Virginia scheme of things and that many of the congressional wives...were resentful, and lampooned them. They lampooned Lincoln, and they lampooned her. The sad thing is that she was a very intelligent, highly educated woman from a good family, but they treated her very badly.

The other thing that might have hit her is that Washington was a swamp; a disease-ridden city. She had a difficult time dealing with that, plus she complained about how worn and drab the White House itself was. Some of the furniture went back to the days of Dolley Madison. So Mary Lincoln had a lot to worry about.

SMITH: If you think of the repercussions for this woman who's arriving from Kentucky, referred to as the "Republican Queen," mocked by people who really don't know her, who are willing to assume the worst about these backward Lincolns—that puts a real chip on her shoulder, even before she arrives in the capital. It may begin to help to explain some of her shopping, some of her preoccupation with fixing up the White House that has become part of her legend.

Mrs. Lincoln looked upon the White House very much as a symbol of this nation and took very seriously her responsibilities not only as a hostess, but as the woman responsible for the appearance of the house. This is a time when the country is literally coming apart at the seams, so the symbolic value of America's house is perhaps even greater, just like the president's order that the half-finished dome of the Capitol was going to be completed. In some ways, she took the same view of the White House.

[Mary Lincoln was criticized for the money she spent refurbishing the White House.] She actually overspent the $20,000 she was allocated by Congress by about $6,000. It's not a huge amount. There was a war going on, so the spending became part of the Mary Lincoln legend, this woman, out of control, a shopaholic.

TERBORG-PENN: When she interviews her African American dressmaker, Elizabeth Keckley, she says, "How much are you going to charge for your dresses because I can't afford to pay you a great deal?" Keckley says, "I will be reasonable," and they came to an agreement. My theory is she wanted a lot of dresses, but she couldn't afford to pay lavishly for them. So, on her budget, she was able to get what she wanted because Keckley agreed not to overcharge her. Maybe that's one of the reasons she got the job.

Elizabeth Keckley made dresses for a variety of people, including Jefferson Davis's wife and General McClellan's wife. She had her own shop. She did not live in the White House. She had her own residence, a place she rented. She was very popular among the congressional wives, who then recommended her to Mrs. Lincoln. She bought her freedom when she was in St. Louis through dressmaking.

Mrs. Keckley was involved with contraband camps. These were filled with people escaping from slavery coming from Maryland and Virginia with their families, or enslaved people who were emancipated but had no place to go. There were several contraband associations across the nation. Mrs. Keckley was one of the founders of the Washington contraband association, and she talked Mrs. Lincoln into donating, and Mrs. Lincoln talked the president into making donations.

SMITH: The Lincoln White House was astonishingly open to the public. It is hard to believe that in the middle of the great Civil War that is raging, that twice every week the president would throw open his office, and people could line up as long as they could wait for what he called his "public opinion baths." These were mostly job seekers. Mrs. Lincoln and the children, they would finesse themselves around all of these folks.

There were the two boys in the White House at the beginning: Willie, who was ten years old when they arrived in Washington, and his younger brother, Tad. His older brother, Robert Todd, had gone off to Harvard, and they'd had a fourth brother, Edward, whom they'd lost years earlier in Springfield.

[After their son Willie died at the White House,] Mary basically disappeared for over a year. Her social life as first lady ended. She gave orders for the Marine band to stop playing their concerts on the White House grounds. When it was suggested perhaps the concerts could be moved to Lafayette Park, she said no, her grief was too great. She indulged herself even beyond the standards of the day. Her compatriot was Queen Victoria, who would spend the rest of her life grieving over the loss of Prince Albert.

TERBORG-PENN: It's hard to determine [whether she got beyond her grief], because she was continually being vilified. Maybe it was years later when her son Robert, who was really a disappointment in the long run, had her incarcerated, in essence, sent to a mental institution. [Perhaps] she woke up then and decided, "I'm going to get out of here." She fought very hard, and she was able to mobilize support to get herself out of the mental institution. It was not just Willie. It was the loss of Edward, then Willie, then the loss of her husband. And then Tad died.

SMITH: You can even go back to her beginnings. Mary lost her mother at age six and then was afflicted with the classic wicked stepmother syndrome, which is what sent her to Springfield in the first place. This is a woman whose life is shadowed by loss.

TERBORG-PENN: Mary was [a good helpmate to President Lincoln]. She tried to advise him, but some of his advisers didn't really want her to be interfering....they were threatened by her sense of significance.

SMITH: She was interested in personalities. She used to refer to [Secretary of State William H.] Seward as "that abolitionist sneak." [General Ulysses S.] Grant was "that butcher." But the fact is, ironically, once the Lincolns actually had attained their goal; once they moved into the White House, her influence over policy diminished. Their partnership was, in some ways, broken. The war consumed him, and it was a source of frustration for her. The relationship that they had had before the presidency was greatly diminished. So, she was not significantly influential in shaping public policy or his conduct of the war, or even who he put in his cabinet.

[As Kentuckians, some of Mary's family were Confederate sympathizers.] At least three or four of her siblings or stepsiblings fought actively for the Confederacy, and some of them died....

Mary made it very clear that her siblings had taken up arms not only against her country, but against her husband, and she saw no reason to mourn their loss.

If you read the press of the day, there was a considerable amount of criticism of Mary Lincoln. We know now how much time she spent visiting soldiers in hospitals, writing letters for soldiers who were unable to write themselves, taking fruit and other gifts, and yet, she never took reporters along with her. If she had been a little bit more PR-conscious, who knows what it might have done for her historical record.

[Mary Lincoln suffered injuries in a] carriage accident. This is, in some ways, the Lincoln presidency in miniature. There was a school of thought that says Mary's condition, whatever it was, worsened after that very severe head injury that she experienced. The date is significant. It was the second of July, 1863, the second day of the battle of Gettysburg. Needless to say, the president's attention is focused elsewhere. He was not in a situation to pay as much attention to his wife as he might have otherwise.

Yet, there is a significant body of evidence that calls into question some of her conduct. For example, she was surrounded by people who very clearly were there to take advantage of her, and she needed money. From the day she arrived in Washington, she needed money. For example, at one point, she was $27,000 in debt to her dressmakers. So the president had to be reelected, because if he was reelected, she could keep those bills at bay. If he wasn't reelected, who knew what might happen.

That debt is quite apart from the public funds she was spending on the White House proper. So, there were always people around her who were eager to serve their own interests by appearing to serve hers. I'll give you one example: There was a shady character named Henry Wikoff, known as the Chevalier, who was with the *New York Herald*. He somehow befriended Mrs. Lincoln, and, lo and behold, the president's annual message to Congress in December 1861 appeared in the *New York Herald* the same day it went to Congress. You get the picture. There was no shortage of people like the Chevalier who were eager to...serve their own interests.

The legitimate criticism of Mrs. Lincoln as first lady has nothing to do with her mental condition, where you can only feel empathetic. But, legitimately, there is criticism about how she conducted herself in ways that always were in danger, if exposed, of embarrassing the president.

One of the really touching counterpoints to this is that Lincoln loved to see her in beautiful clothes. It was one of the few extravagances that he was comfortable with.

TERBORG-PENN: The White House staff apparently liked Mary. Only four of the staff remained when the Lincolns came to the White House. They brought in new staff, primarily freed blacks, who really worked very well with her. Those who were interviewed talked about her in a very positive way. She got along very well with them because they were the ones who helped to raise her after her birth mother died, when she was growing up in Kentucky.

SMITH: In 1864, there wasn't any question that he would seek reelection. There was a profound question whether he would be reelected, as he himself acknowledged as late as August of 1864, wholly dependent on the course of the war. At that point, before Sherman's march, before Atlanta had fallen, before it became very clear that it was only a question of time that the North would win, Lincoln himself believed that he would not be reelected. So you can imagine the mood upstairs around Mrs. Lincoln.

TERBORG-PENN: And Lincoln had bouts of melancholy, a lot of them. Apparently, she was one of the few people who could soothe him and bring him out of it.

SMITH: [Five months after his reelection, in April of 1865, Abraham Lincoln was shot at Ford's Theatre in Washington by actor John Wilkes Booth during a performance of *Our American Cousin*.] Mary was right there, so she witnesses it. She's the one that cries out first, "The president has been shot!" because people assumed that this man who jumps onto the stage is part of the show. They take the president across the street to a boardinghouse. He is [gravely injured]. His cabinet members...are all around him while the doctors are there. Mary is hysterical, and so they get one of her female friends to take her out of the room, and keep her there. It takes him all night to pass away. He died at 7:22 the next morning. The sad thing is that they wouldn't let her see him at the end, because they didn't want to hear her hysteria. Secretary [of War Edwin] Stanton, who took charge of everything in the house that night, at one point said, "Take that woman out of the room." Rob-

The president and Mrs. Lincoln were attending Ford's Theatre in Washington on April 14, 1865, when assassin John Wilkes Booth fired at the president, mortally wounding him.

ert Todd Lincoln was at his father's bedside, but Mary was not there when the end came.

There were, in effect, ten state funerals in cities along the way. By one estimate, a third of every Northern American either looked upon the president's face in his casket or actually saw the train go by. It was an extraordinary pageant of grief, very Victorian, very nineteenth century, and the irony is that Mrs. Lincoln was not along for any of it. In keeping with tradition, she remained behind at the White House, absolutely grief-stricken.

[Mary Lincoln lived for seventeen years after Lincoln's assassination.] Lincoln left an estate of $85,000 at the time of his death, of which she, as a widow, would inherit one-third, and you have to figure that at the time of his reelection, she was in debt $27,000.

She went to Europe, she came back, and then Robert had her incarcerated for several months [for insanity]. There was a second trial, at which she managed to convince the jury that she was perfectly sane. She and Robert never really reconciled.

Mary Lincoln was obsessed with money, and at one point she moved to sell off a number of her White House dresses, which just made the public impression all the worse. She was in debt.... She needed the cash; there's no doubt about it. She petitioned Congress over and over for a pension, which, finally, belatedly, was granted: $3,000.

She went back to Europe and lived in France for four years, and then, in 1880, returned to Springfield. By this time, she was almost blind. She had severe cataracts. She went to live in her sister's house, the house in which she had married Mr. Lincoln, and that's where her life ended in 1882.

Mary Lincoln's legacy:

TERBORG-PENN: Among the nineteenth century first ladies, she and Abigail Adams would be my favorites. I would rank her quite high. You have to look at her vision as a partner. There were several first ladies who considered themselves to be partners with their husbands...to help advise them, to help take care of them, whether mentally or physically or politically. She was a very significant influence on her husband.

SMITH: [Mary Lincoln would want her own legacy to be] that she loved her husband, and her family, and her country, in that order.

I would disagree with those who would rank her at or near the bottom. First of all, that assessment is, to put it mildly, less than compassionate. Her story is really unique in all of the annals of White House history. The fact that, one hundred fifty years later, we're having this discussion, that we're still debating her motives and her conduct, tells you she's an important first lady.

Mary Lincoln is important because of the man to whom she was married. She's important because of the part she plays in the story, which is still being debated after all of these years. We still feel as if we don't know who she was.... To some people, she's a heroine. To many people, she's a victim. But she's a surprisingly contemporary figure, as well.

Eliza McCardle Johnson

> "I do not like this public life at all, and I'll be happy when we're back where I feel we best belong."

Eliza Johnson, c1850
Courtesy Andrew Johnson National Historic Site

Born: October 4, 1810, Leesburg, Tennessee
Married: May 17, 1827, to Andrew Johnson (1808–75)
Children: Martha (1828–1901); Charles (1830–63); Mary (1832–1883); Robert (1834–69); Andrew, Jr. (1852–79)
Died: January 15, 1876, Carter Station, Tennessee

Contributors:

JACQUELINE BERGER, first ladies historian and lecturer; author of a two-volume biography collection, *Loves, Lies and Tears.*

KENDRA HINKLE, museum technician, Andrew Johnson National Historic Site, Greeneville, Tennessee, National Park Service

KENDRA HINKLE: [Abraham Lincoln, a Republican, had chosen a Southern Democrat, Andrew Johnson, as his vice president. With Lincoln dead, Johnson is now president.] A unique situation, and [it was] done because Abraham Lincoln was trying to appeal to a broader segment of the population. In another sense, he was making good on his second inaugural [promise], to bind up the nation's wounds. He was trying to bring the North and South back together again, because Johnson was a Southerner, he was a Democrat, and he was intensely loyal to the Union. He was the only senator who retained his seat when all the other senators from the South left. He had spent time as Tennessee's military governor, restoring a Union government there, and freeing the slaves in Tennessee...so, he was a good choice. He had held nearly every political office that you can hold on the rise to the presidency. It was just a completely different situation going in after Lincoln's assassination; it was a very chaotic time.

JACQUELINE BERGER: It was about four months [after Andrew Johnson's swearing-in] that Eliza Johnson finally came to Washington with her family. They had set up a situation where she took care of the home, took care of the finances. Her life was pretty well set, and the fact that her husband became president didn't change things instantaneously. But she did follow him, and she did bring her entire family with her. She had two daughters. One was married and had two children of her own. Her other daughter was now a widow and brought her three children with her. It was very crowded upstairs in the White House. Eliza was an invalid when she got to the White House, but people think that she didn't participate much, and that isn't exactly true. She was very involved.

She set up her own bedroom upstairs, right across from the president's office, and she was always able to hear what was going on. She was very active. She read daily newspapers, brought different points of view to the president, and was able to calm him down constantly. She was the grandmother of the house, taking care of her daughters and her grandchildren.

Eliza was absolutely terrified [for her husband's safety as president]. First of all, her husband's life was in danger when he was a senator, because he did not want his state to secede from the Union, so he was considered a traitor. Then, when the president was assassinated, she was absolutely terrified. One of her daughters wrote her father before they got to the White House, and said, "Mother is just deranged that you, in fact, are going to be assassinated."

They were an extremely close-knit family. Martha, the oldest daughter, was always watching out for her mother. The grandchildren adored both of their grandparents. Oftentimes, when they were doing some studying with tutors, they'd always come back in and visit their grandmother. The president also spent his mornings visiting with her before he went off to do his business. Everything seemed to revolve around Eliza.

HINKLE: Daughter Martha Patterson was the official hostess, and her sister, Mary Stover, supported her. Mary was back and forth to Greeneville [Tennessee] several times. She was a bit more like her mother and preferred to be with the children.

BERGER: When she was at the White House, Mary was responsible for a lot of the children's education and a lot of their training. She did step in with her sister, but they didn't like the public life. The entire family didn't care for it at all. Mary had lost her husband in the Civil War, so that was difficult on her, having three children and being a widow herself.

The White House was in a period of mourning [because of Lincoln's death]. The war had totally ravaged the White House. I can't even describe what disarray that it was in. They said there was mold in the State Dining Room. There were lice in the rooms. The carpeting was filthy. It took Martha a couple of months while Congress was not in session to get the house all cleaned up. She really scrubbed it down from top to bottom, was very astute at that. Then they had their weekly levees on Thursday nights....

It was also Johnson's intention to have the common people come to the house. He didn't want to have formal dinners, but was more interested in inviting people to come in on a regular basis and see the president's home, the people's house.

HINKLE: [Congress recognized the poor condition of the White House] and gave the family a $30,000 appropriation, which is a lot more money than the Lincolns got. The Johnsons used that money very carefully. Martha oversaw every cent. She refurbished furniture. She would take up strips of carpet, have it cleaned, and if it was a smaller section that was still good, put it in a different area. She took down the wallpapers and she had gilt décor put up that was simple but very elegant.

[Martha Johnson said, "We are plain people from Tennessee called here for a little time by the nation's calamity and I hope too much will not be expected of us."] The public loved this attitude. One newspaper man said there was such a homeliness in that statement. People were craving that after the war; they wanted to know that these were people who had suffered like they had and who were not going to be ostentatious, but who were very respectful of the position that they held in the White House.

BERGER: Many times when a family moved into the White House, they would just stay on either the public floors or the private floors. Martha went down into the basement. She went up into the attic. She was all over. She found portraits of past presidents. They weren't framed but she did show them to her father, and her father thought it was a great idea to frame these portraits and hang them up. President Johnson loved to walk through the halls and refer to a president's picture and tell a story about them.

Martha [got her thriftiness] from her mother, because it was Eliza, when her husband kept going off to whether it be Congress or the Senate, who said, "I remained at home caring for the children and practicing economy."

HINKLE: Eliza was educated about to the eighth grade. There was a female branch of the Rhea Academy in Greeneville at that point, where tradition holds that she went to school. We still have some of the books that Eliza had, one arithmetic and one grammar, that she used to tutor Andrew Johnson in the early days of their marriage.

BERGER: As first lady, Eliza Johnson read lots of things. She loved reading the newspaper. She loved reading the constitutional papers that came out. She certainly read all of her husband's speeches and assisted him with that. She loved poetry. It was a very broad range.

One of the other things that she loved to do was clip things out of the newspaper. Her husband was a great orator and she always wanted to make sure he had some very good talking points. She would read multiple newspapers, and nothing missed her eye. Whenever she'd catch something that she thought her husband might be able to use on a speech, she would bring it to his attention.... We really don't know what her opinions were, because she only shared them with him in private, which many first ladies do. He did listen to her periodically, as well as to their daughter, and asked advice.

Early in their marriage, Eliza Johnson tutored her husband Andrew in their Greeneville, Tennessee, tailor shop. *Courtesy Andrew Johnson National Historic Site*

Eliza was a very friendly person. Initially, historians thought that she only came downstairs two different times during the entire administration. We discovered later on that that is not entirely accurate. Ulysses S. Grant's wife, Julia, said that after the state dinners, the first lady would come downstairs...have coffee and walk around and talk to all of the guests. She was extremely gracious. They said she was always dressed very elegantly and very appropriately. She was a very kind person.

Eliza Johnson has the distinction in history books of being the youngest bride [among the first ladies]. She was sixteen. Andrew was eighteen. As legend has it...she was standing outside school one day, talking with some friends, and Andrew Johnson comes into town. She is the first person he sees. He's asking for directions, and she makes the comment to her girlfriends that that is her beau. Within a year, they did marry. She had four children by the time she was twenty-four years of age. She proved to be a wonderful homemaker and a very good businesswoman as well.

She took care of all of their finances. She would read to her husband in their tailor shop. She herself was a great seamstress. She came from a very poor family, by the way. She lost her father when she was quite young. She and her mother helped support themselves by making quilts and sewing sandals, things of that nature. So she had appreciation for what her husband did, and she would constantly read to him.

HINKLE: The tailor shop soon became the hangout spot for men, where they debated. Students in town, after Johnson started attending debating societies, called him a "Demosthenes," who was a Greek orator.... He had a book called *The American Speaker,* and one of its desires was to "teach the callow young to plead their country's calls with lips of fire." That inspired him to the point where he wanted to break away from life as he had known it, being such a struggle, into something greater.

BERGER: As Andrew became more interested in politics, he was away quite a bit. That's another reason why so much of the responsibility fell on Eliza. She was good at selling and buying stock. Here they came from these very humble beginnings and they owned real estate; they owned other property. She would collect the rent from these properties and basically manage the money very effectively.

HINKLE: [Andrew Johnson served as] alderman, mayor, state representative, state senator, governor, U.S. representative, U.S. senator, military governor, vice president, and president, and he's the only president to this day to return to the Senate. Democrats and Republicans have reversed [political philosophies] as the years have gone by. He was very much a fiscal conservative, supporting limited government and more of the decisions being made by the states.

BERGER: Andrew Johnson definitely believed in states' rights. There was no question about that. He was always putting bills forth for the common man. That was very important to him. He didn't care for the aristocrats. He didn't necessarily care for the very rich planters, as he referred to them. It was basically the blood, sweat, and tears of the common man that he was trying to help support quite a bit.

Johnson was not a drunk. Unfortunately, he got that reputation when he was inaugurated as vice president; he had typhoid fever at that time, and he was pretty down, he was low. He was trying to give himself a little bit of energy, and so he had some whiskey on that day. By the time he got up to give his inaugural speech, he was slurring his words, and people thought he was drunk. But he was not. President Lincoln knew that. People were not willing to let the truth get in the way of a nasty rumor, but he was not an alcoholic, although his sons were.

HINKLE: The Johnsons had a pretty lenient relationship with their slaves.... August 8, 1863, is the day that Johnson freed his slaves. To this day, in Tennessee and surrounding states, that is still celebrated as Emancipation Day. They all stayed on as paid servants afterwards. They all took the last name of Johnson. [Their former slave] Dolly eventually baked and sold pies out of the tailor shop. She started her own business. [Another slave named] Sam wrote President Johnson at one point asking to buy land for purposes of a church and school-house for the African American children in Greeneville. Johnson wrote back and said no, just have the plot of land drawn up and I'll give it to you. He eventually gave Sam land, and he built his own house there in Greeneville.

East Tennessee was very much pro-Union during the Civil War. When Tennessee voted to secede, they were calling Johnson a traitor. They confiscated the Johnson home, and that was a very tragic time for Eliza because she was quite ill.

They had given her thirty-six hours, literally, to leave the home, and she did call on her daughter Mary, and Charles, plus her young son who was only ten years old, Andrew, Jr., whom they called Frank, [for help]. The story is that they were trying to get through Confederate territory, and it was very difficult because the Confederate soldiers were calling out to them and saying things to them that were not very pleasant. One night they slept by the railroad tracks and it was rather cold. They didn't have much food. They would go into various farming communities, knock on the door, and ask if they could possibly spend the night there. By the time they reached Nashville where Andrew was, poor Eliza, she was just pretty well spent.

It's said that Johnson wept at the sight of Eliza when she finally reached Nashville.

BERGER: We do know for a fact that Eliza and Martha had prepared food for the pro-Union guerrilla warriors in the hills. There was no question about that, but there is some question as to who was delivering the food to these guerrilla warriors...

HINKLE: [Lincoln appointed Johnson governor of occupied Tennessee. His job] was to restore Union government in the state. It was a challenging job. He was firing people and standing in the defense of Nashville. He often came in conflict with the generals. He wrote letters to Lincoln expressing his concern, also hoping for the liberation of east Tennessee. Lincoln sided with Andrew Johnson on a lot of the decisions that he made.

BERGER: Their older son, Charles, definitely was in the war. Charles was an assistant surgeon during the Civil War and was killed. Robert was a lawyer, but he also signed up and went to war. That's when his drinking took over. There were stories about him leaving his army [unit].

HINKLE: Robert was colonel in a cavalry unit. He was the only family member who was able to attend Charles's funeral when Charles was killed. Charles fell from a horse and hit his head.

It happened outside of Nashville. Johnson and Eliza were gone during that time.... It was after this that the drinking problem started for Robert.

BERGER: [After the war,] President Lincoln's concept of Reconstruction was to be as lenient as possible. He had said that in his inaugural address when he was reelected, and Johnson believed that, too. Just because the war had ended didn't mean that people's feelings had changed. They were very aware of the fact that there were still individuals that disagreed with that point of view, and they weren't going to accept things readily.... The radicals in Congress and the Senate... thought [secession] was treason, and they really wanted to punish the Southerners. There was a constant battle between them. Johnson would get angry very quickly, and he'd seem to antagonize the people that he was debating with. He had a very difficult time even getting the moderates to go along with him, because of his particular point of view and the way he presented it. He certainly was not politically correct.

HINKLE: [The Johnsons didn't seem to use the White House to advance their policy positions. Daughter] Martha did preside over the state dinners. We have a letter to Mrs. Lincoln that was also passed on to Martha, giving the protocol of where everybody should be seated, and who should be seated first, and how you would pair the people up together, so that they probably played it in that manner.

BERGER: ...Martha became quite friendly with Mrs. Polk, as well as Harriet Lane, who was Buchanan's niece [and his acting first lady]. Martha came into politics through the backdoor, let's say. But I don't think she really wanted to push her particular point of view on her father.

HINKLE: Someone appealed to Martha for clemency for [Lincoln conspirator] Mary Surratt, and she said that, "I feel so terribly sorry for you, but I have no more right to speak of this to [the president] than any of the servants." So, she kept to the background.

BERGER: [The pathway to Johnson's impeachment began when] the Senate passed an act of Congress that said that the president himself could not fire his cabinet members without Congress's approval. That, of course, was not constitutional.

HINKLE: Johnson had suspended Secretary of War [Edwin] Stanton in the fall when Congress was not in session. In December, when they came back in session, he told them what he had done. They rejected that and restored Stanton to office in January. Johnson went ahead and fired him. This was the impetus for them to start impeachment proceedings.

[During the three months of the trial,] it was just very much business as usual at the White House. They went on as if nothing else was going on. The grandchildren helped to keep [the Johnsons'] minds off things.

BERGER: The attorneys told Johnson not to say anything, to reserve comment. "We will handle it." And so, Mrs. Johnson said, "We're just going to go ahead with business as usual." They still had their levees every week, [but the first lady was] reading everything about the impeachment. When there was something good written in the newspaper, she would show him that at night before he went to bed. If there was something very critical in the newspaper, she'd wait till morning to show it to him. My impression of it was, as much as Johnson wanted to fight the charges himself, it was his attorneys that said, "Don't do that. You're the president."

[The impeachment proceedings began in the Congress on March 5, 1868, and went through May 1868.] Eliza honestly believed that her husband would be acquitted, and was very proud of it when he was.

HINKLE: Colonel Crook, who was a personal bodyguard and attendant, writes that he rushed in to tell Eliza that Johnson had been acquitted. He said, "This frail little woman stood up and her emaciated hands took mine, and with tears in her eyes, she said, 'I knew he'd be acquitted.'"

BERGER: [The administration still had ten months to go after the acquittal.] I don't think he had much political capital. He kept trying to instill thought for his point of view, and the things that he wanted to get through, but he had no cooperation from Congress whatsoever, and he just didn't know how to do it. That's the sad part of the administration. They found him surly, basically. They thought that he might've come off a little nasty, and so they didn't want to work with him at all. It was very tough.

[After their term ended,] Mrs. Johnson was absolutely thrilled to be back home in Tennessee. The irony of that is she was thrilled to go back home, and they were no sooner back home when Andrew wanted to get back into politics. Their lives went back to the way it had always been for them. She just was not interested at all, but very proud that her husband did get reelected to the Senate.

HINKLE: He left her behind when he went back to Washington. There are many letters inquiring after her, how she's doing, how her health is, and when he was in Nashville, at one point, canvassing, he says, "Let me know if Mother gets worse and I'll come back home."

BERGER: They were married forty-eight years. It was a tremendous love match. Someone once said that they were the same mind and same soul.

HINKLE: Even though they were completely different. He could be vehement, he was a fighter, but the one person that he leaned on completely was this frail little woman.

[The two died six months apart. When Andrew Johnson died,] there was a big funeral, a Masonic burial for Andrew Johnson. Special trains brought in dignitaries. When Eliza died, the same catafalque was brought in from Knoxville for her funeral, and it was drawn by four white horses and led by some of their former servants.

Eliza Johnson's legacy:

HINKLE: On Andrew Johnson's monument, it says his faith in the people never wavered. Hers might be that her faith in her husband never wavered. That's what she would want her legacy to be.

BERGER: Even the people in the White House, people in Washington, all say that the Johnsons were extremely honorable. They were probably one of the most well-liked families that lived in the White House because they were so gracious. They gave of themselves, of their time, of their energies, their efforts.

Julia Dent Grant

"My life in the White House was like a bright and beautiful dream."

Julia Grant, c1875

Born: January 26, 1826, St. Louis, Missouri
Married: August 22, 1848, to Ulysses S. Grant (1822–85)
Children: Frederick Dent (1850–1912); Ulysses Simpson, Jr. (1852–1929); Ellen Wrenshall (1855–1922); Jesse Root (1858–1934)
Died: December 14, 1902, Washington, D.C.

Contributors:

PAMELA SANFILIPPO, park historian, Ulysses S. Grant National Historic Site

WILLIAM SEALE, White House historian; author of several books, including *The President's House;* editor, *White House History;* academic advisor for C-SPAN's *First Ladies* series

PAMELA SANFILIPPO: Ulysses S. Grant's election started off with the campaign, "Let us have peace." People were really looking to Grant to bring some peace and quiet to the White House and to the nation after the war, and then the years of the Johnson Administration, and so those were Grant's initial efforts as he took office.

WILLIAM SEALE: Grant had the added advantage of being a hero. He was famous, even in the South, if he wasn't beloved. A million young men tried to imitate the particular stance he had. He was wildly popular. He was clean; nothing dirty attached to him. He was a natural.

Julia [Grant] brought an incredibly strong supporting role to the president. Their lives had been that way. She'd argue with him, but she was supportive of him. They wanted to represent, in the White House, the ideal American family…. They put this huge picture of the Grant family in the Red Room so the public could see it on the tours—see that this was their home, this is where they lived. This whole [concept of the] symbolic home, Julia Grant developed.

SANFILIPPO: Julia's parents came to St. Louis in 1816 and established their family in the city of St. Louis, and then at a country home out at White Haven, where she grew up, spending most of her summers there and then year-round. She had four older brothers and two younger sisters. They considered themselves Southerners, and they were a slave-holding family. When Ulysses and Julia were married in the city of St. Louis, none of the Grants attended the wedding, reportedly because they didn't approve of Ulysses marrying into a slaveholding family.

Ulysses was about five-eight, and she was around five-two…. He had been a roommate of Julia's brother, Fred Dent, at West Point. When Grant, after graduation from West Point, was stationed at Jefferson Barracks, about five miles south of the city of St. Louis, Fred invited Ulysses to visit his family out at White Haven.

Grant visited in September of 1843, and then in February of 1844, Julia returned home from the boarding school she was attending in the city. Julia says that initially his visits had been about once a week to White Haven, but once she returned home and he met her, his visits were daily. He proposed to her within three months.

Julia was born with what today we would call a lazy eye. She was always very self-conscious about that, feeling that, especially as Grant rose to fame, she needed to do something about it. On two separate occasions, she attempted to have a surgeon work on her eye. Grant found out about it and told her that he had fallen in love with her the way she was, and he might not like her half as much if she had her eye surgically corrected.

SEALE: [They were married in August 1848. Julia's father didn't approve of their union.] He told Grant that Julia would not like the military life. She had been raised with everything, and would definitely have to do without. It was personal. He thought that Grant was not going to amount to much financially and would not be able to give [his daughter] what she took for granted.

SANFILIPPO: Grant resigned from the military in 1854. He had been stationed on the West Coast. Julia was living at White Haven in St. Louis. She made the journey [home] with him two years earlier because she was pregnant with their second child. Grant came back to St. Louis, and rather ironically, he supposedly told someone: "If anyone hears of me in ten years, they will know of me as an old Missouri farmer." Of course, by 1864, he was general of all of the Army during the war.

SEALE: Grant went through a lot of trouble in the years before the Civil War. He had hard times in business, but half the people in the United States had hard times. It was a national depression of the worst kind—the Panic of 1857. It was only ended by production in the Civil War. He was trying to do business in those terrible years. They said he was drunk all the time.

There's not a whole lot of proof that Grant was a drunk. He drank, but a lot of people drank. There are stories about him being drunk, secondhand stories, and when you lay it all on the table, it doesn't go very far. He was a binge drinker, that's all anyone's ever been able to prove.

SANFILIPPO: Those rumors are greatly exaggerated.... Lincoln is rumored to have said, although it's not a proven story, that when congressmen came to him saying, "Remove Grant. He's a drunk. He can't be running the Army," he reportedly asked them to find out what type of alcohol Grant was drinking, and he would order barrels for all of his generals.

Initially, Julia [held pro-slavery sentiments]. She had been born and raised at White Haven, with the enslaved individuals providing everything that she needed. In fact, at one point, she says that she thought the house kept itself with all the work that was being done by those individuals.

Once she met, fell in love with, and married Ulysses, it put her in the middle between these two opposing viewpoints. She talked about how while growing up, some of those enslaved individuals were her playmates, playing in the yard with her.... These are the same individuals that would provide the work on the farm. The older individuals she considered part of the family, aunts and uncles, a typical Southern way of addressing these individuals. While she considered them part of the family, they obviously did not.

Grant did own one slave that he acquired from Julia's father, that he freed, William Jones, in 1859, before the Civil War started. Julia, although she talked about having four slaves given to her by her father, didn't actually own any. Her father never made legal transfer, otherwise they would have been Grant's property to perhaps free.

[It is true that when Julia made trips to visit Grant on the battlefield, she occasionally brought a slave as] a nurse for her children. [The irony was lost on her.] She needed the help and she even talks about how "Black Julia," as she was called, was almost captured at Holly Springs, and then did free herself and left during one of their trips.

SEALE: In her treatment of the staff at the White House, it was a personal, one-on-one thing with her. I imagine that's how she was with African Americans, as a personal relationship, as apart from this bigger issue.

Julia Grant brought a real order and organization to the White House. She had to manage the money. She had to manage the people. The servants were doubled to thirty, all the payrolls exist, and she very much interacted with them. There was one servant named Henry Harris who had a lot of children. She suggested, to begin with, and then she was very emphatic, that he start buying Washington real estate. He died a wealthy man, and she had forced him to put part of his salary into that.

There was no social secretary then. Usually, the ladies got together and filled out the blanks for their invitations. "The President and Mrs. Grant, in the honor of blank, blank." She had Mary Muller as the housekeeper. They were very close. She called her "a most excellent woman." She helped with some of the events, but for most of the social duties, there might be a clerk from the office that would help. There was no social staff [at the White House] until Mrs. Theodore Roosevelt [became the first lady].

Part of her job, as Julia clearly envisioned it, was to make the White House a model house of the nation. Other first ladies have felt that way too, but it was part of Grant's program, and they entertained very lavishly, not in a fancy sense, but an elegant sense, and she handled that very well herself.

Grant brought his old cronies in as much as he could, and he brought a cook in from the Army as the chef at the White House. At diplomatic banquets, he would serve big roast beef slices and apple pie with cheese on it. The diplomats were horrified, so Julia let him go and hired Valentino Mieli, who was a well-known chef in New York at Sherry's. He turned it into a very cosmopolitan table with flowers and costumes. She was very stringent about rules. All the White House staff had just worn business suits. They were at half-guard. [On Julia Grant's watch,] they had to be in full dress and they had to stand at attention in the entrance hall on shifts.

SANFILIPPO: Julia entertained so much that…frequently congressmen or people who were looking to get in to see Grant would try and do that through Julia, or to gain favor from Grant, they would frequently go through Julia because she was so easy and accessible to them.

SEALE: She considered herself the head of women's society in the capital, and she was accepted. She was friends with all those kinds of people in Washington. She was a go-getter-type woman. Mary Lincoln sat back and waited for people to come to her.

SANFILIPPO: While there was this opulence on one level, it was very down to earth in the fact that, with four young children still at home, Julia, for example, closed off the backyard of the White House so that the children could play.

Their oldest son had received an appointment to West Point under Johnson's administration, so he was coming and going, but the younger children were still there. Julia talked about how Ulysses sometimes would play around with the kids over their dining room table. He would play games and take pieces of bread and roll it into a ball of

The Grants, photographed in Long Branch, New Jersey, in 1870, had a close family life.

dough, and throw it at the boys. She disapproved. She also recalled that upstairs in the White House, in the private family area, all of the children and Ulysses would come into her room about a half-hour before dinner, and they would all just sit and visit and share their day's comings and goings. She recalled that very fondly.

SEALE: One thing I like to tell about family life in the Grant White House makes me want to have been a fly on the wall: General Grant built…a billiard room, which had stained glass in it and a billiard table, and he would invite his old Civil War cronies there to play billiards and smoke cigars and maybe drink a little. They'd end up going into the Red Room and reliving the battles, taking an object off a table, putting it on the floor: "This is Memphis and this is Vicksburg." Imagine being able to see that. That's the sort of informality they lived with their friends. The Hayeses, [who would follow them in the White House,] were very moralistic, trying to show morals more than the Grants did. The Grants liked to have a good time.

One of the most sweeping, romantic, dramatic events to happen in the White House probably since the British burned it down was the Grants' daughter's wedding. Nellie was seventeen. She met Algernon Sartoris, an Englishman, on the ship as she was going to England and they were engaged to be married. The parents disapproved because she was so young. The wedding took place on May 21, 1874. They redecorated the East Room for it, leaving the basic woodwork and adding a lot more mirrors and gold leaf. The nation just went wild. There weren't a lot of invitations, maybe 250. But the streets were mobbed. You couldn't get near the place.

Poet Walt Whitman was there, and wrote, "Oh, bonnie bride, yield thy red cheeks today unto a nation's loving kiss." That was carried in all the papers. It was just the most wonderful thing. She married beneath two huge wedding bells. The presents were assembled according to the stores where they were bought.

There was a wedding breakfast, and then they left on their honeymoon and lived in England, where she renounced her citizenship, which she later very much regretted. She petitioned Congress to get it back, and did get it back. The guy was a womanizer and drank a lot and spent a lot of money. It was not a happy marriage. They had four children. One died in infancy.

SANFILIPPO: [The nation celebrated its centennial during the Grant Administration.] It was huge, almost like a world's fair. There would have been people from all over the world attending it. It was a time for America to shine, and show that it was coming into its own as a world power.

SEALE: Mrs. Grant loved it. She went there and bought two things for the White House with public money. One was a shield that showed characters from Milton's *Paradise Lost*. Then she bought a more endearing piece. It was a centerpiece. She hated the old James Monroe centerpiece of 1818 with mirrors on it, so she bought a Hiawatha silver centerpiece. It shows the Gitche Gumee [lake] with all the cattails and the weeds, and a canoe in the middle of it, and Hiawatha lounging on a bearskin rug…. It's still in the silver closet at the White House.

SANFILIPPO: Most of the people that Grant appointed to his cabinet, he either knew of, or knew personally. For example, Elihu Washburne, a former congressman of Illinois, he appointed as secretary of state as a thank you for Washburne having supported him through the war.

Others were business people that he thought would do the best job. Some of them turned out to be not so deserving of this trust he had placed in them.

Julia talks about the Black Friday incident where James Fisk and Jay Gould tried to take a corner of the gold market. Julia says in her memoirs that the only thing she knew about was when Grant had her write a letter to his sister, Virginia, who was married to Abel Corbin, also reportedly involved in this, in trying to persuade Grant [to join them]. Grant has her write to Virginia, saying, "Be careful." Then Grant turns around and sells off government gold to bring [the scheme] to a stop.

SEALE: [Grant decided not to seek a third term,] but there were many people who wanted him to, and Julia did, too. When he declined it, he didn't tell her. He mailed the letter to the [Republican State Convention] without telling her, but she'd begun to be suspicious. They were upstairs in the hall at the White House and...he said, "I've declined a third term." She said, "You can't do this to me. I want it." He said, "It's done. That's it." She seems to have held up fine until inaugural day, when they got on the train car. She says she went to a bedroom and fell on the bed and sobbed. She hated to leave the place so much.

SANFILIPPO: She said she felt like a waif with no home, because she wasn't sure exactly what was going to happen.

[Going on a two-year world tour] was actually Grant's idea. He said upon leaving the White House, he felt like a boy out of school. He had always loved traveling, and so they embarked on this tour. It was just originally supposed to be Europe, and then it extended all the way around the world. She enjoyed every minute of it, mostly because of the praise and acclaim that she saw her husband receiving, and the shopping that she did, as well, for things that she wanted to bring back home with her. She had a wonderful time.

When the Grants returned from the world tour, there were those who thought that he should run for office again, especially with all of his foreign relations experience. He was interested at that point, feeling again that he could be of service to the country. Julia says they were in Chicago when the Republican convention met, and she tried to encourage him to go downstairs and meet people at the convention and show his face, knowing that would put him over the top with the votes needed. He absolutely refused to do that and lost the nomination.

[After this, Grant and his son began working with Wall Street financiers, and he ended up financially ruined.] This financial failure happened with Ferdinand Ward. Ward comes to Ulysses Junior, and then to Grant himself, and says, "The bank is in a little bit of a financial strait. Can you borrow some money? We just need to get through the next few days." Grant accepts that and borrows $150,000 from William Vanderbilt. Ferdinand Ward absconds with the money to Canada and the fortune is lost. Grant says that he doesn't know if he'll be able to trust anyone ever again.

When word gets out that they've lost all this money, there are actually some veterans from the war who send Grant money that they loan to him, but he's been offered to write some articles for *Century* magazine about the war. He was encouraged from that [assignment] to write his memoirs, something that he had never been interested in doing. It was Mark Twain's publishing company that ends up publishing those memoirs for Grant. Although he completed them just a few short days before he passed away [from throat cancer], he knows that they will bring financial comfort to Julia.

SEALE: The first royalty check was $200,000. The book made over a million. It's a great book, a great classic. I recommend it to anyone.

SANFILIPPO: Grant's was the largest funeral ever held in the country. They brought his body from Mount McGregor, where he had passed away, into New York City, and buried him in a temporary tomb in Riverside Park and then began the fundraising effort to build the tomb that we know today. Julia attended its dedication in 1897, a proud widow, pleased to see the nation recognizing her husband in that way.

[Julia Grant lived for seventeen more years after Ulysses' death. She was the first first lady to write her memoirs.] Julia says that it was her children who, after Grant's death, encouraged her to begin writing her memoirs of her wonderful life with her husband. She says she started it just to satisfy their requests, but then she realized that recalling all of these wonderful times brought new life to her.

She was ambivalent about having them published. Initially, she thought it was just something to record for her children. Then she did try to pursue getting them published several different times; one publisher told her that...it was too much personal information. They remained in the family hands, unpublished, until John Y. Simon, editor of Grant's papers, convinced the family that they should become public in 1975.

Julia Grant's legacy:

SEALE: The first ladies are all women who basically support what their husband is trying to achieve. Julia Grant did it with certain splendor in a very difficult time in American history, and really turned the knob on a dark period that ended with the early Reconstruction, and brightened things for the rest of the century.

Her public popularity, her featuring of the general, the way she did things, the personal way she had; she was a very significant first lady in that way, a public kind of first lady.

SANFILIPPO: Julia Grant would have said that her legacy was that she was a devoted and loving wife, mother to their children; but, more than that, she tried to represent what her husband was trying to achieve: peace and reconciliation in the nation, and in her role as first lady, she was able to accomplish that.

Lucy Webb Hayes

> "Woman's mind is as strong as man's, equal in all things and superior in some."

Lucy Hayes, c1877

Born: August 28, 1831, Chillicothe, Ohio
Marriage: December 30, 1852, to Rutherford B. Hayes (1822–93)
Children: Birchard Austin (1853–1926); Webb Cook (1856–1934); Rutherford Platt (1858–1927); Joseph Thompson (1861–63); George Crook (1864–66); Fanny (1867–1950); Scott Russell (1871–1923); Manning Force (1873–74)
Died: June 25, 1889, Fremont, Ohio

Contributors:

ALLIDA BLACK, research professor of history and international affairs, George Washington University; founding editor, *Eleanor Roosevelt Papers*

TOM CULBERTSON, director emeritus, Rutherford B. Hayes Presidential Center

ALLIDA BLACK: [The aftermath of the 1876 election was] pretty schizophrenic, to tell you the truth. The Hayeses are coming to Washington, but they don't even know if they are actually going to move into the White House because the election is not yet decided. Samuel B. Tilden and Rutherford B. Hayes are in, at that point, one of the closest elections in United States history....

Hayes goes to bed and thinks he has lost, and gets up the next morning and finds out that the Republicans are challenging the vote in three states. If they actually win those three states, he gets the number of electoral votes he needs to become president. They go through all these negotiations; Congress is involved.... Literally, it's not decided until he arrives in Washington, when the deals are finally set. You can only imagine the joy, the fear, the disappointment, everything that they feel as they are on this train coming to Washington.

TOM CULBERTSON: Lucy Hayes made no comments in public. I'm sure she was disturbed by it, but she and Rutherford both felt that he would have been legitimately elected had blacks been able to vote in the numbers they had in the previous elections.

There was a report that a bullet went through their parlor window in Columbus, Ohio, before they came to the White House. There was no Secret Service. They pretty much took it as it came. Their son Webb carried a pistol, and he was their only form of security.

BLACK: The country itself is still very unsettled. The Civil War, even though it's been over for twelve years, is very much in people's minds, because it was such an intensely personal war. Everybody has been affected by it. Plus, you've got all of this technological revolution. The telephone just gets premiered in Philadelphia. You have the typewriter. You've got all of these new kinds of engines that are being built. You have labor unrest. You have great railroad strikes. You have a recession. It's got everything. It's the first major depression that we have. The country is trying to figure out what is going on just as much as the Hayeses are trying to figure out what is going on.

[As the Hayeses work to establish themselves in the White House,] their personalities take over, and they begin by trying to acknowledge the fact that the election is really controversial. They know that he is being called "Your Fraudulency" [and]... "RutherFraud Hayes." What he does with his inaugural address is set the tone.... He makes overtures to the Democrats. He opens the White House up. They begin to try to engage in a public conversation and tackle the issues that tarnished the Republican Party....

Lucy was very shrewd all the way along with him. She understood how politics worked. She understood how to entertain. She understood how to facilitate conversations between people that were difficult. She understood how to bring people to the table in a way that would advance her husband's career. She was charming. Everybody liked her, despite the no-alcohol edict in the White House. She was able to grease the skids for him in a way that made him seem approachable and ethical and blunt.

[Things are beginning to change for American women, but Lucy Hayes was not a trendsetter.] The thing that is really interesting about her is how she is stuck in the middle, in a way, but that doesn't [end up] making her stuck. That sounds weird, but the suffrage movement is totally divided along the lines of race and whether women can vote or not. Lucy Hayes is the first college-educated first lady. She has nursed and stood with surgeons during the Civil War. She's seen more wounds, more battles, more scars, more amputees, more suffering than probably any first lady other than Mary Todd Lincoln. Yet, she's not an avant-garde reformer. She is trying to find her own voice, and so it is hard to put her in a pigeonhole.

Washington looked askance on her with temperance issues, but they also look at her as lovely and vivacious and happy and congenial. Then she orders...shall we say, "eccentric," but gorgeous china, and the press goes insane over it, writing about how difficult it is to eat food [on these colorful plates]. The press really is taken with her. They use the title "first lady" more for her than they had for anyone earlier. They cover her. They see her as vivacious. They see her as somebody who is different. They are fascinated that she went to college, so they really do follow her in her own right.

CULBERTSON: Lucy Hayes was a partner to Rutherford. She was a sounding board for him. She was a gracious hostess. She was able to engage people one-on-one and to make anybody that she talked with think that they were the only person in the room and the only person that she really wanted to talk with. She was a very good politician.

She went to Wesleyan Female College in Cincinnati, Ohio, and got a degree in liberal arts. She studied rhetoric, composition, English, all the standard things, [and] all of that was applicable to what she ended up needing as first lady. She had to deliver speeches [as a student], which was probably good preparation for later on in life.

The Hayeses first met when Lucy was only fifteen and Rutherford was twenty-four. They met at the Sulfur Spring at the Ohio Wesleyan University in Delaware, Ohio. At that point, Rutherford's mother knew about Lucy and thought that they would be a good match. Rutherford rightly thought that she was a bit too young at that point. In 1850, when Rutherford moved to Cincinnati to start his law practice there, he met Lucy again. She was about to graduate from the Wesleyan Female College, and that's when they struck up their relationship. About a year and a half later, they were married in Cincinnati.

BLACK: [Rutherford was forty years old when the Civil War broke out.] He immediately wanted to volunteer, and signed up for a three-year stint, and she was very supportive of him. It was never really a serious discussion about him not going. It was always a question of going to preserve the Union, and also because Lucy had such strong abolitionist feelings.

CULBERTSON: Hayes was fortunate that he spent most of the Civil War in West Virginia trying to keep the Confederates from moving from theater to theater. Whenever he did get out [to the battlefield], he was wounded five times, once badly, and almost lost his left arm. [Future president] William McKinley, who was also in the same unit, wrote later that Hayes turned into a tiger when he was on the battlefield; that he went from being this mild-mannered attorney to being a warrior.

[After he healed from the most serious wounding, his unit was assigned to duty in West Virginia.] The saddest story was the loss of [their fourth child]. Lucy and the children had gone to visit Rutherford in the field of battle in West Virginia, and within a couple of days, their baby son Joseph died. They gave his body to a soldier to take back to Cincinnati for burial, and the rest of the family remained in camp. Rutherford wrote that he never really became attached to the child, but it was really hard on Lucy. She didn't have a whole lot of time to grieve, because she had to take care of the other children and move on.

[The Hayses ultimately had eight children; five lived to maturity.] All four of the boys went to college. They weren't all graduates. Their daughter Fannie did not go to college, which is rather strange, considering the background of the parents. Their oldest son, Birchard, was an attorney in Toledo. Their second son, Webb, was a founder of Union Carbide and became quite wealthy. He...started the Rutherford Hayes Presidential Center, which opened in 1916. Their third [surviving] son, Rutherford, became a real estate developer in North Carolina and in Florida, and their fourth son, Scott, worked for General Electric.

[While still serving in the Union Army,] Rutherford was nominated to run for Congress from his district in Cincinnati. He famously said that he would not campaign. He said a man who was fit for battle who would leave his post should be scalped, and that was used on campaign posters when he ran for president in 1876.

[Lucy Hayes wasn't given the nickname "Lemonade Lucy" in her day.] Her husband made the decision to ban alcohol from the White House. It was a decision that was partly political. He wanted to keep the Republicans in the party who were defecting to the Prohibition Party. He also wanted to set the moral tone, because alcohol was the drug of choice in those days. There were many families that were ruined. You have heard about the sons of presidents who managed to ruin their lives with alcohol. Hayes was never a prohibitionist. He never thought you should outlaw alcohol. He thought that the people who were running the Prohibition Party were political cranks who would also outlaw dancing and card-playing. He just wanted people to learn by education.

BLACK: At the Hayeses' time, the temperance movement was not very popular. It really takes off at the end of the century...when it merges with the women's suffrage movement. When the Hayeses first move into the White House, only twenty-three states allowed women to control their own property, and so one of the big problems with alcohol was, if women worked, their wages legally belonged to their sons or their brothers or their husbands.... Men would take the women's salaries and go into the saloons. The saloons gave you shelter and gave you food and were political bases. They also gave you really cheap beer. It was a complicated issue, because it is really easy to say they are just turning everybody into alcoholics, when what they are doing is feeding people, organizing people, giving them a place to party, encouraging them to drink, and not having women's recourse over their own money.

That's why temperance really takes off, because alcohol leads to prostitution, it leads to bankruptcy, and it leads to venereal disease.

CULBERTSON: [The Woman's Christian Temperance Union commissioned an official portrait of Lucy Hayes.] They wanted to memorialize the decision not to serve alcohol in the White House. Lucy was not pleased by that decision…. She was also not happy that they were trying to raise the money to do this, one dime at a time. She said, "I think I'm worth more than a dime." [Nonetheless, their commissioned portrait became her official White House portrait.]

BLACK: Elizabeth Cady Stanton came to the White House to lobby for Lucy's involvement in women's suffrage. The Hayeses rejected it. They did not support women's suffrage. [However,] Lucy Hayes was absolutely passionate about women's education and encouraged young women to go to college, which was, in fact, a radical thing to say during her time in the White House. She saw temperance, to a certain extent, as a way to help women, but…women's wages, where women worked, women's rights to join a union, women's right to vote, which were the major political issues at that time, she did not associate with all that.

Lucy Hayes was very interested in mental health as well, in terms of the sanitation and the treatment that…shell-shocked soldiers had. She would care a lot about veterans' pensions…especially if they were disabled. Before she was first lady, when she [was still] in Ohio and there would be wounded soldiers who hadn't been paid, she would help set up a system to expedite the on-time delivery of their paychecks. She was interested in orphans, in veterans affairs, in the education of the deaf, and in mental health.

[Mrs. Hayes was also very involved with the indigent population in Washington, D.C.] She did that without making a big fanfare about it. She would give money to some of the employees of the White House to go out and give to the poor. Another one of her causes was the education of Indians and of blacks. She went down to Virginia, to the Hampton Institute, and saw blacks and Indians being educated there and she paid for a scholarship for a woman….

CULBERTSON: In 1879, an old 1812 soldier came to the White House to receive an honor, and he was supposed to have his picture taken.

When he arrived, his uniform came separately and he was distraught that the sergeant's stripes were not on the uniform. Lucy grabbed her sewing kit, sat down on the floor, and sewed on the epaulets. The British minister came in and saw the first lady of the United States sitting on the floor at the White House, sewing on this gentleman's rank. And, it was he who told the story, not her.

BLACK: [Lucy Hayes] is an enigma. She's trying to figure out how to be her own person. She has been stereotyped in a way that Mary Todd Lincoln was stereotyped, and it doesn't show the courage and the incredible guts she had.

I just wish America understood. If I could tell them one thing about Lucy Hayes that I find stunningly haunting, [it would be] how much violence she saw up close during the war, in surgery and out, and not only in Ohio hospitals, but going to her husband's camps where her brother, Joe, was a surgeon. She went in and out of the operating room. She did postoperative care. She saw people without anesthetics suffering in horrific ways. When four soldiers, two of whom were wounded, two of whom were significantly ill, were late and missed their train to Chicago, she opened what she called her back parlor in her house so that they could stay. It makes perfect sense to me that she sewed that sergeant's stripes on....

CULBERTSON: Lucy stayed out of politics. In fact, Rutherford put out a statement that no one from his immediate family would have a paid position in the government to try to keep her family members, mainly, from applying for jobs. At different times, Lucy would write to her son Webb, who was a confidential secretary to his father, saying, "Could you try to influence your father on appointments?" Lucy felt that she was getting nowhere with Rutherford.

BLACK: Lucy Hayes hated state dinners, but pulled them off. She would be very vocal with people that were around her about this. But she was able, with a grace and an ability to put people at ease, to help open the White House up to people in a way that would be very different from Mary Todd, who would be charming, but had an edge to her. Lucy was kind and was able to talk at the level of the person that she was with.

Lucy Hayes in the White House conservatory with two of her children and a young friend (in white blouse), 1877. *Courtesy Rutherford B. Hayes Presidential Center*

CULBERTSON: Lucy loved the twelve conservatories that were in the White House. Every morning, she would make the rounds in there. She would send flowers off to the various hospitals in Washington, D.C. She was a very compassionate person.

They expanded the conservatories. One problem they had was that Congress would not appropriate money to fix up the White House. The carpets had holes in them, so she strategically placed the furniture. She had the curtains reversed so that the worn bottoms were put up toward the top. She went up in the attics and found pieces of furniture. She got a few things reupholstered, even went out and bought some pieces. Once they finally did get money, first she put in new carpets in the East Room, reupholstered some pieces, and added one more conservatory.

[The Hayeses were antiquarians who preserved some of their predecessors' furniture, but were also interested in technology, bringing the first typewriter, installing plumbing. They had the first telephone in Washington, D.C.,] but it only went to the Treasury Department building. She was so thrilled by it that she had a group of singers in and had them sing loudly into the phone. One bass singer hit a particular note and exploded a piece within the receiver of the phone.

Thomas Edison also visited the White House. He arrived at eleven o'clock at night, because Congress had kept him too long demonstrating his recording machine. Rutherford was so impressed by it that he got the ladies up at midnight. It took them an hour to get dressed again, and they stayed up until three o'clock in the morning, playing with the new recording device.

The Hayeses traveled thousands of miles, almost always together.... They were the first to go to the West Coast during their term in office. When they did their traveling throughout the country, the Hayeses wanted to include the South and the West and New England. At the time, he felt that the nomination of James Garfield, and Garfield's election, was a sign that he could have been elected had he chosen to run for a second term in office. He felt that the corner had been turned and the Republican Party was now swinging back.

CULBERTSON: Rutherford Hayes appointed Frederick Douglass as the marshal of the city of Washington, D.C. Hayes was very aware that it was a symbolic gesture on his part. He also had African Americans appointed to a number of positions in the South, mainly. The Hayeses were also the first to have a black opera singer perform for them in the White House, Madame Marie Selica Williams, and had some other black performers on their Saturday performances in the White House.

BLACK: The Hayeses really were progressives, but they were ineffectual in really helping the South adhere to the law.... Hayes pulled the last troops out after securing verbal commitments and written commitments from the Southern states that they would adhere to the civil rights that the Fourteenth and the Fifteenth Amendments guaranteed African Americans.

When Hayes pulls those troops out, equality in the South implodes. You have racial violence escalating. The Ku Klux Klan skyrockets. You have the introductions of the Mississippi codes, which begin in 1877 and are crystallized in 1901, that deprive blacks of being able to own property, and restricts voting rights.

In 1871, ninety-six percent of African American men can vote in the state of Mississippi. When Hayes ends Reconstruction ten years later, less than 0.5 percent of African American men can vote because of the violence and the intimidation, the grandfather clause, the poll tax, and the literacy test. It's really becoming two separate nations where African Americans emboldened by Frederick Douglass in the North begin to organize and begin to secure their rights, while the South has theirs stripped away.

CULBERTSON: [In 1881,] the Hayeses were relieved to be leaving. They said the White House was the best time of their lives to that point, but they felt like they didn't want to wear out their welcome. They had managed to do some of the things that they wanted to do, but they were happy to hand it off to the Garfields and let them sit in the hot seat for awhile.

The Hayeses kept going with their causes. Rutherford Hayes was a trustee of the Ohio State University. Lucy was involved with the Woman's Home Missionary Society, the only organization she ever took a leadership role with. She was the president of the organization. She would go kicking and screaming to the annual meeting and make a short address each year…. She made a comment that there were more immigrants coming in from the "heathen nations," the Eastern European countries, and that in those countries they did not respect women, and that the chore of trying to assimilate them into the United States would be tougher, but they would attempt to do so. She got quite a bit of criticism over that particular speech in 1887.

BLACK: [The press continued to cover the Hayeses after they left the White House.] The Hayeses brought America back, in a way, after the war. They're relatively scandal-free when they leave the White House. Their devotion to each other is palpable. They don't change when they're there; they don't change when they leave, and so the country continues to be interested in them and grateful.

CULBERTSON: Lucy was fifty-seven when she died. They had her funeral in Spiegel Grove [their family home in Ohio]. She was laid out in the front hallway and thousands of people came through. One of the great stories of her funeral was [when] the procession went back behind the home and passed the fenced-in area where her cows were assembled, they lined up like soldiers, they said, and gave her a salute as she left.

Rutherford lived three more years beyond her death. He was still active with the Ohio State University, with prison reform, education of blacks and Indians. He attended lots of conferences. He did a little bit of traveling, finally got out of the United States, visited Bermuda.... He felt that past presidents should really stay out of active politics, though he did rejoice when Republicans were elected, and wasn't so pleased when Democrats got elected.

Lucy Hayes's legacy:

CULBERTSON: Lucy Hayes showed that you could be an excellent mother and a supportive wife, and also a gracious hostess, and be inclusive and welcome anybody regardless of their social strata into the White House. She didn't bend to the whims of society. She didn't change her look. She didn't change her style. She showed that a woman can be a woman on her own terms.

BLACK: She was a transitional first lady. People need to understand the courage that it takes to hold this position, and that she brought her own memories and her own love of country into this role, as well as support and respect for her husband.

[Lucy Hayes made the role of first lady] her own with much less tension than the other women who came before her.... What Lucy gives us is a graceful transition to the end of Reconstruction. The country really understands her strong abolitionist feelings. They also see how graceful she is in receiving Democrats into the White House. She helps smooth the tensions that Julia Grant brought in when her husband was under fire.

The Garfield Administration, 1881

Lucretia Randolph Garfield

> "It is a terrible responsibility to come to him and to me."

Lucretia Garfield, c1881

Born: April 19, 1832, Garrettsville, Ohio
Marriage: November 11, 1858, to James Abram Garfield (1831–81)
Children: Eliza (Trot) Arabella (1860–63); Harry Augustus (1863–1942); James Rudolph (1865–1950); Mary (Mollie) (1867–1947); Irvin McDowell (1870–1951); Abram (1872–1958); Edward (Neddie) (1874–76)
Died: March 14, 1918, South Pasadena, California

Contributor:

CARL SFERRAZZA ANTHONY, historian of the National First Ladies Library; author of several books on first ladies, including the two-volume *First Ladies*

CARL SFERRAZZA ANTHONY: There are so many modern chords in [the story of how Lucretia and James Garfield met]. There's this sense of equality to them. Even though they were mid-nineteenth century people, both of them very much saw each other as equals.

Lucretia Garfield was the great-granddaughter of a German immigrant. Her parents were very religious. They were members of the Disciples of Christ. Her father was one of the founders of the Eclectic Institute, and they very strongly believed in education of women. This is a fascinating phenomenon in Ohio. You see this with all of the presidents' wives who were born and raised in Ohio: equal education for women, and they're all highly educated. Lucretia Garfield...studied the classics. She learned how to speak Greek and Latin. She learned how to speak French and German. She studied science, biology, mathematics, history, philosophy.

If you can think of passion coming through the world of ideas, there was a real passion struck between the two of them. James Garfield came from a very poor family. He was orphaned; never knew his father and had been a canal boy, one of those young guys who would walk the mules along that would pull the canal boats. Everything they got, they greatly appreciated. He felt, like she did, that education was the answer.

He was her teacher at the Eclectic Institute. He then went to Williams College and they began a correspondence. That's really where the world of ideas begins to separate them and bring them together.... One of those ideas was the fact that there was another woman [in James's life,] and that became a point of contention between the two of them.

It was touch-and-go for awhile. But what's really interesting about Lucretia is that even though she very much loves him, she also looked out for herself. She set a course, and she is going to become a teacher. She determined that she would work and earn her own salary. She didn't want to be a burden on her father or, if she never got married, have to depend on anyone else. She not only becomes a teacher, but an interest in art is born in her, and she pursues this on her own and then becomes an art teacher. She shifts the topics that she teaches, and this is all right before she gets married.

Later, James has another affair. The early one was just a love situation before they were married. This later one is a full-blown affair with a woman by the name of Lucia Calhoun in New York, and nearly does in the marriage.

Lucretia really started developing [her keen political sense] once they moved to Washington, D.C., when he was a member of Congress. They lost their first child, a girl. They lost their last born, a little boy. They had a lot of tough times. He [was also gone a lot when he] served during the Civil War.

He came to Washington, and they were separated again, and she finally said, "I'm just not going to put up with this." So they decided to build a home in Washington. When she came to Washington as a congressional wife, she began attending debates on Capitol Hill. She was there during the 1876 election dispute commission.

By the time he runs [for president] in 1880, they are square on the same page in terms of their values, and they both shared a lot of intellectual and literary pursuits, that mutual passion which, during the tough times, kept them together.

At the time she got the news that James had won the nomination, she was in an old bonnet, scrubbing the floor. She didn't want to pose for photographs. She was very reluctant, yet her image is the first that we start to see being used in paraphernalia sold during the campaign. She wrote a private letter to some friends, and said, "The truth is, I really don't want to go to that place, but I really believe that my husband is the right man to lead the country."

[Garfield's 1880 campaign was dubbed "the front porch campaign." Supporters came to the Garfields' home in Mentor, Ohio, to hear him speak.] For Lucretia Garfield, [who was so interested in politics, this meant] that because it was technically the property of her private home, people coming in on horse and buggies to hear Garfield speak didn't find anything at all unusual about the presence of his wife at what was a campaign rally.

[By 1880,] many of the issues that had continued in the post-Civil War era were really in large measure put to rest. The Transcontinental Railroad had by this time been completed. The troops had been removed from the South during Reconstruction. A lot of focus was on power and money. The struggle within the Republican Party for who would control the party, which meant who would control the appointed positions that were at the discretion of people in power, ended up being... between an Ohio-based party, [dubbed the "Half Breeds,"] which was James Garfield's party, and what were called the "Stalwarts," which were New York-based. In New York, that [wing] was headed by a man by the name of Roscoe Conkling, who became a United States senator.

[Garfield was a compromise candidate after many failed ballots at the 1880 Republican convention. When the Garfields came to the White House,] they were largely accepted. This is where Lucretia played a vital role. A lot of that was a matter of cobbling together a cabinet where...the New York wing would be happy, and where Garfield now, as leader of the party and the country, would be satisfied. You had Lucretia Garfield playing a bit of an espionage role post-election, pre-inauguration, where she goes to New York under the alias of Mrs. Greenfield. She is there to deal with this guy she doesn't like, Roscoe Conkling, in negotiating members of the cabinet, who would be appointed and who wouldn't.

The issue of the cabinet really circles around the controversial appointment of the secretary of state, James G. Blaine. Mrs. Garfield is the advocate for him. In fact, Blaine himself writes to Garfield that "the knowledge that Mrs. Garfield wants me in the cabinet is just as important to me as knowing that you, the president, want me in the cabinet."

Lucretia was not a policy person. She was not somebody looking at policy and saying, "You should support this or not support that." She was looking at members of the cabinet who were supposed to be running the government, but from a point of partisan political loyalty... how were these men going to potentially affect her husband's career?

[One of the first decisions that Mrs. Garfield had to make was about temperance policy at the White House.] It ended up, true to what she said, not having a very significant impact politically. A threat was made to her by a woman who said, "You must continue the no-alcohol policy of the Hayeses." Lucretia Garfield said, "Thanks, but no thanks. I feel that by not serving alcohol to my guests, it will take on enormous importance in the press and give it far more attention than it needs." She herself drank wine.

There was very little time for Lucretia Garfield to actually become popular, in the sense of functioning as a first lady. The inauguration was March 4. By the end of April, she had contracted malaria. Through early May, there was even a fear that she might die in the White House. President Garfield, president for three months, writes of how he was unable to work with fear that something would happen to his wife.

[The Garfields' White House] was healthy. It was fun. It was humorous. There was no treacly sentiment. Even though it was the Victorian age, nobody was trying to use them as examples of good living and that sort of thing. They were just a very close family.

The two older boys were to be going to college, but the Garfields were so close that they actually remained in the house and studied there. There were two little boys who were terrors, Abram and Irwin, and then a very openhearted daughter, Mollie, who kept a little diary when she was in the White House. It's a very poignant document because it talks about her father's assassination.

The grandmother was also there, Garfield's mother.... She was of the mind that she had raised her son to be president. When Lucretia was ill and there was some speculation about whether she'd be able to return as hostess, there were suggestions in the press that maybe old Mother Garfield, as they called her, would [stay at] the White House and take over. There's some suggestion within the family that this idea didn't go over too well.

One project we know [she was interested in as first lady] from Lucretia's diary, is going to the Library of Congress to do research on the history of the White House, with the idea of not necessarily historically restoring the house, but bringing a sense of history there. At this point, the White House has been standing eighty years, and all these families back to the Adamses had lived there.... She really had a sense of history and the history of the house.

In her diary, ... she records an incident where one of her guests tells her about the night of the fall of Richmond and being with Mary Lincoln. She writes in her diary that these little stories are the kinds of things she begins to accumulate and feels that there are some ghosts, so to speak, in the house. She has an affinity, a real strong sense of sorority, with many of the first ladies.

She hosted regular receptions, and it's fascinating that at one of those, Charles Guiteau, who would shoot the president two months later, met her. He recorded having a very pleasant conversation with her and really liking her. And then she gets malaria, and there is a fear that she might die. As she's recovering, it's thought that she would do better at the Jersey Shore, with the salt air. Guiteau, ready to shoot the president, is waiting for Garfield at the railroad station. He sees him escorting Mrs. Garfield and he can't bring himself to shoot.

It's extraordinary to think that not even twenty years after the assassination of President Lincoln, that there could be such relatively lax security at the White House.... Members of the public who had some vague connection from a senator or a congressman would be able to go up the stairs, check in with the doorkeeper, and wait in this hallway filled with spittoons and cigar smoke. They would hope to see one of the president's secretaries, pressing their case, usually with letters of introduction, claiming how great and wonderful they were and how they deserved some minor federal position…while the president was in his office at the far end. These kinds of characters were always shifting around in the hallway. Charles Guiteau [Garfield's assassin] was one of them. He never got to press his case, and he took it personally.

[On July 2, 1881, Guiteau gets his second chance at Garfield.] The president is on his way to Elberon, New Jersey, to join his wife, and then he is going to go up to Williams College in Massachusetts. Two of the boys are back in Ohio with their grandmother. Mollie, the president's daughter, is with her mother. Guiteau shoots the president [at the train station in Washington].

…Charles Guiteau, is proudly screaming with the gun in his hand, "I'm a Stalwart. Now, Arthur is president." That was a reference to the fact that Vice President Arthur, elected with Garfield, was from the New York wing of the party.

Garfield right away sees Harriet Blaine, the wife of James Blaine, and he tells her to please immediately wire Lucretia. Mrs. Garfield comes down to Washington, and [at first] she's overwhelmed, of course. She almost faints [when she sees her wounded husband,] and has to be held up by two men on either side of her. She composes herself and says to the doctors, "What will it take to make sure he's cured?" They said, "A miracle." She said, without any sentiment, "Well, then, that's what will happen. It will be a miracle."

[The wounded president was taken back to the White House.] They know he's got a bullet in him. It's beastly hot. There's a rudimentary air conditioning system set up to try and pump cool air up from the ground floor. Not only did ideas for inventions [on how to cool the White House come in from the public], but all kinds of kooky recipes and potions and things like this were being sent to Mrs. Garfield.

It's only after he's shot …that the press really begins to focus on Lucretia Garfield. She becomes not just a national, but an international heroine for her calmness and her control as the president is attempting recuperation for two months. Mrs. Garfield was fantastic in that she was able to compartmentalize what were her very personal fears and the real care and the wear on her emotionally from the possibility of losing her husband. [At the same time, she had] the wherewithal to put out the word that everything was fine, that the president was in charge.

This was a very important thing. She asked that everything written about him be sent to her for review. Vice President Arthur made no rumblings about assuming any presidential duties. He respected her. And you began to see generated, first in the country, and then around the world, the most amazing articles about this woman's courage, this woman's intelligence, her fortitude, her strength, her calm, and how it was pervading the White House. She was cheering up, so to speak, the president, the patient.

The technology of the day permitted pen sketches, so you began to see visual images of Mrs. Garfield with their daughter at his bedside or of her down in the kitchen preparing food for him. It was a bit of hyperbole, because, it was, in fact, a desperate situation.

Alexander Graham Bell offered to bring in a newfangled electromagnetic machine to try and find the bullet. He asked that any metal springs in the bed be removed, but they weren't ... [so, in trying to trace a metal bullet], his machine saw all the bedsprings.

[The president was shot in July, but lingered until September. The decision was made at some point to move him to the Jersey Shore,] to the very place where he had been headed to join her, and that is where he dies in her presence. Among the many [condolence] letters that Lucretia receives is one from a former first lady, Julia Tyler. She not only sends a telegram, as does former first lady Sarah Polk, but then Mrs. Tyler writes her a letter and...uses the word "sister" in talking about this idea of an almost sorority of presidential spouses.

[James Garfield ultimately died of infection.] The bullet was dirty. It was a foreign object that was in him, and so he might have eventually died. Of course, it was also medical ignorance at the time. He had one woman doctor, Dr. Susan Edson, and after the federal government had paid Garfield's doctors, they paid that woman doctor half the amount. Mrs. Garfield wrote a letter and was outraged and used the word "discrimination," and the woman doctor received the same amount as the male doctors.

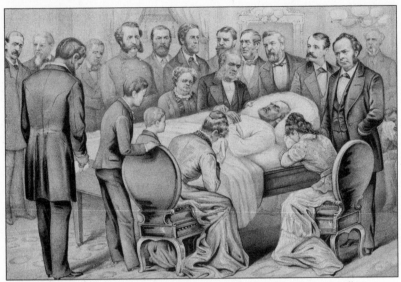

In 1881, the world watched as Lucretia Garfield bravely tended to a mortally wounded president, who lingered for two months after an assassin struck.

Two hundred fifty thousand people came to President Garfield's funeral. There were photographs that show the White House trimmed in the most intricate patterns of black mourning crepe. Mrs. Garfield was strong throughout it. She did not break down, unlike Mary Lincoln and Peggy Taylor, who were unable to emotionally withstand the whole public display.

Mrs. Garfield was seen [by the public]. She also, in a very practical way, began designing and working with the ideas of what his tomb would be like in Cleveland, Ohio.

[There was a fund drive for the Garfield family and somewhere around $350,000, in 1880 dollars, was raised for the family.] It was extraordinary. It was a financier by the name of Cyrus Field who started this in the newspapers, and it really caught on. She really captured people's imagination. We forget it now. It was a brief moment in our history, but it was so different from the way people reacted to Mary Lincoln.

Mrs. Garfield received the balance of Garfield's $50,000 annual salary. She also received his pension as a former member of Congress, and she received that large amount of public funds that were raised. She also received the presidential widow's pension, so she had quite a bit of income coming from several directions.

Because of Mrs. Garfield being awarded almost immediately by Congress a presidential widow's pension of $5,000 a year, that also benefited the other surviving presidential widows, Sarah Polk, Julia Tyler, and Mary Lincoln. True to form, Mrs. Lincoln's reaction was, "I'm sure somebody is going to put the kibosh on that and I won't ever get my money," and Julia Tyler wrote an anonymous letter to the press saying, "This is wonderful, but I think it should be double that amount."

Mrs. Garfield had built onto [their home in Mentor, Ohio,] after his death, a fireproof safe, specifically to house and protect and preserve his letters and papers, because she had been planning on writing a biography about him. She never lived to do that, but later, those letters were published before being donated to the Library of Congress.

[Lucretia Garfield built herself a house in Pasadena, California,] because she couldn't take the cold winters in Ohio anymore; she also maintained a home in Washington as a presidential widow.... California was, in the 1890s, really opening up as the promised land of sunshine. She went out to Pasadena in 1900. She was distantly related to these two famous architects, Greene and Greene.... She had a great interest in architecture, and so she worked very closely with them in designing this extraordinary California arts and crafts mansion, which is still standing, a private home. She was even in one of the carriages of VIPs in the early Pasadena Rose Parade. She had a very full life in California.

She didn't come out on women's suffrage...but her daughter affirmed that her mother truly believed in the equality of the genders. When former president Theodore Roosevelt, in 1912, is mounting a campaign against the incumbent Republican president, she supports Roosevelt. When he makes an appearance in Los Angeles, she comes to that event.

One of her sons was in Theodore Roosevelt's cabinet and another son was in Woodrow Wilson's cabinet, as fuel administrator. She died a year into World War I, and she was actually doing work as a volunteer with the Red Cross in Pasadena when she died.

Lucretia Garfield's legacy:

[Lucretia Garfield died in 1918 at the age of eighty-five.] Unfortunately, her tenure was brief, but we can say this: she was the first to be self-conscious enough not to destroy her papers. She was the first to keep a diary of her White House days. And she might best be thought of as a former first lady, in a sense, in terms of her career.

Lucretia Garfield had such a sense of history that she kept papers, even the ones that might prove embarrassing or personal that related to her marriage. She had a sense of herself and her husband, beyond their own lives, as historical figures.

There are a lot of similarities between her and Jacqueline Kennedy, both in terms of committing to the legacy of their husbands, and yet also not allowing their lives or the lives of their children to be weighed down by grief.

Ellen Herndon Arthur

"Honors to me are not what they once were." —Chester Arthur, following the death of his wife Ellen

Ellen Arthur, c1857

Born: August 30, 1837, Culpeper County, Virginia
Marriage: October 29, 1859, to Chester Alan Arthur (1829–86)
Children: William Lewis Herndon (1860–63); Chester Alan II (Alan) (1864–1937); Ellen Herndon (1871–1915)
Died: January 12, 1880, New York City (one and a half years before the Arthur presidency)

Contributor:

CARL SFERRAZZA ANTHONY, historian of the National First Ladies Library; author of several books on first ladies, including the two-volume *First Ladies*

CARL SFERRAZZA ANTHONY: With Garfield's assassination, you have this man come into the White House, and everyone is thinking, "Oh, my gosh, this is the worst." Talk about a man who has benefited from political patronage: Chester Alan Arthur has never been elected to any office. He was the collector of the Port of New York. He had a high position in New York State during the Civil War, quartermaster, but it was all political patronage.

Roscoe Conkling, who was the kingmaker of the Stalwarts in New York, thinks, "Aha! Now the doors will open and we'll get all the political plums." But President Arthur says, "No, I'm going to change my stripes and we're going to be honest." Chester Arthur is the man who initiates the first civil service reform.

Of course, the focus in 1881 really remained for so long, well into October and November, on President Garfield and his family. Chester Arthur's permanent home was in New York City on Lexington Avenue. He himself was still in a state of very deep mourning...because his wife, Ellen Herndon Arthur, had died in January of 1880, so it wasn't yet two years that he had lost her.

Ellen Arthur was very fashionable, very rich, largely through the wealth of her mother, and very ambitious. There are a lot of stories about how she got behind her husband's career. She really didn't like that politics kept him away from the home so often, but on the other hand, she was very socially ambitious and ambitious for his career.

Ellen had come from a very powerful, well-connected Virginia family. She grew up in Washington, D.C. They went to St. John's Church on Lafayette Square, and for about five years between the time she was five and ten years old, she knew Dolley Madison.

Her father was a very famous naval commodore who took a ship, the *Central America*, on a commercial trip. It went down [in a hurricane], but his was a great act of bravery, because he made sure that all of the passengers who were on board got off first. His widow and his daughter, Ellen, who was an only child, then living in New York City, were given all sorts of honors and awards. Even today, there is a monument to Herndon in Annapolis at the Naval Academy.

Ellen went to Abraham Lincoln's 1865 inaugural. She attended the White House wedding of Nellie Grant. She knew the parents of Theodore Roosevelt in New York City. She bought at the best stores. They took summers in Cooperstown, New York, and Newport.

Because she was an only child, she was very close to what were her double cousins; her parents' siblings had married each other. Even though she was a Southerner, and it was during the Civil War, Chester Arthur was able to secure the release of one of these cousins from Union prison.

[As president,] Chester Arthur made several appointments that we know of, specifically of people who had known his wife. One cousin...

was made assistant attorney general. Another was put at Treasury. It was very controversial, that for the superintendent of the Naval Academy, he appointed somebody who had been a childhood friend of his wife's. [One of his appointments] created a political problem with the Senate. Before Washington, D.C. had mayors, there was a ceremonial role...and [the Senate] liked the prerogative of appointing the position, yet Arthur insisted on making that appointment, because it was somebody who was a friend of his and Ellen's.

He kept Ellen's picture on the wall with fresh flowers nearby. He had a stained-glass window put in at St. John's Church so he could see it from his bedroom window in the White House. There was some remorse on his part, perhaps, because he was quite married to his career and his political advancement. Mrs. Arthur, who was an accomplished singer, died of pneumonia while he was in Albany on political business.

You have the administration coming in without a wife and without a vice president. His ten-year-old daughter is living with his sister, Molly, up in Albany. It was all sorts of loose ends, and the press at the time begins speculating in a series of articles about who will be lady of the White House.

It got a little unseemly, because there were a lot of wealthy women, or women who wanted to be wealthy, who began flirtatiously appearing wherever President Arthur did. He had no interest whatsoever in remarrying. He really became depressed.

He basically said, "I'm not going to have a first lady. Nobody is going to take the role of my wife." He starts having these events once the social season begins again, when Congress comes back into session. It was like first lady for a day,...a cabinet wife [acting as hostess], then a Senate wife. None of it was really quite working.

The following year, 1883, New Year's Day, his sister comes down from Albany. There's an indication that Arthur knew he had a terminal illness, Bright's Disease. He wanted to be close again to his little daughter, Nell, so she came down from New York...with her aunt, Mary Arthur ("Molly") McElroy.

Molly lived in the White House with her brother, [the president, and the two were extremely protective of the little girl]. In fact, that was part of the reason Arthur kept her away from the White House for

President Chester Arthur, a wealthy widower, worked with designer Louis Tiffany to refurbish the White House, installing a fifty-foot wall of glass in the main hall. *Credit: Library of Congress. Courtesy White House Historical Association*

nearly a year, making sure she lived at his home in New York City. Then he was having that home remodeled, so she went to live with her aunt. Molly McElroy's daughters, Jessie and May, a little older than their cousin, also came to live with their mother in the White House.

[Even though a president had just been assassinated, there was no extra security at the White House.] There were guards at the front door, but it still had a sort of lazy, old hotel quality to it. This was one reason why Arthur was very protective of his daughter. In fact, it isn't until the 1886 New Year's Day reception, two months before he leaves office, that he allows his daughter to appear publicly.

[Arthur's White House was a] very interesting situation, because it really showed us that the country had come to expect a female presence, whether it was a wife or a sister or a daughter. Molly McElroy really walked a fine line; she made public appearances, sometimes on her own, sometimes with him. He was ambivalent about how public a role she should take.

[Arthur began to entertain lavishly in the White House, and he undertook an amazing redecoration of the White House led by Louis Tiffany.] This wall of Tiffany glass was put up in what is the main hall, the central hall, of the state floor…. In those days the draft was so bad, people were complaining about it, so Arthur put up this wall of garish Victorian Tiffany glass. It was considered high style. It didn't last but twenty years. Teddy Roosevelt's famous words were, "Smash that wall to bits."

If we could credit good old Molly McElroy, who is basically forgotten in history, with anything, it's bringing the first ladies together. She invited to the White House Julia Tyler and Harriet Lane, to publicly receive with her, as sort of co-hostesses. Because of the pension issue, Mrs. Lincoln and Mrs. Tyler were back in the news again, along with Mrs. Garfield. And, finally, when Molly McElroy left the role of substitute first lady, she handed it over to the Cleveland White House; Cleveland, who's a bachelor at the time, has a sister, Rose Cleveland, who will be assuming that role. So, there was a lot of press about these two sisters passing along the role of first lady.

In conjunction with all of this, the very first book is written on the history of first ladies, a collective biography called *Ladies of the White House* [by Laura Carter Holloway]. It's a very famous book, and came out in many editions.

Ellen Arthur's legacy:

Ellen Arthur is really interesting [among first ladies]. She doesn't become first lady, but she influences the administration, very similarly to the way that Rachel Jackson did, her ghost, the memory of her.

Frances Folsom Cleveland

"I want you to take good care of the furniture and ornaments in the house, for I want to find everything just as it is now when we come back four years from today."

Frances Cleveland, c1886

Born: July 21, 1864, Buffalo, New York
Marriage: June 2, 1886, to Stephen Grover Cleveland (1837–1908) (widowed); February 10, 1913, to Thomas Preston (1870–1955)
Children: Ruth (1891–1904); Esther (1893–1980); Marion (1895–1977); Richard Folsom (1897–1974); Francis Grover (1903–95)
Died: October 27, 1947, Baltimore, Maryland

Contributors:

ANNETTE DUNLAP, author of *Frank: The Story of Frances Folsom Cleveland*

TAYLOR STOERMER, Graduate School of Arts and Sciences fellow and instructor of public history, Harvard University, focusing on the American Revolution and its modern relevance

ANNETTE DUNLAP: If you think about the 1880s, it was probably the age of newspapers. Every major city had multiple newspapers, and every one of those newspapers was looking for a way to make money. The best way to make money was to get the best story, so whoever could find out where Frances Cleveland was staying, what she was wearing, what she was doing, what she looked like, who she was seeing, that was going to help sell papers. It didn't hurt if they made a little bit of it up, either.

From the time that Grover Cleveland came into office in March of 1885, there was all of this speculation about who possibly could be his bride. It would waver between some of the women who would help his sister, Rose, with her receptions at the White House; and then, there was this competition in the minds of the public between whether or not it was Frances Folsom or her mother, Emma. People were pretty convinced that there was no way he was going to marry Frances. She was way too young. It had to be Emma. Then, right about the time on what they used to call Decoration Day, now we call it Memorial Day, in 1886, Cleveland sent out the wedding invitations. Frances, her mother, and her cousin came back from Europe, and at the Decoration Day Parade in New York City, Frances was introduced to the public.

[The wedding was held in the Blue Room of the White House with music by John Philip Sousa.] The president thought that he had been able to outsmart the press [about their honeymoon destination,] because they had arranged for a special two-car train. It was going to be on a side rail. They figured that they could get up to an area around what is now Deep Creek, Maryland, on some privately owned property, but there was a telegraph agent who was able to be bribed to reveal the destination of that train. Because it was pouring rain that night, when they got to the train station they then had to take a carriage from the station to their actual honeymoon location. The carriage got bogged down in the mud, which gave the press even more time, and the press was actually staked out by the time they got there.

Cleveland ranked the press: he had what he called the respectable papers and the not-respectable papers. He invited reporters from the so-called respectable papers to come into the cabin where he and Frances were staying. They had stacked these telegrams from well-wishers on the table. They shared some of those. It was very nicely staged, very choreographed. They allowed the press to see some of these papers, allowed them to see him and Frances engaged with one another. It was a way to say, "Okay, boys, you've had your fun. Now, would you leave us alone so that we can get about the business of being married?"

Grover Cleveland was law partner and friend with Frances's father, Oscar Folsom. When Oscar and his wife had Frances Emma Folsom, Cleveland supposedly gave them their first baby carriage and became a

The White House wedding of President Grover Cleveland and Frances Folsom, twenty-seven years his junior, as depicted by *Harper's Weekly* in 1886.

fixture in their house. As Frances grew up, she started to call him "Uncle Cleve." Then her father was tragically killed just a couple of days after her eleventh birthday in a carriage accident.

Oscar was not a good money manager. Some people who knew a little bit more about the family history said he was a little bit of a rogue or a rake. He actually owed more money than he had in his estate. Cleveland stepped in as executor and money manager to help handle the affairs and then worked with Emma to oversee Frances's education through high school and into college.

People who...grew up in the Wells College area, which is Frances's alma mater, will tell you about the special train that came to the depot so that Grover could come and visit her. He did write her letters. He did send her flowers. She also accompanied him on campaign appearances when he ran for governor of New York in 1882. So, his interest in Frances is definitely well [before the] White House years.

You will find some language in the press that called them "Beauty and the Beast," because they didn't like him. He was forty-nine, he was portly, he wasn't necessarily the handsomest man in the world, and she was an absolute stunner, dark hair, blue eyes, tall for that age, very good-looking, and there were people that thought there was something a little strange about it. But for the most part, because they fell immediately in love with her, they just accepted him as part of the package.

Frances loved Grover. She started out, as most people do early in a marriage, thinking that it was romantic, but the age difference was pretty significant. Over time, that love matured into a deep caring.

In that time period, there was still this attitude of "spheres of influence," where women were supposed to stay pure, and take care of the home, and take care of the children, and that's exactly where he wanted Frances to be. He didn't want her pretty little head upset with notions about being first lady or being affected by all of the demands of being in the White House or being the wife of the president. He also didn't think that women should vote or work outside the home.

TAYLOR STOERMER: Politics in the 1880s is brutal.... You have Grover Cleveland, on the one hand, who has very little political experience of this sort. He was elected mayor of Buffalo in 1881; he was elected governor of New York in 1882, and two years later, he's the Democratic nominee for president. That's all the major political experience that he has, but he has developed a reputation of being honest and trustworthy and a reformer. On the other hand, you've got a guy named James G. Blaine, the "continental liar from Maine," who, if anything, has too much political experience. He's been speaker of the House. He's a senator from Maine. He's one of the major figures in the Republican Party. He has a reputation for probably having private virtue, a good family man, but he's also tainted by public corruption. He's an "inside-the-Beltway" guy. The whole campaign of 1884 ends up revolving around these things. If the... greatest opportunity that the Democrats have had since James Buchanan to get back the White House is the reputation of Cleveland as being a man of public virtue, then, as any good political operative would point out, go right after it. And so they did. The Republicans went straight after probably his most weak point, which is the illegitimate child.

DUNLAP: In 1874, a woman by the name of Maria Halpin gave birth to an illegitimate child in Buffalo, New York.... Maria named him Oscar Folsom Cleveland. Cleveland stepped up to the plate and said that he would take responsibility for her and for the child. Maria apparently had problems with alcohol and was not taking care of him, and an opportunity developed for Cleveland to be able to place the child in the home of a family. It was the family of Mr. and Mrs. James King, and so this young man, who started his life as Oscar Folsom Cleveland, became James King, Jr.

It was all pretty quiet [in the campaign] until they uncovered the dirt and found out that Cleveland had assumed responsibility for this child. Therefore, the assumption was that he also was the father of the child. There were some efforts initially to cover it up, and then the famous line that Cleveland says was, "Tell the truth."

Cleveland was very obviously courting Frances at this point. It's 1884.... One of her Wells classmates came into her dorm room and happened to see a picture of Cleveland on the desk and wanted to know who it was. Frances referred to him at that point as the mayor of Buffalo, and her comment was: "A man more sinned against than sinning." Her mother apparently wrote a letter to Frances saying that she hated to see Cleveland going through all of this trouble with the issues with this boy, but there's never any discussion in those letters about who they thought the real father was.

STOERMER: [Parlor politics was practiced] less in the Cleveland White House than probably in many of the previous White Houses. Frances is involved in at least one occasion...she actually attends a Senate debate. She's sitting in the gallery watching over his major piece of legislation on tariff reform. It's one of the only pieces of direct evidence that we have of her involvement in any kind of political influence.

Other than that, they're using the White House for very different kinds of things. She's able to improve his standing in D.C. simply by standing next to him, because he has a reputation coming into the White House. He likes poker, he likes hanging out with his guy friends, he likes smoking cigars, he likes hunting and fishing...

DUNLAP: And drinking bourbon.

STOERMER: Frances socializes him and civilizes him almost immediately, which gives him some political cache.... She is doing things like getting involved in copyright legislation. A focus on intellectual property, this is in the woman's sphere, in order to be able to protect the arts, protect authors. She holds a reception at the White House for authors, to bring attention to the need for intellectual property legislation. [However], she's going far beyond just the parlor politics of having people over and talking. She's even doing things like going to rallies... unaccompanied by the president, to make sure that she was being directly associated with this legislation.

Everybody else knows [Frances's political potential]; everybody else seems to know it except for him. The *New York Times* has editorials about how she is his great card to play, and he's not going to play it. Instead, he's going to focus on vetoing as much legislation as possible, ticking off as many people on the Hill as possible, which actually continues to undermine his political capacity.

DUNLAP: [During his first term, the Clevelands undertook a historically significant tour.] This was the first time since the end of the Civil War where a president embarked on this extensive a tour to cover the South, as well as the West, which was gaining in population. The crowds were [huge]. Richard Watson Gilder writes letters to Frances saying, "Get some bodyguards, get some protection. You're going to be crushed to death." She writes letters back,... "We're finally on the way home. It's been a wonderful and terrific tour. I'm so thankful that nobody got killed and no child got trampled," because the crowds were just enormous.

STOERMER: The people of St. Louis actually made coins with her image on them to hand out during her visit.

DUNLAP: Frances took a temperance vow probably about the time she joined the Presbyterian church, which was at the age of fourteen, and she honored that up until the latter part of her life. However, she served alcohol in the White House. She had some very fine wines served at some good state dinners. Cleveland, on the other hand, enjoyed his whiskey.

STOERMER: It's not a broader public policy issue for her. It's just a personal issue, and the Woman's Christian Temperance Union wasn't just about temperance. The WCTU were actually her biggest critics in the first term about the kind of clothes she was wearing.

DUNLAP: They didn't like her sleeveless dresses or her low neckline. They said she was being immodest.

STOERMER: And she ignored them.

DUNLAP: Cleveland was not as wealthy as maybe some of the earlier presidents who owned large amounts of land, and who were slavehold-ers, but Cleveland was not a poor man, either. Once she married him, there was money for her to be able to purchase very nice clothing.

Frances set some trends. The one that she is the most famous for, although it may not be a true story,...is getting rid of the bustle, a wire contraption that was on the back of your dress.... Some reporters were looking for a story, and they said, "Well, anything about Mrs. Cleveland sells. Let's say she's quit wearing the bustle." The story went out...and all the women quit wearing bustles and had all their dresses remade.

STOERMER: [The 1888 election pits Grover Cleveland, who stands for reelection, against Benjamin Harrison of Indiana.] In terms of our understanding of this election, there are really two things: The first thing is that it really is the first of the big-money elections. This makes campaign finance history. Then, the other issue is really about, what are you going to do about Grover Cleveland's greatest card, Frances? A Republican said at the time that it's one thing to go after Grover Cleve-land; it's another thing to try to defeat them both. We are back into these bare-knuckled politics: the Republicans bring up this story that Grover Cleveland is abusing Frances.

DUNLAP: I'm convinced it's untrue.

STOERMER: There are these contradictions when we're talking about Grover Cleveland and the deployment of Frances in political ways.... Obviously, you've got to tamp down this particular issue. And this elec-tion is the one election in which the image of the first lady is employed in direct political ways, more than [in] any other election in American history.... In the '88 election, the Democratic Party is rolling out Fran-ces Cleveland. There is the creation of the Frances Cleveland clubs.

DUNLAP: [Grover Cleveland lost the 1888 election] but Frances is supremely confident [he will return to power]. To be honest, the minute they hit New York, which is where they lived for the next four years, she started campaigning for him.

STOERMER: Part of it is that he didn't lose the 1888 election. He actually outpaced Harrison by tens of thousands of votes, but was swamped in the electoral system, and so, he's the only president, other than FDR, to win more than two elections.

DUNLAP: New York City was probably a good place for Frances, with her interest in the arts. Cleveland got a job there. He worked for a law firm with Francis Lynde Stetson, who was the attorney for J.P. Morgan and several other extremely well-known and financially well-off and influential people. He was considered "at counsel." He wasn't actually a practicing attorney as much as [he was] overseeing activities within the law firm.

[Frances also gives birth to the couple's first child, Ruth, while they were in New York, and the Baby Ruth candy bar was named for her.] The story there is that the Curtiss Candy Company developed this candy bar. Ruth Cleveland tragically died of diphtheria in January of 1904....

STOERMER: [The 1892 election was a rematch between Benjamin Harrison and Grover Cleveland.] The major issue is that the economy is going to tank, and there isn't anything that Harrison can really do about it. And the Republican Party is splintering...whereas the Democrats are finding a better recipe to coalesce.

DUNLAP: [Grover Cleveland wins reelection and is the only president to serve non-consecutive terms. Soon after,] he found a soft spot in his mouth. He called his doctors because it bothered him, and they decided that it was probably cancerous. Frances was pregnant at the time with their second child, their only child to be born in the White House, Esther.

The original plan was for them to go to a rental house that they had been renovating in the Cleveland Park section of D.C. Then, all of a sudden, you get this announcement in the papers that they've changed their plans, that Mrs. Cleveland wants to take her baby to Buzzards Bay in Massachusetts for the summer, so that Ruth can enjoy the winds and the breeze. Frances and Ruth depart, and they go onto their friend's yacht, and they go up to Buzzards Bay....

In the meantime, to dispel some rumors that he may be losing weight...they're saying that Cleveland is on this diet program. Cleveland gets on the yacht. They perform the surgery on the yacht and he's basically gone for a month. The press starts to say, "What's going on? Where's the president?" They are asking Frances questions, and she's putting them off, saying, "Oh, he's just having a good time fishing. He needs the rest. Things in the country have been terrible. He really needs this time away."

They are able to cover it up with the press. Then he has to go back for a follow-up operation to get fitted with this rubber jaw, and, again, the press is looking. There is a reporter who eventually broke the story, but the administration, unfortunately, discredited him. Frances was very complicit in this cover-up....

STOERMER: Cleveland and his supporters firmly believed that any hint that the president was in danger at all in terms of his health would send the markets even further into the tank, and all the Wall Street investors would pull out and accelerate a panic that was already in full swing. They had to maintain stability in the markets, and the only way that they could do that was to keep this [health scare] completely secret. We're not just talking about a little secret; they make sure that they do the surgery so there are no external scars, and he gives an interview to a reporter three days after his second operation, with his rubber jaw [to help assure the public he's okay].

DUNLAP: Frances really scaled back the social calendar [in their second term]. She did what was absolutely necessary from a diplomatic standpoint during the typical Washington social season, and then they tried to get out of the White House to this rental house that they had in another part of Washington.

[Mrs. Cleveland began to be concerned about the safety of their children.] That's also part of the reason why people decided they did not like her as much. She started closing the White House gates so that the public could not see the children or her when they were out on the grounds. She also uncovered a kidnapping plot, which made her even more vigilant toward the children.

STOERMER: [By the time they finished their second term, the public's view of the Clevelands was] very dim, for the most part, especially of him. The economy was in the midst of the worst depression in American history up to that point. It lasted for five or six years, with unemployment...as high as 18 percent. He was seen as being able to do absolutely nothing about it....And his great card that he had to play, Frances, was seen as being much more withdrawn. These questions about the security of the first family, as being "owned" by the American public, creeps in for the very first time.... The White House security staff goes from four to twenty-seven. They spend much more time outside of the White House, so she's seen as being much more aloof from the American people. She's not the same first lady that the public came to expect during the first term. When you combine these two things, the Clevelands can't wait to get out of the White House by the end of their second term.

DUNLAP: They couldn't go out and look for property on their own.... Cleveland contacted the president of Princeton University, who then found the property that they purchased called Westlands. This was probably the best [period for them] from the time they got married. They were a real family unit. They got very active in Princeton University. Frances got involved with the growing number of women who had graduated college.... They "adopted" young men who were Princeton students who didn't have family close by or have money, and opened their home to them, provided support to them. Cleveland worked with the Equitable Life Assurance Association. He wrote articles, worked on his letters and they had more children. When they left the White House in 1897, Frances was pregnant with Richard, who was their first son and fourth child. In July of 1903, she gave birth to their last child, another son, Francis Grover Cleveland.

Grover Cleveland died in June of 1908.... It sounds like he probably had stomach cancer. It was a slow, drawn-out, painful death. He died in the house at Princeton.

STOERMER: Frances married again in February 1913, about five years later...to a professor.... He had moved to Wells from Princeton, and he was a professor of archeology. They were roughly the same age. His name was Thomas Preston. They had a lot in common, whereas she made a point of saying that she and the president had very little in common, that he found boring what she found interesting. It was much different with Mr. Preston…in terms of their interest in traveling, their interest in the arts, their interest in broader culture, the kind of things that really did bore Grover Cleveland, that he found rather tiresome.

DUNLAP: People were still very interested in Frances and she had to manage the press. It waned over time, but she was always a news item. She got active during World War I. She was active with an organization called the Needlework Guild, which made handmade garments as gifts to other nonprofits for giving out in emergency disaster situations. People followed her. You could still read news items about her, but the obsession wasn't nearly as heightened as it had been during the White House years.

She was the second vice president for the New Jersey Association of Anti-Suffrage from 1913 until women got the right to vote. She went ahead and voted, but she still didn't think that women needed the right to vote.

STOERMER: The fact is that Frances Cleveland, although she exercises her own right to vote, is still part of a way of thinking about women and their place in American society that develops in the 1870s, 1880s. It's first wave feminism: if you want to be the best woman you can possibly be, through education, through understanding of the world around you, that is done by exercising authority within your own special sphere, so that you're not interfering with what men are doing. It's very consistent with what Grover Cleveland is thinking about what women should be able to do.

[Frances opposes women's voting] for the rest of her life, thinking it's a silly, unnecessary thing. Yet, her involvement in World War I, and what she's doing in terms of trying to be very active in supporting American patriotism, and the kind of speeches she's giving throughout World War I, are extraordinary pieces of rhetoric, and things that you would suspect Grover Cleveland would have no truck with whatsoever. She becomes a very different woman after her marriage to Preston.

DUNLAP: [She was interested in the kindergarten movement throughout her life.]…She was instrumental in the founding of Douglass College, the women's college that's now part of Rutgers in New Jersey. She stayed very active with her alma mater, Wells College, for forty years as a trustee.

For the most part, people embraced her remarriage, embraced her. She was back in Washington a number of times. She met Margaret Truman [daughter of President Harry Truman] and [President Dwight] Eisenhower. She maintained her level of celebrity.

Frances Cleveland's legacy:

DUNLAP: Frances Cleveland has been somewhat lost to history, but shouldn't be. She was very strong in education, very strong in the arts, and those are things that we still think are very important today.

She changed the role of first lady in terms of putting education in the forefront, and getting involved with education and taking care of children. She was really concerned about how children were cared for, and that was something she definitely emphasized.

STOERMER: Frances Cleveland is the first national celebrity first lady. When we talk about the development of our understanding of the institution of first lady, then Frances Cleveland is the first one in which we get to start thinking about what are the uses of that celebrity in good ways and bad. There are concerns that have developed about the first family being owned by the American public, but also [we see] how celebrity actually can be a positive tool of the broader presidency. If only Grover Cleveland would have been able to see that.

Caroline Scott Harrison

"I am disgusted with newspapers and reporters. Truth is a characteristic entirely unknown to them."

Caroline Harrison, 1885
Courtesy Benjamin Harrison Presidential Site

Born: October 1, 1832, in Oxford, Ohio
Married: October 20, 1852, to Benjamin Harrison (1833–1901)
Children: Russell Lord (1854–1936); Mary Scott (1858–1930); unnamed baby girl (1861)
Died: October 25, 1892, at the White House in Washington, D.C.

Contributors:

EDITH MAYO, curator emerita, First Ladies exhibit, Smithsonian National Museum of American History; academic advisor for C-SPAN's *First Ladies* series

WILLIAM SEALE, White House historian; author of several books, including *The President's House;* editor, *White House History;* academic advisor for C-SPAN's *First Ladies* series

WILLIAM SEALE: [Benjamin Harrisons's administration] was a very tumultuous time politically.... It was a very tense time between the Democrats and the Republicans, and the motivations were clearly drawn. The Republicans were protectionists. The Democrats were not. The Republicans wanted high tariffs, and the Democrats did not. Harrison was a man who was of a conservative nature, in that he wanted the debts paid, he didn't want a lot of spending, paradoxically, because it was a time of very great spending in his administration.

[It was also a time of grief in Washington. There were fifteen deaths during Harrison's term, including associate justices on the Supreme Court; also, the Navy secretary and his family were burned alive in a house fire.] The Homestead Strike of Carnegie's steel plant was a terrible thing, and twenty men were shot dead among the protestors. While it seemed justified to the plant and Carnegie, it horrified the American public. They just could not believe it. Harrison got a lot of the blame for that.

EDITH MAYO: Caroline Scott was born and brought up in Oxford, Ohio. Her father…was a professor at Miami University, and then went on to found the Oxford Women's Institute, which was a college for women. Her parents were both extremely well-educated, and her father was a supporter of women's education, so he made certain that his daughter had a good one. That interested her for the future in women's accomplishments and the progress of women.

[First ladies having a college degree] was something that was relatively new. Mrs. [Rutherford] Hayes was the first college graduate among first ladies. Frances Cleveland also graduated from college, and Grover waited to pop the question while sending flowers to her the whole time she was there. Caroline Harrison also had a college degree, so it was something that was coming into vogue for women in the later part of the century.

[Benjamin Harrison was also] from Ohio, and they met there in college. He was taking a course from her father in mathematics. Then he began to visit the Harrison home under the pretense of creating a relationship with his professor, but in actuality it was because he wanted to see more of Carrie.

SEALE: President William Henry Harrison [was his grandfather]. He died after thirty days in the White House and [Benjamin] Harrison, as a little boy of maybe nine years old, saw him in his coffin. That's the only time he saw him.

They were from a very distinguished family in Virginia. They lived at Berkeley Plantation on the James River. The two Harrisons would be the only grandfather and [grandson to serve in the presidency]. The grandfather's father had signed the Declaration of Independence, one of the Virginia signers.... Benjamin Harrison...was very conscious of being the great-grandson of a founder and the grandson of a president.

[The Harrisons moved to Indianapolis, where Benjamin] Harrison quickly rose. After the Civil War, his law practice flourished in business law and divorce. Indianapolis was the Reno of its day; lots of people went there to get a divorce. He was the best divorce lawyer in town, and his fortune increased. He made quite a bit of money as a lawyer.

MAYO: [Because they had children, it was a big decision for Benjamin to fight in the Civil War. During the war,] Caroline worked with several women's patriotic associations. She visited hospitals, attended wounded soldiers, helped with the Women's Loyal League and those kinds of... patriotic organizations [like] the women's sanitary commissions, which were helping nurse wounded soldiers; the women's side of the war.

SEALE: Caroline was psychologically set for doing that because of her upbringing; that's what her family believed in. I'm sure her father, as a widower living with them in the White House, encouraged everything she did in that direction, too. They were deeply religious people, Presbyterians, [and community service was part of their ethos].

MAYO: Harrison became the secretary of the Republican State Committee, and through that he began to make all these contacts in the state...and campaigned for other Republicans, which then stood him in good stead in his own right, as far as [being a] possible candidate. [After a failed gubernatorial bid, he was elected to the United States Senate.]

[Harrison defeated Cleveland for president in 1888. The Harrison Inaugural Ball] was in the Pension Building ballroom, [which was] all decorated inside.

SEALE: The Marine band played, and the Harrisons danced. They had not done so in a while. And so, the dancing custom was brought back to the White House, where it had been missing since Harriet Lane.... The ball was held in a rainstorm, but it was a very glamorous and happy event.

The Harrison White House was crowded, and there was lots and lots of entertaining.... Remember, the [president's] office was in the house at the other end of the hall from the family quarters. There were about fifteen servants, mostly federal employees from the agencies, and they are paid from the agencies. And with all these children and the routine of a private house, plus the public activities, it was a very busy place.

There were their children and grandchildren. Their son was in and out; he lived out in Helena, Montana, but his wife was [in the White House with] their children, as was the Harrisons' daughter, Mary, who's called Mamie, or Mrs. McKee. She was the mother of the celebrated Baby McKee, the little boy who became world famous...for doing nothing, except just being Baby McKee.

MAYO: This is the period when photographic studios started taking enormous numbers of pictures of the White House, the furnishings, the occupants, and particularly, the children. It was a new pop culture kind of sensation, and fixated on Baby McKee.

Caroline was very savvy in knowing that people were going to demand photographs of the grandchildren and the family. Instead of letting them descend on her willy-nilly, she called in a pioneering woman photographer, Frances Benjamin Johnston, and had the children photographed. It gave her and the family much more control over how the photographs were taken, and where and when and how these children were pictured in the press. She was very smart about doing that. It was very modern.

One of the things that Frances Cleveland complained about in their second administration was that she was afraid people were going to kidnap her children. They'd found ways to get into the White House grounds, and she was constantly fearful. So what Caroline Harrison did was very smart.

SEALE: It was a time of big spending in his administration. The government was spending a lot of money and she got into it by wanting to create a house; they were crammed in the White House. They only lived upstairs…. The family quarters were seven rooms, that was all, and a bath-and-a-half. She wanted something big to live in, but something also to entertain in, because the Harrisons entertained all the time.

Mrs. Harrison had this plan done [for an expanded White House]. On the right side was to be the National Gallery, or the National Museum, and then other public rooms on the other side. The second floor then had guest rooms, family quarters, and such as that to make it a much more livable house, as well as the office.

MAYO: She went about lobbying [for her plan] through her entertaining, but she also called in the press, and showed them the plans, and got them to sign on that this was really a good idea. They were in the White House at the centennial of the presidency, so she thought this would be a wonderful plan as a memorial for the one hundredth anniversary. The nation had grown in land and in power, and she wanted a residence that reflected the global power of the United States, so this was a perfect opportunity. She got a lot of major people in Washington interested. She lobbied the Senate. She lobbied the House…. She brought in [former first lady] Harriet Lane, and she also used the name of George Washington and how this would be a fitting memorial.

SEALE: Speaker Tom Reed from Maine was a great adversary of Benjamin Harrison; they fought a lot over bills. Leland Stanford of California was Mrs. Harrison's great ally [for the White House renovation], and he spent the night sleeping in the House cloakroom, hoping the act of appropriation would go through. Speaker Reed was a very razor-tongued guy, and he cooked up this story that Harrison had dared to appoint a postmaster in Maine without his approval and crashed the whole thing. He wouldn't let the plan come up for a vote.

[Unable to renovate,] she redecorated, thinking and hoping it was a minor thing to do, and she became interested in the historic house and began researching the attics, pulling out antiques and putting them in the different rooms. She had a decorator in Boston make things spiffy. Tiffany had been the last one to do the rooms, and they were very run down, with special effects that nobody could reproduce.

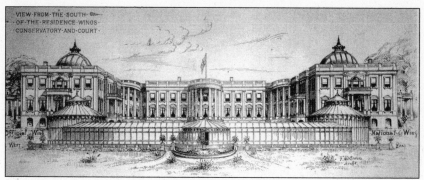

Using architectural drawings like this, Caroline Harrison lobbied Congress to greatly expand the White House, adding a wing that would house a National Gallery.

MAYO: [When Caroline got into the attic of the White House, she discovered it was full of rats.] Washington has a very prolific and well-known rat community, and they had infested the White House and were both in the basement and also in the attic. Apparently, a man with ferrets was brought in to help reduce the rat population, but there was also a man with a gun who was shooting the rats whenever he saw them.

SEALE: He would precede her through the attic. Now, strangely enough, the attic had no access to it. When the elevator was put into the White House, the little back stairs that Lincoln made famous [were] taken out, and the elevator was put in there. So they had to go on a ladder up above the elevator. Caroline, this little, tiny woman, went up there with this guard with a gun, and they began pulling things out of boxes, and a rat would appear, and he'd shoot it. And they were big ones, too. She'd scream, and he'd shoot.

She furnished the upstairs hall from the attic. The corridor that runs the full length of the White House on the second floor was just an old hallway with white wardrobes and things in it. At one end of it was a waiting room. Mrs. Harrison furnished it as a room, as it is today. If you went up in the elevator in the family quarters, you would find a big sitting room divided by doors. She furnished that from old things she found in the attic.

MAYO: She was trying to make more room for the family. The family quarters had become so cramped and overrun by the presidential offices that she was looking for space anywhere she could find it, so she turned that hallway into a large living area with defined spaces for seating and conversation.

The decayed furnishings they also found at the White House, stored for years and years, all these things that were thought to be out of date, were sold at auction. They had huge auctions, and [painful to imagine], all of this marvelous stuff migrated out of the White House.

SEALE: [In 1891, the Harrisons brought electricity into the White House, installed by the Edison Company. This was] extremely important. The Harrisons were terrified of it. They wouldn't turn it on or off. When they were ready to go to bed, they'd call one of the employees up to turn the lights off. They never got used to it. They were scared to death of it. They were used to gas.

MAYO: [Caroline Harrison established the first White House china collection, organizing past sets for display.] The cups and saucers ordered for the Harrison china did not arrive at the White House until after Caroline's death, which is very sad that she didn't get to see them. Her china was reordered periodically in later administrations, so it became a very popular service, ordered again by McKinley and Roosevelt and even as late as Jacqueline Kennedy and Mrs. Clinton.

SEALE: [Caroline was an avid painter of china, and gave classes in this art, along with language classes, at the White House,] which may have been a political move. She had little classes, and only twenty-five could attend. It rather smoothed the feathers of some of the people in Washington. They silenced themselves about her because they all wanted to be part of those classes. They were ladies' classes.

MAYO: [Mrs. Harrison was criticized by the press for being overly domestic.] They thought that she was doing actual housework, which was what was rumored. Rather than looking for historical treasures and trying to salvage the history of the White House and the presidency, it was looked at as [though] she was actually engaging in housework. This was seen as very much beneath the dignity of a first lady. However, one of the things that she mirrors in the time is the growing home economics movement, which organized itself around 1890. She was very much a part of her times in anticipating what was thought to be the professionalization of housework. Instead of being praised for what she did, she was criticized. She could not fathom why there was all this scorn and mocking in the press of what she was doing in the White House, but people didn't quite understand what she was trying to accomplish.

SEALE: Washington is hard on first ladies...until they prove themselves. Caroline had been around—he [Benjamin Harrison] had been in the Senate, they'd been in Washington many times. She was a popular woman in Washington socially, but when she got into the White House, it was a little different, and she was hurt.

MAYO: Plus, she was following this absolutely gorgeous young woman, so that must have been very difficult.... Frances Cleveland was ten years younger than Jackie Kennedy when Jacqueline entered the White House, and so she was very popular.... [Then the Harrisons arrived, and Caroline] was a matronly woman by that age.

SEALE: [Caroline Harrison agreed to become the president-general of the DAR, the Daughters of the American Revolution.] The DAR is always misunderstood. The DAR was founded by working women who were supporting themselves, and their children, perhaps. It was founded in the fall of 1890. In some way, Caroline Harrison became involved, probably because of the centennial of Washington's inauguration. They persuaded her to be first president. She made the first recorded address ever made by a first lady to their convention. The DAR had a lot to do with working women who were in the field and not being treated like ladies.... Mrs. Harrison saw political promise in it, and she is the one that thought the DAR ought to be political. They never intended that. They met in the Blue Room at their first meeting, and she told them how to do it.

MAYO: She gave the DAR visibility, legitimacy, a place to meet, helped smooth over the political differences within the group, people wanting different offices, and so forth. By taking the president-general position, she quelled a lot of that.

Women did not have the right to vote..The suffrage movement was finally coming together in 1890, after having been split since the end of the Civil War. One group wanted to go the constitutional route; the other group wanted to have...a states' rights approach. They had fought each other for a generation, and finally, they had a meeting in Washington, in 1888, and decided to unify the suffrage movement. That was going on at the national level. The home economics movement also began in 1890. The club movement had progressed from local and state groups to national groups in 1890. You have the white clubs, the black clubs, the Jewish women's clubs, and they all get started in the early '90s. Women are really beginning to organize and lobby very loudly for women's progress.

SEALE: Caroline provided much more [political guidance to her husband than many earlier first ladies]. This woman was very much attuned, savvy to what he was doing. She was very interested in the position of women. She was not an activist in the street, like the suffragettes who wanted the vote would be later on, but she believed that the power of women was very great, which it was. She believed in women getting out there and getting involved.

The Harrisons were both committed to civil rights. He had a very legalistic mind, and he looked for ways of assuring the vote to the African American male.... His whole administration fought for the African American vote, everywhere. Of course, remember, this was only for African American men to vote, not women.

MAYO: [Caroline Harrison got involved in a campaign to admit women to Johns Hopkins's new medical school.] Johns Hopkins had built a hospital, and was going to build a medical school with graduate education...but they ran out of money for the medical school. A young woman whose name was Mary Elizabeth Garrett, daughter of the owner of the Baltimore and Ohio Railroad, had a group of women, all of whom had their fathers on the board at Johns Hopkins University. They would meet regularly in a group they called "The Friday." They referred to themselves in their memos as "girls." Well, the girls decided to take on this project. Mary Elizabeth Garrett had been her father's right-hand person. She'd traveled with him, watched him make, as Donald Trump would say, the art of the deal. She was very aware that this was the time that they should tell Johns Hopkins that they would raise the money that was needed for this medical school if the medical school would admit women on the same equal basis as men.

It took the men on the board a little aback and took them a while to come around to the idea, but there were all these incredible women that she had contact with. Here are some of their names: They were Mrs. Leland Stanford, of Stanford University, and Mrs. Potter Palmer, whose husband had built the Palmer House in Chicago; Julia Ward Howe; Elizabeth Blackwell, who was the first female doctor in the country; Louisa Catherine Adams, who was a granddaughter of the first Louisa Catherine, the first lady; and M. Carey Thomas, head of Bryn Mawr.

These women decided that this was going to be their mission and they were going to raise $100,000 to help Johns Hopkins put up this medical school. The men acquiesced, and the women divided the country into fifteen geographical regions and invited Caroline Harrison to be the person in charge of Washington, D.C., with all her connections. She had several receptions in the White House. This was wonderful publicity and legitimacy for this group of women and their mission. Mrs. Harrison also went to Baltimore several times, and was the guest of honor at the receptions that Mary Elizabeth Garrett held. It was very successful lobbying, and the women came through and raised the money.

SEALE: The Silver Purchase Act of 1890 led the economy into a depression. Harrison lost the election of 1892, and he was lucky, because the economy crashed in the autumn of 1893 for President Cleveland, who returned to office.

Mrs. Harrison, by that time, had died. She had had tuberculosis, but she fought it and stayed busy; and depression has to be added to it. Finally, she couldn't fight anymore; but it was just the last two months of her life that she really ailed. Everything in her life happened in October. She was born in October; she was married in October; the DAR was founded in October; and she died in October.

Caroline Harrison died in the White House in 1892, the second of only [three] first ladies to have died in the White House.

MAYO: [Her funeral] was in the East Room, but it was not of a state nature. [Four years later, Harrison] married Caroline's niece, who had been her social secretary and also an aide to him as the president. She had lost both her parents when she was very young, so they brought her into the family as another daughter into the family. She looked at both of them, for most of the time, as substitute parents.

SEALE: [Harrison and Mary Dimmick] married in '96. There was a great kerfluffle about it. It was considered the wrong thing to do by a lot of the public and the family. The family was shocked because she had been there with them almost like a sister. And then they had a child, [which further alienated people].

Caroline Harrison's legacy:

SEALE: [In the pantheon of first ladies,] Caroline Harrison fits obscurely, for some reason, because she was stronger and she did more than most. There are seeds in what she did that were later to be measured.

Ida Saxton McKinley

"I will be glad when he is out of public life. I do not want him to run a second time. I thought he had done enough for the country and when his term expires, he will come home and we will settle down quietly and he will belong to me."

Ida McKinley, c1900

Born: June 8, 1847, in Canton, Ohio
Married: January 25, 1871, to William McKinley, Jr. (1843–1901)
Children: Katherine (Katie) (1871–75); Ida (1873)
Died: May 26, 1907, in Canton, Ohio

Contributors:

CARL SFERRAZZA ANTHONY, historian of the National First Ladies Library; author of several books on first ladies, including the two-volume *First Ladies*

RICHARD NORTON SMITH, presidential historian; executive director at five presidential libraries; author of several books, including *Patriarch*; history consultant for C-SPAN; and academic advisor for C-SPAN's *First Ladies* series

RICHARD NORTON SMITH: [William McKinley was felled by an assassin's bullet at the Pan American Exposition in Buffalo, New York, on September 6, 1901.] It was a world's fair that could not have been better timed, because it was a celebration of America's new place in the world. The McKinley presidency was very surprising in many ways. McKinley has been identified all of his political career with protectionism and, in fact, he would be the president who took the country onto the world stage, annexed Hawaii in 1898, fought the Spanish-American War. He turned America, it was argued, from a republic into an empire. At the end of his life, in the last speech that he gave at that fair, in effect, he recanted his earlier protectionist outlook and talked in ways that one hundred years later, we could all appreciate, about opening America to the world.

CARL SFERRAZZA ANTHONY: Ida McKinley has been grossly miscast by history as this Victorian invalid on the fainting couch. That wasn't the truth. There were times when she was that way. She actually had three chronic illnesses. One was seizure disorder, otherwise known as epilepsy. She had some neurological damage along her left leg which often led to immobility, or periods of it. She also had a compromised immune system, which made her susceptible to colds and infections.

SMITH: The assassin's name was Leon Czolgosz,...a drifter. He was an anarchist in his politics. He believed, with many people at the turn of the century, that the existing systems of government, particularly monarchs, for example, in Europe, existed to the detriment of the common man. Some anarchists were against all organized governments. They certainly were against the system that was topped by the powerful. Czolgosz said McKinley had power, while he had none, in effect.

He had planned on killing the president early in the year. The king of Italy had been murdered. Czolgosz's family later said that Leon would stay up late at night reading newspapers about the death of the king. It may have been the thing that triggered it, but in any event he made plans to kill the president. There was no Secret Service protection. There was just one guard at the White House, and he retired early at night.

George Cortelyou, who was the president's secretary/chief of staff, wanted very much to cancel the reception at the Temple of Music at the fair. He worried about just such a threat. Ironically, Czolgosz got in. He managed to wrap his gun in a bandage around his hand, so it was unnoticed, and shot the president twice. At first, it was thought that McKinley would recover, and then, about a week later, he took a turn for the worse.

ANTHONY: [Ida was not at the president's side when he was shot.] Among her string of doctors, she had one who really committed to helping her in trying to control her seizures. Part of that required a very strict regimen of diet, but also rest at regular points. She had been with the president on the opening day there, and then they went to Niagara Falls. The doctor said, "It's time for your rest." Both the president and Mrs. McKinley had bought off on that, and so she was taking her scheduled rest. She suspected something had happened when the hours started going by and he didn't come back. She was very calm when she was told, and really rose to the occasion, in fact, almost in an extraordinary way. There's a story of her during this period of his convalescence, when there's hope that he will recover, where she's going out walking or for a carriage ride. She walks along the sidewalk on her own and talks to the reporters, which defies the perception of her.

SMITH: The country was convulsed [by McKinley's death]. It's hard for us to realize one hundred years later… but, the fact is, if you talked to the man on the street in September of 1901, he would have told you McKinley was certainly the greatest president since Lincoln. He wasn't simply admired. This was the man who had brought us out of the greatest depression to that date in American history. He projected American power, economic and military, onto the world stage. He was a very large presence for someone to have become almost forgotten. When he died…there was enormous grief in the country. One reason why people loved McKinley, even people who didn't vote for him, was because of what they saw as his tenderness and devotion to this invalid wife.

ANTHONY: [Ida Saxton was born in Canton, Ohio, in 1847.] Her parents were not only well-off, but they were what you almost would call radically progressive, particularly on the issues of abolition—they were rabidly against slavery—and on equal education for women. Ida's mother was extremely well-educated. Ida McKinley is the most formally educated of all the first ladies up to that time.

Ohio was very much like the California of its day, in the earlier part of the nineteenth century, representing almost the Far West. That's where you really find this movement for equal education for women. Ida's father helps bring a famed abolitionist to Canton. Ida then follows her when the teacher goes to teach at Delphi Academy during the Civil War; then she goes on to study in Cleveland, and then to Brooke Hall Seminary in Pennsylvania. What you see is a worldly, educated young woman with an interest in finance and a capability for mathematics and also great physical activity. She's an unusually physically fit young woman who hikes upwards of ten miles a day on her 1869 trip to Europe [with her sister].

SMITH: [Ida Saxton was good at numbers. Her father, who owned a bank, gave her a job as a teller and she worked her way up to bank manager.] This was not common for women, certainly not in a professional or managerial capacity like this. And second, it does tell you a lot about the relationship with her father.

[She met Major William McKinley at the bank.] It must be said that McKinley married up. There's no doubt that this was a young woman with a cosmopolitan and sophisticated background, neither of which could be said of McKinley. He was born in Niles, Ohio, from a family that had been in the iron-making business. There are people who think that's maybe where the seeds of his interest in protectionism were planted. He went to a place called Allegheny College for a year and came back homesick, and perhaps genuinely sick. The real classroom, as for so many of his generation, was the [Civil War, which] began in 1861. He entered as a private. He ended the war as a brevet major. Along the way, he found the patronage of his fellow Ohioan, Rutherford B. Hayes, of the Twenty-Third Ohio Regiment.

Hayes took a liking to this young man. He became a protégé of sorts and, years later, Ida would spend a good deal of time in the Hayes White House. She babysat for the Hayes children while the president and first lady were away for a couple of weeks, so that relationship became a very significant one.

ANTHONY: [The McKinleys married when she was twenty-three. He was twenty-seven.] Their early years were, frankly, a little bit conventional. She stopped working and he was interested in politics. There's no question that you see the very first legal cases, the business he was handling, it was all through the Saxton family. That family really helped build the city of Canton, which went on to become a major and important industrial center in Ohio at that time. Certainly Ida's father and grandfather helped build it, and McKinley helped sustain it and make it famous, but he rose in prominence largely because of her.

[Ida's problems began in 1873.] She gave birth on Christmas Day 1871, to their first daughter, Katie, who was a very healthy little girl, the central focus of their lives. Then, Ida's mother became very ill, it turns out, with cancer. Ida was very close to her mother and grandmother. She was pregnant a second time at the time her mother had cancer. Two weeks before Ida gave birth, her mother died, and there was a fall either stepping into a carriage or out of it, at her mother's burial service. Ida, from firsthand accounts at the time, struck her head. She may have had some kind of very bad injury to her spine. She gives birth two weeks later to a child who lives only four months. At this time, at this relatively advanced age, Ida starts developing seizure disorder.

After their child died, they moved out of their house…. They moved into the Saxton-McKinley House…. Katie came with them. And then, she died of scarlet fever. This is after Ida has already been through trauma and is dealing with this very bewildering new factor in her life of seizure disorder. She began, some years later, to take comfort in certain tenets of Buddhism, and one in particular was reincarnation. You began to see Ida McKinley…essentially keep Katie alive, keep her memory alive. She always had her picture on the wall. She kept the girl's clothes and rocking chair visible. She spoke as if the child sometimes was still alive. There are also a lot of firsthand accounts of her looking [rather oddly] at young children, because she believed that perhaps Katie had been reincarnated.

SMITH: McKinley had…been gerrymandered out of his congressional job. The Democrats tried twice, and the second time, they got him. They should have reconsidered, because the next year, he was elected governor of Ohio. He was reelected two years after that. One reason why he is today thought of as almost a prisoner of big business, of the trusts, as they were known at the turn of the century, is his association with Mark Hanna, [Ohio Republican kingmaker].

ANTHONY: [When McKinley served as governor,] their home was a residential hotel. The suite overlooked the plaza in front of the Capitol, and William would go out [every day at three o'clock and wave his handkerchief in the direction of his wife]. Stories were written about him and tourists started to come. At three o'clock, they'd say, "Oh, there's the governor—look how devoted he is." …Legislators were bent over in laughter, because they were watching Governor

McKinley wave his handkerchief and they all knew that Mrs. McKinley had been back in Canton for about a week, so he was putting on a good show. He began to use that devotion to Ida as presidential timbre. He was disciplined, and he was focused, and he was devoted, and he was loyal. These were the kinds of things you could look for in him as president.

SMITH: [William McKinley, U.S. congressman, then Ohio governor, became the Republican presidential nominee in 1896, a year that matters] because it's a realigning election. We don't have a lot of those. They couldn't know it in 1901, but William McKinley had transformed American politics for the next almost forty years. Up until FDR and the New Deal, Republicans would be the dominant party. He's the man who broke the logjam after the Civil War when power went back and forth. That's important.

One other case of presidential power that is relevant to our own time, is that McKinley unilaterally dispatched five thousand American soldiers to combat the Boxer Rebellion, which was always referred to as a secret society of Chinese who were fed up with the exploitation of their country by Western imperial powers. They had laid siege to the Western delegation in both Peking and in Tientsin, where a young, honeymooning couple named Herbert and Lou Henry Hoover were ensconced.... McKinley sent these troops along as part of an international expedition. In the nick of time, they arrived in Peking and were able to save about nine hundred Westerners who were there.

But the thing is, he did it on his own power. He never talked to Congress, and subsequent presidents would use that example in situations that may or may not have been similar. That's just one way in which war, which McKinley never wanted in the first place, transformed his presidency and the presidency.

ANTHONY: [At the national political level, Ida McKinley's illness] was really brilliantly handled.... You would see her with a gold-handled cane; the wheelchair didn't really come until towards the end of his administration. He would always give his arm to her, and it was very easy to focus on that, which is what he did. She would talk to reporters, and say, "Oh, I have lameness in my leg." That, for a while, kept the public satisfied. Occasionally, you would start hearing expres-

President McKinley, standing with blanket, was always solicitous of Mrs. McKinley (seated), who suffered from numerous health issues throughout his public career.

sions like "nervous affliction." They never used the word "epilepsy" in her lifetime. What was really going on, and what's tragic in and of itself, is the ignorance of the vast population at the time about seizure disorder. Even as the age of neurology is dawning, people equated seizures with insanity, mental problems, as opposed to physiological issues. McKinley was trying to contain this from the public learning about it, because there was a fear that it would damage his career. There were ideas that his wife had a form of mental illness.

He contracted, well-intentioned, with a doctor in New York, John N. Bishop. This guy really broke the Hippocratic code by giving McKinley bromide salts, which…could control the onset of seizures. The doctor started writing reminders, "I gave you these on the condition that I would get a weekly report of her symptoms because it's a very precise measurement that has to change week to week based on that." McKinley would never write because he didn't want to put anything in writing about this situation. Over time, it actually created a greater harm called bromism. Bromide salts dulled the nerves, but over time, it could damage the nerves.

For almost the entire first half of the McKinleys' years in the White House, Ida McKinley was fine. Ida McKinley was traveling on her own to New York and to Baltimore. She was really relatively active. She was still disabled in the sense that she had the mobility problem, but she adapted [to] the role of first lady, and she didn't hide the fact that she had this occasional walking problem.

She took a real interest in a wide variety of music. She loved the opera. She was really big on the theater. One of the great things she loved about being first lady was having all of the stars of the stage—of course, this is before Hollywood—come to the White House. She had all kinds of music played at the White House. She had native Mexican music. She had a British club. She had glee club. She had African American music. She even had the very first bit of ragtime performed at the very first Valentine's Day dance held at the White House.

Mrs. McKinley was very involved with two organizations. One was called the Crittenden House, and the other was the Red Cross. The Crittenden House was very interesting because it specifically helped women who had been battered, who were homeless, and provided them with shelter and with education and helped them reestablish their lives.

Apart from her illness, and even before she was having her seizure disorder, she was not interested in housekeeping. She was not really interested in menus or entertaining. They had basically lived in hotel suites in Washington, and then in Columbus.... So McKinley took control, and he was the one who actually planned a lot of the dinners, and she was at them. She had weekly receptions. She did a lot of the traditional stuff, but she was not particularly interested in making those decisions.

[There are stories that when Ida had seizures during official dinners, the president would place a dinner napkin over his wife's face until they abated.] They're true stories, but they've been exaggerated and distorted. Here is the truth: this only occurred in private.... The three or four eyewitness accounts that I found are all in reference to private dinners. This never happened at state dinners. This never happened in public.

...The reason it didn't happen in public was she was being kept on these bromides that were dulling her senses; instead, you begin to have firsthand accounts from John Hay, from Henry Adams, talking about how vague and distorted her conversation was becoming. This is 1899 and afterward. It was the effects of the bromism, of the nerve damage that was occurring.

There are one or two times [when her health affected his presidency]; periods right after the battleship *Maine* is sunk in Havana Harbor, in February 1896. He's reluctant to go to war. The negotiations with Spain broke down and we went to war. There were times when he stayed up late at night, but the truth was that was the period when she was worried about him. There is a strong record that shows that she was trying to talk to Cortelyou, his assistant, saying, "We need to do something about him." She was playing the protective role.

This is a period when Ida is physically strong. It's the later period… when we took the Philippines, and they did not welcome us; they resisted. It was bloody and horrifying, and there were atrocities committed on both sides. That's when she was [at] her neediest. That's when the pressure really did get to him, where he had to constantly make this choice between his work and his wife.

SMITH: [It's been reported that] Ida's constant harping on all the good work done by Methodist missionaries heavily influenced her husband's ultimate decision on keeping the Philippines. He always said it had religious connotations to take the Philippines and "educate and civilize and Christianize them."

ANTHONY: But what's interesting is Mrs. McKinley is not what you'd consider a traditionally religious person…. The suggestion is, though, that she really believed from the reports they were getting, although they were slanted and untrue because the whole population was summarized as if they were living in a primitive way,…that the Filipinos' lives needed to be improved in a way that only the Americans could do.

[One way Ida McKinley countered her illness and depression was by knitting what became thousands of slippers.] It was actually pretty brilliant because Ida McKinley was a very witty woman and a little bit subversive. The one area politically where you do see her really having an influence, is in judging the character of people that [her husband] is considering for higher positions or to be around him. If she didn't like someone or didn't trust someone...she gave him a very rational explanation. She also indicated how she felt about people by the color of the slippers she gave them.

[In 1899, McKinley went to Massachusetts for college graduation ceremonies at both Smith College and Mount Holyoke.] Ida went with the president, and he became the first president of the United States to address the issue of women's education. Back in that day, people thought this was going to be the end of American society; if you educate women, they're going to want to get jobs and the fabric of the family will fall apart.

We don't have the text of her speech, but Ida McKinley also delivered a short speech at Smith College, not on the main stand, but in one of the rooms inside a building, where she was presented with a silver cup. She was very decidedly in favor of women's rights—the equal right to vote.... She was the first incumbent first lady to publicly support suffrage.

[It was on this trip to Massachusetts] that she had a massive epileptic seizure and her health really began to deteriorate. It was June of 1899. What also happened was McKinley had purchased the original house where they spent the first two-and-a-half years of their married life together [the site of the 1896 front porch campaign]. She was already very depressed because of the onset of the seizures, and he unrolled these blueprints of what they were going to do: "I'm buying the house; we're going to expand it." He got her into this idea that, finally, they were going to retire.

She had a very strong and stated-for-the-record fear of his assassination. It was based, very rationally, not on any kind of hocus-pocus, but because of the movement of the anarchists killing leaders around the world. She did not want him to run for a second term, and he refused to say whether he was or not. As that summer of 1899 unfolded, it [was becoming] very clear to her that they were expanding that house not for their retirement use, but to house his campaign and campaign staff.... John Hay writes, as do others, that this is the most depressed and the lowest that Ida has ever been.

[Ida was very frustrated] when she found out that McKinley was going to run for reelection and he hadn't told her. At this point, she is more physically disabled; this is going into the year 1900 and his re-election campaign. Later in life, as a widow, she wrote something that was really remarkable. It was basically saying, "The longer I live without him, the more I realize how completely dependent I was." Their story has always been painted like he was the great hero and the protector, but he was also controlling. He controlled her medicine. He controlled a lot of things. From her point of view, she was willing to accept her limitations and adapt herself, and there were times he didn't want that.

SMITH: The 1900 election was a rematch of 1896. McKinley again ran against William Jennings Bryan, but the issues were different, which in some ways is a testament to how much McKinley had succeeded. He was, by 1900, seen as the man who brought us out of the Great Depression of the 1890s. The new issue was America's place in the world, and a word that was new to most Americans: imperialism....

Theodore Roosevelt joined McKinley on the Republican ballot in 1900.... McKinley seemed to have been ambivalent about this. Vice President Garrett Hobart had died in 1899, so there was an opening. The convention went wild for T.R., who had tried, in advance, to indicate that he didn't want to be vice president. He knew his own temperament. It was like taking the veil, and that was not T.R.'s style.

ANTHONY: Ida McKinley...was crucial in at least two instances at very important points in the rise of Theodore Roosevelt. Perhaps the most dramatic one is when Roosevelt was with the cavalry in San Antonio, with the Rough Riders. He was trying to get onto a train so he could get to the transport ships in Florida, so they could go to Cuba; nobody would give him permission. He was sending wires and telegraphs to the secretary of war. He sent one to Mrs. McKinley. She brought it to the president. She had met Roosevelt and trusted him. That is what got Roosevelt to those transports in Florida. Roosevelt responded to the president, "Please tell Mrs. McKinley to think of the Rough Riders as her very own, and we will make her proud." From that point on, Roosevelt curried favor with Ida McKinley....

[Six months after his second inaugural, McKinley was shot. He lingered for] eight days. She wanted to be with him. She wanted some privacy. She wanted to have a moment with him. On the night before he died, in the late hours, she was brought in to be with him and they did have some private words together. McKinley said something that has never been quoted widely before. After she was brought out of his room, he said to the doctor, "What will become of her?" [It sounds] almost a little bit cold. It wasn't. He loved her, but he knew he was dying.

They would not allow Ida to attend any of the public ceremonies. She was in the White House. She had some time downstairs with the closed coffin in the East Room, and then she was brought to the train, and brought back to Canton. The coffin was an open coffin for the public to file by and pay their respects in Canton City Hall, but she was not permitted to go. She said, "I want him one last night in this house alone with me, so I can look at him one more time." They brought the coffin but they had sealed it, so she was very bitter, frankly. I very rarely found instances of her saying things that were really sharp and frustrated, but she did after that.

President McKinley wasn't buried because they were building a monument. His flag-draped coffin was on a stand in what looked like a church. In it were large floral displays, and then, eventually, banners of various groups that came. Every day she went. At first it was thought therapeutic, that, in a way it was healthy to physically get her out. Over time, it became rather ghoulish and grim for her, because she was focused on death. She was even focused on the flowers that were dying, trying to keep them alive.

There was a really an incredible little moment that happened: Her two nieces both had a daughter each, and suddenly, at the end of her life, there were these two little girls in Ida's life. She stopped going to the tomb every day, and she started walking again on the porch in the middle of winter, and gardening and talking about the flowers and the new McKinley building. She really returned to life.

SMITH: Part of this is the times, the Victorian obsession with death. To me, the eeriest chapter in this whole story is [that] allegedly she never had another seizure after the president's death.

ANTHONY: We only know so much. The paradox of this is that part of the reason she would sometimes get very stressed out, is that she was worried about him being shot. With him now being gone, that stress was removed.

Ida McKinley's legacy:

ANTHONY: [Ida McKinley died in May of 1907, just shy of her sixtieth birthday.] There was almost nothing said about her as a person; everything that was said about her was as a symbol. It was all through the lens of him. The truth is, in her lifetime, she really didn't care what people thought about her. She didn't really care whether the public loved her. She only cared about what they thought about William. She would attack somebody who attacked him.

Edith Carow Roosevelt

"I take the keenest pride in seeing Mrs. Roosevelt at the head of the White House—a gentlewoman, who gives to all the official life...."—Theodore Roosevelt

Edith Roosevelt, c1905

Born: August 6, 1861, Norwich, Connecticut
Married: December 2, 1886, to Theodore Roosevelt (1858–1919)
Children: Theodore, Jr. (1887–1944); Kermit (1889–1943); Ethel Carow (1891–1977); Archibald Bulloch (1894–1979); Quentin (1897–1918); stepdaughter Alice Lee (1884–1980)
Died: September 30, 1948, Oyster Bay, New York

Contributors:

STACY CORDERY, professor and chair, history department, Monmouth College; author of several books, including *Theodore Roosevelt*

KATHLEEN DALTON, instructor of history, Phillips Academy; author, *Theodore Roosevelt: A Strenuous Life*

KATHLEEN DALTON: Theodore Roosevelt was climbing a mountain in the Adirondacks when he heard the news that McKinley was shot. He rushed down the mountain and came to Buffalo. At first, it looked like McKinley was going to survive, but then blood poisoning set in, and T.R. came to Washington and took over a mourning nation. It was a national tragedy. It was really hard to come to the presidency because of an assassination, but he reassured America, and he turned out to be a very successful president.

STACY CORDERY: He was very young, forty-two, but he had a lot of experience behind him in government.

DALTON: New York state assemblyman, assistant secretary of the Navy, civil service commissioner, New York State Police commissioner, governor of New York. Politics defined his life, but he wrote thirty books. He was a serious naturalist. He did a lot of things. He read widely, traveled a lot, and had a very expansive and interesting life. It was his spirit that triumphed and made the country look forward instead of behind.

Theodore and Edith grew up in the same neighborhood in New York City. T.R. grew up at East Twentieth Street, and she grew up near Union Square. They were tutored together. She was his younger sister, Corinne's, best friend. They watched the invalid corps of the Civil War, the men who lost arms and legs, marching down Union Square together from his grandfather's window. They were playmates. They read books together. They were like family.

CORDERY: [People believed there was a romance between T.R. and Edith, but] there's the mystery of the summer house. There was an argument. We don't really know happened, but T.R. and Edith were together, things seemed to be going very well, and then there was some sort of fight. After that, they broke apart; Theodore went off to Harvard and there, across the room, he saw Alice Hathaway Lee. He told a friend, "I'm going to marry that woman." And, indeed, he did.

DALTON: Alice Lee was the daughter of a wealthy banker and was a very beautiful woman, and really quite charming and athletic. T.R. was incredibly taken with her, but she had many suitors, so he had to work hard. He surrounded her; which is to say, he charmed her little brother and sister and her cousins and her uncles. Finally, he became so familiar, she gave in.

[They married in] 1880; he was just twenty-one and she was something like nineteen, so they were very young, but that's not unusual in that time period.

[On Valentine's Day in 1884, there was a great family tragedy.] Baby Alice had already been born two days before; Alice, the baby's mother, had Bright's Disease, which is a kidney disease, and she was fading. T.R. was up in Albany with the state Assembly and he got telegrams saying, "Come down, your mother is ill." She had typhoid fever. But then, he would get more telegrams, "[Your wife,] Alice, is not doing well, either." He finally came down on the train to New York and came to the house. [Sadly, his mother and his wife] both died that same day.

It was a tragedy that broke his heart. He was distraught. He had already been West, and so he did flee to the West, and was very, very sad for a long time. [Baby Alice was cared for by his sister, Bamie.]

CORDERY: When Theodore Roosevelt went out to the Dakotas, he vowed he was never going to marry again. This was very much a Victorian notion, that you were committed to your wife, even though she had died. He was heard to walk the floor out there, saying, "I have no constancy, I have no constancy," after he met Edith [once again].

There was an impromptu meeting [between Theodore and Edith], and they discovered that old flame that had died was rekindled. They courted in secret and didn't tell anyone about it.... Other people noticed that they must have been in love, because it was printed in the newspapers that they were engaged. Roosevelt had not yet told his sisters. So then he had to explain this in sad letters to his sister, saying, "Well, actually, it's kind of true."

He was devastated [by Alice's death], but he was also very young and very vigorous and very much alive. Of anyone in his life, Edith had known him the longest and had been through the death of his father, had been through the death of his mother, the death of his wife. It was, in that sense, a lovely destiny that he would find solace in his old, dear friend.

February 14, 1884, is when Alice, his first wife, died, and then T.R. married Edith in December 1886....

DALTON: T.R. said that he would never have been president if it hadn't been for his time in the Dakotas.... Edith understood. She had visited the ranches that T.R. had and understood that his time being a rancher meant everything to him. She put up with some people whom she might not have chosen as friends, desperadoes and farmers and cowboys whom T.R. loved, so she accepted them.

He [eventually] had to sell the ranch. Basically, he was a failed cattle rancher. The [cattle] froze. Those were hard days.

Theodore's family had merchant wealth, banking wealth. His grandfather was very successful, helped found the Chemical Bank in New York City, and they also owned a lot of property and collected rents. T.R. spent a lot of his inheritance from his father on ranching, and wasn't very careful about money. They really lived on his writing and just his salary, so that's why they were strapped.

CORDERY: Edith was very poor as a child, compared to the Roosevelts, and so she was always in the habit of pinching those pennies. It wasn't really until they got to the White House that she felt that she had enough money, finally, to entertain, and could relax a bit.

DALTON: Theodore Roosevelt adored Edith Roosevelt, and she was devoted to him. Not that they didn't have their little difficult moments. He was not an easy husband—he forgot birthdays and could be very inconsiderate.

CORDERY: He wasn't there when children were born. But, he truly did love her. He wrote about her to friends of his, highly complimentary things.

DALTON: The Roosevelts were different kinds of parents. Edith could be fairly strict, a descendant of Jonathan Edwards, a Puritan. She thought children should behave. She would turn to Theodore and ask him to do the spanking, but he did it reluctantly. He was an indulgent parent who liked to play bear and hide-and-seek and have pillow fights with the kids. The kids looked at him as a large playmate, so she really had to be the main parent.

CORDERY: [They raised six children together; five of their own, plus Alice.] Edith said she did her best by Alice. She once said, "I'm not the best kind of mother for Alice; she needs someone who's more outgoing and a little less staid than I am." She was actually a very good mother.... But as Alice got older, she was seeking attention that she never had. To find that attention—couldn't quite get it from her father, couldn't quite get it from her stepmother, didn't get it from her stepsiblings—Alice

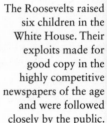

The Roosevelts raised six children in the White House. Their exploits made for good copy in the highly competitive newspapers of the age and were followed closely by the public.

looked on a much bigger stage. Once Alice began to cross these lines of propriety, as Edith saw them, the relationship became much more strained.

CORDERY: The public was delighted, to use Theodore Roosevelt's word, [to have the Roosevelts in the White House]. It had been a long time since there had been children in the White House…. The children's antics were in the newspapers, and there was very little attempt to stop that, particularly after T.R. learned that this was pretty good press for him. The children and their antics, their pets—these were very important parts of Roosevelt's public persona as president.

DALTON: There were all these yellow journals, newspapers like Pulitzer's and Hearst's, that would put pictures of the children in their newspapers, and then, all of these magazines, like *McClure's*, that people would buy. There's a much more active media, and they could publicize what was going on in the White House very much more actively.

CORDERY: They were all photogenic and they did great stuff. They would steal the cookie trays from the kitchen and slide down the staircase on them. The children would pop out from behind potted palms and scare the guests. They would roller skate and walk on their stilts, throw ice at the policemen. The White House staff had their hands full, but it was all terrific press for Theodore Roosevelt.

[It soon became evident that the White House was too crowded for the family.] Edith picked up on some plans that had been underway since Caroline Harrison's time in the White House, and pretty quickly got together with a very influential firm called McKim, Mead, and White. Edith Roosevelt worked very closely with Mr. McKim and decided that she was tired of, as she put it, living over the store. She wanted to separate the living areas from the public areas. And so, the upstairs was renovated, the downstairs was renovated, and most people really liked it.

DALTON: Congress voted [to allocate $475,000] for this. They wanted a better house. It was the moment when the United States became a world power. T.R. was modernizing the presidency. The United States had really arrived as the most successful manufacturing power on earth, and they were in the process of becoming a very serious world power. Congress thought of it as a matter of national pride to have a president's house that would be as distinguished as the equivalent in another country. Oh yes, and there were rats in the White House.

CORDERY: The renovation was important for all kinds of reasons. It was a marvelous reflection of these changes that...as the country takes on a new aspect, so does the executive mansion, which is now renamed the White House, because Theodore Roosevelt said, "There are executive mansions in every state. There's only one White House."

DALTON: It took most of one year. It was in 1902. Edith took the children back to Sagamore Hill over the summer. The renovation started before she left. They were staying in Jackson Place at Lafayette Square. T.R. was hit by a trolley in the middle of this when he's settling the anthracite coal strike, so they have some difficult moments where he's negotiating with labor and management in a wheelchair....

In order for the United States to be taken seriously as a world power, the United States president had to entertain like the heads of state elsewhere. Changing the White House really made a difference. With all of those diplomatic receptions and cabinet dinners and open events, big dinners, it was something like forty thousand people that came through the White House in the first year. It is just amazing. It creates goodwill. If you've had dinner with someone, you're more likely to be able to agree with them or work with them afterwards. Sometimes we underestimate the power of face-to-face interactions. The Roosevelts really did a good job of this, because they knew how to socialize and they were very energetic entertainers.

CORDERY: Edith hired a woman named Isabella Hagner, who was very interesting in her own right…. She came into the Roosevelt White House at the time when the first lady was inundated by all the details of Alice's debut. There were letters to write. There were invitations to offer. There were flowers. All these many things to be taken care of. That's when Belle stepped in. She stayed until the end and was quite a member of the family. At one point, Edith said, "I think of you as my daughter," so they had quite a close relationship.

DALTON: [Edith had strong opinions about her White House guest lists.] She didn't want people who were adulterers or who were unacceptable socially to be a part of their entertainment. Most people were white, and there weren't that many Jews invited to the White House in those days. Keep in mind, this is the WASP ascendancy era of social life…[for] Washington elites and people in government, foreign diplomats, and people like New York society. It was an exclusive group.

CORDERY: She begins what is a much longer tradition now of the bureaucratization of the office of the first lady. Belle was not the very first social secretary ever to work for a first lady, but she is the one who stays the longest and starts us down this path.

Edith loved classical music. She worked with the Steinway Company, and in this way brought amazing entertainers to the White House, including Pablo Casals and Jan Paderewski, the pianist. She brought the entire Philadelphia Orchestra, at one point. She was much attuned to this. Edith had tastes that weren't quite in line with her husband's family. She loved the Corcoran Art Gallery, for example. Theater and art and music, classical music, were very important to Edith.

DALTON: [They also brought to the White House] what they would call then "Negro spirituals." T.R. brought Indian songs. They are cultural nationalists and they want people to discover America, so he helped encourage [musicologist] John Lomax to discover cowboy songs. They wanted people to understand that America had culture. It was not a colonial society anymore that depended upon great European cultures for borrowing artists. The White House had really arrived culturally. The Roosevelts are really important in that sense, too.

CORDERY: Edith played a fairly large role in T.R.'s White House, but behind the scenes. One of their friends called Edith "the perfection of invisible government," which she would have liked. For example, [with her largely Victorian sensibilities,] it was Edith who said, "We are not going to call the president by his first name anymore; he will be Mr. President." She never called him by his first name in front of people in the White House, making that much more formal.

She played a role in personnel. At least at one point in time, we know that she suggested…James Garfield for the civil service commission. She tried to get rid of an ambassador from Britain she didn't like very much, and tried to get [Cecil Spring Rice] in. She said, "I pulled every string that I knew to pull to try to get you here," and alas, she failed.

She was a back channel to Theodore Roosevelt. Men in the White House, Henry Cabot Lodge, for example, would talk to her about the post office scandal, rather than talk to him about it. She could also be a pathway for Roosevelt to discuss matters of diplomacy that he could not discuss with the diplomats themselves.

[Then, there was] all the time they spent together walking. She read four newspapers a day. He didn't like to read newspapers; I guess he read a lot of [other] things. She cut out stories and handed them to him, so she made sure certain topics were in front of him.

DALTON: She favored his conservation policies. We have her on record with that. Later on, when he ran for president in 1912, she cried the day after he lost. She was really behind him. And she edits his speeches and his articles and he clearly talks with her about policy. She sits in political meetings like Rosalynn Carter [would do later]. She was knitting, looking unobtrusive, but then they discussed what happened at the meeting afterwards. She was a very active first lady.

On October 16, 1902, Theodore Roosevelt invites Booker T. Washington, who was the leader of the Tuskegee Institute and a very important figure in African American history, [to the White House]. Booker T. Washington was somebody who rose up from slavery and was recognized as a very important educator, but also dealt with political patronage for the Republican Party. Edith and T.R. had him to dinner…. People in the South went crazy. People threatened to kill T.R. They said they should put a bomb under his chair, that he advocated social equality between blacks and whites. In African American history, after Reconstruction, this is the nadir of legal segregation passed by Southern states. African Americans in the South were treated very badly, so it was controversial to cross the color line socially.

[There's another side to T.R.'s record on race. In 1906,] African American soldiers were falsely accused of shooting up the town of Brownsville, Texas, when they faced terrible segregation and local hostility. T.R. didn't really want to know the details; he just assumed they were guilty. They got dishonorable discharges, quite unjustly. T.R. has had a fair amount of African American support in the North, where black people could vote, and he lost them over this.

[On the other hand,] he appeared on a stage with W.E.B. Du Bois, and said, "Justice has not been done to black people, and this is something I really want to face."

CORDERY: And their daughter taught African Americans at Sunday school, as well. Race and the Roosevelt family is a very interesting topic.

DALTON: [Edith created a family retreat in Virginia called Pine Knot.] Especially in 1905 and 1906, where he had a lot of political conflict and a lot of difficulty, such as the Pure Food and Drug Act…times when he's really having a rough time in the presidency, and he has gained a lot of weight, she wants him to have an overnight out in the cabin.

I've been to this cabin. It's very primitive. There's no plumbing, there's no electricity, there's nothing. She didn't cook, so T.R. had to cook for her on a kerosene stove. They had to do everything for themselves.

CORDERY: Pine Knot was important because there was no more privacy at the White House and very little at Sagamore Hill by this time. In order for Edith to get her husband away, she had to go far, far off the grid, as we would say today.... She did hike. But after a certain number of children, she decided that, [instead of] these point-to-point hikes that Theodore Roosevelt promoted so strongly, she would take a book and sit on a porch and read, and let the family go about it.

DALTON: Walking through the swamps or climbing, he would take his kids and any neighbors on these big hikes. She didn't like that. But she was not a classic Victorian lady. She was willing to hike. After he died, she traveled around the world. Then she went on a canoe trip to a distant waterfall. She did a lot of adventurous things for someone of her age. [But] she always had servants. She was proud that she had never made a bed in her life, except maybe at Pine Knot.

The press left them alone [out there]. Edith lost some sleep when they first went there because she was worried about intruders, and she didn't feel entirely safe. Finally, the Secret Service protected them.

CORDERY: At Pine Knot, John Burroughs...the great naturalist, went out to take a little walk and thought he heard something, and discovered it was Secret Service men that Edith had secretly put there to protect them. She didn't tell T.R. about the extra Secret Service.

[Following McKinley's assassination,] she beefed up security on the quiet whenever she could. Those were her greatest fears, and she wrote about it in letters to her sister. She wrote about this fear of Roosevelt's assassination in letters to friends as well. That was really scary for her.

DALTON: T.R. carried a pistol. He was cavalier about it, whereas she was very worried because people would come [up to him directly]. He was eventually shot in the 1912 campaign, and McKinley had been shot, and there were other attempts to get at him. She had reason to be nervous.

[After the 1908 election, when T.R. declines to run for reelection, they believed their lives in politics were over.] They moved back to Saga-more Hill. T.R. goes on a safari in Africa for a year, and then she joins him. They ride camels together in Egypt, and they travel to revisit the sites of their honeymoon in Italy and other places. They travel around Europe. But then he comes back, and Taft is in political trouble because the Republican Party is split between progressives and conservatives. Taft hasn't really done a great job at holding the party together. So T.R. gets back into politics in 1912.

[She supported his run as the Bull Moose candidate in 1912.] It was a painful moment because they knew that he couldn't win. This is when the primary system comes in. They voted to have preferential primaries instead of having caucuses choose candidates. He won a lot of the pri-maries, but they were all new, so nobody knew what that meant. So when it came time to go to the Republican convention, Taft controlled the delegates and got the nomination.

[Soon after, T.R.'s health began to decline.] He explored the Brazilian jungle in 1913 and almost died. He had a leg injury, he had fever, and he had rheumatism. He was in bad shape, and part of it was the way had lived his life. It was a strenuous life.

CORDERY: [T.R. died at Sagamore Hill, at age sixty, in 1919.] His heart gave out. Edith was just fifty-eight.

[After he died, Edith's life was] travel, travel, travel, travel. She traveled a lot of places. She went to South America many times. Kermit, her son, was down there.

DALTON: Edith did contribute to a travel book after T.R. died, and she did do a family history. But she never wrote memoirs, and she did burn most of his letters, but not all of them. She wanted to be very private. Some of her letters, especially her letters to her sister, survived. She tried to erase a lot of the record because she didn't want people snooping into her private life, even in death.

CORDERY: That's part of the Victorian [mindset]. This was very much part and parcel of being a woman of the nineteenth century.

DALTON: By the 1920s, Ted Roosevelt, T.R.'s oldest son, has political ambitions, and some people accused him of being involved with the Teapot Dome scandal, which, it turns out, is really not fair. Eleanor Roosevelt drove a car with a teapot on the top of it to embarrass her cousin. That created bitter feelings for a while....

CORDERY: [Ultimately, Edith lost three of her sons.] Awful, horrible, unbelievable. Quentin died in World War I, and then she lost sons in World War II.

DALTON: Ted was on the beach at Normandy [for D-Day]. He was a war hero. Kermit kills himself and the family didn't want to talk about that for many years. Archie lives a very long life.

CORDERY: Ethel lives a long life, and Alice will, of course, outlive everyone. She married a man about fifteen years her senior, Nicholas Longworth, who everybody thought might become president, which would have put Alice in the White House as first lady.... She will become a wise political observer, and people sought out her dining table, sought out her advice for sixty years. Alice was an icon in Washington, D.C.—the "other Washington Monument," she was famously called. And she was funny, very witty.

Edith Roosevelt's legacy:

DALTON: When Eleanor Roosevelt and Franklin Roosevelt came to the White House in the middle of the crisis of 1933, they told friends, "We'd really like our White House to be like Uncle Theodore's and Aunt Edith's." [T.R. and Edith] were role models for other presidential couples, because they were vigorous and active, but also, they maintained a homey sense and kept their personal life alive. She's a really important organizational pioneer in some ways.

CORDERY: The first lady has a fine line to walk between being the embodiment of the ceremonial aspects of the job and the global stage that the first lady needs to occupy, and that folksy, home-like, "this is your house as well as mine" [personality]. Edith did that very, very well. The changes she made, the professionalization of the office itself, all reflected that very clear sense that Edith had that we were stepping into a new century, and the future was going to be terrific.

Helen Herron Taft

"Mr. Taft was all but impervious to any friendly advice, which being followed, would have tended to enhance his own political advantage."

Helen Taft, c1900

Born: June 2, 1861, Cincinnati, Ohio
Married: June 19, 1886, to William Howard Taft (1857–1930)
Children: Robert Alphonso (1889–1953); Helen Herron (1891–1987); Charles Phelps (1897–1983)
Died: May 22, 1943, Washington, D.C.

Contributors:

JANE HAMPTON COOK, author of seven books, including *American Phoenix: John Quincy and Louisa Adams, The War of 1812, and the Exile that Saved American Independence*

LEWIS GOULD, historian and professor emeritus, University of Texas at Austin; editor of the *Modern First Ladies* series, University of Kansas Press

LEWIS GOULD: [Helen Taft is one of the more obscure twentieth century first ladies, but deserves better.] She did some things that were very constructive: the cherry trees, bringing classical musicians to the White House, and, generally, trying to make Washington the cultural center of the nation. That was her ambition. It didn't work out because of medical reasons, but she had an agenda that would have made her rank with Eleanor Roosevelt or Lady Bird Johnson in terms of transforming Washington had things gone the other way.

[She is remembered as being ambitious for her husband's career.] Sometimes, Helen Taft is portrayed as a cross between Mommie Dearest and Lady Macbeth, which isn't really the case. She was a much more constructive influence and a nicer lady than history has treated her.

Her father and the Herrons in Cincinnati were friends with President Rutherford B. Hayes and Lucy Hayes, and they went to the White House. She went only once, but she had not yet made her debut, so she couldn't participate in social activities.... In the Taft family lore, she was supposed to have said, "I'm going to come back." It's not clear that that's really what she said, but, like many people, she says, "I want to marry a man who may become president."

She came from a political family. Her father was [also] a friend of Benjamin Harrison, and they had also been involved in Ohio politics on her mother's side. There had been a congressman in their background. She was quite the intellectual. She was reading Darwin and Goethe in school, and she had the ability to play the piano, which she studied quite seriously. She had a salon in Cincinnati, which was a very culturally rich city in those days, as it is now.

She and Will Taft knew of each other; it was a small community. It was really after he had gone to Yale and come back to Cincinnati Law School that their lives began to intersect and they began to court. She was in her mid-twenties, which was late for marrying in those days, and he was almost twenty-nine by the time he got married. They started going out to some of the beer halls and other offerings of Cincinnati, and gradually fell in love. He was much more smitten with her originally than she was with him. He proposed, but she rejected him, which was the standard in those days; the woman never accepted the proposal right off. They had a rather lengthy courtship by our standards;...she made him wait a while, but then they got married in June of 1886.

Helen Herron didn't go to college. She studied a little bit at the University of Cincinnati, but she really almost was self-educated.... She took some courses, but she didn't have a degree like her husband did.

William Howard Taft wanted to be a lawyer, and he wanted to get to the Supreme Court. He would later say that like any good politician he had his bowl turned upward when offices were falling into his lap, but he definitely wanted to be chief justice of the United States almost from the time he learned about the law. [Ultimately, Taft became the only person to serve as both president and chief justice.]

At the initial stages, she had relatively little influence [on his career path], because he became a state judge, then he became solicitor general of the United States and was appointed to the Court of Appeals in Ohio. The big turning point came in early 1900 when President McKinley called him and said, "Come to Washington." He offered him the chance to go to the Philippines and establish a civilian government in the Philippines. He asked, "Do you want to do this?" and Helen said, "By all means." She said this would give her husband the sphere of power and influence that he wouldn't have had any other way. That was the decisive moment in their lives, when he was in his mid-forties, moving toward being in politics in a new way.

He pursued a political career with more zest than we sometimes realize. What Nellie Taft, as everyone knew her, would say is that Will had a way of getting people to push him in a direction that he wanted to go....

[Serving as] the governor general of the Philippines made Taft a national figure. Then, when he serves in Theodore Roosevelt's cabinet, he presents himself to Roosevelt as the logical choice in 1908, once Roosevelt had said he was not going to run. As Roosevelt looked over the cabinet to see who might be his successor, Elihu Root was probably too old, so there was Will Taft from Ohio, a state that really mattered to Republicans in those years. He became the logic of the situation.

JANE HAMPTON COOK: Their time in the Philippines was very important to Helen's development. When she returned to the United States, she met a military wife in the Army who had known her in the Philippines, who said, "In the Philippines, you were a queen and here, you are a nobody." I do not think Helen ever thought of herself as a nobody. When she was in the Philippines, she wasn't a queen in a royal sense, but in an American sense in that she invited people to her table, Philippine women and American women, and really brought those two cultures together. She served her husband very well by doing those things.

GOULD: The American Army in the Philippines drew what they called the color line, which meant that they didn't socialize with the Filipinos, so for Taft and Nellie to shake hands with the Filipinos, to dance with them, was seen as quite radical. There were elements in the military who were not thrilled with what Taft was doing. He wouldn't have been able to do this in the United States, ironically, at the same time, but in the Philippines, this accounts in part for his enduring popularity. Though, [it should be noted that] the Filipinos wanted the United States out as soon as possible, in the way of most colonial people.

Will Taft and Theodore Roosevelt got to know each other in the early 1890s. What is significant is, almost from the beginning, there is not the same rapport between Edith and Nellie. In fact, Nellie would later say she never liked Edith Roosevelt. There was a competition between them that pulsed through the 1890s. When the Tafts were in Cincinnati, it was not so [evident], but when they got back to Washington… they seem to have been two women who just struck odds when they started out. You had these two men who were very close, but their intimate families, not so much; and so, there was not a strong underpinning for the T.R. and Will Taft relationship once the two women got in closer proximity. It had something to do with Cincinnati versus New York, with Edith Roosevelt being from a onetime aristocratic family and Helen Taft being from Cincinnati and wanting to be upwardly mobile.

[As first lady,] Edith Roosevelt did have weekly meetings with cabinet wives; they met in the White House library from eleven to twelve [o'clock] once a week. Helen did attend, but she thought that they were a little too gossipy or that the topics of conversation just bored her. It wasn't something that she really enjoyed. She made it known to the press before she became first lady that she would not be continuing these meetings because they had not been successful. That was quite a slam to Edith to say that publicly. Helen could have been a little more genteel in how she transitioned….

The [Roosevelts] supervised some of the women in the Washington community. If you had a dalliance with somebody who wasn't your husband, you heard from the White House that you'd better stop. There was a certain amount of nitpicking and gossiping. Helen Taft, who liked to have a beer, smoke a cigarette, play some bridge, was not as hoity-toity as Edith Roosevelt. That was another source of tension. Helen Taft wanted to set a cultural standard of sophistication, but not

Helen Taft, shown here en route to the Philippines in 1900 with husband William Howard Taft (center right), had a fondness for playing cards, one of many "newer attitudes" she held about women's comportment.

be a busybody about it. Edith Roosevelt, who was somewhat priggish, wanted to pull the higher moral standard.

COOK: The Tafts were both born during the Civil War, and so they didn't [experience] it. They are post-war baby boomers with some newer attitudes.

GOULD: [Some of those newer attitudes included Helen's fondness for playing cards, smoking, and drinking alcohol.] I don't think the public really knew much about that, that she played bridge for money and she would win $10 or so, which sounds pretty tame. But if you put it into today's currency, she was winning about $200 or $300 in purchasing power when she won $10. If it had come out that she was playing cards, it would have been another political difficulty for her.

In 1906, Roosevelt begins to convince himself that he and Taft agree on more than they, in fact, agree on. There's a courtship where both invest each other with the qualities they want to have. Later on, they would find out that they had somewhat deluded themselves. But from 1906 to 1908, Roosevelt becomes a staunch backer of Taft.

COOK: Helen Taft was very influential [in Roosevelt's decision to support Taft]. She did meet with Theodore Roosevelt at least on two occasions to talk about this. Once, when he wanted to offer Taft a position on the Supreme Court, he called her in and she said, "Oh no, he wants to remain as your secretary of war." Wink, wink, nod, nod, he wants to succeed you. Roosevelt didn't see enough passion in Taft, and he was trying to nudge Taft, "Hey, there are other men who want [my nod]. If you want it, you need to be more aggressive." Taft did go out and do some campaigning for congressional candidates in 1906 to prove that he could campaign.

GOULD: The Republicans held on to the House and Senate in 1906. They suffered some losses, but basically, Taft came out of it as the frontrunner and would get a first-ballot nomination in 1908.

In 1908, Taft beat William Jennings Bryan. It was a pretty decisive victory.... Bryan essentially carried the South and a few Western states. Taft, who was a better campaigner than anybody thought, did very well.

COOK: Helen Taft seemed to have a good relationship with the press. They interviewed her after his nomination, and she said, "I love public life. This is exactly the position that I think my husband should have. I'm enthusiastic about Roosevelt." She really wasn't, but she said that to the press. One of the reporters commented that she would be an intellectual and that she had all these spheres—the intellectual, the cultural, and the domestic—all in one package. What a great opportunity for America to have Helen in the White House with her husband.

GOULD: There really was no mechanism for the transition in those days. There hadn't been a transition from one first lady to another in that way before for almost twenty years, so they were making it up as they went along. Helen was eager to get started and talked about changing the footmen who would be at the White House door. Edith had a gentleman who was white greet people when they came to the White House. Helen wanted to have African Americans in livery. Mrs. Roosevelt bridled at that. Nellie wanted to change the furniture. She had other changes that she wanted to make right away: "Let's get started." Edith was thinking, "I'm going to be first lady until March 3"; she said, "Not so fast."

There began to be [tensions between the two camps pretty quickly]. In the Taft family, they would say to the president-elect: be your own king; you need to take over. The Roosevelt people, who had put Taft in because he would extend Roosevelt's ideas, said: Wait a minute, what's going on here? What about the cabinet? What about the appointments that are being made? The friendship began to erode...and it started the doom of Taft's presidency.

[Taft's inauguration was held in a blizzard.] Theodore Roosevelt said, "I knew it would be a cold day when I went out." Then he went off to the train station and went off Oyster Bay. The Tafts rode back to the White House [after the ceremony] and created the precedent-breaking moment when she [became the first first lady to ride in the president's car] back to the White House.

COOK: She wrote later, "I had a secret elation in doing something that no other woman had done." This was really her proudest moment, riding in that car and being by her husband's side. She set a precedent; first ladies who followed her have done that since. It was definitely something she was excited about. She did have a little inaugural fashion emergency with her hat: the feathers caught on fire the night before and she had to trim them down.

GOULD: It turned out that day was really the high point of her time as first lady. It was almost all downhill after that, because, two months later, she has this stroke and [her] life changes forever.

[Helen Taft's desire] was to make Washington the cultural center of the United States. This made people in New York very uneasy. There were some newspaper columns asking, "What is she trying to do?" Washington at that time did not have a symphony orchestra, didn't have opera, and she wanted to bring those musical things here. She also wanted to have the city generally embody American values. This was a very ambitious agenda, to transform Washington into a city that would be as it was under Dolley Madison, a focus for national and international attention.... She hit the ground running, and she also started going to see Congress, visiting the Supreme Court, advising Taft on the cabinet. She was...very active as first lady for two months.... And, overall, the who's who of classical music moved through the White House in those four years. It was as stunning a group of artists as would later come in with the Kennedys....

[And, here is the backstory on Helen Taft and Washington's famous cherry trees:] Taft was not pro-Japanese in his foreign policy. He was tilted more toward the Chinese...so [Japan's gifting of the cherry trees] was a gesture by the Japanese government to try to make nice with Taft. But it did turn out to be one of the great beautification moves of the twentieth century.

Taft would say in the 1920s to his daughter, "Your mother's work with the cherry trees is now coming to blossom and because of her contribution it's making the city better than it has ever been."

On May 17, 1909, the Tafts went out to take a cruise on the Potomac in the presidential yacht, and one of the cabinet members noticed that there was something wrong with Mrs. Taft. They realized that she had had some kind of seizure, and they turned around and took the presidential vessel back. Military aide Archie Butt said, as he looked at the president, that he had this face of a stricken animal, he was in such pain seeing his wife with this seizure. It was a moment that transformed the presidency and their lives.

COOK: She had some temporary paralysis in her limbs, but that came back pretty quickly. [The problem] was her voice; she could not articulate. She got to the point where she could speak [sentences] and could read something aloud, but you couldn't understand her fully because she lost that articulation....I don't know that she ever fully was the same.

GOULD: There are stories of Taft sitting on a couch with Helen saying, "Now, say 'thee,' darling. Say 'thee.' That's very good. Now, let's try to say 'thee' again." He was running a kind of rehab in the White House for his wife while he was also being president.

He carried forward the duties of the White House. But what is striking to me is what emotional stress it must have been, because at any moment she could have had another stroke, as she would have in May 1911. The concentration and the distraction of knowing that your wife is upstairs vocally impaired and suffering is [such] an element of the Taft presidency that even in the book I wrote about it, I don't think I gave it enough importance.

COOK: It comes at a very critical time in his presidency, when they are debating the tariff act, and he loses her input to him on the political ramifications, if it goes this way or that. This was a highly stressful time for him and for her, obviously.

GOULD: He really had no other close friend because T.R. had been the close friend. None of his brothers were very good at giving him advice; there was no structure in the White House, no chief of staff, no aides. There was just the secretary and the clerks. She was his most intimate advisor, and in an afternoon she was gone, in terms of giving him advice. Roosevelt had left him in a tough position. He had delayed the tariff debate until it was dumped into Taft's lap, so it wasn't exactly a profile in courage for T.R.

COOK: In reading her memoir, Helen downplays her role [in advising the president on policy], but it seems to me that she had more of an advanced role than a lot of first ladies up to that point, but not nearly as advanced as we've come to expect today. She was very Washington-centric in her outlook as first lady. She was not going around the country making stops. She might have traveled with him had she not had that stroke. That might have been the influence that we're missing on his presidency.

GOULD: [Helen went to the Massachusetts coast to recover.] She couldn't be in Washington in the summer without air conditioning, as it was in those days....But he would dictate some letters, and then she said, "Please, handwrite them." So, he did that, too.... He wrote to her every day when she was away, and these were handwritten, six-, seven-, eight-page letters.... Here was Taft at the end of a very busy day sitting down and writing two thousand to three thousand words to his wife. That's devotion.

[William Howard Taft weighed] about 350 pounds in the presidency, and he neglected his health. He hadn't been to a dentist in a couple of decades.... There were many stories about his weight. In fact, Chief Justice Melville Weston Fuller said, "The president got up on the street-car the other day and gave a seat to three women."

There's one biographer that says this was the source of some marital tension. She, of course, from a health point of view, wanted him to reduce his weight, but this was an area in which he didn't take much dictation.... Emotional stress operated. There's a story of him at a cabinet meeting where they had a bowl of fruit and he just picked each one off until the bowl was completely empty. He didn't find the presidency very enjoyable, and he ate to forget.

[The rift between Taft and Roosevelt grew so great that Roosevelt decided to challenge Taft in 1912.] This was a disaster for the Republican Party that still echoes in its DNA to this day.... Helen was convinced that T.R. was going to run almost from March 4, 1909; Will saw it developing in a more measured way.... Helen didn't trust Theodore Roosevelt one minute in their whole relationship.

[Helen Taft attended the 1912 Democratic Convention, the only first lady to attend the opposite party's convention.] The Democrats met in Baltimore, which made it a road trip for her, and she went with a couple of Democratic women. Most of Washington society went over to see the Baltimore convention. It lived up to its billing.... Nominating Woodrow Wilson went forty-six ballots. It had drama, it lasted a week. William Jennings Bryan was going to introduce a resolution attacking President Taft, but he withdrew it, because he said he didn't want to embarrass the first lady...while she was sitting in the gallery.

[Roosevelt's third party Bull Moose challenge split the Republicans and threw the election to Democrat Woodrow Wilson.] Taft took his defeat with unusual grace. He was not a bad loser. When the press asked, "Do you feel disappointed?" he said, "the American people gave me the gift of the presidency for four years. How many men have had that gift given to them?" ...Taft was disappointed, but he was not embittered. That redounded to his credit over the long haul.

COOK: That makes sense because what mattered most to Taft was the rule of law, and the people had spoken...so he could accept that much more easily, probably, than some people.

GOULD: Helen had eight years of transition. Taft, after he left the presidency, became a professor of constitutional law at Yale. It was really quite nice for Mrs. Taft because, in those days, you could get on a train and go to New York, eighty miles, go to the theater, have a nice meal, do some shopping, and get back in time for dinner at night. She enjoyed that part of it after the pressures of the White House.

COOK: Right after the White House, Nellie did write an autobiography with a ghostwriter. That was a first, to have it published. Louisa Adams wrote an autobiography, but it was not published in her lifetime. Helen's memoir was published in 1914.

GOULD: Taft played things very carefully for eight years, hoping that the Republicans would come back in.... The Democrats were repudiated in 1920, and [Warren] Harding became president. On Christmas Eve of 1920, Taft is in Marion, Ohio, and goes to see the Hardings, and Harding asks, "Would you like to be on the Supreme Court? I'll put you on that court." Taft said he could only be chief justice, and Harding, in effect, says, we'll work it out. Six months later, Chief Justice Edward Douglas White dies.... [and] Taft is appointed chief justice about July 1, 1921.

Then, of course, the Tafts went back to Washington. The role of the chief justice was very much less social than had been the presidency, so Helen sort of took the veil in the 1920s. They also differed over Prohibition. Chief Justice Taft wanted it enforced, and Mrs. Taft, not so much.

COOK: Being first lady is what she had always wanted to do, so she didn't have a big ambition after that other than to live a quiet life. That's why we don't see her as much.

Her oldest son, Robert, ran for the Senate and was a successful senator, and so was his son. Taft's great grandson was the governor of Ohio. Their daughter, Helen, went on to earn a Ph.D. She married and had children. Their youngest son was the mayor of Cincinnati, so they had their own legacy in politics.

GOULD: [Even though she suffered two strokes, she outlived her husband and lived until the age of eighty-one,] interacting with her children and grandchildren. They continue going to Murray Bay, Canada... where they first had a cabin, which then grew into a Taft complex. He would have made it the summer White House in Canada, but the president, in those days, by tradition, could not leave the continental United

States during his time in office. Somebody once said, if they could have annexed Murray Bay, Taft's presidency would have been a lot happier....

COOK: [She was invited back to the White House by Eleanor Roosevelt in 1940.] That's a quiet tradition that first ladies have. Helen invited Frances Cleveland back to the White House when she was first lady.... They were only three years apart in age. They got married the same year, in 1886. And so, there was a little club of first ladies to share and talk about their experiences.

[Helen Taft died on May 22, 1943, and is buried] at Arlington Cemetery. She is the first first lady to be buried there. [Jacqueline Kennedy is the only other.]

Helen Taft's legacy:

COOK: Definitely, [Helen Taft should be recognized for] all of the firsts that she had as first lady. Also, she made it okay for a woman to have an interest in politics. We can look back and see that she was ahead of her time, and ... the first ladies that came after her, more of them had that natural interest, as well.

GOULD: She should be remembered because of the cherry trees, because of the musicians that she brought in because of her role in making Taft president, because of her role in the split between T.R. and her husband. She was a consequential first lady in a cultural and political and marital sense. She deserves much more from history than she's received.

Ellen Axson Wilson

"I am naturally the most unambitious of women and life in the White House has no attractions for me."

Ellen Wilson, date unknown

Born: May 15, 1860, Savannah, Georgia
Married: June 24, 1885, to Thomas Woodrow Wilson (1856–1924)
Children: Margaret Woodrow (1886–1944); Jessie Woodrow (1887–1933); Eleanor Randolph (1889–1967)
Died: August 6, 1914, at the White House, Washington, D.C.

Edith Bolling Wilson

"I, myself, never made a single decision regarding the disposition of public affairs. The only decision that was mine was what was important and what was not, and the very important decision of when to present matters to my husband."

Edith Wilson, c1915

Born: October 15, 1872, Wytheville, Virginia
Married: April 30, 1896, to Norman Galt (1862–1908) (widowed); December 18, 1915, to Thomas Woodrow Wilson (1856–1924)
Children: None
Died: December 28, 1961, Washington, D.C.

Contributors:

JOHN MILTON COOPER, professor emeritus, University of Wisconsin-Madison; author, *The Warrior and the Priest: Theodore Roosevelt and Woodrow Wilson*

KRISTIE MILLER, author of several books, including *Ellen and Edith: Woodrow Wilson's First Ladies*

JOHN MILTON COOPER: [Ellen Axson was born in Georgia in 1860.] Her early life was very difficult. Her father was a Presbyterian minister. He had served in the Civil War, but had to leave because of some stress-related conditions. He later developed a mental illness and [ultimately] died in a mental institution, possibly a suicide. Ellen was very close to her mother, but her mother had died in childbirth with her fourth child when she was forty-three. Ellen really had to take over the family.... She became a very competent manager.

Ellen was very well-educated for a woman of her time and place. She would have gone to college if she'd had the money. After her father died, she had the money to go to the Art Students League in New York for a year. She had been very unsure that she would ever meet a man who could be her intellectual equal, which she felt was necessary for marriage. In fact, she had plans to open up a boardinghouse for women and support it with her artwork. People around town had started calling her "Ellie, the Man Hater," because she was so clearly not going to be satisfied with anyone in the town. Then, [Thomas] Woodrow Wilson came to town. He was a lawyer at that time and had a case there. He went to the church where her father was preaching and met her there.

[Woodrow knew instantly that he was in love with Ellen.] I wish I could say that he was a man of great enlightenment and forward-looking views. He wasn't. He wasn't bad, though. By the standards of that time, he comes off pretty well as believing strongly that women are very bright and very capable. Generally, though, he still liked the subordinate role [for women]. Basically, he liked women, and more so than men of that time. He enjoyed the company of men very much, but he just generally enjoyed the company of women, and he enjoyed their intellectual companionship.

KRISTIE MILLER: Woodrow Wilson was very passionate and very eloquent, and...the letters that he wrote to Ellen after they were engaged are just the most astonishing love letters you will ever see. She was quite eloquent, too.

They got married two years later. Woodrow had a great strategy. He had had a girlfriend before, and she had refused his offer of marriage. He was once burned, twice shy. He had decided that he was going to propose to Ellen just before getting on the train to go to Baltimore to attend Johns Hopkins in political science. If she refused him, there would be no awkward lingering, he later said....

When he proposed to her, she was so startled that she blurted out, "Yes." She hadn't meant to.... They had hardly known each other, but he was going off to study for two years. So they had a two-year engagement and it was these marvelous letters through which they became intimate.

COOPER: ...His first teaching job was at Bryn Mawr, a brand-new college for women. He liked teaching there. He liked the women at Bryn Mawr better than Ellen did; Ellen objected to these modern women more than he did. He got to Princeton in 1890 and he became the most popular professor there. He was one of two real stars of the faculty. There was some intrigue among the trustees to get him into the [college] presidency, and he was chosen president in 1902. He tried to reform Princeton and succeeded a bit and failed quite a bit. He really got stymied, then the New Jersey political bosses came along and offered him the ... governorship.

He took [the governorship] from them, and then he turned and immediately became a reformer.... Wilson made a remarkable transition in two years. He went from being a university president to being president [of the United States]. The governorship is just an interlude there, although he was a very effective governor.

MILLER: [As his career progressed,] Ellen was building on each of the things that she'd done before. She had been involved in a small way with some social outreach during the time that she was a private person. When she became first lady of New Jersey, she became very interested in social welfare. She took Woodrow on a tour to look at state welfare institutions like the homes for the insane or the prisons, so she had an early record of activism. She also had to do a great deal of entertaining...as the college president's wife, and more when she moves into the governor's mansion.

What was interesting about the 1912 campaign was that she was the first ...[candidate's wife] to go on a campaign before the convention. She and Wilson went down through the South, especially in Georgia where she was hailed as much as he was. Unfortunately, they didn't get the delegates from Georgia. She had a hand in trying to get Woodrow to patch up relations with William Jennings Bryan, who had three times been the Democratic nominee and was the leader of the Democratic Party. He was very key in helping Woodrow get the nomination.

COOPER: Wilson had come from a different wing of the party. He'd said some things about Bryan that some of his enemies had publicized to try to make trouble. Ellen saw a chance to mend the fences there. She brought them together, and they hit it off very well. Bryan and Wilson had a good relationship, right down to some of the unfortunate stuff in World War I. She was playing the same kind of role that she played in his academic career: a very shrewd tactician, a very good facilitator. Not out in front.

MILLER: Woodrow Wilson was involved with another woman during the time he was married to Ellen. He met Mary Allen Hulbert Peck in 1907. By 1908, he had scribbled on a little note somewhere, "My precious one, my beloved Mary." I don't think he sent it to her; he was just venting his feelings. Ellen was very upset. She accused him of emotional love for this woman, but she tolerated Mary and tried to protect Woodrow from the scandal. There still was some scandal, and Theodore Roosevelt was invited during the 1912 election to make use of it. Somebody said that they had letters between Woodrow and Mary, and although they were never as ardent as his letters to Ellen had been, they were certainly compromising. Roosevelt said that using this would be wrong, and also, that nobody would believe him.

COOPER: People said this was very noble of Theodore Roosevelt, but frankly, he said, "I can't believe that somebody who looks like an apothecary's clerk could be a Romeo. Nobody will believe that." So, he said no, it's not going to work [as a campaign tactic against Wilson].

MILLER: [The Taft-Roosevelt split threw the 1912 election to Democrat Woodrow Wilson. The Wilsons made a decision not to have an inaugural ball.] It was partly because of Ellen, who felt that it would be a commercialization, something frivolous, at what should be a solemn occasion. She was a very thrifty woman. Woodrow did not make a lot of money in his early days, and she had a habit of frugality. Somebody once said, "Mrs. Wilson looks sweeter every year, and that brown dress she wears looks sweeter every year, too," because she never got new clothes....

Ellen felt that as long as she was in the White House, not a place where she particularly wanted to be, she would use her position to do as much good as she could. She connected with a group called the National Civic Federation that had been around for ten years or so. They were very interested in trying to clean up these little alleyways in between the bigger streets of Washington, where there were tumbledown shacks, great squalor. They wanted to tear down these buildings and do what we would now call urban renewal. Ellen was so interested in this project that she took some of the congressmen in the White House car through the alleyways to show them the conditions of these houses that were right behind the Capitol. She lobbied them to pass a bill that would enable this because at that time Washington's government was run by Congress; they didn't have their own government. She was the first first lady who lobbied for a cause that wasn't her husband's, and she was very effective at doing this.

COOPER: I love Ellen.... That being said, she was a Southern woman, and I don't think we could honestly say that she believed in the equality of African Americans. She was a wonderful, warm, loving person, but African Americans occupied their place. This was in a [maternal] way that she wants to help [the alley cleanup cause], and it was also to beautify Washington, not just to be helpful.

MILLER: [An avid gardener, Ellen Wilson created the White House Rose Garden.] Ellen also did earn money from selling her paintings that she donated to a charity that she had set up in the memory of her brother who had died. The only other first lady who earned money while she was in the White House was Eleanor Roosevelt. That did not become a first lady tradition, and it's just as well.

[Ellen was ill her entire time in the White House.] She first developed kidney trouble in 1889, when her third child was born…. She probably had been suffering for some time before she got to the White House [from] something called Bright's Disease, an archaic term that means kidney disease. I was impressed that they were able to diagnose it as early as 1889.

[The three Wilson daughters] were all roughly of marriageable age when they get into the White House, so they go to balls and parties…. Two of them did get married in the White House, and considering that [Ellen] was only in the White House for seventeen months before she died, that's quite an accomplishment. She had a very big wedding for her first daughter, who was married in November. She had a very small, quiet wedding for her third daughter, who got married in May, very shortly before Ellen was bedridden.

I don't think Ellen knew how sick she was. She was hoping she would get better. The doctors kept telling her she would get better. The doctors were in denial, so I don't think Woodrow really knew she was dying until…the day she died.

The day that she's dying, she tells the chief of staff, Joe Tumulty, to go up to Congress and say she will die more easily if they will just pass an Alley Bill. The Senate takes action in time for her to learn about it, before she loses consciousness for the last time. The House passes it later, but it is never implemented because of World War I breaking out…. This whole issue is dropped until 1933. There was a young woman whose husband was in the Wilson Administration, Assistant Secretary of the Navy Franklin Delano Roosevelt. Eleanor Roosevelt went to the White House many times and met Ellen Wilson…. The first week that Eleanor Roosevelt was in the White House, she went back to the National Civic Federation women, the same women that had worked with Ellen Wilson, and began to lobby for an Alley Bill…. I firmly believe that Ellen set an example to Eleanor, and that Eleanor, of course, set an example to many first ladies who came after her.

COOPER: Those last days of hers, the president is literally at her sick bed every possible minute; on the other hand, the world is literally falling apart with World War I, and he has to deal with that. It was terribly affecting. [The period after Ellen's death is] the worst time in Wilson's life, except for his stroke, because he was absolutely devastated by Ellen's death.

MILLER: He had to [focus on the affairs of state]. In fact, he said that's what held him together. He had to be president. He had to pay attention to these things. Otherwise, the man really could have deteriorated badly if he had been on his own. The presidency was his crutch at this point....

I don't think that there was a great rush of women to meet [the widower president]. His doctor was very concerned about him and thought that a friend of his, Edith Galt, might be somebody that would cheer him up. He arranged for Helen Bones, the woman who was serving as official hostess after Ellen's death, to go walking with Edith. Because Helen herself was having some health problems, he thought it would benefit her to go walking with this nice, hearty, vigorous woman. They took a number of walks together, and that led to a meeting in the White House between Edith and Woodrow. They were immediately drawn to each other. Just as with Ellen, he very quickly fell in love and very quickly proposed to her.

He said, "Time is much quicker here than it is on the outside." I hate to call it a ploy, but one fact that he pointed out to all three of the women that he was involved with was that he needed them so much. It was a real, genuine need, that he often said that he couldn't do his work unless he was assured of their love. That was definitely one of the things that he said to Edith, and she responded. She said, "To know that you have needed me is very sweet." That was another very successful courtship tactic. Although she refused him the first time, two months later, he proposed again, and she accepted.

COOPER: We both read all the correspondence [between them], and I'm impressed that Edith's refusal looked pretty pro forma. You just knew that she was going to accept this guy.

MILLER: One of my favorite quotes [about her initial refusal] is from a Secret Service man, Colonel Sterling, who said, "The lady was retreating, but how fast and with what intention?" We don't know.

Mrs. Wilson (seated, left) laughs as President Woodrow Wilson throws out the first baseball on Opening Day of 1916.

COOPER: Wilson would go over to Edith's house. He would spend the evening there, and then, sometimes, he would break into a dance walking back to the White House.

They tried to keep it out of the press as long as they could. The reactions in the cabinet were mixed; mainly, they were worried about the political fallout.... There's the old phrase "a decent interval of time." How do you define that? The longer, the better, perhaps.... Several of them tried to hatch something to warn him off there, and that backfired very badly.

MILLER: Fortunately, it was not as his advisors feared. The public loved it. They went on a tour about six weeks after they were married to drum up interest in preparedness in case America got into the war, and she was seen as a great asset. The press really loved her. The crowds really loved her. They loved the idea of the two of them still essentially being on their honeymoon. It was a great public relations asset.

The daughters were very happy to see their father married again because he was in deep despair. They were very worried about him, and they were among the happiest people in Washington about the marriage.

COOPER: Wilson courted the widow Galt with the presidency and the secrets of the state, and she ate it up. There's no question about it. She frankly admits in her memoir later that this was a good bit of her attraction to Wilson. She was attracted to him, too, personally, but definitely, this made him a much more glamorous figure to her.

MILLER: Poor Edith gets pitched into the White House in the middle of the war, in the middle of his term without any preparation whatsoever. She really rose to the occasion.... Edith had the doubly trying situation of having to have two receptions because she couldn't have all the warring ambassadors with each other, so she had to have a party for the Allies, and a party for the Central Powers. She really was terrific and everybody was impressed with her good, firm handshake, and very impressed with her sense of style. No poor little brown dress for Edith.

Edith really did not have Ellen's acumen for understanding [public policy]. Wilson liked to show her his papers, but mostly what she would do is get all fired up and say, "You should put this note to Germany more strongly," or "You should put this note to the Secretary of State William Jennings Bryan more strongly." He liked her to be fiery like that...but she didn't really have any understanding. A lot of people thought that she had influenced him to lobby, as he finally did, for women's suffrage, but that was not the case at all. She really didn't approve of women's suffrage. So, I wouldn't say she had any effect on his legislative programs.

COOPER: [Once the decision was made for the United States to enter World War I, the country was all in....] It was a race against time for us to get our Doughboys there. The British and the French—bless their hearts—held on that one last time and blocked that German offensive, but they were able to do it because they know the Yanks were coming.... We provided the Doughboys and the dough. [Ultimately, there were] about one hundred forty thousand American casualties in the war.

Armistice Day was November 11, 1918. Wilson becomes peacemaker-in-chief. He decided very early that he was going to go to Paris and was going to be our chief negotiator because he wanted to shape the peace as best he could there. He knew we had come into the war later than the others, and for different reasons, and he knew that there were real differences [among the participating nations].

MILLER: [The Wilsons traveled to Europe for the peace conference by ocean liner.] They were received, especially in England, in terms that would have been accorded to royalty. Everywhere they went, they were cheered by the populace. In the beginning it was wonderful, but once the negotiations got underway Edith suddenly went from this fairytale existence to being extremely concerned for Wilson's high blood pressure.

He had had some kind of episode when he was only thirty-nine years old where he had a lot of numbness in his hand…. During those negotiations, he couldn't rest or exercise. Edith was trying her best. Her secretary said that she would never go out if there was a possibility that she might be able to take Woodrow for a walk. But it was not enough.

COOPER: [His stroke occurred] more than halfway through his second term. It was in October 1919. He had just returned from a whirlwind speaking tour. He was trying to sell the country on ratifying the peace treaty and going into the League of Nations, and he'd really worn himself out. His doctors aborted the tour and got him back to the White House. After about five days back in the White House, he suffered a massive stroke.

MILLER: There are some conflicting reports about what happened, but the most accurate portrayal is, Edith had been going in to check on him during the night, and in the morning she found him slumped to the floor… She went out into the corridor to use a telephone that did not go through the switchboard. She did not want to have this [situation] universally known. She asked the chief usher to call the doctor from this other phone. The doctor came in. They helped him into bed, but he was paralyzed on his left side.

COOPER: The worst effect of the stroke on Wilson was really on his emotional balance and his judgment. His intellect wasn't impaired. His speech wasn't impaired, so he could function that way. But so much more goes into being a leader, being a president, than being smart and being able to do these things. Another thing is…they isolated him and…now the neurologists say that is exactly the wrong thing to do. What you want to do with a person who's had a stroke is get them back into social interaction as soon as you can. So, with the best of intentions, they were doing exactly the wrong thing.

MILLER: [Wilson continued in office, but] I don't think it was with the doctors' consent. Not a bit. In October, Dr. Cary Grayson wrote a memo so that should he be subpoenaed to Congress he would have something on paper early on saying exactly what was wrong with the president.

COOPER: Edward Weinstein, [who] was a very distinguished neurologist, wrote a medical biography of Wilson. He takes it straight on that Edith said that their doctors said, "Keep him in office." He said no responsible physician would have said that; Edith was making that up.

This is the one time that we really have had a disabled president, and how do you deal with it? I have a lot of sympathy for Edith. She was scared. This is a very scary thing she was in, and you make it up as you go along.

MILLER: She had had exactly two years of formal schooling in her whole entire life…. Her grandmother was a very opinionated woman and taught Edith that it was good to have opinions and to make decisions. Edith had been widowed relatively young and had inherited Galt Jewelers, which was like the Tiffany's of Washington…so she brought this very decisive personality. In addition, Woodrow had courted her by showing her a lot of secret papers…. So, she probably knew as well as anyone what he was doing and what he was thinking, because he was a real lone wolf when it came to being a president. He didn't have a lot of close advisers.

COOPER: He or she who controls access to the president, to some extent, is president. He was pretty well embargoed for well over a month. Nobody from the outside got to see him, but also…Edith would decide what was best for him to see and what not. One of the raps on Edith in this was that she was putting her husband's health ahead of the good of the country, and that somehow her priorities were wrong there. I don't think that was entirely why she did what she did. She knew what he wanted, and that if he couldn't express himself, she knew he would not want to resign, that he would want to hang on to the [presidency].

MILLER: There were two senators who were detailed to come in and assess the condition of Wilson…. Edith and Dr. Grayson really stage-managed that very well. The accounts differ exactly on what they did, but whatever it was, it was enormously successful. Senator Albert Fall, the Republican, who would have been most anxious to show that there was something wrong with Wilson, said to the press afterwards that the president grasped his hand with both of his. That was manifestly impossible because Woodrow couldn't move his left hand, but the senator was taken with Wilson's apparent animation….

COOPER: [It was April of 1920 before the president had his first post-stroke cabinet meeting.] Wilson was a great delegator, except in foreign affairs. Other than that, he gave his cabinet secretaries lots of leeway, so they were used to running things on their own. It's just very lucky, and something of a tribute, that government functioned as well as it did; not all that well, but it kept going.

MILLER: One aspect to Edith's role during this time that's been overlooked is the extent to which she tried to make Woodrow give way on some of his intransigence about the League of Nations….

She and [adviser] Joe Tumulty had discussed some of the places where they hoped Woodrow could give a little ground, and then where the Republicans could give a little ground. They hoped to find some compromise. She took some notes, almost shorthand notes, of what was obviously a speech that she was going to give to Wilson that wound up saying, "For the sake of the country and the peace of the world, please consider this." It didn't work, apparently, because he didn't change.

COOPER: Wilson should not have continued as president because he wasn't functioning and there was this warped judgment of his that would not compromise. If he had resigned, or there…was something to get him out of the way, we would have joined the League…. It would have gotten us into a leadership role in world affairs a generation before we did. What was lost was a generation of experience in leadership.

MILLER: Edith was first lady to a functioning president for about four and a half years, and she was nursemaid to a president another four and a half years, [including the three years he lived after they left the White House].

COOPER: [He died February 4, 1924, at their home in Northwest Washington D.C.] President Coolidge offered the Capitol to have a state funeral. Edith declined. They had a service at their house, presided over by both a Presbyterian clergyman and the Washington Episcopalian bishop.... There was a procession up Massachusetts Avenue to the National Cathedral, where there was the interment. It was a lovely ceremony. One of the nicest touches was at the end of the service, a bugler played "taps" and they had a hookup via a telephone to Arlington Cemetery...where the bugler in Arlington also played taps.

MILLER: Edith lived...thirty-seven more years; it was an extraordinarily long time. He died in 1924, and she died at the end of 1961. She spent all the rest of her life being Woodrow Wilson's widow. She chose his first biographer. She controlled access to his papers very closely. She controlled how his image was portrayed. She wrote her own memoir, with her own spin on it. She collaborated with Darryl Zanuck, who made a movie about Wilson. She really had a tight rein on what he was allowed to do. The most important thing that she did was when she supported...the Woodrow Wilson Foundation. They helped create the United Nations, and they also collected his papers...so that there are sixty-nine volumes of Woodrow Wilson's letters and other significant papers, many of the letters from the first ladies, even letters from Mary Peck. That's Edith's biggest legacy.

When FDR went to Congress on December 8, [1941,] the day after the bombing at Pearl Harbor, he invited Edith Wilson to come and sit in the gallery, as she had sat in the gallery when Woodrow Wilson called for war in the First World War.

Ellen Wilson's legacy:

COOPER: [Without Ellen Wilson, there may not have been a President Woodrow Wilson.] Absolutely. This man blossoms. He met her just as he was about to depart for Johns Hopkins. He'd been playing around with the law, trying to write, trying to find himself. Love concentrated his mind wonderfully. It's extraordinary. His two years at Hopkins, he's…writing these letters to her—long, involved, wonderful letters— and writing his first book and best book, *Congressional Government*. It's amazing.

Any academic would love to have Ellen as a wife…. She was such a help, such a support, and such a terribly shrewd adviser, and such an emotional support to him. It really is extraordinary.

Edith Wilson's legacy:

MILLER: Unfortunately, her biggest contribution is what not to do. Even as late as 1987, William Safire was writing a newspaper column that said to Nancy Reagan, "Don't you be an Edith Wilson. Don't you meddle in presidential politics." I'm afraid that, in some ways, is Edith's greatest legacy as first lady.

COOPER: Although Edith had to handle the country in this crisis of presidential disability, she has set a pattern of how not to do it because it was a cover-up…. Grayson acted on Edith's orders and said, "We're not going to admit he had a stroke." The White House never admitted that. One of his consulting physicians let it slip out of the bag later, but they never admitted it. This uncertainty about what the president's condition was really contributed to the political downfall that comes.

Florence Kling Harding

"The happy woman is not one who has married the best on earth but the one who is philosophical enough to make the best of what she got."

Florence Harding,
c1920

Born: August 15, 1860, Marion, Ohio
Married: (**common law**) March 1880–June 12, 1886 Henry deWolfe (divorced); July 8, 1891, to Warren G. Harding (1865–1923)
Children: Marshall Eugene deWolfe (1880–1915)
Died: November 21, 1924, Marion, Ohio

Contributors:

DAVID PIETRUSZA, presidential historian; author or editor of several books, including *1920: The Year of the Six Presidents*

KATHERINE SIBLEY, history professor, Saint Joseph's University; author, *First Lady Florence Harding*

DAVID PIETRUSZA: The mood of the country [in 1920] is really bad. It's a year when just about any Republican can win. The trick is to get to the nomination. Theodore Roosevelt was supposed to be the nominee. They had the big split in 1912; the Progressives are still in tatters. That's patched up. Unfortunately, T.R. died in his sleep in January 1919. There are some people who want to fill the bill, [and in the end, they turned to] Warren Gamaliel Harding. He's not too hot, not too cold, not too interventionist, not too much of anything except he is really handsome. He is a fairly good speaker. He's been on the national stage at the 1916 Republican convention. He nominated Taft in 1912. So, he is the alternative, and in that year, the alternative to Wilsonism wins.

KATHERINE SIBLEY: The *Marion Star* was a very small paper when Harding acquired it, and he made it into a much more successful paper over time, thanks to the efforts of his wife Florence....

She was a key element [in his road to the 1920 nomination, as well]. What happens is, they are working at the newspaper and it's going very well, but it's a little dull for her and she'd like to see him get involved in some other things. He does go on the Chautauqua circuit, and he was a very good speaker. He was quite successful, and she thought, "He could go for bigger things." So he did. He ran for state Senate. He was elected two times in Ohio, then tried to go further than that with lieutenant governor. He later ran for governor. It was not successful, but he was positioned. He was visible in Ohio, and by the time of 1913, when there was a new law in this country which allows senators for the first time to be elected popularly, he was positioned to run. In 1914, he was elected to the Senate for Ohio. He thus becomes the first popularly elected senator from that state, and the first senator to become president as a sitting senator. Florence, his wife, is right there alongside him. Her role is quite significant in developing this trajectory.

Florence was someone who saw the potential in Warren. She saw that he could be someone who could rise to a higher position with her strength, with her backing. Sometimes we hear that she made him president, and that's too simple. That takes away from his own abilities.... He wasn't just a pretty face and a senatorial-looking man, but she certainly had a key role in pushing him into the place where he got to be.

PIETRUSZA: [Harding's personal life was a mess going into the 1920 campaign, but] scandals of public figures were not written about unless there was a divorce case, unless something went into the courts. The papers would not touch it.... You also see in that era that there are other infidelities going on.

SIBLEY: Warren Harding did have this affair with Carrie Phillips; they met early on and were old friends. They were couples—the Phillipses and the Hardings—who all were in a connected way in Ohio. What happens over time is that Warren falls in love with Carrie and Florence eventually finds out. Sometime between 1905, when Florence gets sick for the first time, and 1911, she discovers this affair. The [Phillipses and the Hardings] were still friends, and they were still vacationing together…. Florence asks him to consider a divorce, but Warren refused. He knew very much that he needed her…so he agreed to downplay this affair and he committed to ending it, but, in fact, he did not, as it turns out.

By 1920, as he is running for president, the affair is a bit of an embarrassment. It's been on and off. It hasn't been a very active affair for some years at that point, but there are flaring moments of it…. Because of that, in the end, Carrie Phillips is essentially bought off by members of the Republican Party and others who come up with funds to get her out of the way. Florence was not happy about this at all. There are some wonderful quotes we've read in her diary where she expresses the difficulty of dealing with an unfaithful husband like hers.

PIETRUSZA: [There is a] long letter which Harding sends to Carrie Phillips regarding [her attempts to] blackmail him. She had Harding's letters. There were approximately ninety-eight of them, not all torrid love letters, but a lot of them were….There's a certain charm and skill to his language, but she has got the goods on him. This is the smoking gun, and she's got it. She finally had become so incensed at Harding that she tells her husband and they determine that they are going to put the hammer to this want-to-be president, and they will drive him out of office or they will drive him bankrupt.

The Republican Party made Carrie Phillips an offer of $5,000 a year. They give her $25,000 upfront and an all-expense paid trip to the Orient: both she and her husband "go far away during this election campaign." The excuse is that he's in the dry goods business and they have lots of dry goods there.

SIBLEY: [With this deal,] Carrie is pretty much out of the picture at that point. I argue that this is the end of this relationship. I would also argue that it's the end of all his relationships. Many might suggest there were other relationships, Nan Britton and other names have been heard…. I would say absolutely, I do not believe that Harding is the father of Nan Britton's child. Britton's papers are now available…. Seems to be she was a young woman, she obviously had a crush on Warren, she hoped perhaps he could help her with a job. She knew his sister. She was from Marion. [But] to me, there is no credible evidence.

[Florence had had a prior marriage and did have a son by her first marriage.] This is a sad story. She married early on to escape her overwhelmingly powerful father. We don't actually have any record that she literally married this man next door, Pete DeWolfe, but she certainly eloped with him and they had a child. He was someone who had a difficult past and a difficult future.

DeWolfe left her. He was a ne'er-do-well, he was a drunk, and there she was trying to raise his little boy, Marshall, on her own. In the end, her father steps in and says, "You obviously can't do this. I will take over." She was trying, though. This is a very interesting part of her story. She was a single mother who taught piano. She had gone to a conservatory and she was a very good pianist. She was making money doing that, but not enough to sustain both herself and her son. So, in the end, she has to allow Marshall to live with her father. Nevertheless, she sees her son quite a bit.

PIETRUSZA: There could have been more public sympathy generated for Florence because her life is so tremendously hard.... She comes from the richest family in town. She has to go and elope with this fellow when she [becomes] pregnant at the time of their non-marriage. And when she is abandoned, it is on Christmas Eve, and she has to hitch a ride, beg a ride, on a train to get home. Even then, she is afraid to go see her father and must break into an abandoned home to spend the night. Then she sees her father and it's, "No, I will not help you." Finally, a deal is brokered after quite a while that, "I will take your son, but not you." ...This is real nineteenth century melodrama, and it happened to her. This is a very hard life...and, in that way, she's a very sympathetic person because she's a survivor.

SIBLEY: ...Warren Harding didn't necessarily want to be president. He enjoyed being in the Senate, and it was his friends who wanted him to [run]. They loved him, and he was popular, and it just seemed like, over time, increasingly, there were urgings on him. Also, the situation back in Ohio didn't look good for him to be reelected.

PIETRUSZA: [However, Warren and Florence] are two people who, physically, should never have gone to the White House. She has nephritis, and she's laid up for months and months, literally dying. It's really a horrible thing, the pain she's in. They say the pain is so intense, she was digging her hand in and making a fist, and it goes in so deep, the nails cause her to bleed.

SIBLEY: [Florence was the better politician on the campaign trail.] She is more out there with her strengths. He gets exhausted in some of these encounters, but she continues. When we think about how ill she was, back and forth with her illness and nephritis, the kidney ailment, it's really pretty astounding. It would take her sometimes forty-eight hours [to recover], with her hands sore and swollen from shaking so many hands, thousands of hands, but she had this strength. She was determined to do what she wanted to be accessible. She wanted to be a people person.

By 1920, the number of actual voters jumped from something like eighteen million to twenty-five million because women were voting [for the first time nationally]. This was a really significant shift. It's also very important in the election because Florence becomes someone who was very much attuned.... She was very interested in women's involvement in politics.

Florence listens closely to many who come to the White House, and the vote itself is a moment of real triumph for her. She was there for the front porch [campaigning], and she travels about twenty thousand miles with him in the fall after they leave the front porch. She's reaching out. There are a number of problems they face during the campaign, some of the scandals, but she is very much excited about women's possibilities.

PIETRUSZA: [The big issue for women in elections] is always the economy, and the economy is very bad in 1920. There is tremendous unemployment. There is inflation and there are strikes ravaging the country. The country is a mess economically. There's all this dislocation of veterans coming back [from World War I] and causing all sorts of problems. Also, the League of Nations is the big issue that year for everyone. If you don't want another war, you don't want America to be dragged into things. The Harding who is the most vociferous against the League of Nations was not Warren; it is Florence. Florence is really the hard-liner there.

Prohibition had just passed. It was going into effect. Harding had voted for it without any great enthusiasm. He would take a drink or so, but as Edmund Starling of the White House Secret Service said, he'd take one shot and that would be it for the night. He was not a heavy drinker despite some reports. It is the temperance movement of the women which largely puts Prohibition in. They see the men getting their paycheck on a Friday night and blowing it in the saloons, leaving them hungry.... The saloon was established as an evil place.

SIBLEY: Reporters really gravitated to Florence.... They were very popular in the White House, in part because they could deal so well with the press. During the campaign, the press was used extensively. They were very media savvy, the Hardings. They were also close to this fellow, Albert Lasker, who sold Van Camp Pork and Beans, and were able to use [his marketing savvy] to sell their campaign. They shared pictures of themselves with the public. They had recordings made of themselves, and all of that played very well with the press as well.

[They also brought Hollywood into their campaign.] The Gish sisters came to their front porch as did singer Al Jolson. It's interesting today to think about a Republican candidate with all this support from Hollywood...but at that time, the Hardings were very popular in Hollywood. The Hardings loved the movies. They showed movies in the White House extensively. This was something that they really, really gravitated to, the Hollywood crowd and that kind of celebrity culture....

She was certainly the first first lady to use photography in [photo ops].... She liked to do this. She also had this very photogenic dog called Laddie Boy, and he was featured regularly. Part of her whole interest in animals and animal rights was put forward by these photo ops with Laddie Boy....

PIETRUSZA: The Hardings had quite the zoo, but Laddie Boy was particularly popular. There's a famous picture of Florence shaking hands with Laddie Boy, but even before that, she's the first candidate's wife to go to a convention and [actively] campaign for her husband and to be accessible to the press. She's not just there as an ornament; she's very effective.

Warren and Florence Harding at their home in Marion, Ohio in 1920, site of the famous "front porch" campaign.

SIBLEY: [The Wilson Administration had closed the White House lawn during the war and had sheep grazing there. The Hardings opened the lawn back up to the public.] It was so positive. In fact, the public already knew this was going to happen; they had heard about this during the campaign. People were excited; they said, "Speed the day when Florence comes into office," and Warren, too, of course. This is going to open things up.

Even *The New York Times* talked about how there would be "four shoulders" coming into office. There was a sense that they would be sharing the burden, and this opening of the White House was an absolutely refreshing moment. People now could come onto the lawn.

PIETRUSZA: There's a story about those sheep: Florence is walking by the White House when Warren is still a senator and Wilson is in the White House. She sees the sheep grazing, and the police are guarding the sheep, shooing the people away from the White House. She gets nervous and trips and falls into the mud. She is tremendously embarrassed by this, and says, "I tell you, if I ever run this place, the policemen will have better things [to do] than guarding sheep on the damn lawn."

SIBLEY: [They also reinstated the White House Easter Egg Roll,] one of the biggest days for visitors. They had the Shriners visit;...all kinds of people came. At one point, just before their trip to Alaska in 1923, seven thousand people were in the White House. They were wandering the floors. This is how open they were and how accessible. [Because of the Hardings' illnesses,] this was probably not that healthy for them; not just the germs, but the exhaustion of greeting people and seeing them all the time, but they made themselves wide open. They had concerts on the lawn. They had visitors coming constantly. Harding was a kindly and dear man. He felt there was no reason why he shouldn't be accessible to people.

PIETRUSZA: One of the people who was a very popular visitor was Evelyn Walsh McLean, who was a very wealthy heiress, [owner of] the Hope Diamond. Florence got very ill in September of 1922, so from then until March, the visits really stopped. Very few people came, and the White House was a silent place, a difficult place. But she recovered, and one of the reasons she recovered was because...the whole country prayed for her. There were hundreds of people who went to Keith's Theater and had this mass praying for her to get better. Across the country there were many groups who did this independently. Finally, she's just at death's door and the famous Dr. Charles Mayo is set to come [tend to her]. Movie cameras are there to watch him come in. Evelyn McLean [is already there] to cheer Florence up and that seems to have really turned the corner for her, her dear friend, this much younger woman. She was twenty-nine; Florence is fifty-five. Both of them didn't have the greatest health, but they had a real bond, and Evelyn certainly added some pizzazz to the White House.

SIBLEY: Veterans' issues were very much of a passion and interest for Florence. Before the war, she'd been involved with some of the other Senate wives on various things to help out soldiers.... but because of her kidney ailment, this made her particularly sensitive to the suffering of veterans after the war. There were many people going around in wheelchairs, with limbs missing. She would invite them to the White House. If she saw some veterans walking along the street, hobbling, she would stop her car and make sure they had a ride. She would go to the hospitals. This was very close to her heart, and she was particularly disheartened when it was discovered that there was a scandal in the Veterans Bureau, another new initiative of Harding's. He created a Veterans Bureau for the needs of the returning veterans. Unfortunately, the man he chose, Charles Forbes, turned out to be a real crook. Forbes stole many of the goods that were supposed to go to the veterans' hospital supplies. He sold them cheaply and made money from kickbacks. It was a real scandal.

PIETRUSZA: Forbes was a Wilson appointee running Pearl Harbor in Hawaii. The Hardings ran across him in one of the trips and he flattered Florence shamelessly. She was the person who said, "Warren, you should appoint this Forbes fellow." Her other great friend, Dr. Charles Sawyer, took an immediate dislike to Forbes, always hated him…. When you talk about the Harding scandals—Teapot Dome or whatever [Attorney General Harry] Daugherty or Jeff Smith did in the Justice Department—the great shame of the administration is what they did to the veterans.

SIBLEY: When Florence found out [about this scandal], then she was even more forceful than Harding. He was always a little reluctant to turn hard heart on his old friends, but in the end, he did have to accept the resignation of Forbes.

PIETRUSZA: [The Harding presidency was beset by scandals, but] I don't think Harding is corrupt at all. That's a canard…. There are the bad appointments, but there are scandals under Truman with mink coats and deep freezes. There is Sherman Adams under Dwight Eisenhower. There are scandals under Lyndon Johnson. There are scandals of a much more recent vintage. They are not necessarily connected to the man in charge. They are unfortunate but they do not prove [those presidents'] corruption, and it's unfair to tar them, certainly in Harding's case. I would criticize him for not being as vigilant with Forbes, and that he should not have allowed him to flee the country. Eventually, Forbes goes to jail after Harding is dead.

SIBLEY: [In the summer of 1923, the Hardings took a fifteen thousand mile trip to Alaska.] It had long been a goal of the administration.

There have been suggestions that somehow this was to escape the scandals, but they had wanted to go and they gave it a grand name, the "Voyage of Understanding." They were going to go all the way to Alaska, and then they were going to come down through the Panama Canal, which had been a wonderful place they had enjoyed right after the election as a vacation visit.

This trip was aimed to create a greater connection between the American people and Alaska. Unfortunately, it was the trip that would be the end of Harding's life. What happened on the trip is that he gives many, many speeches. He is welcomed around the country, but it turns out that San Francisco, which he had planned to visit and [where he had planned to] give more speeches, is the place where he dies, at the Palace Hotel.

His health was already not so strong, but…Florence's health was so dire that on this trip, in the ship they took, there was a coffin packed secretly…for her. Her dear doctor, Dr. Joel Boone, as well as Dr. Sawyer, were aware of this. The fear was that she wouldn't survive the trip. Well, she did survive the trip and…then, Harding gets sick. The thought is it was the crab meat that he ate in Alaska, but it turns out, no. Everybody else who had had that crab meat recovered from whatever that was, and he did not. In fact, he gets sicker. He recovers, and then slowly gets sicker again. In the end, he dies of what at the time they thought was apoplexys. Some have alluded to poisoning, but it seems he simply had a heart attack. It was a very sad moment for Florence because she loved him dearly despite their difficult history.

She called to Dr. Boone when he died. Boone had just stepped out. He finally was getting a breath of fresh air downstairs because they had been there for days in the hotel. She called for him, but it was too late when she called.

[Florence practiced] self-mastery of her emotions. She kept saying, "I will not break down," and she kept her emotions in check. All around her, Daugherty and others are in tears and falling apart, but understandably, she would not. She knew she had to organize a little ceremony in San Francisco, and then this huge ceremony, including a visit to the Capitol rotunda, with thousands seeing the body in Washington. And then there was another ceremony in Ohio. There was also a ninety-six-hour trip across the country, which took even longer than they expected.

PIETRUSZA: The trip back is remarkable, because his body has to go all the way across country, and then has to go out again to Marion, Ohio. The scenes, which people write about, are of crowds gathering silently in the middle of the night, in remote areas, breaking into songs and hymns. God knows how many people saw him pass through. The feelings were quite genuine.

SIBLEY: There were a number of rumors circulating [about his death, some suggesting that Florence had poisoned the president].

PIETRUSZA: [Florence Harding contributed to these rumors because of her] burning their papers under the circumstances of his death and the scandals. She burns a lot of stuff at the McLean mansion. It appears that she burned…an unopened suitcase of Harding's. We really don't know. Were there letters between the two of them [that she burned] because they wanted some privacy? T.R.'s widow burned a lot of his papers—any conspiracy there, or the desire for privacy?

SIBLEY: Warren Harding was buried in Marion, Ohio. Twice. First, he had to be exhumed and reburied in a beautiful mausoleum.

If Florence had stayed in Washington, she might have lived longer. She got her nephritis again in July 1924. She had just come back to D.C., and she was beginning somewhat of a second act of life…. Unfortunately, she got sick again and Dr. Sawyer encouraged her to come back to Ohio. At that point, she just gave up….

PIETRUSZA: Warren's life was her life, and that was gone, and her kidneys were gone, too. [She died on November of 21, 1924, in Marion, Ohio at age sixty-four. They were the only president and first lady to die before what would have been the end of their first term in office.]

Florence Harding's legacy:

SIBLEY: Florence…has been even worse treated by history, yet there's more to her now than we probably have ever known. She belongs in the top ten. She was a transitional first lady. She made the cracks in the mold that Eleanor Roosevelt broke. She had causes for the first time, many causes, that people embraced. She created this culture of celebrity that's still attached to the first lady today. She was a caring, kind person who really wanted to make the world better for the underprivileged, prisoners, women, and minorities. I hope people will look into her further.

PIETRUSZA: She's a transitional figure because the times were changing so rapidly then. So, part of it is just a function of the times, but she's also a forward-looking person.

In terms of setting precedents, [or] opening up the...office of the first lady, she'd have to rate very high on visibility. In terms of reopening the White House to the public, that's very significant, but we've seen it close down since then.

Grace Goodhue Coolidge

"This was I and yet, not I. This was the wife of the president of the United States and she took precedence over me. My personal likes and dislikes must be subordinated to the consideration of those things which were required of her."

Grace Coolidge, c1924

Born: January 3, 1879, Burlington, Vermont
Married: October 4, 1905, to Calvin Coolidge (1872–1933)
Children: John (1906–2000); Calvin, Jr. (1908–24)
Died: July 8, 1957, Northampton, Massachusetts

Contributors:

CYNDY BITTINGER, writer and Vermont historian; former executive director, Calvin Coolidge Memorial Foundation, Plymouth, Vermont

AMITY SHLAES, board chair, Calvin Coolidge Presidential Foundation; author of several books, including *Coolidge* and *The Forgotten Man*

AMITY SHLAES: [Calvin Coolidge became president upon the sudden death of President Warren Harding. Coolidge was] quite prepared because he'd been a politician all his life. President Coolidge was one of those men who started small in city council, was a city solicitor in Massachusetts where the Coolidges lived, and went all the way up the ladder of the state of Massachusetts, and then to vice president. One could never be prepared for a shock like the death of a president, but he was quite prepared professionally.

Grace Coolidge didn't think she was [prepared for the responsibilities of the White House]. She wrote to her sorority sisters and said,

"Pray for me, friends." But she was ready, too, because she had been a politician's wife, and she had quite a realistic view of politics and that particular job. She called this kind of marriage "a double harness...." [meaning she] had pulled her load along with the president even when they were local politicians.... It was clear even when they were courting that Calvin, her future husband, was ambitious in politics, and that was part of her deal in the marriage.

CYNDY BITTINGER: It was sudden, but she had been second lady for a little while...and she got to know the personages in Washington, D.C., so that was very good.

She was to set the tone in that she was very joyous, very vivacious. Some people said she was the fun one, she was the front door greeter; whereas, her husband was the thoughtful one behind her. It's an interesting dynamic, because we often don't see that with first ladies and presidents.

SHLAES: The famous thing that Harding did was invite his vice president, Calvin Coolidge, to sit in on the cabinet. Vice presidents hadn't always done that, so that was...very useful for Coolidge. He never did hear all of the dirty details of the Harding Administration, but he had heard some. Being the president of the Senate, he got to know the Senate, which he recalled as quite an experience.

Between the two ladies, it was a little bit rougher. Mrs. Harding was much older. She was a bit envious of young Grace Coolidge, who had a beautiful complexion, and that was much treasured in that time, and still had the bloom of youth upon her....Mrs. Harding could be snippy with Grace. We have some letters that suggest she was indeed thinking about the next election, and maybe Coolidge wouldn't be the [vice presidential] candidate the next time.

The Harding marriage was more like a business.... In the Coolidge case...Grace was deferential in public, and in private, maybe there were some fireworks. In public, she didn't talk about politics. Her husband didn't want her to talk about politics. He kept her in quite the proscribed area. One time Mrs. Coolidge tried on a riding habit and went riding. She looked very good in the riding habit; he said he didn't want her to do that: "I advise you not to try anything new while we're in the presidency." So, Mrs. Coolidge in some ways was a very old-fashioned wife, but it is complicated.

BITTINGER: [Grace Goodhue and Calvin Coolidge met in Massachusetts.] She's the urban one. She's from Burlington, Vermont; he's from little, rural Plymouth. They were quite different in that respect. She found him engaging and thoughtful, and he found her beautiful, but he didn't quite know how to romance her. He asked one of his friends, who happened to be the shoemaker in town, what to say to Grace. The shoemaker said, "Just compliment her. Tell her that her dresses are beautiful. Do that kind of thing." Grace saved the letters that Calvin wrote to her. Even though they were neighbors, he wrote her letters, and they were very affectionate letters between them.

Lemira, [Grace's mother,] adored her only child, and thought that after Grace had graduated from the University of Vermont, she would stay in the Burlington area. Grace had a mind of her own and had met deaf children through the Yale family, who were neighbors. She said, "I'd like to teach at the Clarke School for the Deaf. I'm moving to Northampton." Lemira said, "Oh, that's a woman's town. That's the home of Smith College, and most of the men are married, so it will be all right." Lemira could still look for a husband for Grace....Grace, with a mind of her own, finds Calvin; Calvin finds Grace, and the rest is history. Lemira didn't get what she really wanted. On their wedding day, Lemira has a headache....

The couple met in 1903, and they married in October of 1905.

SHLAES: [They were married at Grace's parents' home] and a bit earlier than her mother would have liked, and with some trepidation, writing her friends that she was going off into this adventure, but they were quite determined. This was a modern thing; they chose one another. She had been to college. She had been to a co-ed college. She had a trade. She taught the deaf. It was a very modern marriage compared to many of the preceding presidencies.

BITTINGER: When they get married, Calvin delivers to Grace fifty-two pairs of socks to be darned. Grace says, "Did you marry me to darn socks?" He said, "No, but it comes in pretty handy." And she started doing it. It was okay. They did kid each other quite a bit. She adjusted to some of his personality. He was a little tough when he was writing speeches, and she said she was his safety valve. She would listen to him and be positive when he was doing something like that.

He was interested in clothing for both of them, right from the beginning. He even wrote his father to get funding for their clothes because he wanted to look good. This was part of their image as a couple. It's fascinating. Frank Waterman Stearns, his backer, owned the Stearns Department Store in Boston. I have a feeling that Frank Stearns was able to get some discounts on some of this clothing so that Grace could wear it. That could have been part of it. Calvin would go window-shopping as president, and he would buy a hat and bring it back for Grace to wear. He was very interested in what she wore.

SHLAES: If she didn't like it, she didn't always say. She saw how important it was to him, but she certainly enjoyed the clothing. And that was something they could do together, wasn't it? She enjoyed how lavishly he attended to her. This was one of the happy parts to their marriage, and she was so beautiful. That's what we forget, how beautiful she was. She became a great and important symbol for Americans—her joy, her beauty, all of that.

BITTINGER: Howard Chandler Christy is [the painter of Grace's official portrait.] He was having Grace pose, and said, "I really like this because of this contrast between her red dress and the white dog." Calvin came by, and he said, "Oh, I like Grace much better in her white dress. I think we should just have her wear her white dress and dye the dog red." There was that kind of joking [between them].

That painting is also important because the Pi Beta Phis gave it to the White House, and they came thirteen hundred strong. It was the biggest gathering of women at the White House up until that time. She was a…sorority sister. She had started the Pi Phis at the University of Vermont and then always stayed interested and involved, and was appointed to higher and higher offices there. She had to recede once they reached the national office, but she always loved her sisters. In 1915, she started round-robin letters with her sisters. That means writing letters to them, and they write letters to her, and pass this around. The

Pi Phi's were very important for us, the historians, because we have those letters to read.

SHLAES: Grace was very good [for American businesses,] to have a first lady like this. She didn't speak much in public, so everyone loved her. She never said anything you wouldn't like because she didn't talk very much.... She absolutely was [a master at the photo op]. He played the silent one and she played the big volume. Some of this is theater, and in marriage, we trade off roles, don't we? They had their act down, that's what we could say.

She wanted to dance. She took dancing lessons in Washington. But Coolidge wouldn't have liked that. He didn't want her to have short skirts.... He didn't like her to wear pants. Grace didn't wear pants until after Calvin passed away. He didn't really like the idea of bobbing hair. She didn't bob her hair until after the presidency, either.

BITTINGER: She did have music, though, wonderful music at the White House. It was more traditional, such as [pianist] Sergei Rachmaninoff. She loved to showcase people at the White House who were very talented, but it wasn't jazz. That was going a little too far. So, we're in this transition time period where some people feel this couple was quite traditional as the nation was becoming very wild in some ways. The Coolidges believed in Prohibition, too.

SHLAES: People came through by the thousands [to meet them]. So, when Calvin did Grace a favor, it was that he would shake hands so she didn't have to. She might stay out of a reception, but more often, she had to be there, or she had to entertain. The very physical obligations [of the office] were hard to endure. At one point, she did become ill later in the presidency. You can see how much they had to do just in terms of pure reception. This idea of the White House as the democratic place, that meant that people came in; the Hardings had set that precedent.

BITTINGER: Presidents are the head of state; we don't have royalty here, but they are somewhat our royalty, and that's what...all of this adulation by the public [is about]. When they would travel, people swarmed them. She brought a little more discipline into the role of first lady, though. She had two secretaries instead of one. Florence Harding let people come any old time to the White House. Grace said, "No. I think you should meet me at noon on the steps or at three o'clock for the reception." She was a little bit more organized about these things.

People forget that they had the *Mayflower* yacht. That was their Camp David...a place they could go and be themselves. The military ran it, and the public really didn't know a lot about what was going on there, even though, of course, it was all very upright. Still, it was a time out for them, a little bit.

SHLAES: Each place they escaped to, they found was often no escape, because of the crowds. [At Coolidge's hometown of] Plymouth Notch, especially, people camped out, shopped, and the neighbors created a tea house. Coolidge wasn't sure people should exploit the presidency in that way, but he wanted his neighbors to do well. There was always this ambivalence, so they began to go on summer retreats...in Swampscott, Massachusetts one year, in a house called White Court. They went to the Adirondacks, or they went to South Dakota, or they went to Wisconsin where they could have distance.

BITTINGER: [There were rumors of Grace having an affair with Jim Haley, a Secret Service agent.] It was in the Black Hills when they were there for the summer White House. She and the agent were lost for a few hours. When they returned, Calvin was not happy mainly because he thought she had been hurt. A Secret Service agent is supposed to be taking care of the first lady and making sure she's not hurt, so he sent Agent Haley back to Washington, D.C. Grace tried to explain that no, nothing had happened. She was okay. She hadn't fallen down. It was all right. They had just been lost. That was all that happened.

I say there is nothing to this. She kept up letters, communication with his family. She felt embarrassed about the whole thing. This was very much in the public. There was no affair. It's just that a few people thought that Jim Haley was handsome [so there must have been] an affair.

The Coolidges just loved their animals. Grace typed [a list] of her animals and their nicknames, and who they were. The best story is Rebecca Raccoon, who was sent to the Coolidges for Thanksgiving dinner. The Coolidges, being animal lovers, were outraged at this and decided to raise Rebecca at the White House. This is the only time that the staff was not terribly happy, because Rebecca was sitting in the bath of the first lady's room, throwing the soap up, climbing the curtains. It wasn't the best for the staff, but Grace just loved Rebecca. She even sent Rebecca out to the Black Hills to play with her. It was quite something. But Rebecca got rambunctious; it was a bit too much… even though Grace designed a house for Rebecca on the grounds, so she eventually was taken to the zoo.

SHLAES: This was the president of savings and economy…. You can find the tension over the spending on food in the Coolidge White House. There was a housekeeper, and Coolidge didn't like the way she spent. She went to the specialty stores. He thought she should go to the Piggly Wiggly and save. Soon, she was gone and they brought in a New England lady, Ellen Riley. Miss Riley kept a record of every penny that was spent, and indeed, she spent less. Grace had to be the wife in all of this, had to appear to save with all these social demands. What tension that must have caused for her.

BITTINGER: This is a couple that did have to pay for everybody's food, but they had a diplomatic budget. They have an entertaining budget. Some historians said they entertained more than many presidential couples because they had this separate budget. Remember, this is a very middle class couple coming into the presidency and the first ladyship. They don't have their own wealth, as we've seen with others.

SHLAES: It was said Grace was rabid [about] baseball. She loved baseball even more than the president did. She loved that it lifted him up. I noticed when I was writing about some of his great battles, say over taxes or fiscal problems or vetoing that he had to do, Grace would take him to a baseball game. That's what they did in Washington, and later, when she was alone, she went to baseball with her friends in Boston herself. She was a Red Sox fan.

BITTINGER: [The Coolidges had two sons.] They were teenagers. When Calvin was vice president, they were still at home in Northampton, and that was difficult. Grace and Calvin conferred with Admiral Boone, who was the assistant White House physician, and some others, and decided that the boys should go to Mercersburg Academy in

Mercersburg, Pennsylvania. That would only be a couple of hours from the White House, and maybe she could see them a little bit.

John was born in 1906; Calvin, 1908, so they were fairly close together. She felt she really raised them, because Calvin commuted to the general court in Massachusetts, which was in Boston. She's the one who put out the toy train tracks. She's the one who built the little roadsters. She's the one who played with the boys, and their father came home on weekends....

The boys loved tennis, and...the White House had tennis courts. The boys played on the tennis courts. One day, Calvin, Jr. went out without any socks and got a blister on his toe. Nothing much was made of this, but when Admiral Boone, arrived one day to play tennis again, he noticed that Calvin, Jr. was quite ill and had a fever. He did look him over and found that there were streaks of red on his leg, so Admiral Boone was alerted right away to do something about this. He called in military physicians, and he called in civilian physicians. The family knew this was quite serious. They took samples and found out it was first staph, and then it was septicemia. Even today, you can die of septicemia. This went so quickly. Calvin and Grace were shocked that anyone could lose a son this way, so innocently and yet so fast.

SHLAES: They were not the only ones in this period who lose a son. It was a much more common event—Charles Dawes, the vice president, lost a son. T.R. lost a son in World War I. All around them were people who had been through this singular experience that no parent would wish for. Lincoln had lost a son, and there are echoes of Lincoln in the way this was handled. The carts rolled in with flowers. They set up stations in the White House. People came to call. Then the train took the sad cargo to Vermont where Calvin, Jr. was buried. It was new and horrible and yet very familiar, a very American event.

Coolidge pursued his policy plans as the president; he did good things, notwithstanding the loss of his son. [He was] more joyless, as he notes in his autobiography, but still with that perseverance. Coolidge did not give up, and Grace did not give up.

BITTINGER: The difference between the two is interesting, though. When there were holidays, Calvin would know who wasn't at the

A year after they took office, tragedy struck President and Mrs. Coolidge when their son Calvin Jr. died at age 16 of an infection.

table; Grace took joy with whoever was at the table. They just were very different in the way they handled it.

SHLAES: Hollywood celebrities…were brought around at various points to show [that] the Coolidges were jolly, and they had this elaborate friendship with Will Rogers who was a superstar…. He had columns, he did acts, he had movies, and he was very funny. He called Mrs. Coolidge his favorite first female. They had a whole courtship going, the Rogerses and the Coolidges. There was also Charles Lindbergh, the flier who had become a celebrity by going over to Paris; they hosted the Lindberghs at the house on DuPont Circle while they were out of the White House.

BITTINGER: Helen Keller wanted to use the White House to publicize the need for support for deaf education, and Grace and Calvin were both happy to accommodate her. Grace did as much as she could to bring deaf children, children with disabilities, veterans with disabilities to the White House and highlight their needs for the American public.

She was very involved [in renovating the White House]. We always think of Jackie Kennedy as the first one to want antiques at the White House…. Grace got to the White House and said, "I'd like to have a committee; I'd like to have Congress allow gifts to be given to the White House." That did go through, and she then was able to accept gifts. She went through the attic trying to find colonial antiques. Her committee got a little ahead of itself, though, and the American Institute of Architects got a little upset at them. At one point when they're off at one of the summer White Houses, Calvin says, "We've really got to stop. We can't pursue this attempt to change the Green Room and the Red Room." She drops that, but she's really one of the first ladies to say the White House is a museum, and we must honor it.

SHLAES: [Coolidge's legislative proposals] took enormous political capital to get through, and each one of them was hard for Calvin. When you look at their marriage and his view of scandal, the reason that he avoided scandal, and indeed, any controversy, right down to her wearing a riding habit or redecorating the White House too loudly, was because he wanted that capital to pass laws…. You feel like redecorating the house, but maybe you shouldn't because it attracts too much attention, and then you might have one fewer vote for this or that. It was quite cold, but also quite a concentrated and focused presidency in that way.

In the summer of '27, [he announced his intention not to seek reelection]. He happened to be near Mount Rushmore. Coolidge was a man who was concerned about having his head turned by power; …the presidency makes narcissists…. And there he was at Mount Rushmore, with its big heads coming, they weren't sculpted yet, of giant presidents, and he was grossed out by it. He said, "That's not the kind of presidency I want to have or be remembered for. Therefore, I will not run again, though I might."

BITTINGER: Grace did know about it in advance. I found the letters to her girlfriends, and she told them in March, "I'm getting ready; I will soon be [back riding] on the trolley. I won't have these cars." She did know about it, and she kidded around about how pleased she was…. However, when he announced it that day, she acted as if she didn't know. Maybe it was, once again, "I've got to stay out of public policy. I don't want to comment."

SHLAES: They returned to Northampton, Massachusetts, where Coolidge had begun his career as a county seat attorney. They went back to their house on Massasoit Street, which is half of a two-family with not much distance to the sidewalk. Of course, people did come up, and as much as they wanted to "fit back into their old clothes," which was the metaphor Grace used, they couldn't....

Eventually they retreated to a house with a bit of a border around it, the Beeches, also in Northampton. The president said, "Well, the doggies can run here." It was also a bit more fenced. They could have some privacy; still quite modest by presidential standards. After the president passed away, Mrs. Coolidge built yet another house somewhere nearby.

One of the stories that is a background for understanding them is the story of great love.... Coolidge had to raise money for his library, for his papers, and he did get his friends, led by Clarence Barron of the *Wall Street Journal,* to raise $2 million.... In the end, he gave all of the money from his friends to his wife's favorite charity, the Clarke School for the Deaf.

[He did it] because he was giving back. After all she had given to him, Coolidge wanted to give back to Grace, and therefore, there was no great monument for the Coolidge papers; there was only her charity. He knew he would pass, and he knew that it would be wonderful if after he died, his wife could be the most important lady in the town and lead the charity that meant something to them both. The Clarke School was where she had begun her career so many years ago. You can't think of a greater act of love than that. You have to juxtapose this action with his statements that sound un-modern to our ears, and decide what you make of this marriage. We find it quite wonderful and intriguing.

BITTINGER: It wasn't very long [after their move that Calvin Coolidge died]. It was January of 1933. In his retirement, he did write his daily articles. He turned to Grace and said, "I think you could write, too." She started writing some articles for *American Magazine,* and those are very important to those of us who study the first ladies because she does tell about her life. He seems to feel strongly about what's happening in the nation, but his friends say he's not good at figuring out his own medical problems. He denies medical treatment. One day, he goes up to shave. Grace goes out and walks back and, just by happenstance, goes upstairs and finds him, and he has died.

When Calvin died, she asked about fifty friends to write up their views of Calvin Coolidge, and that softened his image quite a bit. She contributed the last love letter that he wrote to her, which was just before he died. So she did somewhat manipulate his image a little bit at the end.

SHLAES: Grace didn't have to [accept the contemporary analysis that Coolidge's policies deepened the Depression]. That was her license, because she'd never been political and that's the great liberty of not being political. She did charity work throughout the 1930s. It was a terrible time, but she didn't have the burden of it having been her policy.

Crashes came all the time. Coolidge had six or seven serious crashes in his career, when the market went down more than 20 percent, but they never led to a decade of double-digit unemployment. It's not the crash so much as the depth of the unemployment and the duration of it that makes the Depression great in our memory. He was bewildered by it, and also by the policy applied to it. She was bewildered as well.

BITTINGER: Grace Coolidge lived until 1957. In the run-up to World War II, she was a champion of the Jewish children in Germany. She was part of a Northampton committee, and she wanted to rescue children, and she proposed that about twenty-five children come to the town. I wouldn't have been surprised if she wouldn't have taken a couple in herself. Her proposal was sent to the State Department; it was folded into the Wagner-Rogers Bill, which, in 1939, did not pass. She was rather brave with that stand and strong about America's participation. She urged Americans to get involved in World War II.

Grace Coolidge's legacy:

BITTINGER: We should remember her for treating the White House as a museum. She took her job very seriously. She thought she was the national hugger: she was to hug everybody, greet as many people as she could, keep the doors open for the public, so to speak, and also keep her husband and her children happy. It was very important to be a good wife and mother, provide a solid home life for them. That's what she saw as her role, and to be an advocate for people with disabilities.

SHLAES: [She should be remembered for] her great joy, that she could transcend any troubles through her faith and her joy.

Lou Henry Hoover

"I was incensed at much reading about the president's having no thought for the little man, but bending all his energies towards saving the bloated plutocrat. The absolute injustice and downright lying of these statements infuriated me."

Lou Hoover, c1928

Born: March 29, 1874, Waterloo, Iowa
Married: February 10, 1899, to Herbert Clark Hoover (1874–1964)
Children: Herbert Charles (1903–69); Allan Henry (1907–93)
Died: January 7, 1944, New York, New York

Contributors:

EMILY CHARNOCK, former fellow, presidential studies, the Miller Center, University of Virginia; 2015 Keasbey Research Fellow in American Studies at Selwyn College, University of Cambridge

ANNETTE DUNLAP, first ladies biographer; author of the forthcoming *Lou Henry Hoover: A Biography*

ANNETTE DUNLAP: This was a woman whose story has not been fully told. There are so many layers to her, so many different activities that she has been involved in, and a legacy that she's left for women, particularly, even to today, that I would like to see the rest of the public know about.

[Lou Henry was born in Waterloo, Iowa. Her father really wanted a boy,] so they say. And so the name, Lou, which is not short for Louise or any other type of genuinely female name, and he did pretty much raise her as what we would call a tomboy. One of the earliest pictures of her with her father is of the two of them fishing in a stream. [There are photos of] her carrying a rifle and sitting on top of a burro. A lot of her diary talks about her joy at being able to hunt, fish, and be outdoors.

She stayed somebody who was totally fascinated with the outdoors through her entire life. Obviously, her decision to study geology at Stanford University was an outgrowth of that.

Her father was in banking, and he started out as a clerk at a bank in Waterloo....[Banks] went up and down with the economy and with farm economies, so her father, Charles, was looking for other opportunities. He was given the opportunity to come and start a bank in Whittier, California. At the time that they moved, which was in 1887, they were building a brand-new community. It had been founded by the Quakers, but they said they were open to any fair-minded people of any religion.

[Lou's choice of geology as her field of study at Stanford] was very unusual. We aren't 100 percent sure, but we think she may have been the first woman in the entire country to get a degree in geology. The male students went out on field trips and she was not allowed to go, because she was a woman. Knowing how much she loved the outdoors and some of the field trips she had taken when she was at normal school, the teacher training school she went to before Stanford, I can imagine how upset she was.

[Lou met Herbert Hoover at Stanford.] ...Herbert was a senior at the time that Lou started, even though, interestingly enough, Lou is six months older. They were both born in 1874, but he was born in August, she was born in March. He was what we would call a lab assistant in the lab of Dr. John Banner. Dr. Banner had delivered a lecture on geology that had inspired Lou to go ahead and apply to Stanford and study there.

Bert Hoover took an instant liking to her. He writes about her whimsical smile, her laughing blue eyes, what an intelligent and delightful young woman she was. The part that I find so totally humorous is that he says, "And I believe that she needed some assistance."

Obviously, there was a strong connection and a strong interest. His jobs took him to Nevada, and then to Australia. He was working in Australia and they were continuing to communicate. Then he was offered a position in China, and he sent her a telegram. The telegram went through the post office, and the post office saw these names, Lou and Bert. It wasn't really a formal proposal. It just said, "Heading to China, will you join me?" and so, the postmaster posted it on the bulletin board for everybody to see. It was an invasion of privacy, to be sure.

One day after they got married, February 11, 1899, they were headed off to China on a steamer. They spent a couple of days in Japan, and then [in China,] and they were there when the Boxer Rebellion occurred. Their lives were threatened. They were under siege. They had barricades, and Lou went out and manned the barricades. She was out there when the weaponry was drawn. She was involved with the Red Cross, getting supplies to aid people. She was sitting in her house one day when a bullet came straight through the front door. She pulled out a deck of cards and started playing solitaire and didn't even miss a beat. It didn't faze her. She also wrote a letter to…friends, and said, "You have missed the most exciting summer. You should have been here."

Their stays…in a lot of different countries influenced them. One of the things that they were very interested in when they got to the White House was looking for ways to help us keep our freedom. They saw what it was like to be in countries where freedom had been taken from people. They had been in China during the Boxer Rebellion, they were in Europe during the outbreak of World War I, they had lived in countries where people's freedoms had been curtailed. As Americans, being taught the importance of individual freedom, and then being in countries where they saw people not enjoying that same freedom of choice, they realized that this was something that was very important. Also, this [philosophy] enabled the Hoovers to acquire quite a bit of wealth and be very successful in their chosen fields. They were multimillionaires by 1914.

EMILY CHARNOCK: [After serving in the Harding and Coolidge cabinets, Herbert Hoover was the Republicans' choice for president in

1928.] The American economy has been growing in leaps and bounds through the 1920s. Herbert Hoover had been this incredibly prominent secretary of commerce; the verb to "Hooverize" has come into the language; and, there's a lot of hope and a lot of expectation surrounding Hoover. He is the great humanitarian. He is the great engineer. He is able to get the nomination in 1928 partly from the reputation that he's built up through his service in World War I and as secretary of commerce, but then also, the incredible relief effort that he managed in 1927 with the Great Mississippi Flood.

DUNLAP: Lou Hoover was extremely involved [in the 1928 campaign]; she went with him on all of the campaign appearances. She was very visible. Part of the press that was out at the time in conjunction with Al Smith being the Democratic nominee was that his wife, Katie Smith, was from the Lower East Side of New York. There were comparisons of this woman who really wasn't that knowledgeable or that sophisticated... against a Lou Henry Hoover who's a graduate of Stanford and who's traveled the world.... Lou had also already gained national prominence on her own from some of her other activities, as well.

CHARNOCK: It was a landslide. Hoover wins almost 60 percent of the vote. He wins an enormous proportion of the Electoral College.... Herbert Hoover, in a way, is a beneficiary of a divide that happens on the Democratic side, where Al Smith is essentially opposed from within because of his Catholicism and partly on concerns about his position on Prohibition. Hoover escapes an internal battle, and it shows at the polls.

When Lou Hoover came into office, it was with the same expectations and the same enthusiasm that greeted Bert's coming into office. A lot was expected of this couple. Lou had been involved nationally with the Girl Scouts. She had been involved with the National Athletic Amateur Federation, the women's division. She had chaired a conference on women in law enforcement back in 1924 to try to get equal enforcement of the Prohibition laws. She was very well-known.

One of the things that she did early on [suggests] she was unorthodox in some ways. ...She inherited Grace Coolidge's social secretary, but the two did not get along. Mary Randolph, who was the social secretary, wanted Lou to learn how to do things the Washington society way, and that wasn't exactly how Lou wanted to do things. Those two parted company after the end of one year, and Lou did not hire another social secretary. She did introduce a lot of changes, and she, indeed, was very unorthodox, and it told over time.

In terms of their White House functions, they respected Prohibition. Hoover had campaigned in 1928 on a law enforcement plank. He was officially in favor of Prohibition. Lou had chaired this committee in 1924 on law enforcement. I have heard certain rumors that on his way home from work, when he was secretary of commerce, Bert sometimes liked to stop by the Belgian embassy, which was obviously foreign territory, and maybe have a cocktail after the end of the day. They weren't teetotalers. Herbert Hoover had a Quaker background, which in some ways would have lent itself to a more pro-temperance stance, but they occasionally indulged themselves.

DUNLAP: It was very common for the first lady to have teas for the wives of the members of Congress...usually one tea where all of the wives came for one event, and then it was over. In the same year that Hoover was elected, 1928, Chicago elected an African American congressman by the name of Oscar De Priest. He was the first African American to get elected to Congress in twenty-eight years, and so the issue arose about what to do about inviting Mrs. De Priest to one of the teas.

Lou instructed her secretaries to start having communication with the political side, with Bert's secretaries, about how could this best be handled. One of the decisions that Lou made early on was...to break it into six teas where congressional wives were selected as a group. Some of what was going on behind the scenes was that particular wives who they thought might not be offended by having a tea with an African American woman, would be vetted during one of these teas, and their racial views sounded out.

On June 6, which is the day after the fifth tea, Lou sends a private invitation to Mrs. De Priest for a tea to be held on June 12. Mrs. De Priest comes. Congressman De Priest publicizes this and gets a lot of attention. Everything seems to be okay. And then, a week later, Representative De Priest hosts a musicale and tea as a fundraiser for the NAACP. All of a sudden, the Southern delegations and the Southern state legislatures realize that this is getting out of hand, and this is all because Mrs. Hoover has had an African American to the White House.

The entire summer you have censure in the state legislatures of several of the Southern states, but also a threat on the part of Southern members of Congress to censure Mrs. Hoover in the Congress. It becomes quite a brouhaha throughout that summer.

CHARNOCK: Hoover and Lou have to negotiate the aftereffects of this brouhaha, because it has really substantial political effects. Hoover does not necessarily have a solid base in Congress at this time. The Southern Democrats are outraged at him. There are what are known as lily-white Republican organizations in the South that are trying to become competitive by essentially respecting traditional race mores in those areas, and they're not very happy at what's happened. So, on the one hand, it was this very positive gesture that Lou and Herbert Hoover do; on the other hand, they don't necessarily build or maintain momentum beyond it.

This was part of a larger picture of difficulties that Herbert Hoover had with the Congress, both the Republican Congress...in 1928, and then, in 1930, when the Democrats actually win back the House, that's even more problematic from his standpoint. The problem is that Herbert Hoover is not a politician. He has risen to the heights of secretary of commerce, and then president, without ever having held elective office...so Hoover doesn't have this background in deal-making and dealing with politicians. He acts [as though he's] quite superior towards politicians. He says of one senator that he's the "only known person with a negative IQ." Hoover doesn't necessarily...do what he needs to do to make deals.

DUNLAP: Lou and Bert were basically two sides of the same coin. In the same way that Hoover was not a politician because he had always been a very effective administrator and an effective leader, Lou was the exact same way. She almost always started an organization or very quickly rose to the top of an organization, so she was always in some type of leadership role where negotiating was not necessarily a skill she had to develop. She was, in some respects, a little bit better able to pour oil on troubled waters than Bert was. She did try to help Bert by inviting people for dinners where they could have an exchange of ideas and perhaps get him to talk about some of the issues that were going on, but a lot of the time she was probably doing the same types of things that he was. When she got rid of her social secretary, and was no longer really engaged in that social side of Washington, that was an area that was shut down for them, as well.

CHARNOCK: [They were in office just eight months when the stock market crashed.] There were warnings that were probably more apparent in hindsight. There had been a stock market wobble just as they were coming into office in March.... There were certainly some bad economic signals in the air, but certainly nobody expected what happens on October 24, Black Thursday. The stock market just tumbles. It seems to regroup a little bit the next day. Hoover makes a statement that the basis of the American economy is sound. He's trying to build confidence and then, the following Tuesday, October 29, Black Tuesday, the stock market just crashes.

DUNLAP: [During the Depression,] Lou Hoover's big cause was volunteerism, getting people to pitch in and help, particularly people who were not severely impacted by the Depression. She used her youth organizations that she was involved in, the Girl Scouts and 4-H clubs. She encouraged Girl Scouts and members of 4-H who were in agricultural communities where...it had not really bottomed out, to get in there and to share, to provide for their neighbors, to see where there were needs, and to get involved in that way.

CHARNOCK: Hoover does try to do several things [to assist those affected by the Depression]. He tries to do it, though, in a complementary way to what Lou is doing, through volunteerism. He creates the President's Emergency Committee on Employment. He's trying to get together all of the agencies of the state and local governments and the Red Cross to try to coordinate information about unemployment, but also to coordinate relief efforts. He was trying to use the weight of the federal government in a non-coercive way to try and encourage voluntary organizations to get more involved....

DUNLAP: We have to realize that nobody ever expected the Great Depression to be as deep, severe, or as long-lasting as it was. The Hoovers had seen volunteerism be successful in the short term when they were involved with the commission for the relief of Belgium during World War I, during Hoover's time with the U.S. Food Administration, and asking people to have meatless Fridays and wheatless Mondays so that they would conserve food. Volunteerism had its limitations, but those limitations were really dictated more by what was going on with the economy and the fact that this was a much more serious problem than anybody could even understand at the time.

CHARNOCK: By 1932, you have over 20 percent unemployment. Everyone knows someone who has lost their job, is facing economic hardship, and there starts to be increasing protests, the Bonus March being the most prominent of them. These were veterans from World War I who, in 1924, had been promised a bonus as additional payment for their service in World War I that was going to mature in 1945.... What they wanted was a full payment of their bonus early.... They come to Washington; they camp out. There are over ten thousand of them. They're trying to push Congress to pass the full bonus, which the House does, but the Senate doesn't. Now, we have ten thousand people camped out in Washington, and they have effectively failed in their mission in Congress. What do we do with them?

Hoover makes a prophetic move, where he asks the Army to help disperse the Bonus Marchers, and this turns into an incredibly graphic, violent episode. General Douglas MacArthur essentially exceeds his orders and uses pretty violent means to make them move on. This is in the summer of 1932. There's an election in November....

This doesn't look good at all for Hoover. This does not look like he is really concerned for what, at that time, is the forgotten man.

DUNLAP: Probably the most difficult thing [about the Depression for Lou Hoover] is what she saw it do to Bert.... They had always been very close partners, but they were not as close in their partnership during these four years in the White House. Bert pulled into himself a little bit, wasn't as communicative as he had been, and it took a toll. One of the Hoover sons supposedly told one of his cousins many years later that he felt that his parents being in the White House for those four years was a mistake, because of the stress that it put on their relationship.

...Fairly early on, realizing that they needed to find a way to get out of Washington on a regular basis, the Hoovers located property in the Shenandoah Mountains [and built a retreat they called Camp Rapidan]. Lou designed a house and laid it out, and they went there as frequently as they could...with friends and sometimes with people from government. There was one report that $100,000 was spent on laying phone lines [for the president,] which was a pretty considerable sum of money in that time.

The Hoover School, or the President's Mountain School, was established by the Hoovers after they had encountered some of the local families that lived in the area where they built Camp Rapidan. They realized that these children had never attended public school, and so they went about with their own funds building the school, and then worked with the state of Virginia to hire a teacher. They actually interviewed the teacher. They contacted Berea College, in the Appalachian portion of Kentucky, which really does a good job of preparing people for working with communities such as this one.... That school stayed in place [for years] until the national park took over that area.

[This charitable act was not known by the public] because public relations was not the couple's strong suit. Bert's press secretary absolutely begged Bert to let the public know about his acts of charity, his acts of kindness, his reaching out and caring for youth.... In a lot of ways, what made them so wonderful also set the stage for them to have so much difficulty in the public perception of who they were.

CHARNOCK: Lou Hoover was the first first lady to make a national radio address. She was using it to try and push this volunteerist message, which is very much in keeping with what President Hoover was doing at that time.... In 1932, she comes up with a plan called the Rapidan Plan, after the camp where they formulated it. It's basically this effort to try and muster the resources of the Girl Scouts into a more coordinated, organized effort to help local and state relief agencies. She has an individual who helps her with that called Lillian Gilbreth, who, at the same time, is working with the president on an organization for unemployment relief.... Lou is complementing his policies.

DUNLAP: The Hoovers had two boys, Herbert, Jr., who was born in 1903, and Allan, who was born in 1907. They happened to have both been born in London, because this is where Bert was working at the time, and the Hoovers lived there. Both of them were extremely successful.

Their older son was diagnosed with tuberculosis in 1930 when he went for his physical for his annual time to serve in the reserves. Tuberculosis, at that time, was a very serious disease. It was not always cur-

In 1931, Lou Hoover used radio addresses to encourage more volunteerism to offset the suffering caused by the Great Depression.

able. This was, of course, pre-antibiotics. The Hoovers had Herbert, Jr., living in Camp Rapidan for the beginning of his convalescence until the winter season started to set in, and then they located a sanitarium in Asheville, North Carolina, for him to continue his convalescence.

During the year that Herbert, Jr., was convalescing, Lou invited her daughter-in-law and their children to live in the White House, so there were children running around the White House during that time. That wasn't necessarily successful in softening their image, because they didn't want the children photographed and they didn't want things written about them.

CHARNOCK: There was increased security after the Lindbergh baby kidnapping in order to protect the White House and whatever children might be in there at the various times. There's also an increased concern about assassination threats against Herbert Hoover himself, especially as protests about the scale of the Depression continue. Security is certainly a very important factor in the White House at this time and the Secret Service is very much vigilant.

At first, Hoover…was not necessarily committed to running for reelection [in 1932]. The idea of an incumbent president actively seeking reelection was considered maybe a little bit unseemly. Herbert Hoover has immense respect for the office that he holds, so he decides that he's going to make a couple of speeches, but he's going to be very dignified, very restrained. It becomes clear as the fall of 1932 progresses that he is in serious, serious trouble.... He then essentially embarks on what we would call a whistle-stop tour, crisscrossing the country, giving a number of addresses and radio addresses, and returns home to his home in Palo Alto to wait out the results. It's a landslide against him, bigger than the one that brought him into office only four years earlier. It is a very rapid turnaround for a man who had so many high hopes around him when he went in.

DUNLAP: Lou participated in just the same way she had in '28. She was with him on all of this whistle-stop tour.... There was disappointment [with their loss], but she basically says, "We are still here and we are moving on." It's one of those combinations of hurt at the way they've been treated when they've tried so hard, and a bit of relief that the responsibility is not going to be theirs much longer.

Returning to Palo Alto when they left the White House, Lou did use her personal funds to help build a cultural community, and particularly, a musical community there. The Hoover Institute came later, possibly after Lou passed away.

West Branch, Iowa, is where Bert was born, and Lou attempted to purchase the land and the home that he was born in, but the family who owned it at that time was not interested in selling. At some point, they were able to acquire that property, and it is now the Hoover Presidential Library with a restoration of the buildings from Bert's childhood. [It was dedicated in 1962, almost two decades after Lou Hoover died.]

Lou Hoover continued to be very physically active. She was still riding a horse and camping and sleeping on the ground in her late sixties. She had wanted to continue to live in Palo Alto, but Herbert had found that he enjoyed the intellectual stimulation of New York City, so they had this East Coast-West Coast kind of marriage until about 1940, when he convinced her to make her base with him in New York City. They lived in an apartment in the Waldorf Astoria.

She had gone out to dinner with a friend in January of 1944, and she started to say, "Let's walk back, it's such a lovely evening," and then changed her mind and said, "No, let's take a cab." She said good-bye to her friend and went upstairs to her apartment. Bert was getting ready to go out to dinner with a friend of his, and he said, "Let me just say goodbye to Lou." When he went into her room, she was collapsed and already dead on the floor. She died of a heart attack.

She was originally buried in Palo Alto; then, they exhumed her body and [now] she is next to Bert in West Branch.

Lou Hoover's legacy:

CHARNOCK: Lou's legacy is the way in which she tried to utilize her role as first lady to both make a call to action to the public for issues that she believed in, but also ones that really dovetailed with the kind of approach and philosophy of government that her husband had. They have a legacy as presidential couples for the delicate balance between the political sides of what first ladies are increasingly expected to do. Lou Hoover really starts along that path.

DUNLAP: If she had not been succeeded by a woman who served in the position for thirteen years, Eleanor Roosevelt, we would remember a lot more of Lou Hoover now. Lou's activism and her non-political agenda in working with youth through the Girl Scouts and through 4-H set the stage for future first ladies to have causes and things that they supported that did not necessarily have to have political repercussions or political connections.

As far as remembering them for the Depression: I don't think that anybody knew how to handle this, as we had had depressions before, and we had managed to pull out of them within a couple of years. This was the first one that lasted as long as it did. Another thing to remember is we really did not pull out of that depression until we entered World War II. Even with all of the legislation that Franklin Roosevelt was able to get Congress to pass, that in and of itself did not help improve the economy until things changed very radically.

The Franklin D. Roosevelt Administration, 1933–1945

Anna Eleanor Roosevelt

"Courage is more exhilarating than fear and in the long run it is easier. We do not have to become heroes overnight. Just a step at a time, meeting each thing that comes up, seeing it is not as dreadful as it appeared, discovering we have the strength to stare it down."

Eleanor Roosevelt, 1940

Born: October 11, 1884, New York, New York
Married: March 17, 1905, to Franklin Delano Roosevelt (1882–1945)
Children: Anna Eleanor (1906–75); James (1907–91); Franklin Delano, Jr. (1909); Elliott (1910–90); Franklin Delano, Jr. (1914–88); John Spinal (1916–81)
Died: November 7, 1962, Hyde Park, New York

Contributors:

ALLIDA BLACK, research professor of history and international affairs, George Washington University; founding editor, *Eleanor Roosevelt Papers*

DOUGLAS BRINKLEY, professor of history, Rice University; presidential historian and biographer; author or editor of more than twenty-seven books, several on Roosevelt and World War II era.

DOUGLAS BRINKLEY: Franklin Delano Roosevelt didn't get to walk into [the White House after his inauguration]. He came in on a wheelchair. Somebody who was crippled in the lower half said, "We have nothing to fear but fear itself," and that's perhaps the most famous phrase out of any inauguration.

What people feared was unemployment, chaos, Hoovervilles, agricultural angst, topsoil blown all over, dust bowls—the October 1929 crash of the stock market. Our country was really in tatters, and there was Franklin Roosevelt, this man who had overcome such odds in his personal life, overcoming polio and being sidelined from politics, now ushering in a new progressive era and offering one hundred days of the New Deal programs right off the bat....

ALLIDA BLACK: Eleanor struggled to define her role because she was exceedingly active before she went into the White House. She was a party operative. She edited all of the national Democratic Party publications, as well as their New York State publications, covertly. She was on the board of labor unions. She was on the board of social reform organizations. She taught civics, history, and literature at a girls' school. She was a major political force in her own right, so much so that, during the campaign, all of the major newspapers in the United States would run full-page stories on her own political career and her own ambitions.

When she came into the White House, FDR said, "You have to resign all your positions; you have to…be the traditional first lady." She tells a friend that the thought of living in the White House filled her with the greatest sense of possible dread, that the White House eats women, that she fears a lifetime of white glove tests, where she's running her gloves down the banister to see if the dust has been taken off…. Literally, from the first day she's in the White House, she is trying to figure out how to resurrect her own voice in a way that will give her the latitude she needs to be herself while, at the same time, not undercut her husband's agenda.

BRINKLEY: She's the great first lady; as Harry Truman said, she was "the first lady of the world." She got very involved with getting African Americans more equal rights, working in West Virginia with coal miners and the working people of America, the forgotten people, the downtrodden, and also, women's issues, getting women into the forefront of American political life. She had no role model as first lady. She created this role all on her own. There is really nobody quite like her.

BLACK: She did [spend a lot of time on the radio]. She was on the radio before FDR. She had her own radio show. She will have become her own syndicated columnist by the beginning of 1936. By the end of her life, she will write over eight thousand columns, more than five hundred articles, more than twenty-seven books, give seventy-five speeches a year, and write an average of one hundred fifty letters a day, all without a ghostwriter.

Eleanor hit the ground running on policy in ways that we don't really think about.... The day after FDR closes the banks, he sends the Economy Act to Congress, which is going to cut federal employment by 25 percent. People are freaking out. The official unemployment rate is 25 percent, but anybody with a brain over [the size of a] squashed pea will know that it's really about 40 percent.... To take 25 percent of the federal payroll out in the middle of the Depression, and to say to federally employed women that you're going to lose your job if you're married to a federally employed man, Eleanor hits the roof. She issues, in this first week of her husband's presidency, her own opinion piece saying this legislation is wrong. FDR and Eleanor have dueling editorials in all of the Democratic Party press over the injustice of this act. She does win out, which is why she's so intense about women in that speech.

BRINKLEY: It's something that FDR and the White House staff doesn't like. Eleanor Roosevelt is very cognizant that you can't [oppose your husband's message] all the time, that you're going to have to find common ground. Otherwise, you're going to create a shambles of things.... She handled it very well, but [this is] the one time they caught a bit of a crossed wire early out of the gate; but she fell in line well.

BLACK: ...FDR knew that she was going to do this. The correspondence shows that, so what they were trying to do is to bring this issue front-and-center and buy support and curtail some of the backlash.... So they coordinate. When they go at each other, they go at each other deliberately to get the country engaged.

BRINKLEY: I don't think it was just one day or on one particular point [that FDR and his inner circle learned to use her as an asset]. It depends on who it was. Smart people knew that she was important and had the president's ear and that what she said mattered. She represented the liberal wing of the New Deal. FDR had to win over Southern Democrat conservatives. FDR was very scared on issues of race during his presidency because he had to run for reelection, and he was worried about things Eleanor Roosevelt really pioneered, [like] an ability to be with African Americans, talk to them, be in photo ops. In that way, she helped FDR a lot. They were working in unity. But she was a force to be reckoned with. In World War II,…she went to the Pacific, and Admiral "Bull" Halsey said, "We never had somebody that was so beloved by the troops quite like her before." She became an ambassador for the president…. There is a *New Yorker* cartoon that was famous showing a coal miner underground, and saying, "What's Eleanor Roosevelt doing here?" [She was, in] many ways, a stalking horse for some of his policies, putting up trial balloons.

BLACK: Henry Wallace writes in his diary that "Mrs. R. finally gets to go to the Pacific, because the 'Negro situation' is too hot." She goes right after the race riots in Detroit, where she's blamed for those race riots. But to really understand her progression, we need to look at Eleanor before she really starts [talking about] race, because Eleanor really doesn't start on race until '35 and '36.

BRINKLEY: Eleanor Roosevelt was born in New York City, part of that social swirl, social society. The Roosevelt name is as good as a name as you're going to get. Her father is Elliott Roosevelt, who's the brother of Theodore Roosevelt. Elliott was quite a character in his own right. He ended up having problems with alcohol and opiates, but he was a great outdoors person, a great hunter, a great bon vivant, and somebody whom Eleanor Roosevelt loved madly, even though he was an absentee [father] quite a bit.

A key thing for Eleanor Roosevelt is both of her parents die when she's quite young. She loses her mother and loses her father, and that's quite dramatic. Beyond that, [another significant childhood event is that] as she moves up to Tivoli [her grandmother's estate] in the Hudson River Valley…she grew up just down the road from Springwood, the home of Franklin Roosevelt, her distant cousin.

BLACK: [She did not have a happy childhood.] She writes that the only place that she ever felt safe in Tivoli was climbing to the top of a cherry tree, pining for her father to come get her. There's significant evidence that some of her uncles, who were alcoholics, took potshots at her out of the windows. The thing that is very remarkable about Eleanor Roosevelt is the extent to which she's able to transcend that sadness.

Marie Souvestre was the headmistress of Allenswood Academy. Elea-nor went to [school there in] London when she was fourteen. Her mother died when she was six. Her father died when she was ten. She was dividing her time between Tivoli with her maternal grandmother, who loved her, but who was very strict and wouldn't let her play a lot. She really didn't see to her education, so much so that Eleanor's lack of education became an embarrassment to other members of the fam-ily. Her mother's sister said to her grandmother, "We promised Anna, [Eleanor's mother] that we would send her to Allenswood." So, she went to Allenswood Academy, which was located basically where cen-ter court of Wimbledon is today. It was a school of thirty-three girls, and she worked with Mlle. Souvestre, whom she later calls a closet Bolshevik.

Mlle. Souvestre saw in Eleanor this spunk and this mind that no-body had seen. She taught her that the only way to really be sure about what you think is to be able to argue both sides of an issue with equal conviction. Eleanor wrote…"I finally learned that I have a brain. I have argued the Boer War with Mademoiselle and I have won each time."

When Eleanor left Allenswood at the age of eighteen, Mlle. Souves-tre wrote her a letter that Eleanor will carry with her for the rest of her life, that says, "Of course, you must go home and make your debut. You, after all, are a Roosevelt, and Teddy is now president of the United States. But first and foremost, you are my Eleanor, and I expect great things from you in your own right in this world."

Eleanor had an exposure to [important social issues by this point in her life]. She had an interest, but she was still very caught between two worlds. She was caught between the world in London that she loved and wanted to stay in. She wanted to teach. She wanted to live there. She didn't want to come home. She was caught between the demands of being the daughter of the most beautiful debutante in New York, as the *New York Times* repeatedly called her mother, and the social expec-tations of the niece of the president. So, she was trying to figure out that dance.

BRINKLEY: [Her uncle, President Theodore Roosevelt,] loved her.…
He was very hard on her father, Elliott…but he loved his brother tre-mendously.… When Elliott committed suicide, T.R. felt a special kin-ship to Eleanor, but also nicely said that Eleanor Roosevelt had a great

sparkle in her eye and a great intelligence. She developed her courage over a period of time. Theodore Roosevelt admired that about her, so he was there to give her away when she married Franklin Roosevelt in New York City on St. Patrick's Day [1905].

[Eleanor and FDR became reacquainted in 1903.] They had first met, apparently, when they were young, at Springwood, and so they were cognizant of each other, but they met on a train ride out to Tivoli. They started a romantic interlude through letters and seeing each other, and it just snowballed.

Franklin Roosevelt was Sara Delano Roosevelt's only child. FDR had a half-brother, Rosy, and his father, James Roosevelt, was a fine, upstanding man. He died when FDR was a freshman at Harvard in 1900....

Sara could be very domineering. She was very overprotective of Franklin in a good way. He used to go bird-watching, which was a big avocation of his; he joined the American Ornithological Union.... She kept a very tight eye on him. There are even photos of young FDR wearing a kind of dress and having long hair, being "mummy-fied" to a very large degree.... Historians often feel bad for Eleanor Roosevelt having to deal with Sara out of the gate, but, as mothers go, she was very, very intensely loving and caring. FDR cared the world about her. He seemed sometimes to be happiest when she was around.... Sara was opposed to their marriage, very much so. She said, "Please, you're going to put the family in shame. Why are you doing this?" This was really his coming out, saying, "Mother, I've got to marry Eleanor. I'm going to do this." So, Sara came along, to some degree, with the marriage.

BLACK: ...The relationship with Eleanor and Sara is very intricate and very intimate, and it changes over time. When Eleanor fell in love with FDR, she very much hoped that Sara would be a surrogate mother to her, and so you'll see lots of overtures to this. Sara created this cocoon of love around FDR.... Sara's love for FDR gave him the cushion to take the risks that he needed to take to lead later on.

...Eleanor burned their courting letters when she found out about [FDR's relationship with] Lucy Mercer, so we can't reconstruct [their early days together]. What we can do is suppose, based on the best evidence that we've got, that FDR confided in Eleanor his early ambitions.

She didn't laugh at him. She saw him as this virile, handsome, charming hunk. Everybody else saw him as a dapper pretty boy. Franklin was a hunk…. He made her laugh. He could see in those sparkling blue eyes something that was there that other people didn't see. So with the level of trust that's there, they stay together for a year, despite Mama's best intentions to keep them apart, and they have this very teenage, idyllic crush….

BRINKLEY: [They married in 1905 and then, in the next ten years, they had six children, five living to adulthood.] That's important. Franklin Roosevelt, Jr., the first one, died as an infant, but she ended up raising a lot of boys; only had one daughter. When you're raising a lot of boys, it's a lot of work. Sometimes we lose sight of that. Hers was a remarkable life, but she was also a remarkable, loving mother with her kids. FDR was an absentee father a lot, and Eleanor was the one that kept the unit together, kept the rhythm of it. In fact, when FDR would show up, the kids went crazy for him, but it was only because he was gone so much and he didn't have to be the disciplinarian. He could be the fun, playmate type of father.

Franklin wins, in 1910, the state senate, so he's in Albany, promoting a lot of different issues, [such as] conservation, and they're interested in the union movement. After being in Albany, he becomes assistant secretary of the Navy for the Wilson Administration, and is in D.C.

BLACK: Eleanor discovered, [in 1918,] that Franklin had fallen in love with [her social secretary] Lucy Mercer. In the interest of historical accuracy, we don't know if it was or was not a [physical] affair. What we do know without a doubt is that they are emotionally in love with each other. Eleanor reads the letters, which she finds when she's unpacking his trunk coming home, and she leaves. She offers him a divorce. She takes the children, and he considers it.

[FDR's political advisor Louis] Howe says to him that, A, there's never been a divorced president; and B, that Lucy is Catholic, and that the Pope will never bless a marriage where a man leaves his wife and five children to marry another woman. His mother says to him, "Son, if you do this, I will cut you off and you will never have a penny." So, the Roosevelts come back together and they learn to develop a new relationship which gives them space that goes beyond their infatuated high school...crush love story. [They became] two adults finding ways to love each other, learning to trust each other in different ways, but living two independent and somewhat overlapping lives. Polio changes that.

BRINKLEY: In 1920, Roosevelt teams up with [Democratic presidential nominee] James Cox, of Ohio. Cox is a progressive. FDR goes like a banshee across country promoting the League of Nations and Wilsonianism. They go down in hard defeat, and it ushers into the 1920s the era of the three Republican presidents: Harding, Coolidge, and Hoover.

FDR lost in '20, and now, in '21, he gets polio.... We think he contracted polio from a Boy Scout pool at Bear Mountain, New York, where he picked up the virus. He then went up to Maine and went putting out a forest fire with his sons, and just had terrible chills. He tamped out the light and went to bed with the shakes, and then woke up and couldn't feel his lower half.

Eleanor Roosevelt was there for him like nobody else. With that utter hell he was living, that anybody would feel, she showed her true colors of friendship, loyalty, and love.... That realigned their marriage. After that, he adored her for more reasons. She became somebody who took care of him when he was beyond down.

Once FDR was struck with polio, in 1921, Howe and Eleanor Roosevelt still believed in FDR's political future, whereas Sara said, "You have polio. Retire. Be a country gentleman. You have money, you love forestry, and you can run your property." Eleanor and Howe double-team FDR and say, "Let's go." So it's a tripod, in some ways, on the political front.

BLACK: By [1921], Eleanor has become exceedingly political.... What she doesn't know how to do is speak in public, and so Howe's big first tutelage of her is how to speak without that modulated voice going all over the place. Then they form an intractable team for FDR. This man is so disabled, [concerning] the intimacy in their marriage; polio so debilitates him that Eleanor has to give him enemas. She has to insert a glass catheter into his penis. She has to lift him up and turn him over, this man who was so incredibly virile. At the same time, in her mind, she is thinking, "I love this man. What is happening to him? We have to keep his spirits up." And, at the other half, she's thinking, "Oh my God, I have finally gotten my life, and now my life is gone, and I could be here doing this for the rest of my life." They figure out how to navigate that, and that is a remarkable testament to both of them.

BRINKLEY: [Val-Kill] was Eleanor's place of peace of mind, a place she could get away. There's a swimming pool there where she would swim. It's now part of our National Park Service as a stand-alone home. She would have inner city kids come there, poor people, come and talk. She would have world leaders, and presidents would visit her there. It's quite a spot.

BLACK: Val-Kill was built in 1925, along the Val-Kill Creek. It was built because the Roosevelts loved to picnic, and they loved to picnic away from Springwood, the main house, because they could get away from Mama and just hang with their friends. A lot of the political cronies that Mama did not like would come up for picnics.

Eleanor remarks to FDR in the beginning of winter how sad it was that it was their last time that they could picnic this year. They were picnicking, at that point, with Nancy Cook and Marion Dickerman, two women with whom Eleanor had developed a close political working relationship, both of whom were very involved in the Democratic Party, one of whom had run for office. FDR offers to give them a ninety-nine-year lease [on the land near the picnic spot,] and the three women will each put in a third to build a cottage. The cottage would be called Val-Kill. That was an extraordinary place for Eleanor, but it's also a political experiment, because the women build a furniture factory there to help farmers in the Hudson Valley learn marketable skills in the winter. The women have a falling-out in 1935...and, in 1937, Eleanor buys them out. She converts the furniture factory into her own home, and that was her only home of her own and her most special place. She will live there until she dies.

BRINKLEY: She had people visiting her all the time, but she lived so simply. I've been impressed about how spartan both Franklin and Eleanor can live. Right next to Val-Kill, FDR was building his dream house, Top Cottage, that would have no electricity and be on a rustic mountaintop.... I can't emphasize enough what a special place that part of the mid-Hudson is in Dutchess County. The great love and friendship of

Franklin and Eleanor, from shared neighbors, shared friends, shared topography, in knowing all the little back roads together; it was a big part of both of their happiness.

BLACK: Val-Kill is Eleanor's home and her office. Eleanor was very rarely alone at Val-Kill.... Eleanor was always surrounded by hordes of people at Val-Kill that she would invite. There would be neighbors; there would be dignitaries; there would be friends; there would be reporters; there would be painters; there would be performers; there would be Winston Churchill. John Steinbeck came to Val-Kill, [civil rights activist] Pauli Murray came to Val-Kill. Val-Kill was a hub; it was Eleanor Roosevelt's unrestricted space.

BRINKLEY: [When FDR wins the 1932 election, Eleanor is ready for the role of first lady.] She came from a famous family. She had uncle Theodore Roosevelt, who was already in the White House. She had been first lady of New York from '28 to '32, and New York was a big deal back then, being governor. She had a lot of scrutiny, and also, she shared in these New Deal type of programs that FDR started doing when he was a governor.... She's very equipped policy-wise, for the difficulties that you might find being a first lady under all that kind of scrutiny.

BLACK: They had also learned to live separately. The Roosevelts are never together for more than six months out of the year, from the time he gets polio until FDR dies. What she learns through the governorship years is specifically how to develop her own voice and her own alliances and to support policies in ways that will get FDR to pay attention to them. In many ways, the '20s for Eleanor was her own political laboratory.

Eleanor took profoundly controversial stands on the issues of civil rights, on women working, on women traveling unescorted. She spoke out, by the second term, on legal and constitutional questions that made people a little nervous, and especially the Daughters of the American Revolution, who called her an unfit woman and really did not want her in the White House. Her poll numbers throughout, and the letters that she received, as well as the hate mail, and the largest FBI file that we'd had in American history up until that time, show the extent

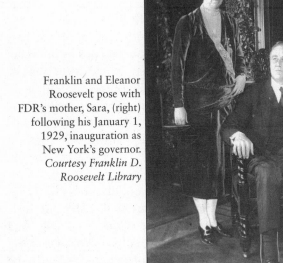

Franklin and Eleanor
Roosevelt pose with
FDR's mother, Sara, (right)
following his January 1,
1929, inauguration as
New York's governor.
*Courtesy Franklin D.
Roosevelt Library*

to which the American public really revered her. But the people that
disliked her, disliked her intensely. She really was a Rorschach test for
what you thought about democracy and the social upheaval of the
time....

BRINKLEY: She would have done very well on the modern circuit. She
wrote "My Day" columns from 1936 to 1962, six days a week; that's
sort of what blogging is today, isn't it? ...People liked her because she
told people what she thought. Authenticity comes through in the end,
and she had a genius for that.

As first lady, she said, "I want women journalists in there." They were
all being excluded, short of one or two, and she started having regular
press conferences for women, and bringing journalists in. Looking today
at all the great women foreign correspondents we have, Eleanor Roosevelt, in many ways, is their patron saint, because she began saying
they are doing just as great work as the men are.

BLACK: It's hard to overestimate the impact that "Hick," as both Eleanor and FDR called Lorena Hickok, had. Hick was the leading political journalist of the era. She was the only woman who would write for the front page of newspapers and get her own byline. She had been assigned to cover Eleanor, fell in love with Eleanor during 1932, and there's an intimate trust…and a love that develops between the two. [We don't know if the love was just emotional or actually physical,] but there's no doubt in my mind that Hick was in love with Eleanor…. Hick taught Eleanor how to deal with the press in a way where Eleanor could define her own message. When Eleanor became first lady, Hick resigned her position and moved into the White House because she has fallen in love with Eleanor, and she can't be objective.

Eleanor then goes to FDR, who also liked Hick, to say, "I want to send Hick out and investigate what the New Deal is doing, what it's not doing." [To Hick, she said,] "I want you to get the hopes and fears and put your journalist craft on paper in very private reports to us." What we get is the most incredibly honest and powerful assessment of how the Depression is affecting individual people. Hick is involved in that, and [thereafter,] Eleanor will never make a major career decision without talking to Hick.

[The Roosevelt family quarters in the White House was regularly filled with family, visitors, friends, and senior advisers such as Lorena Hickok.] It was very clear who was coming and going, especially when "My Day" starts getting published, because Eleanor says who's there, who's spending the night, what they talked about, and what they had for dinner. She also would have her own press conferences where she would tell people who the guests were and who was living there. So, yes, people knew [that Lorena Hickok lived in the White House].

BRINKLEY: It was a different era with the press and the media. People wouldn't even take photographs of FDR in his wheelchair. We only have a couple of him incapacitated…. Could you imagine that in our YouTube era today? People didn't start covering people's affairs or dalliances in that way—although they would be rumored. Things would percolate, but it didn't take on a cast…. People left them somewhat alone.

BLACK: Eleanor and Franklin both saw the Depression as a war on the American spirit and a war on the soul and the economic soul of the United States. And so, Eleanor absolutely refused to have Secret Service protection in the White House. She said, first of all, it would impede her ability to have a conversation with the American people, and she saw her number-one job responsibility as helping bring the government to the people so that people could understand its human face.

This woman traveled without Secret Service from 1933 until 1962. I can document fifteen assassination attempts on her life.... We know the Ku Klux Klan placed the largest bounty in its history on her head. We know people shot at her. We know they dynamited trees outside clapboard churches where she spoke. We know that they wrapped dynamite around the axles of her tires. We know that they placed nitroglycerine in lecterns where she stood. She said that it was her responsibility to be able to have a talk with the people of the United States. She wanted to meet her neighbors. Anybody that interfered with that interfered with her ability to do her job, and she would have no part of it.

[In 1941, it was Eleanor who addressed the nation by radio after the Japanese attack on Pearl Harbor.] She was in her own element. She's now saying what she wants to say and she very much appreciates the gravity of Pearl Harbor. She's got boys in the Pacific. She had toured battlefronts in World War I. She had seen hundreds of dead soldiers piled up with their stomachs exploding because they had not been buried yet.... So, for her, this is a defining moment. And [in her address,] she is telling FDR, and has told FDR for at least two years prior to that—they both understood that war was inevitable; they were trying very hard to stay out of it—but she says to him that we must remember that the lesson of World War I is that we won the war, but we lost the peace.

BRINKLEY: This was a period where she was pioneering on civil rights, in a way.... She supports the Tuskegee airmen, even flies in a plane with one of them, and she promotes women working in factories and industrial places, including our first day care for women that are working in factories and have children. So she's constantly pushing the envelope, and FDR allows it, which is remarkable. If you're a real liberal, you preferred Eleanor Roosevelt to FDR, because as president, he had to modulate himself in a certain way for votes.

BLACK: [Eleanor certainly had her share of critics.] The first campaign button that the Republicans made in 1936 was "We Don't Want Eleanor, Either." There's a long history of mocking Eleanor in political cartoons. Also, there are lots of cartoons of Eleanor coming out of a mine with soot on her face, inferring that she had black blood. In fact, J. Edgar Hoover was convinced that she had... "colored blood." He tried to convene a secret meeting of the Senate Judiciary Committee to have her declared "colored," stripped of her citizenship, and sent to Liberia to live with her people, the "coloreds."

[During her 1943 tour of American troops in the Pacific, Eleanor flew over in an uninsulated military aircraft]. Her eardrum shatters. She goes deaf in one ear. She will walk fifty miles of hospital corridors in two days. The arches will fall on her feet. She will never be able to stand again without special shoes. This trip changes Eleanor Roosevelt. She begins to carry a prayer in her wallet that says, "Dear Lord, lest I continue in my complacent ways, help me to remember that somewhere someone died for me today. And if there be war, help me to remember to ask and to answer, am I worth dying for?"

Eleanor did not know about the arrangements that some of the staff had made for Lucy Mercer to return to FDR's life.... Anna Roosevelt, their daughter, brings Lucy back into her father's life at her father's request during the war. Lucy is [among those] with FDR in Warm Springs the day that FDR dies of a cerebral hemorrhage.

BRINKLEY: [April 1945 was Eleanor's final month as first lady. She heard about FDR's death] when it got reported. It was unfortunate. She wasn't down there in Warm Springs with him.... Whatever the wounds were of having [Lucy Mercer] down there around him,... Eleanor ran the funeral service wonderfully at Hyde Park. FDR wanted a very simple headstone, his name and his years and Eleanor. It tells you his love of her. He wanted to rest in eternity [with her]. When she finally dies in 1962, she gets buried there with him.

BLACK: [After Franklin's death,] she was out of the White House within a week. Truman said that she could stay longer. She said, no, she wanted to get out. She famously said, "The story is over," but the story was not over, and she knew it would not be. People were already lobbying her to run for the Senate, to be governor, to be secretary of labor, to be president of one of the major colleges, to run one of the major political action organizations in the country.

She moved back to Val-Kill to settle the family estate. Meanwhile, she kept in constant contact with the first American delegation to the planning meeting of the U.N. in San Francisco. By August, she is so frustrated with Truman that she begins a full court press on Truman's politics, so much so that Truman appoints her to the first American delegation to the United Nations to get her out of the country.

BRINKLEY: FDR's great legacy is the United Nations, and Eleanor Roosevelt started working very closely with the U.N. in the postwar era, most famously authoring the United Nations' Declaration of Human Rights. There's no figure more synonymous with human rights than Eleanor Roosevelt.

BLACK: We would not have the Universal Declaration of Human Rights without Eleanor Roosevelt. She was not only chair of the Human Rights Commission; she was chair of the drafting commission.... You have a small window in which to come up with a vision that will stand up in opposition to the horrors of the Holocaust, the atomic bomb, and the fear that another world war may start in ten years. Without Eleanor Roosevelt's negotiating skills...everybody would have dissolved into conflict, and there would have been a great bloc opposing the declaration, rather than having the declaration passed unanimously. It took three hundred meetings of more than three thousand hours.

BRINKLEY: [Eleanor died on November 7, 1962. There was] deep and incredible mourning. President Kennedy came to the funeral, Dwight Eisenhower came, Harry Truman came, and everybody else you can think of. It's a little village, the town of Hyde Park, and all the world came to be there. She had become beloved as a champion of the underdog and the underclass.

Eleanor Roosevelt's legacy:

BLACK: She would say it was the Universal Declaration of Human Rights, but I would say something else.... She has seen everything that is [sometimes] horrible to see about democracy—slaughter and violence and poverty and discrimination—and she never gave up. She kept going when people tried to kill her, when they disparaged her husband, when they mocked her children, and when it hit her income. She believed in democracy and the promise of America and the promise of human rights so profoundly that she risked everything she had to try to make us get there. I think that showed undaunting and fierce courage.

BRINKLEY: I'd say that, and civil rights…. It was her voice on a national level that started bursting through. She has a place of honor in the civil rights movement. She's in the same pantheon as Martin Luther King for her caring about equality.

Elizabeth (Bess) Wallace Truman

"We are not any of us happy to be where we are, but there's nothing to be done about it except to do our best—and forget about the sacrifices and many unpleasant things that bob up."

Bess Truman, c1944

Born: February 13, 1885, Independence, Missouri
Married: June 28, 1919, to Harry S. Truman (1884–1972)
Children: Mary Margaret (1924–2008)
Died: October 18, 1982, Independence, Missouri

Contributors:

NICOLE ANSLOVER, assistant professor of history, Indiana University Northwest, focusing on twentieth century U.S. history and the presidency; author, *Harry S. Truman*

WILLIAM SEALE, White House historian; author of many books, including *The President's House;* editor, *White House History;* academic advisor for C-SPAN's *First Ladies* series

NICOLE ANSLOVER: [When Vice President Harry Truman got the news of Franklin Roosevelt's death,] he was having a drink with his cronies, as he was often wont to do. He thought a lot of politics was accomplished by relaxing and having a somewhat more cordial atmosphere. He received a phone call, and he said he just knew [it was news of Roosevelt]. The story goes that he ran to get to his car to get to the White House.

WILLIAM SEALE: [Harry Truman was sworn in as president two hours later at the White House.] Mrs. Roosevelt was at a luncheon at the Sulgrave Club, and they went and got her, but didn't tell her anything. Steve Early, the press secretary, told her when she got to the White House, but it wasn't a surprise to anyone in the White House at all. They knew Roosevelt was dying.

ANSLOVER: The Trumans thought they could stay in their Washington, D.C. apartment until they moved into the White House. They offered Mrs. Roosevelt as much time as she needed. She took about a week. By then, the Trumans realized that, security-wise, they could not stay in their apartment, so they were living in Blair House. As Eleanor Roosevelt watched the staff pack up the last of her belongings, she went across the street to Blair House to say goodbye to the Trumans, and she warned Bess, "Watch out for the rats." She and one of her female friends had seen a rat run across the terrace recently.

That was the Trumans' introduction to their new home. Bess and daughter Margaret went over to take a tour of the White House, and they were appalled [at its condition].

Bess Truman's first problem as first lady was that Eleanor Roosevelt had, probably meaning well, set up a press conference for Bess, because Eleanor had established the tradition of press conferences. Bess Truman went to the [first female cabinet member,] Secretary of Labor Frances Perkins, and said, "Do I have to do that? Is it okay to set my own tone?" She was assured that she could do what she wanted. She put a lot of thought into it. At the last minute, she decided that this was not something she was going to do, and she never did hold a press conference.

SEALE: Bess sent Edith Helm, the old-time White House social secretary, who went there with Mrs. Woodrow Wilson II and stayed through the Roosevelts, through everything. She was Admiral Helm's wife. She commuted in a limousine from Leesburg, Virginia, every day, and she knew everything to do. She knew where the bodies were buried. She handled the press conference.

ANSLOVER: At first, the press were clamoring to get more information [about Bess,] and they were very aggressive, and calling her secretaries and asking where she was going to go and what she was going to wear. It's not that Bess wouldn't speak to people. In those days, largely women journalists covered the first ladies and she would invite them over for things like teas, or she would go to their luncheons, but she would insist on it all being off the record. So they did get to know Bess Truman a little bit, and they understood that she wasn't trying to do this out of spite. She was just a private person and wished for a private family life.

SEALE: [She didn't want to take on anything] extra. She did what she had to do. She had the parties, the receptions for the military. She did those kinds of things. Mrs. Roosevelt had had a newspaper column, and Bess just wasn't going to do that. This was her life.

ANSLOVER: The Trumans certainly didn't get much time to relax [during their initial years in the White House]. It was very busy. Bess did spend a lot of time traveling back and forth to Independence. Now, that's not just her being spiteful. She still felt that she had to be the caretaker for her mother [and Harry's mother, who] was still alive during his early years of the White House. They had family business to take care of. When Harry and Bess were in the White House together, they would do the same things that they did at home. They read. They enjoyed an evening cocktail. They liked to listen to music. They chatted with Margaret…. They used [the Truman balcony] the same way they used their porch in Independence, as a [place] to spend time together.

One of my favorite Truman stories is he often wrote Bess letters when she was home in Independence and he was in the White House. He was just convinced he could hear the ghosts of his predecessors wandering the halls. He really enjoyed imagining they were there to keep him company. Bess thought it was silly, until one night, she and Margaret heard a crash, and then they thought for just a minute that maybe there were ghosts there….

[The Bess-Harry dynamic informed his presidency] greatly, because he asked her before he did pretty much anything. There's a little bit of controversy over whether he consulted her about dropping the atomic bomb. The story has it from some sources that he didn't consult Bess about that, but be sure that he consulted her about everything else. Their dynamic was very important, and you can see his spirits got lower when she was home in Missouri. He just didn't function with quite as much vigor when Bess wasn't near.

[Margaret Truman explains that,] when Harry was in the Senate, he had time to come home in the evening and talk things out with Bess, and they could discuss it over their "old-fashioneds" [cocktails], which they liked to have in the evening. When he became president, his decisions multiplied rapidly, and it's not that he didn't want to consult her, [but that] he did not have time to consult her on every little thing. She grew frustrated at first, but she came around.

SEALE: The president was away at the Potsdam Conference when the atomic bomb was dropped, and Mrs. Truman was in Independence. It was such a scary thing. Even Roosevelt had trembled at the thought. [She spent] an awful lot [of time in Independence]. She was gone a lot of the time, but Washington had the social season and she was always there for the December-to-spring season in Washington where you had five or four official White House dinners. She presided over those with great panache, all with good reviews.

Mrs. Truman was no cultural backwater to Washington. She had been in Washington. She'd been a senator's wife. She was active in the Congressional Club. She was active in things in town, and when they got to the White House, she knew exactly what to do, and that bears discussion, too. They were among the most formal entertainers the White House had ever had.

There had been no formal entertaining at the White House during the war. So when the social season was revived after all these years, they were sticklers for having it exactly as it had been: black tie, evening clothes, and all that. The chief usher, Mr. West, in his memoir, says the White House had never been so formal and so devoted to diplomatic precedent as it was under the Trumans. Everything was done exactly as it had been before the Roosevelts. They only got one [social season, in 1946-47 before the White House construction started,] because they had to move, but they did entertain at the Mayflower from time to time...

ANSLOVER: The Trumans met when they were about five years old in Sunday school. I'm not sure whether Bess distinctly remembers it, but

Harry always spoke of the girl with the beautiful blue eyes and the long golden curls, and he claims that he fell in love with her that day. As far as we know, he never did look at another woman.

SEALE: Her family owned a store in town and manufactured Queen of the Pantry Flour, and they were considered a little more upscale than the Trumans, who farmed other people's land. There was a Truman farm, but, in fact, some of the land they farmed [belonged to] Mrs. Wallace, Bess's mother. There was that difference [in social status], and that difference surfaced all during their lives.

ANSLOVER: Mr. Wallace committed suicide when Bess was eighteen, and in those days, it was a huge scandal—a great stigma on the family. This really explains why Bess wanted to keep her family life private. She saw how this shattered her mother. She wanted to shield her mother; she wanted to shield her brothers from having the press dig through her family history and bring that up again.

SEALE: It was a terrible thing for everyone. Nobody ever understood why he did it. Mrs. Wallace left right after the funeral with her children for Colorado and lived there for a year, and then came back and moved with [Bess and her brothers] into the house with her own mother.

ANSLOVER: Bess and Harry Truman never have their own marital home, and then her mother lived in Blair House or the White House with them a lot of the time. It's even thought that that was part of Bess Wallace's hesitation for accepting Harry Truman's proposal, because her mother didn't approve of Harry.

Harry first unofficially proposed in about 1913, after their courtship started in 1910. She didn't write him a letter back, but you can tell from his second letter to her, when he says, "If I bought a ring, would you wear it on your left hand?" There was no answer, but she agrees to still be friends with him. They keep courting, and then they get close to a formal engagement, and then World War I intervenes, so that's why it's delayed even further.

[During the war, he was in] great danger. He was in combat at the front, leading his men. He was writing to Bess and carrying her picture with him every day.

[After the war,] he ran a store in Kansas City for a while, a men's clothing store with his good friend, Eddie Jacobson. That's where he gets into some debt, which he did insist on paying off, and he eventually does pay it off. He was still involved in the family farm. He was trying to do all of these things to make himself more, and he does become interested in public life at that time.

[After he was elected to the Senate, Bess worked in his Senate office, and received a salary, which was criticized. They handled this] the same way they did everything: straightforwardly. They said other people did it, and Bess did the work [she was paid for]. This was just people trying to start problems. They knew that people would try to start problems, but it was an okay thing for Bess to do.

Financial reasons were why he put Bess on the payroll [of his Senate office]. Margaret Truman always described her mother as a penny-pincher, but Margaret also admitted it was a good thing she did. The Truman finances were often very tight. It was somewhat ironic that for Truman's second term, no one had expected the Democrats to win, and that pesky Congress had approved a bill that would double the president's salary from $50,000 to $100,000, which is a huge leap. So imagine Congress' dismay when Harry Truman received that money, instead. Presidents did not have pensions before Truman. They were just kind of put out of office. They didn't even have security.

Harry started calling Bess "The Boss" in the mid-1930s, we think, because she was very organized with his Senate office. She didn't mind the nickname until he introduced her during the 1948 campaign as "The Boss" and Margaret as "the Boss's Boss." The reason that irritated Bess so much was she thought people were going to think Margaret was spoiled.

Bess didn't try to stop him [from running for election in his own right in 1948]. In her heart of hearts, does she want to keep being first lady? No. But, again, this is a partnership. She might have been able to persuade him not to run, but she knew that it was what he believed was best for the country, so she supported him.

[Most people believed Truman would lose the 1948 election because] Truman was not popular at the time.

SEALE: He made a cross-country [campaign trip] and went out and spoke to people, and got in front of courthouses, and he won it on his own personality. He must have had enormous personality as a stumper, as they say, on his stump speeches. [Their whistle-stop campaign tour was] very, very [important because] it got him elected, brought him to the people. [Media coverage at the time] was mostly radio and print, and Movietone News, that sort of thing. Of course, there was television, but it was coming in at the end [of the campaign].

ANSLOVER: Republican Thomas E. Dewey was so far ahead that they stopped polling a couple weeks before the election actually took place; that's why the numbers were so off. The Trumans spent a lot of time on that train. They were all exhausted and ready to head down to Key West after that.

The first year [of his first full term] was said to be their happiest in the White House. Harry thought, here was the chance to be president in his own right. This is when his "Fair Deal" started really kicking off. But then things go horribly wrong, largely because of Korea. It shattered the economy. It shattered the people's faith in him and their willingness to understand. Then he fired General Douglas MacArthur, [and public opinion of Truman tanked].

Bess was still going back and forth [to Independence] a lot. But, again, that's largely because of family issues. They reestablished their partnership. They got over the personal tensions that they had during those early days where she was feeling a little bit left out. They found their rhythm again. Their union was happier and steadier the second term.

SEALE: [Soon after the 1948 election, they confirmed that the White House was literally falling down around them.] The trouble started right after Pearl Harbor, when the Army Corps of Engineers, the old enemies of the White House, came in and did an engineering survey.... The ceiling in the East Room had dropped forty inches. The room is so long, eighty-five feet, you can't tell...but it was considered a fire trap, and they recommended that Roosevelt move out. Of course, he wouldn't do it....

The Truman family's whistle-stop campaign tour was critical to President Truman's success in the 1948 election, defying the polls.

After the war, when Truman was there, the house was [creaky] in the upstairs and the floors jiggled and all that…and the plaster would begin to trickle down from the light fixtures, so they decided that they had to get out.

They moved across the street [to Blair House], and great plans were made for redoing the White House. Now, I bet you he consulted on this with Mrs. Truman. The Corps wanted to tear it down. That was the easiest thing to do, but George Washington built those walls and Truman wouldn't hear of it. He had the house gutted, but the stone walls on the outside never were touched. In fact, they wanted to take a bulldozer in through one of the doors, and they were about to open the door up with pickaxes He saw them, and said, "Stop!" They took the bulldozer and a dump truck apart, and reassembled them in the cellars of the house to dig the lower cellars.

ANSLOVER: Harry did definitely consult with Bess [about remodeling the White House]. She wanted the original structure to remain. Why wasn't this renovation done in their first term? The house was falling down then, but Bess and Harry were both convinced that somehow the press would blame the Trumans for bringing down the White House, so they waited until he was reelected to tackle this project.

SEALE: Mantelpieces were preserved [in the White House renovation,] some doors. Not much of it was to be preserved, because it was cheaper to put pressed wood in, but Lorenzo Winslow, the architect, really was the hero, as far as saving the original things. He saved what he could. [When the house reopened,] people thought it was beautiful. *National Geographic* did a beautiful issue on it after Truman was out of office.

The decorating was all done by a department store in New York [called] B. Altman. Chuck Haight made the decisions. Mrs. Truman and the president refused to make decisions about wallpaper and things like that because they said it was not their house. It was for the future. So Mr. Haight and the staff made most of those decisions. It was done cheaply. They beat everybody down. Franco Scalamandre gave fabrics for $3.50 a yard, which are hundreds of dollars a yard, just for the prestige.

Mrs. Truman had as much influence as she wanted [in the rebuilding of the White House,] but they both felt that they weren't going to live there long and that it was something more important than them.

ANSLOVER: [When the 1952 election came around, the Trumans had a decision to make.] The Twenty-second Amendment not only did not apply to the incumbent, but it would have only been his second time being elected. Bess said to him that she could not take another four years as first lady, and she didn't think he could take it, either. They were in good health for their age, but Korea and McCarthyism was starting to spread, and they were getting worn down.

SEALE: And, once Dwight Eisenhower turned Republican, it was pretty clear he was going to win....

ANSLOVER: Truman was highly offended during the transition period, when Eisenhower did not appear to want to take his advice. A big social snub occurred on Inauguration Day. It's customary for the incoming president to stop by the White House, have tea, pick up the outgoing president, and ride together. First, Eisenhower, it was said, wanted to be picked up at his hotel. The Trumans said no. So President-elect Eisenhower and Mamie arrived at the White House, but they would not come inside and greet the Trumans. They sat in the car, and the president of the United States had to walk out to him. You can feel the tension, if you look at the pictures of that inauguration.

SEALE: After the inauguration, Truman was almost forgotten. He was almost thrown out. Guards were taken away. He had no pension coming to him. One member of the Secret Service detail took annual leave to accompany the Trumans back on the train to Independence. No one bid them goodbye until they got to the train station....

ANSLOVER: ...When they returned home, there were thousands in Independence. So the Trumans were gratified but still somewhat offended.

They did not expect the crowds; and people just kept walking by [their home] and wanting to see them. There's a story about Margaret one day coming out onto the porch and yelling at someone to go away, and they later found out he was an escaped mental patient who had a gun. It was a very different time.

Harry Truman wasn't necessarily unpopular at home. He was still the hometown hero. Independence, Missouri, has not had any other presidents. People probably thought they could just walk right up and say hello to the Trumans as they had in the past.

SEALE: The city of Independence put a retired...policeman on the back porch, and that's the only guard they had until after President Kennedy was killed. Then the pensions started, and the Secret Service detail began for former presidents.

ANSLOVER: Theirs were long [post-White House years]. He wrote his memoirs, first of all, because he had to make money. He wasn't getting a pension. Several lucrative offers came his way, but he never believed anyone should trade on the presidency. So he wrote his memoirs and Bess edited every single word, and that was their first project.

SEALE: He was intimate to [the establishment of the Truman Library,] and believed very much that it was a matter of interpreting history. He did the original design himself for the exhibit.

ANSLOVER: [He could see his gravesite from the window of the office he kept at the Truman Library.] The great story with that was that he said, "I can just see, Bess, you're going to lay there next to me, and one day I can see myself saying, 'Oh, I feel like going into the office,' and you'll say, 'Harry, you oughtn't'." So that's how they expected to spend eternity.

There's not a lot of scholarly work on Bess Truman. A lot of what we have are the works by Margaret, and then Bess's grandson, who compiled some letters. Those letters are in the Truman Library and they're available for people to use to do research. Any book that you read on Harry Truman is going to talk about those letters and use them as a reference.

SEALE: [We don't have any letters from Bess because] she burned them. Truman came upon her when she was throwing them in the fire, and he said, "Don't do that. Think of history." She said, "I am." Mrs. Washington, Mrs. Harding, and Mrs. Truman are three first ladies who burned their letters, and what a loss it is.

ANSLOVER: We're fortunate that she didn't burn the letters from Harry, at least. She left us those. But she did not want her words recorded. It was a partnership, but she was a silent partner.

[Harry died in 1972. Bess died ten years later, in 1982, at age 97. She spent those last ten years] at home. She tried to keep up her correspondence.

SEALE: She had a caregiver, finally, and then several of them at the end, but she died at home.

ANSLOVER: And I imagine that's the way she wanted it.

Bess Truman's legacy:

ANSLOVER: Bess Truman's greatest contribution to the role of first lady was demonstrating that you can be a strong, influential partner and you don't have to be on the front page or on the TV every day. Your influence can be strong without it being public.

We should remember her the way she wanted to be remembered, that you can be a wonderful, influential first lady, even if people don't know it at that time.

SEALE: She was her own person. It's not really possible for first ladies anymore. Mrs. Reagan once said she was going to play cards with her friends, which is something Bess Truman would have done and, my goodness, you'd think she'd committed treason.... But Mrs. Truman would have responded to that by saying, "It's my life, and I'm not elected."

The Eisenhower Administration, 1953–1961

Mamie Doud Eisenhower

"Why, this comes naturally. I've been training for it for thirty-six years. When you're in the Army, you get used to chasing after your husband."

Mamie Eisenhower, May 1954

Born: November 14, 1896, Boone, Iowa
Married: July 1, 1916, to Dwight David Eisenhower (1890-1969)
Children: Doud Dwight (Icky) (1917–21); John Sheldon Doud (1922-2013)
Died: November 1, 1979, Washington, D.C.

Contributors:

MARILYN IRVIN HOLT, historian and author of several books, including *Mamie Doud Eisenhower: The General's First Lady*

EDITH MAYO, curator emerita, First Ladies exhibit, Smithsonian Museum of American History; academic advisor for C-SPAN's *First Ladies* series

MARILYN HOLT: Mamie Doud was born in 1896, in Boone, Iowa. She was our very last first lady to be born in the nineteenth century. Her family lived in Boone until she was about eight years old, and then they moved to Colorado, and that's where she grew up.... The family would winter in San Antonio partly because of one of her sisters' health problems, rheumatic fever; she was almost an invalid. While they were in San Antonio, they went with some friends to Fort Sam Houston, and that's where Mamie was first introduced to Ike.

Dwight "Ike" Eisenhower was a second lieutenant; very serious. She says when they've written about this meeting that he was really not interested in any kind of girlfriend. He was very [focused on his] duty and his job in the military, and Mamie just kind of swept him off his feet, or vice versa.

Her father warned her off [the hardships of military life]. Mamie's parents really liked Ike.... They thought he was a wonderful young man. Her father even told her when he was coming around to visit that she ought to quit being so flighty and going off with other young men to parties, that she should pay attention to Ike. But when they got married, her father told Mamie they absolutely could not expect any money from him. They would have to live on Ike's military pay. Mamie's response was, "Well, I didn't care about that. I just wanted that man."

[She had been] living a very comfortable life with plenty of money. It was quite a shock for her, but she had learned from her father about budgeting and how to spend money and how to save money. So, though it was difficult in the early days of their marriage, she always managed to live on Ike's salary.

EDITH MAYO: And not only that, but in an atypical role-reversal, Mamie is the one that handled the family's finances.

Mamie took a domestic science class when they became engaged, but because they moved their marriage date up to July first, rather than in November, after she turned twenty, her domestic science classes were cut short. I'm not sure she was that serious about them anyway. So, he did the cooking. He knew how to do that.

HOLT: [Three years after they were married, their first child was born.] "Icky" Doud Dwight.... was just the apple of their eye. Wherever they were, he was like the little mascot that everybody just took to. He died at the age of three of scarlet fever. It happened so quickly. In that time period, it sounds strange to say today, but couples could almost expect to have at least one child die of some childhood disease. Because of the available medical care, there just weren't the things that you could do about it. The Eisenhowers were absolutely devastated.

MAYO: It's a recurring theme in most of the presidential families all the way from the beginning [that first couples have lost children]. It's always a horror story, no matter when it happens. In an era before antibiotics and modern drugs, you have it happening frequently.

HOLT: Then their son, John, was born. One of the things that John said is that his parents never made him feel as if he was a replacement for the child that they lost, that he was his own person, his own special self. That was the way the Eisenhowers were as a couple. They took people as they were, but that didn't mean that they totally forgot the first child. They just made another place for another child in their lives. Mamie was, I would say, overprotective of John.

There was one year in which they moved three times. Sometimes, when Ike was posted for a very short time, Mamie might go back to Denver and live with her family.... So, they were back and forth. That's something that every military wife faced at one time or another. You might live in who knew how many different posts in a very short period of time. You could expect multiple moves, and sometimes long separations.

MAYO: That's why they, number one, treasured their years in the White House, because it was a permanent home for eight years. And then, when they purchased the farm in Gettysburg, that was their first family home.

They did a lot of entertaining on their various posts. Many times, the Eisenhower home was called "Club Eisenhower" because of their entertaining of the troops and the military personnel....

HOLT: Even when they were first married and they were at Fort Sam Houston, they very quickly became a couple that invited other military couples into their home. They would have Saturday or Sunday evening potluck, play cards, and were very social. They had a rented piano that Mamie played, and they sang.

MAYO: For most of the time [during World War II], Mamie lived in Washington, D.C., in an apartment. She wanted to be in Washington, hoping that there would be times that Ike would be allowed to come back home, which he did a couple of times. Their son, John, was at West Point, so any opportunity that he had for vacation time, like Thanksgiving or Christmas, she wanted to be close at hand in order to see John. It was only later in the war that for a period of time, that she went to stay with a sister.

HOLT: [Ike was rumored to have had an affair with] Kay Summersby, who was often referred to as Eisenhower's [World War II] driver, but there were several people that drove Ike around. Summersby's primary job was to keep his appointments calendar, to make sure that the right people got in and out and to meetings. She was at Eisenhower's headquarters. She was engaged to an American officer who was tragically killed in the fighting in North Africa, and she stayed on at the headquarters. Rumors began that Eisenhower and Summersby were having an affair.

I don't believe that there was an affair because it's hard, for one thing…to imagine that Eisenhower, the Allied commander of the European theater, was acting like a schoolboy, puppy love, following Kay around, which is what she alleges in her book, *Past Forgetting*.

Did Mamie know? There wasn't anything for Mamie to know, except the rumors were extremely hurtful to her. It was the kind of gossip that went on and on, especially after Summersby's book, which later was a made-for-TV movie. That was very hurtful for Mamie.

[After the war, Eisenhower became president of Columbia University, and then, in 1951, President Truman appointed Eisenhower the Supreme Allied Commander of NATO. There was a] grassroots movement, Citizens for Eisenhower, with little groups of people all over the country forming and pushing for Eisenhower to run for president and to run as a Republican. When they were in Europe and he was at NATO, there were people actually flying to see Ike, to try and talk him into running on the Republican ticket. He doesn't come out and say what he will or will not do because of his position and what he's doing at NATO.

One of the stories Mamie tells is they were in France, he was with NATO, it was about Christmastime, and people were sending Christmas packages from the United States. They opened this one package and it was from the group Citizens for Eisenhower. There were all these little beanie hats and ties and "I Like Ike" pins. They were having guests over, and while Ike was in the library on a phone call, Mamie got this box and they all put this paraphernalia on. When he came back into the room, there they were. She said he took one look and his face turned red with anger and then he just burst out laughing because they all looked so ridiculous.

MAYO: [Once the decision to run for president was made, Mamie got involved in the campaign] very wholeheartedly. She loved the attention. I am not sure that her part in the campaign was scripted. She just threw herself into it, and it turned out to be a watershed for presidential wives and political campaigning. She was a great boon to the Republican Party.

They liked the fact that she connected with the women of America, and people started asking for her on the Eisenhowers' campaign train. They did a whistle-stop across the country, and people at the end of Ike's speech would say, "We want Mamie," and there was a lot of clapping and calling for Mamie to come out on the rear of the train. Then he began saying, "And now, would you like to meet my Mamie?" She was a tremendous hit. She would court local politicians; she would give little interviews. She turned out to be quite an asset.

...The Republican Party just went completely wild with putting out materials that promoted the campaign and Mamie herself. This resonated with people, and this is the first time that the women's vote caught up with the number of men voting. Women had gotten the vote in 1920, but their voting participation had always lagged behind until 1952.

Ivy Baker Priest, who was the head of the women's division of the Republican Party, had come up with three areas that would appeal particularly to women in the campaign. They emphasized bringing the boys home from Korea, which was imaged in the sense of bringing your husband, your son, your boyfriend home. Ike was the great military hero who was going to do that. The second thing that they emphasized was the so-called mess in Washington, with supposed scandals within the Truman Administration. It was imaged in the sense that any housewife could clean up a mess in her home. So, there were all kinds of cleaning pails and scrub brushes and brooms and lapel pins in the shape of brooms that were put out by the Eisenhower campaign, so that women would identify with cleaning up the mess in Washington. The third thing was the economy, and that was imaged as every woman has to stay within her budget, and why shouldn't the government do the same? They put out enormous grocery bags that said "Ike and

Crowds would yell, "We want Mamie!" during the Eisenhowers' 1952 whistle-stop campaign tour. *Credit Republican National Committee. Courtesy National Archives and Records Administration*

Dick" on them.... The grocery bags were going to be extra-large, because this was how much farther your budget was going to go if you elected Ike Eisenhower and Dick Nixon.

There were a lot of advertising men who migrated bodily into the campaign and imaged Ike and Mamie as a commodity, a product that could be sold to Mrs. American Consumer.

HOLT: With Mamie, even though you have these campaign managers, image-makers, she is not someone that the image-makers are not making [into] who she is. She is being herself.

MAYO: Mamie was extremely popular. She set off a rage for pink. She set off a rage for bangs. Everybody wanted to look like Mamie. It seems a little strange to us post-Jacqueline Kennedy, but she really epitomized the best in taste and dresses and accoutrement, if you will, for the 1950s, and everybody tried to copy her look.

She first started wearing bangs in the 1920s after the death of their son, Icky, had resulted in the Eisenhowers growing somewhat apart. When they were sent to Panama, his commanding officer's wife took her under her wing and said, "You have to do something to rescue your marriage." One of the things she decided to do was to take a renewed interest in her personal appearance, and that's when she had her bangs done. That was a symbol to both of them of the rapprochement in the marriage.

Later, when she was in Paris, when Ike was head of NATO, she started frequenting the Elizabeth Arden Salon in Paris.... After the first inauguration, Elizabeth Arden wrote to her and said, "Now that you're in the public eye, I noticed that when you first came back, your hair looked absolutely beautiful but it hasn't been quite the same since. So I asked our stylist to render these structural drawings...of the steps that a hair stylist must take in order to achieve the 'Mamie look' and the 'Mamie bangs.' In your travels across the country and around the world, you can take these structural drawings with you and go into any Elizabeth Arden Salon and have your hair turn out beautifully."

HOLT: [Truman decided not to run for reelection in 1952 and Eisenhower won by a landslide against Democrat Adlai Stevenson.] Obviously, there's been a great deal said and written about how badly Truman and Eisenhower came to dislike each other, but Mamie and Mrs. Truman were good friends. Mamie went to Mrs. Truman's Spanish classes. There's a photograph of Bess showing Mamie around the White House, and they look like two girlfriends giggling in a corner. Mamie knew, regardless of what somebody's political affiliation was, she could get along with them. And that was the case. If their husbands were having problems, that didn't affect how Mamie and Bess Truman would get along.

MAYO: [The gown the first lady wore for the 1953 inaugural ball was] "Mamie pink." It was a pastel peau de soie. She decided that she wanted to have a little extra flair, is the way she put it, so she had Nettie Rosenstein, who was the designer, put two thousand pink rhinestones on the gown so that it would sparkle and glitter. "Mamie pink" was a color that was very popular in the '50s, part of not only a wardrobe color scheme, but also as a household color scheme. Charcoal gray and pink was also a big color combination in the '50s, and she had a number of formal gowns that were charcoal gray and pink.

[Mamie visited the Oval Office just four times during Ike's presidency. In the 1950s, there was] very much a division of labor. The women would handle the food, the entertainment, the family. The president would handle the country, the politics.

HOLT: Part of that was Mamie's military background, too. She once made the comment that a wife never went near her husband's command post, his point of operations. It just simply wasn't done. So again, there was that separation of their spaces.

MAYO: She did not discuss issues publicly. That was not her job, as she saw it. Privately, she was very opinionated. She had some very strong ideas on a number of social issues, but she simply was not an activist the way that we think of women speaking out today. In fact, she was probably the last presidential wife that didn't have a particular cause while she was in the White House. That was something that Eleanor Roosevelt had done, but Bess Truman had not done. Mamie's whole background would not have lent itself to her doing that, but she's the last first lady where that's the case.

HOLT: She launched lots of charity drives. She was a spokesperson for the American Heart Association, but you can't say that those were causes and projects the way that it became institutionalized [for later first ladies].

The Eisenhowers entertained more heads of state, more foreign dignitaries, and had more state dinners than any previous administration. Certainly, part of that has to do with the change in transportation [air travel became common]...and his position...in NATO. When Queen Elizabeth and Prince Philip came to the United States, Eisenhower said, "We reacquainted ourselves with old friends," because they knew Queen Elizabeth when she was still a princess. They felt that way about so many of the people that they had met; they were just re-meeting them and entertaining them in a different place.

MAYO: Interestingly, it's Mamie Eisenhower who returns large-scale, elegant entertaining to the White House. Most people think of Jacqueline Kennedy as the person who did that, but it's really Mamie Eisenhower, after several decades of curtailed entertaining in the White House with the Depression and World War II, and then the Truman renovation of the White House when they were living at the Blair House and couldn't entertain in the White House.

For Mamie, the entertaining of heads of state while he was commander of NATO was something that really prepared her for entertaining in the White House. She knew how to do it. She was confident about doing it. She actually loved that part of the first lady's role.

[Mamie also encouraged Ike to use the presidential retreat in Maryland.] There had been previous presidential retreats. The Hoovers had set up Camp Rapidan in Virginia, but that had been unused because it was a rocky, hilly terrain that Franklin Roosevelt couldn't access. And so Roosevelt had set up this presidential retreat [in Maryland] called Shangri-La. When Eisenhower was in office, he renamed it Camp David, after his grandson.

HOLT: Mrs. Joseph McCarthy, wife of the senator from Wisconsin, was invited [to the White House]. She was invited to teas, and receptions. She did not attend. Mrs. McCarthy was making a political statement on her husband's behalf not to cross the door into the White House.

MAYO: Senator McCarthy was the senator that went after so-called Communists in government positions. It was like a Salem witch hunt, if you will. They saw Communists under every desk, under every chair. He went after all kinds of people that were supposed to have had some affiliation with the Communist Party, or a Communist Party front, or somebody who leaned toward the Communists in the '30s and '40s. He did a great deal of harm to a great number of people's careers and personal lives. The reason that Mamie would not invite him to the White House entertainments was that she disagreed with the methodology that he used and the ruining of people's reputations and careers.

HOLT: [Mamie Eisenhower was a big fan of the television show *I Love Lucy*.] Lucille Ball had been brought before McCarthy's committee, and, of course, she and Desi Arnaz were terrified that their careers were over with.

It was Ike's birthday...and Mamie invited Lucy, Desi, and Vivian Vance and...William Frawley...[the cast of the popular TV series] to the

White House, to entertain.... Mamie made a point of having Lucy and Desi sit with her and Ike for the dinner portion of the evening. She was not saying anything about it. She was just making a very public statement about who she invited, where they sat, and how they were treated when they arrived.

[There was a televised Mamie] birthday celebration in March 1956, and obviously, it was an election year. Immediately, the Democrats wanted equal time because this was, in their view, a campaign ad. William Paley, who was president of CBS, and a very close friend of the Eisenhowers, said, "No. It's not equal time because this is nonpolitical entertainment with the first lady."

Mamie's birthday is in November, and this special celebration was in March, so obviously, there was some political background to this. But, if you watched the show at the time, what you saw besides the singing and the celebrating were a lot of people talking about Mamie, and with real affection, and wanting to get across how really popular she was at the time.

MAYO: ...Part of the excuse, if you will, about having this celebration for Mamie was that she so epitomized the '50s, particularly with American women, that if she hadn't been there to do it, someone would have had to invent her.

Mamie Eisenhower's legacy:

HOLT: [After they left the White House in 1960, the Eisenhowers returned to their farm in Gettysburg, Pennsylvania. Ike died in 1969, and in 1979, Mamie had a stroke and was taken to Walter Reed Army Hospital, where she eventually died.] Perhaps one of the things that is most telling is she didn't think about having a legacy. She thought about what she had done as a first lady as an important job, her contribution to American life. Her legacy would probably be what she said to Barbara Walters in a [television] interview, that when asked, "How do you want to be remembered?" she said, "Just as a good friend."

MAYO: That's how she felt about the American people, that she was a good friend to them.

She would say that [her greatest contribution to the role of first lady] was giving Ike a comfortable home life where he could relax and get away from the pressing issues of the day. Her greatest contribution was in institutionalizing the first lady as the campaigner. That's the role that has really carried on with later first ladies and in American political life.

HOLT: I would agree that, privately, it would be creating that home. When she said "homemaker," she meant it in the truest sense: making a home that was comfortable and welcoming and gave Ike a place to escape, and for their friends and family to enjoy themselves and to be together.

Publicly, her contribution as a first lady was [in] projecting someone who really was interested in anyone and everyone without any consideration for their political, social, or religious background. To say that she was nonpolitical, it almost sounds like it's too good to be true. Basically, she was interested in people for who they were, and they realized that in her and responded to her.

Jacqueline Bouvier Kennedy

"So many people hit the White House with their Dictaphone running.... I never even kept a journal. I thought, 'I want to live my life, not record it.'"

Jacqueline Kennedy, 1961

Born: July 28, 1929, Southampton, New York
Married: September 12, 1953, to John F. Kennedy (1917–1963) (widowed); October 20, 1968, to Aristotle Onassis (1906–1975) (widowed)
Children: Caroline Bouvier (1957–present); John F., Jr. (1960–99); Patrick Bouvier (1963)
Died: May 19, 1994, New York, New York

Contributors:

MICHAEL BESCHLOSS, presidential historian and author of nine books on mid-twentieth century leaders; Introduction to *Jacqueline Kennedy: Historic Conversations on Life with John F. Kennedy*

BARBARA PERRY, presidency expert; White Burkett Miller Professor of Ethics and Institutions at the University of Virginia's Miller Center; biographer of the Kennedys, including *Jacqueline Kennedy: First Lady of the New Frontier*

BARBARA PERRY: Jacqueline Bouvier was born in the Hamptons in 1929, just before the stock market crash, in the summer of that year. Her parents were John and Janet Bouvier. He had been an investment banker on Wall Street, but he lost his savings in the stock market crash. She continued to summer with her grandfather Bouvier, whom she

called "Grampy Jack," and he was the one who introduced her to reading and literature at such a young age. She loved him dearly, and they
would write poetry and memorize poetry together.

Her mother was a pretty strict disciplinarian, but both sisters, Lee
and Jackie, grew up in a broken home. Their parents separated when
Jackie was only seven, and then they divorced when she was twelve. It
was a very bitter, acrimonious divorce, because her father was a womanizer and somewhat of an alcoholic.

MICHAEL BESCHLOSS: [Her father's nickname was] "Black Jack"....
She had this insecure childhood, and the interesting thing is that if you
looked at her and didn't know any of this, you would've thought that
she had just the most perfect early years and was probably an heiress.
Her father was so short on money that when she was at Farmington, in
high school, she later said that sometimes she would worry that he
would not be able to pay the tuition at the end of the term, and she
might have to leave. That's where this strength of will came from. This
is someone who lived in a way that was much more elite than 99 percent of human beings, but at the same time, it had its difficulties.

Her mother then married an affluent man named Hugh Auchincloss,
but he was not in the business of endowing his new wife's two children, so
when Jackie took on a job [as an "inquiring photographer" for the *Washington Times-Herald* in the '50s], it was because she needed the salary.

PERRY: She made her first trip to the White House when she was a
pre-adolescent, about eleven or twelve years old, and that was because
her mother was coming to [Washington to] date Hugh Auchincloss,
who lived in Northern Virginia. Then, when her mother married him in
the early 1940s, Jackie and her sister lived with them at Merrywood,
their Northern Virginia estate. [It was an] all-Republican family, and
they would summer up at Newport, Rhode Island, at Hammersmith
Farm. That was her introduction to the culture of Washington. Jackie
Kennedy would say her first trip at that time to the National Art Gallery, was when she fell in love with art, and the wonderful feelings it
gave her to view art and sculpture.

BESCHLOSS: Jackie lived on huge estates both in McLean, Virginia,
and in Newport, but she was always sort of the poor relation.... I'm
not making an argument that she lived a life of hardship, given the way

that most of humankind lives, but this was someone who felt that there were challenges.

PERRY: Jackie didn't know what her future would be in terms of money except to marry well, which she did. [The fact that John Kennedy's family was very wealthy] had to be some of the attraction, certainly. It appears that it wasn't love at first sight, and that there wasn't chemistry immediately. When they were first introduced at the famous dinner party by [journalist and JFK friend] Charlie Bartlett in 1951, there were no sparks, really. He seemed to want to ask her out, but supposedly when he went out [the door] with her, there was another male friend waiting for her. So he was stopped short, and it took another year for them to get together at another dinner party at the Bartletts'.

BESCHLOSS: Jack Kennedy was born in 1917, she in 1929, [so the age difference was] twelve years. She had actually first met him on a train, and she wrote about it. She [called him] "this congressman with reddish-brown hair I met on the train." I don't think she had ever even heard of him, although already he was by then in Congress, and had written a bestselling book, and had a father, Joseph Kennedy, who had been a rather famous ambassador to England.

PERRY: [In the beginning, their relationship] was very tough. [There were] medical problems that she had with childbearing, that he had with his back, and his other ailments. He was gone so often, and they also didn't have their own home.... They did not really have their own home that they had bought and stayed in for any time until 1957, in preparation for Caroline's birth, on N Street in Georgetown.

Smoking, we think, could have been [a contributing factor to her difficulties with pregnancy]. She was a chain smoker, several packs a day, and if it didn't lead to the problems with the actual pregnancies themselves, there were lung conditions that some of her children were born with: John, Jr., and then Patrick, who succumbed to it. They also think possibly that some of the president's medical conditions, perhaps even STDs, could have led to problems with pregnancy.

[JFK's infidelity] is one thing that she kept her counsel on most of the time, and...I think that's a great credit to her.... We think that she may have a couple of times let out in anger, perhaps in French [in] both instances, references to someone who might be having an affair with her husband. One can only speculate about what that was like in the marriage and what tension it must have brought to the marriage, especially the early marriage when he was having all of these medical problems...and she was having trouble with her pregnancies, as well.

She had just a terrible record in her pregnancy. She had lost a baby to miscarriage in 1955, and then she had lost a baby, stillborn, a little girl in 1956, right after that very hot, non-air conditioned [political convention]...

BESCHLOSS: And she remembered the jostling in the crowds...

PERRY: So she was really just afraid to go [to the 1960 Democratic convention]. From about April onward in 1960, she did tend to stay home, though she did go with the president-to-be, to a jostling parade in October 1960 through the canyons of Manhattan with lots of tickertape. But she was definitely great with child—the child would be, of course, John, Jr.

BESCHLOSS: And, JFK, who always had this great sense of humor, had as his friend [journalist] Ben Bradlee, who also had a wife who was great with child. And so right after the election was won, JFK said to the two women, "All right, girls, you can take the pillows out. We've won."

The moment that [JFK] began to [appreciate Jackie as a political asset] was when they went to Paris in the spring of 1961 and there were a lot of people who turned out both to see John Kennedy, and also to see Jackie, who had been a student in Paris, had French ancestry, spoke French, and certainly knew French art and history. That was the first time she began to get enormous crowds. And then domestically, what really did it is the program in February of 1962 when she did the tour of the White House that she had worked so hard to restore.

She spent an awful lot on clothing. And that was, by the best information we have, actually supported by Joseph Kennedy, Sr. who said, "Dress as you need to and send me the bills," because they felt that this was something that would be very important to that presidency. And in those days, it turned out to be a great asset.

PERRY: It did become a bit of an issue in the '60 campaign. There were some statements in the press that she must have spent perhaps $30,000 a year on her wardrobe.

BESCHLOSS: It turns out she spent a lot more. She put out a statement saying, "I couldn't spend $30,000 even if I wore sable underwear," which she did not wear.

PERRY: And then she wore a cloth coat to the inauguration instead of a fur.

BESCHLOSS: She felt that for the first lady to dress in the best of American fashion, and to try to bring the best of American art and culture to the White House would show the rest of the world—and she said this a little bit during the televised tour in February of 1962—that the United States was no longer this young, adolescent, unformed, stripling country but a country...worthy of being considered as a superpower. She understood this was a part of diplomacy.

PERRY: There was just an upping of the level of the style, and that all goes to Oleg Cassini. First of all, she picked him because he was American, though he had European ties and Hollywood ties. He said, "I will create a wardrobe for you on the world stage," and indeed, he did.

BESCHLOSS: She wrote to him, saying, "I want Jack and myself to dress as if Jack were president of France." In a way, that happened. It's not something she ever would have said in public.

PERRY: By and large, [the American public] loved it. Now, every now and again, she was a little too youthful, like when she'd show up in a bathing suit or be waterskiing. So you'd have some conservatives [who would] say, "Oh no, a first lady shouldn't do that." The previous three first ladies, Eleanor Roosevelt, Bess Truman and Mrs. Eisenhower... were in their sixties when they left office, and they were somewhat matronly, and they had grandchildren in some instances. So she seemed like everyone's older sister or cousin, rather than their maiden aunt or their grandmother.

Her political contribution... [was her assessment of people], because she didn't have a major impact on policy and that by her own admission...

BESCHLOSS: Nor did she want one.

PERRY: And the president didn't talk to her about it very much. He might on occasion mention something, but he didn't seek her out for advice, so if he was going to have any connection with her at all in terms of politics, it would be as...they were coming back from political trips. She did go to 46 of the then 48 states with him, in 1959 and '60, when they were really out with the rank and file. I'm sure that she was on the plane with him coming back, saying, "That person's a phony, that one's real. That one's stupid, that one's really smart. Make sure you keep up with that one."

BESCHLOSS: If you go through [her audiotaped interviews] as I have, you hear the people that she criticizes, like Adlai Stevenson, or Dean Rusk, the secretary of state. These were people who tended not to do too well in the Kennedy administration, though people she praises like Robert McNamara did very well, so I think he really did listen to her.

PERRY: I counted up sixteen state dinners in those 1,032 days that they were in the White House.... The Kennedys loved entertaining, and they would [invite] these third world leaders, and they would draw them in. The arts were then part of that entertainment.... She had her fine arts committee bringing paintings to the White House, [like] the *Mona Lisa* coming to Washington and to New York....

BESCHLOSS: If you see the way a president nowadays receives a state visitor, that's all Jackie Kennedy's doing.... It was her idea that you should have round tables that encourage conversation and you should have a pageant on the South Grounds, perhaps with performers that harkened back to the Revolutionary period. She even had Air Force One repainted with the design that we see nowadays. She knew that even that plane landing at a foreign airport, looking the way it does, would be a tool of America's diplomacy.

PERRY: It was her idea to greet the foreign visitors on the lawn of the White House and make it a beautiful ceremony. Otherwise, it would have been at Union Station or National Airport.

BESCHLOSS: Jackie got to the White House after the election of 1960 and was shown through it by Mamie Eisenhower. She was aghast. She said it looked like a Statler Hotel, which she did not mean as a compliment, meaning that it had not very convincing reproductions. So, this mother of two, with other things to think about, took on what was this enormous project of raising a huge amount of money and also getting donations of furniture and art and artifacts.

She wanted the White House to be the equivalent of the great houses in Europe. She felt that for foreign leaders to come to the White House and have it look like a hotel that was in some cases threadbare and full of reproductions, it cast a bad light on the United States. So, if you like the way the White House looks nowadays, you should thank Jackie Kennedy.

[The White House Historical Association was created during this time.] The thing that she was most concerned about was that when she was no longer first lady, the next first lady might not be so interested in history, and might have a sister-in-law who ran a curio shop somewhere, who decided that they would redecorate, perhaps, in the style of the late 1940s or something that was more contemporary. She thought that if there was a White House Historical Association, that would be one bulwark that would prevent future first ladies from turning it backwards, back to before the period in which it had become such a great museum.

PERRY: CBS televised [the White House tour when the project was completed, though it aired on all three networks]. It was with Charles Collingwood. She goes throughout the White House. Remember, we're now talking about 90 percent of households having televisions. Even though it's in black and white, and we can't see her bright red dress on Valentine's Day, and even though, again, by today's standards, it's a bit stilted, people fell in love with it. They think there were about fifty-six million viewers. They think three out of four [homes] watched it.... She even received a fan letter from Barbara Bush, future first lady.

It [was televised] behind the Iron Curtain. It went to 106 countries around the world. She won a special Emmy for it. It was a real high point of her first ladyship.

BESCHLOSS: Sometimes her influence on historic preservation is forgotten.... If John Kennedy, and particularly, Jackie Kennedy, had not been the president and first lady in the early 1960s, the executive office building next to the White House would've been torn down, which Dwight Eisenhower was very eager to do; he thought it was an eyesore. Probably half of Lafayette Square, the president's park north of the White House, would've been torn down.... It would've been replaced by federal office buildings of the time that would look roughly like a federal penitentiary and a prison yard. That shows what a difference that it made that she was there, and it really helped the historic preservation movement to accelerate.

[The Kennedy marriage] was probably perhaps happiest at the very end. She certainly said that their happiest years were in the White House.... Also, there's a lot of evidence that suggests that after they lost a son, Patrick, in August of 1963, they became a lot closer. For instance, you see them holding hands at the airport, on the last day of his life, in a way that you had not seen before.

PERRY: As they came out of the hospital after poor Patrick had passed away after two days, the president is holding her hand as they come out in front of photographers. When they take the helicopter back to Hyannis, [Massachusetts,] and they come down the steps, he's helping her because she's gone through this Cesarean section and it's just a week later. JFK is helping her down the steps, and then he gingerly comes down himself. I had not seen that before.

BESCHLOSS: For all the reasons that she was distraught and devastated by what happened on the twenty-second of November 1963, it was that much worse because if you assume that there was new hope and new warmth in that marriage, then suddenly this happens. You can imagine what was going through her head.

PERRY: [Prior to the final trip to Dallas], the president had suffered in the Gallup polls [about twenty points] because of civil rights. He had fallen particularly in the Southern states, so he was concerned. He was going to Texas to try to cement the party there and raise money for the '64 campaign. It was really the kickoff for the '64 presidential reelection campaign. Gallup did not take regular polls about the first lady at that time, but early on, in '61, she was polling at about 59 percent. In '62, she finally supplanted Eleanor Roosevelt, who had been the most admired number one for about twelve years....

BESCHLOSS: There's also an irony, because when John Kennedy was planning his campaign in 1960, he once made an offhand remark: "During this campaign, we'll have to run Jackie through subliminally." What he meant by that was that Jackie was someone who he thought had been raised in a rather elite way, and rode horses, and would have a life experience that might not be too politically helpful. There was no one who was more astounded and absolutely delighted [than he] that she had turned into this vast political asset. When JFK was planning this trip to Texas, John Connally, the governor of Texas, said, "You have to bring Mrs. Kennedy because she is so popular; you'll have much bigger crowds." As, indeed, he did.

[She was] just thirty-four years old [when John F. Kennedy was assassinated]. We know so much about this story, you sometimes forget he was shot, and, in fact, [was in] her arms for the five minutes that they were going to the hospital. He was there with sightless eyes. She felt, almost from the moment that they left the hospital to go back to Washington, that her great mission had to be to do something to make sure that he had the historical reputation that he deserved, but would not be there to fight for.... She felt that one thing that would be very important for his legacy would be, as horrible as Dallas was, to wipe out the view of that and restore the American people's dignity by having three or four days of ceremony. That, she hoped, would be what they remembered, rather than the tawdriness of what had happened in Texas.

PERRY: She knew that she wanted to go back to the funeral rites for Abraham Lincoln, our first assassinated president, and that is indeed what she did. She asked her brother-in-law and the president's various friends and aides to come to her aid and to find books on the Lincoln funeral, and they did. Then all of this played out on television.

By this time in 1963, probably 90 to 95 percent had televisions. I can remember sitting in our family's living room on that night of November 22, 1963, and seeing Mrs. Kennedy walk out of Air Force One behind her husband's casket. I can remember my parents and my two older brothers gasping to see Mrs. Kennedy in her blood-stained suit.

BESCHLOSS: We now know what she was saying to people [about that suit]. Lady Bird Johnson said to her on that plane, "Please, Jackie, let me get someone to help you change your clothes." She said, "No, I want people to see what they have done to Jack."

PERRY: [After the assassination, President Lyndon Johnson treated Mrs. Kennedy] very well.... Jackie was very grateful to both Mrs. Johnson and President Johnson that they were so gracious to her, and let her stay in the White House until December 6. She was able to stay there with her children until she got a sense of where she was going to go. She had no home to go to. As one writer has said, in those seconds of carnage in Dallas, Mrs. Kennedy lost her husband, her home, and her job. She literally had no place to go until [Ambassador] Averell Harriman opened his home to her in Georgetown. She needed a place to live. Caroline was going to nursery school and kindergarten there.

BESCHLOSS: During the days of the funeral and the ceremony, she said to one of her associates: "Just keep on moving right now. We can all collapse later." Until she left the White House, there were enough decisions that she had to make—where to live, even early decisions about the presidential library, trying to make sure that her children were in as normal an environment as possible. You can't think of anything that's more abnormal than for the children to lose their father this way. Once they got to Georgetown, that's when she really did almost collapse. That was late December through the beginning of the spring. She went through a terrible depression, quite understandably. Before then, you couldn't ask for more than she did in terms of keeping this whole situation together.

A week after the assassination, Jackie Kennedy asked Teddy White, who was a family friend and a journalist, to come up to Hyannis Port

First Lady Jacqueline Kennedy leads grieving family members out of the U.S. Capitol following November 25, 1963, memorial services for her assassinated husband.

and interview her, with the idea that what she wanted to say would get into *Life* magazine. The presses were held for this.

She said, "Late at night, before Jack and I went to sleep in the White House, we had this little Victrola, and we used to play the record of *Camelot*, the play." Needless to say, editors at *Life* and Teddy White saw this was going to be the big theme. Actually, she urged him to make Camelot the major theme of his article…. In the end, it may not have been something that helped, because to say that those years, which had their lights and darks, were all [filled with] knights and great noble deeds was almost setting him up for the revisionist movement of the 1970s, as indeed did happen.

PERRY: She also must have known that these [revisions] would come along and that she could get out in front of them perhaps with, as the lyric said, "one brief shining moment." All you have to do is look at the imagery to see that they were a shining couple with two beguiling, shining children.

BESCHLOSS: Jackie Kennedy, right in the wake of the assassination, was reading all sorts of stories about how her husband wouldn't amount to very much because it had only been two years and ten months [in office]. So, she was so determined to try to help him win this reputation that she felt he deserved. One of the things that was urged on her by Arthur Schlesinger, the White House aide and historian, was there was a new movement called "oral history".... Schlesinger interviewed her at her house in Georgetown about eight times—ten hours in the end—only a few months after the assassination, when her memories were very fresh. The idea would be that she would speak freely. He told her, "Speak to the historians of the twenty-first century." These recordings were closed until about 2011, when daughter Caroline felt that they should be published, and [they] were.

JFK, about a month before the assassination, went to Harvard and saw a football game against Columbia. He also looked at what was going to be the site of his presidential library on the Boston side of the Charles, across the river from most of Harvard.

[After the assassination, Mrs. Kennedy] very quickly began talking to his friends and aides about what kind of exhibit should be in the library. She started raising money for it, and she also began thinking about who should be the architect.... She chose I.M. Pei, who is famous now, but at that point was very little known, because she thought that he was much more in the spirit of JFK, who was young and had not been that well-known himself.

PERRY: [She was] terribly concerned [about security for herself and her children after the assassination of Senator Robert Kennedy, her brother-in-law]. She supposedly said, "They're killing Kennedys. My children could be next." So, once again, financial security and physical security became so important to her, and surely, that was part of her attraction to [Greek shipping magnate] Aristotle Onassis.

BESCHLOSS: Four months after RFK's death, she married Aristotle Onassis. [After she married him,] she was pulled off the pedestal. People were outraged. Probably many people were outraged that she would marry anyone at all, rather than be an eternal widow, but particularly, to marry someone who was this much older, and who was not an American, and who was under some suspicion by the United States government in some of his financial activities. One person said, "She has gone from Prince Charming to Caliban."

PERRY: Her sister, Lee Radziwill, who had, by the way, also had a romance with Onassis prior to her sister's, said, "He was really quite charismatic." She said [about] the way he moved and the way he looked, he might not have been a typical *GQ* representation of a beautiful, attractive man, but she said that he was. She also said Jackie liked all things Greek. She liked Greek mythology. She liked Greek poetry. She also found great comfort in the tragic poets of Greece. So, we can't say that she wasn't attracted to him at all, but certainly the money and the physical security [were attractive]. As she pointed out, he had his own island, Skorpios.

[The Onassis marriage lasted] from '68 to when he died in 1975, but they were somewhat estranged. She lived a good portion of the time in New York.

BESCHLOSS: She would say that the marriage was quite good until January of '73, when Aristotle Onassis's son died in an accident. She [returned to New York City] and did something that many people would not have expected. She decided to go to work and get a real job. She became an editor first at Viking, and later on, at Doubleday. This was not just someone who was there for show business and acquiring books. She actually edited with great intensity. Her authors were hugely loyal to her.

[Jacqueline Kennedy Onassis died of cancer at her apartment in New York City in May, 1994.] For the last years of her life, by all accounts, she was actually in certain ways happier than perhaps she had ever been in life. Plus, she had a relationship with a fine man, Maurice Tempelsman, and this was a relationship of equals. It was very different from, certainly, her second marriage, and perhaps her first.

PERRY: [She was] always close with her children and always so proud of them. Her brother-in-law Senator Edward Kennedy's eulogy for Jackie talks about how, whenever she would speak of them, her face would light up.

BESCHLOSS: She once said, and this gives you so much of her mindset...when she was in her deepest grief in 1964–65, she wrote to British

Prime Minister Harold Macmillan, and said, "If I raise my children well, that will be my vengeance against the world." She really felt that she had achieved that vengeance.

Jacqueline Kennedy's legacy:

BESCHLOSS: Here's a case where Jackie Kennedy had a much bigger impact as first lady in all sorts of areas that may not have been the ones that people thought about at the time she served.

PERRY: Very much the way her generation was a bridge between traditional wives and mothers and the post-women's liberation of the modern era, that's exactly the way Jacqueline Kennedy was as first lady. There were traditional first ladies immediately preceding her, and afterwards, they were much more modern, much more full partners with their husbands.

The Lyndon B. Johnson Administration, 1963–1969

Claudia (Lady Bird) Taylor Johnson

"It's like shooting the rapids, every moment a new struggle, every moment a new direction—trying to keep the craft level and away from the rocks, and no still water in sight."

Lady Bird Johnson, c1960s

Born: December 22, 1912, Karnack, Texas
Married: November 7, 1934, to Lyndon Baines Johnson (1905–73)
Children: Lynda Bird (1944–present); Luci Baines (1947–present)
Died: July 11, 2007, Austin, Texas

Contributors:

BETTY BOYD CAROLI, first ladies historian; author of several books about presidential spouses, including *America's First Ladies*

COKIE ROBERTS, journalist for NPR and ABC; author, including *Founding Mothers* and *Ladies of Liberty*

COKIE ROBERTS: [The challenges for the Johnsons after the Kennedy assassination were] enormous. First of all, nobody knew whether there was a widespread plot, and so the country was in terror for a period of time. [Then they had to make] sure that there was a peaceful transition to power without seeming to take over, because of the image of pushing the Kennedys out of the way; they had to be very careful in how they handled it. Lyndon Johnson was very lucky that he had Lady Bird to help him with that because she had a good ear for knowing exactly what to say and when to say it.

BETTY BOYD CAROLI: Lady Bird said she felt like she was on stage for a part that she'd never rehearsed. In fact, it would be hard to find a first lady better prepared than she was. She immediately started taking notes. We have her shorthand notes while she was still waiting to hear whether President Kennedy had died. On the way back [to Washington, D.C., after the assassination,] on the plane, she started making plans for putting her radio station into some sort of blind trust so that they would not be accused of profiting from it. She really took over very fast. She was a good study.

The amount of documentation [that took place during their administration] was new. She didn't record every day because some days were just too full, but she had a little recording machine, and on days that were too busy, she would stuff brown envelopes with menus or lists of people she had seen. Then she would get an hour or so some days, and she would sit down and record. Those recordings are still being transcribed. They are wonderful. Her White House diary, which people may have read, is eight hundred pages, but that's only an eighth of what she has on those tapes. We're waiting for the rest of it to come out.

ROBERTS: Before this, there were recordings, of course. We have some Kennedy recordings; we have some Roosevelt recordings. Louisa Catherine Adams, John Quincy Adams's wife, wrote, when she was first lady, *The Autobiography of a Nobody*, which tells you something about her state of mind at the time. Most first couples have an awareness of the magnitude of the job, but Lady Bird Johnson had such a sense of history. She said she dared herself to keep a diary. She understood that this was something special.

CAROLI: [In her recording about the day of the Kennedy assassination,] she's very specific, and she gets so many details. Her description of...walking into the hospital and seeing that the Kennedy car was still there, and she saw this bundle of pink blossoms and the blood around it; she's a very astute observer.

ROBERTS: She's also a wonderful writer, and she's aware of that. She writes intentionally. She's also clearly upset in that recording. You can hear it. She's trying to describe the situation, but at the same time, give homage to Jacqueline Kennedy, "this [immaculate] woman, caked in blood," all of that. She's trying to tell you what was happening, but not to sensationalize it.

CAROLI: To Lady Bird Johnson, many people said [that Jacqueline Kennedy] was a daunting act to follow, and she said, "Well, feel sorry for Mrs. Kennedy, not for me, because I still have my husband." She made a special effort not to imitate in any way some of the projects that she considered [Mrs. Kennedy's]: for example, beautifying the Mall. Lyndon Johnson had advised her not to do that because the Kennedys had done something similar.

She didn't have envy of anybody. She seemed to consider the Kennedys a different generation. I find her amazing in that regard, that she knew that Jacqueline Kennedy was extremely popular, and yet she knew that she had a lot to offer, too.

Claudia Taylor was born outside of the town, which is really not much of a town, of Karnack, Texas, in December 1912, in a big house. One of the things I found in studying first ladies is how many of them married down; that is, they married into families considerably below theirs economically, socially, sometimes even education[-wise]. It made a big impression on me to drive past the house where Lady Bird Johnson was born, that seventeen-room house with six fireplaces, and the big white columns, and then go three hundred miles west and see that low-to-the-ground, four-room cabin where Lyndon Johnson was born. She came from a far wealthier background than he did.

She was only five when her mother died in what I consider mysterious circumstances. She was a very lonely child, although she said she wasn't, but how would she know what any other kind of childhood would be like? She had two older brothers.... They were a good bit older, and they were sent away to boarding school. Tommy, the older brother, she said she really never knew him. When he died in 1959, of pancreatic cancer, she said she cried harder than she had ever cried in her life. So it was a lonely childhood.

Even her name, Lady Bird; the typical story is it came from a nurse, but she says in her interview with [historian] Mike Gillette that it was really two little African American playmates, the children of hired help, who decided to call her that, because they didn't like "Claudia." But it was not considered somehow acceptable to say that she had African American playmates, so the nurse was brought in, and [her nickname] was attributed to the nurse.

ROBERTS: There she was, this little girl all by herself in this big house with a father who was around, but had no clue what to do with her, and this sort of nutty, old Southern aunt, and some playmates here and there, but the big advantage to that was she became a world-class reader.

[It was] slightly [unusual that she went to college], but by that time, more women were going to college. We were now talking the 1920s and into the '30s, so it was more common than it was a generation before that.

CAROLI: She was interested in [journalism in] high school, so it was obviously an early interest. It was part of her plan to get out of that part of Texas. [She not only got a college degree, but also a teaching certificate and learned stenography.] That's what a girl did to prepare for all possibilities, right?

ROBERTS: But isn't it interesting that she felt the need to prepare for all possibilities with as much money as she had?

CAROLI: She was inheriting about $7,500 a year in the 1930s, which was about what five schoolteachers could make. Her aim was to get out of there, she said, to some faraway place like Hawaii or Alaska. She went to the same journalism school as Walter Cronkite.... We forget how very well-trained she was as a journalist.

[She met Lyndon Johnson] by chance, supposedly, but it was certainly through a woman that they both knew, and they must have heard something about each other. It was a September afternoon when Lady Bird had dropped into the woman's office. Her name was Jean Behringer, a woman that Lady Bird had grown up with, although the woman was older than she. Lyndon dropped by the same office on the same day. It was, as Lady Bird says in one of the interviews, electric going from the first minute.

The love letters, which are the courtship letters, were released by the library last Valentine's Day, and everybody should read them online....

They were conducting a hot and heavy courtship there, because he was in Washington.

ROBERTS: Lyndon was not going to waste any time. She was either going to marry him or not. [He was a Capitol Hill staff member and you could be an aide and not run, but he clearly had [political] ambitions, and she was [supportive of] those ambitions.

From her own oral history, she basically says, "Hold on here," as anybody would. He essentially said, "Are you going to marry me or not? Because if you're not, let's just not see each other." She didn't want to have him gone, so she finally said, "Okay."

CAROLI: They met on September 6, and Lyndon showed up on Halloween. So, what is that, seven weeks later? The time they'd spent together was about five days, and he was ready to get married right then. Even her father said, "This is a little too fast." The woman who introduced them thought it was too fast.... Against all the family counsel, she went ahead. What she said was when she got in the car that Saturday morning, and they drove down to San Antonio to get married, she didn't know whether she would get out on the way. She really didn't make up her mind until about six o'clock when she went down to the church. [He was twenty-six when they married and] she wasn't quite twenty-two.

When she married him, he was a congressional aide, and that's when she first started out [in Washington]. She got there New Year's Eve, 1934. She'd been married [five or six weeks], and he served about a year before they went back to Texas so he could be head of the National Youth Administration.

She goes back to D.C. in 1937 when he's elected to Congress, and she's there for about a dozen years, as a congressional wife. She's very good at networking with other women. She's a very loyal member of the Congressional Wives Club. Then he gets elected to the Senate in 1948, and she's a very loyal member of the Senate Wives.

In the House years, in 1941, after Pearl Harbor, Lyndon enlisted. He had been in the Naval Reserves, and he went on active duty, and she ran his congressional office. I don't think we have another first lady who ever ran her husband's office. Bess Truman worked in her husband's Senate office for pay, and Lady Bird Johnson was always very careful to say in all the letters that she sent out that she was volunteering her services.

ROBERTS: Lyndon just left her in charge, and off he went, and then various friends of his reported to him that she was running the office a whole lot better than he had.

Coming back to…Lady Bird's networking with the political women, it was an extraordinary group of women, to begin with. What they were doing was not sitting around drinking tea and tending to the tatting. They were very politically active, both in their husbands' campaigns and in the broader campaigns, voter registrations, organizing conventions, all of that.

They were also very active in the District of Columbia. It was before home rule. No matter where they were from, and at a time when it wouldn't have been popular were it known where they were from, they worked with the African American women here in Washington on all kinds of social service issues, and they really did create a social safety net.

CAROLI: Lady Bird inherited some money and some land from relatives, and she bought a radio station in 1943. The figure generally given is $17,500. Then she was very active in seeing that it was turned around from a money-losing operation to a money-making operation. She went down and lived in Austin for six months or so and mopped floors and cleaned windows.

ROBERTS: She took over a radio station and started running it. How do you do that? And she did it. She just went in, she changed the building, and she changed the staff. She got the station up, and CBS came in, and [she] got it as an affiliate, and it became this highly successful station that she was running…. She drove back and forth constantly between Washington and Austin.

CAROLI: …Lady Bird demanded weekly reports, and people said she went over them with a fine-toothed comb, suggesting different sales pitches to use to sell airtime. She was very active in who got hired. She was managing a good station….

ROBERTS: [That station] was just the beginning; it became a communications empire.

[During the 1960 presidential campaign, when Lyndon was the Democratic vice presidential nominee on the ticket with John F. Kennedy, the campaign reached out to people living in the South] mainly by identifying with them, and Mrs. Johnson was very key in that. She emphasized her Alabama roots, which is where her mother was from, and she had spent time there with cousins as a child. She insisted on spending time in the South.... Texas did go for the ticket and, had it not, Kennedy would not have been elected president. Whenever we're talking about the pick for vice president, the only time we can ever actually prove that a vice presidential pick made a difference is the Johnson pick.

CAROLI: She held those teas all across Texas and insisted on shaking hands with all of the four hundred or five hundred women who showed up. After Texas did go for Kennedy-Johnson in '60, didn't Robert Kennedy say, "Mrs. Johnson won Texas for us"?

The vice presidential years for her were great, but they were terrible for him. Everybody says they were his worst years, but she loved it. First of all, she traveled a lot. She talked about arriving in Senegal and feeling like she'd been put down in the middle of *National Geographic*.... She really thrived on being a second lady, if that's what we're going to call it. And, she filled in a lot for Mrs. Kennedy.

ROBERTS: ...There were lots of times that Mrs. Kennedy was [unavailable]. She was pregnant, she lost a baby, she wasn't well a lot of times; a lot of things she didn't want to do. Mrs. Johnson filled in, so she knew the role well.

She was a quintessential Washington political wife. She had been on this scene since the 1930s, and she really knew it well, and she had a cadre of other political wives who were just extraordinary women, and they all gathered around her, and that also made that transition somewhat easier.

She started these women-doers luncheons, and she had them in places like Senegal. People think that this is something new under the sun, that only recent first ladies have been interested in women and women's issues and promoting the role of women around the world. Mrs. Johnson was doing that back when she was second lady.

CAROLI: She tried [to keep Lyndon happy in his political career during the vice presidency and keep their domestic life enjoyable]. She was always trying to get him to go to the gym, because he put on a lot of weight, and she tried to get him to watch his diet. She invited a lot of people that he would like to see, but they were really not good years. Everybody will agree that he did not do well. The vice president's job is a little difficult for strong people.

...After President Kennedy's assassination, there was a month of mourning, and so there was no White House entertaining. But by early January of 1964, they were having two or three evenings a week when they were getting congressmen and their spouses into the White House in small groups. They could have done it in one big reception and gotten some footage, but they did it a dozen at a time and got much closer to the congressmen.

...Many of the congressmen's wives had never been upstairs, and certainly the Kennedys didn't open the second floor, but Lady Bird had them and the women reporters up there on January 8. She had only lived in the White House about a month, and she had the women reporters going through the family bathrooms and looking at the living quarters. It was completely different from Jacqueline Kennedy's attitude that the upstairs was off-limits and it was private.

ROBERTS: Don't underestimate the power of that, because people, when they feel that they're in the inner sanctum and they've gotten something special, they're likely to be nicer to you.

CAROLI: I'm sure [the women reporters] appreciated her being so open. I was struck by the fact that when she had the women reporters through the upstairs quarters, she said, "I felt good about it, because I've always been open about my life, and I think that's why I am pleased to share most aspects of that with the reporters." She said one thing she'd do next time was put away the books she was reading, because a week later, an article appeared—which may have been coincidence—listing the books that Mrs. Johnson liked....

People who knew them said that Mrs. Johnson always acted as though [Lyndon's reported infidelities] didn't happen, but that she must have known they existed. It's important to realize that journalists changed how they covered presidents during the Johnson years. She had lived in Washington all those years and watched Franklin Roosevelt's relationship with Lucy Mercer and John F. Kennedy's relationship with other women, and reporters didn't write about that.

In the Johnson years, and perhaps encouraged a little bit by President Johnson himself, they did start writing about the women who were around him. *Time* magazine, in April of 1964, when Lyndon Johnson had been president only three or four months, had this article about Johnson driving around the roads of Texas at eighty-five miles an hour with a glass of beer on the dashboard and a beautiful young reporter at his side, cooing into his ear, "Mr. President, you're fun," [which] was the headline. I don't think you'll find any articles like that on previous presidents. So, it's important to remember that she came into the spotlight at a time when the spotlight had changed.

ROBERTS: As she went into office, Lady Bird hired Liz Carpenter as press secretary and chief of staff, and Bess Abell, who had been working for her, as social secretary. They really took over the East Wing and then hired others, obviously, to help. That was the first time that there had been a press secretary and chief of staff for the first lady...

CAROLI: I tried to find out the number [of people on her staff], and I was told by her office that it varied, because not only did she hire a large competent staff herself, but she also brought in on loan, people from other departments. For example, for the beautification campaign, she brought in people from the secretary of interior's office, so it was not on her budget. So, it's really hard to come up with a number. It was somewhere in the twenties.

ROBERTS: She also still had this cadre of political women who worked with her on many of these things, particularly when she got very engaged in creating Head Start.... So, she had a lot of volunteers, very highly trained, very smart volunteers, as well.

CAROLI: In that first year in the White House, the year that they had the rest of the Kennedy term, she didn't choose a project. She didn't even change the curtains that needed changing because she said the next family might not like it. She acted as though that would be the last year in the White House. Then, after Lyndon Johnson won so big in 1964, she sent out requests for advice on what she should do. The word came back that she, like other first ladies, should do something about Washington, and the beautification of Washington really came out of that.

Very quickly, it became clear that her beautification committee had split. Some wanted to go more national, and that's where the emphasis on national parks and highway beautification came from. [Her friend and philanthropist] Mary Lasker said, "These highways are terrible." She was thinking particularly of the New Jersey turnpike. She said...it can be better. So, it's good to think of her beautification project as being national, and that was highway beautification, getting the junk-yards either removed or covered up with fences.

Even the Washington part split into two. One group wanted to plant tulips. They were called the Dogwood Set. These people wanted to polish the statues and make it a more beautiful city for tourists. Others wanted to go into the poor neighborhoods where [there were no] sports fields, recreation facilities...and do something for those neighborhoods. The important thing about her is that she incorporated them all.

ROBERTS: She tried to do it all, but what she also did was, she personally lobbied the United States Congress. There was no hiding behind the man; she did not pretend that she was not doing it. She was up there lobbying, and it was very tough.

It sounds all nicey-nicey, beautification, but, in fact, you can imagine, the billboard lobby was completely against any of this. There were people, as there always are in these situations, pushing harder, saying she wasn't doing enough, that it needed to be a much bigger emphasis on cleaning everything up, and there were people saying you're going way too far. She just hung in there, and she kept it up. Even as the Congress was ready not to reauthorize, she kept it up. She was a very powerful force.... First ladies have always lobbied, from Martha Washington on, but that was the first time there had been such public lobbying.

CAROLI: It was both [a complement to Lyndon Johnson's Great Society programs and an independent program of her own]. That's some-

Lady Bird Johnson, a faithful diarist of her days in the White House, is seen here in her sitting room, recording events for November 15, 1968. *LBJ Library Photo by Robert Knudsen*

thing that we've required of almost every first lady since her: What will be your project?

Remember that Lady Bird continued that work—the beautification, if we want to use that terrible term...after she left the White House, up until 1990.... She continued to give that highway beautification award out of her own pocket to workers in Texas who had done the most to beautify the highways there. I'm always interested in which first ladies continue their projects afterwards and which ones forget that they ever did them.

The Vietnam years were very hard on everybody. They were hard on the whole country, but we also were going through this huge generational fight. Having people outside the White House screaming, "Hey, hey, LBJ, how many kids did you kill today?" Can you imagine? This is somebody that wants to do the right thing by the country, and it is a horrible thing to have that.

But Lady Bird kept going out and giving speeches in spite of those protests.... She said, "I don't want to shut myself up," which would have been easy to do.

...She wrote in her diary in 1964, "I know when the time to leave [the White House] will be, and it is exactly"—and she picked March of 1968. She was such an authentic person that I don't think she dreamed that up later. Certainly, as 1967 wound on, there was a big meeting in September of '67 at the ranch. She talks about being called in with the top advisers, and she says, "I don't want another campaign; I don't want to ask people one more time to help out."

It was hard for Lyndon Johnson to walk away from the presidency. She very much wanted him not to run in March of '68, and he found it difficult to walk away.

ROBERTS: It was a terrible time. 1968 was...the beginning of America's loss of innocence, in a way.... Just trying to keep the country together and keep it in some sense of not falling into despair was something that all the political leaders had to do. The president tried, but it was very hard for him, because he was seen as the symbol of the problem by so many of the people.

Partly, she was worried about his health. His heart attack in 1955 was really a massive heart attack. He was quite affected by it, and the whole family was affected by it. That was something that they always had hovering over them. She had been very protective of his health and of his diet, as best she could be. It was something that was always on her mind. And, in fact, he did die [of a heart attack] in January of 1973.

CAROLI: He lived about four days beyond what would have been a [second] term. He couldn't have [still] been president. He had that serious heart condition during that time, then another heart attack.

[After President Johnson died, Lady Bird continued to be very active] into the 1990s. With her macular degeneration in the nineties, she had to stop reading, and that's when she really stopped giving speeches, because she couldn't see the notes well enough, but certainly until the nineties, she was very active.

Even after [a 2002] stroke, she continued to see people, just so valiantly going out to restaurants. Even though she couldn't voice her reaction, she laughed and made people feel that she really appreciated them.

ROBERTS: She was very active at the LBJ Library, and very interested in the work, and very proud of the work of the library.... She was always there.

CAROLI: Lady Bird was so important in the building of the Johnson library. She looked into the smallest detail, how they were going to attach certain things to the wall. She had herself raised in a crane so she could see what the view would be from her office, which is on the top floor. She was very important in... where it would be located, because she had traveled to the FDR Library and thought the president's hometown might not be the best place. She wanted it at a university.

ROBERTS: Her work at [Lyndon B. Johnson School of Public Affairs at the University of] Texas was very much a part of her work at the library. It was all of one piece, and she was very interested in that work. That's a great place. It's a wonderful school.

CAROLI: [The Lady Bird Johnson Wildflower Center is located] in Austin. When she first started it, it was called the National Wildflower Center.... It's really quite an operation, answering questions from all over the world about what species will grow where and showing people model gardens. Mrs. Johnson continued to visit that right up until she was in a wheelchair with an oxygen tank. She knew the people who worked there. She really continued to be active in that.

[When she died in 2007, at the age of ninety-four,] there was an outpouring of...respect and love.

ROBERTS: Lady Bird's sense of history is something that really we can enjoy so much.... Mrs. Johnson has made it possible for us to see their home movies, read their love letters, and, most important, from my perspective, hear those Johnson tapes [the president's taped White House phone conversations]. She allowed those tapes to be open to the public without knowing what was on them, which is very gutsy. We have learned an enormous amount about American politics and American history from listening to those tapes.

CAROLI: [President and Mrs. Johnson are buried near Stonewall, Texas] just down the road from their ranch house, in the family cemetery. You can walk from the ranch, to the cemetery, to the birthplace, to the school in ten minutes, a very short time.

Lady Bird Johnson's legacy:

ROBERTS: People don't realize that [Washington, D.C.,] is much more beautiful because of Lady Bird Johnson and Mary Lasker, her friend, who was a wonderful philanthropist. This profusion of flowers and trees, and the fact that you just come into the city and are greeted by total beauty, is a result of her having been here.

The first ladies who have succeeded her, particularly both Michelle Obama and Laura Bush, have quoted her, … "I realized I had a pulpit and I could use it, and I could use it to do good." Lady Bird determined that she was going to do that. They have taken those words and followed them very consciously, quoting her.

CAROLI: She was an outstanding first lady who really wrote the book for modern first ladies, what they needed to do to be noncontroversial and yet contribute to a spouse's legacy.

Patricia Ryan Nixon

"I've never had it easy. I've never had time to think about things like...who I wanted to be or whom I admired, or to have ideas. I never had time to dream about being anyone else. I had to work."

Pat Nixon, c1969

Born: March 16, 1912, Ely, Nevada
Married: June 21, 1940, to Richard Milhous Nixon (1913–94)
Children: Patricia (Tricia) (1946–present); Julie (1948–present)
Died: June 22, 1993, Yorba Linda, California

Contributors:

MARY BRENNAN, professor and chair, history department, Texas State University, focusing on modern U.S. history; author of several books, including *Pat Nixon: Embattled First Lady*

TIMOTHY NAFTALI, Cold War historian and author; former director, Richard Nixon Presidential Library

MARY BRENNAN: Pat Nixon was fun and funny. People who knew her talked about her sense of humor. And she was adventurous. As a young woman, she worked for a hospital in New York City, and she would go out with the patients who had tuberculosis and take trays from the cafeteria and slide down the hills. That's the kind of thing that she would love to do.

TIMOTHY NAFTALI: She was a working woman. In many ways, she was a pioneer. Her wit was strong and, at times, biting. She didn't always take herself seriously, and she probably did not want to be first lady.

She was always much more popular than Richard Nixon. In fact, a lot of the public felt a great deal of sympathy for her, particularly as the demonstrations got raucous outside of the White House, because of Vietnam and later, because of Watergate.

It's really important when we think about her image to think about how much of it she didn't control, because the Nixon White House in many ways was a model of the modern White House in the television age. The White House decided how the presidential family would be used or not used.... Pat Nixon did not have the opportunity to control as much as she would've liked the way in which she was presented to the American people....

BRENNAN: [Critics dubbed her "Plastic Pat," which] came from very early on during the first controversy that she had to deal with during [Richard Nixon's 1952 Republican vice presidential bid, his famous] "Checkers" speech. There was only one camera, and so the cameraman told her, "We never know when we're going to come onto you, so just keep a smile on your face," and so she kept that smile the whole time. There were other reasons she was holding that smile as well, but that started this idea that she was this rigid personality. Afterwards, [public perception] just kind of kept coming back to that.

She was [born] Thelma Catherine Ryan. When her father came home, he wanted to call her Patricia. He didn't really like Thelma Catherine, so he said she was his "St. Patrick's babe in the morning," and he always called her "Babe." Her friends in school called her Thelma, and in high school they all called her "Buddy." When she went to junior college, she enrolled herself as Pat Ryan, but that was the first time that she consciously renamed herself.

As a child, she had a very hard time. Her mother died when she was not quite thirteen, then her father died four years later. She kept house for her brothers. They lived on, basically, a hardscrabble farm, so they were always working. She had jobs sweeping out banks. She did all kinds of things, because they had to make money to be able to pay the bills, to keep the farm. Eventually, they rented out the farm as they had to pay their father's medical bills.

NAFTALI: She wanted to go to college, but she couldn't afford it....

BRENNAN: Another way Pat Ryan made money [was] she drove a couple... [to New York City]. They paid her to drive their car across the country. She was going to visit some of her father's relatives on the East Coast.... One of her aunts was a nun who worked at Seton Hospital and gave her a job. It was the middle of the Depression, so she stayed on her own in New York City. She worked different kinds of jobs in the hospital. She worked in the lab. She did all kinds of things, because she needed the work.

NAFTALI: It belies the "Plastic Pat" [image]. This is a woman with a great deal of gumption and drive, who knows what she wants and wants the world. She's really interested. She comes from Southern California, from an agricultural part in Los Angeles County, and she wants to go to New York. She gets this opportunity to go to New York, and she stays. She only comes back when her brothers tell her that they've raised enough money so she can go to college. She goes to the University of Southern California.

BRENNAN: [After graduating *cum laude* and earning a special teaching certificate,] she was teaching at Whittier High School, and she loved theater. She had been in theater all throughout high school and in college. There was a community theater production that was going on, and one of the older teachers suggested that she try out. It was not just a suggestion; she kind of got the idea she should do it.... Richard Nixon, who was a young lawyer in Whittier, was trying to make connections every way that he could, and he was also trying out for the show, so they were both there at the same time.

Richard Nixon said that he fell in love with Pat at first sight. He offered to drive both her and a friend home. He said in his memoirs that he asked her to marry him that first night. The friend said that took him three times driving back and forth, but he was very persistent. He ran after Pat, and she kind of held him at arm's [length].

Pat did eventually come home and tell her roommate that this guy had really put the moves on her, and that she wasn't sure she was going to go out with him, but that she thought he probably could be president someday.

NAFTALI: It was their intelligence [that attracted them to each other]. They're both highly intelligent people, and they're both quite determined. Richard Nixon could not walk over Pat Ryan. That both drew them together and at times, it pushed them apart, but there are some similarities in their characters. They both have strong characters.

BRENNAN: I would add ambition. They both wanted things. Pat was not going to be happy staying in Whittier. She wanted to see the world. She saw that in Dick Nixon that she wasn't going to have to stay where she was. [They married in 1940.]

When Richard Nixon came back [from in the Navy in World War II], he was in D.C., still on active duty, and he was contacted by someone from California. They were looking for somebody to run against Jerry Voorhis in the state's Twelfth Congressional District [in 1946]. Dick talked to Pat, and they agreed that he would go back out and he would talk to these people.... They said, yes, this is a good thing, and they decided to run.

By this time, Pat was pregnant with Tricia. They...have to go all the way back across to California, because they have to start campaigning. She packs everything up, eight months pregnant, gets everything moved back out to California. A month or so after they get back out there, she delivers Tricia while they're still campaigning.

This...tells something about her ambition, because she delivers the baby and, six hours later, she's up typing, doing research for his speeches. Now, granted, they didn't have a lot of money for the campaign, but she had a perfect excuse to stop participating. She had a brand-new baby that she had to drop off at her mother-in-law's to go work on this campaign, but she doesn't do it. She makes the choice to go ahead and participate. This first campaign, where they didn't know anything about what they were doing, Richard calls their sweetest victory....because they had worked so hard to get this. This was really the beginning of what became the Pat and Dick team.

...There were things in politics that she hated, and I don't think she realized in 1946 what those would be. I don't think she realized how much of her life she would have to give up, how much privacy she would have to give up....

But when she becomes second lady, [in the Eisenhower Administration,] and they get to visit all of these places, she sees not just the world that she'd always hoped to see, but how she can touch people. She can do things and make a difference in people's lives; for her, that almost balanced out all of the parts of politics that she hated. She loved exploring the world. She got to do a tremendous amount of it as second lady. That did help later on, as she planned [how] to be first lady.

[The 1960 presidential campaign experience] was devastating.... All you have to do is look at that picture of her from Nixon's concession speech in 1960 and it's written all over her face. It just sucked the life out of her. Whenever she talked about the campaign in 1960, it was, "We're running for election." When the American people rejected him, she really saw it as a rejection of them. She couldn't recover from that the same way that he could.

NAFTALI: What's also clear from [her daughter] Julie's book [*Pat Nixon: The Untold Story*]...is that Pat Nixon did carry some resentment about the 1960 election. She did feel that it had been stolen, and she did not hide her disappointment. Look at photographs of her in 1960; she's not wearing a poker face. So, there is no doubt in my mind that some of the anger that Richard Nixon had for the Kennedys, she did [as well].

Something happens after 1960.... After that very bitter defeat and that very difficult defeat, she wanted out of politics.... I think she wanted to be first lady in 1960. I'm not sure if she wanted to be first lady in 1968.

[After his loss in both the 1960 presidential election and the 1962 election for governor of California,] Richard Nixon goes back to being a lawyer, but he never stops thinking about returning to politics.... It's especially difficult to understand the inner workings of a presidential family. There are bits and pieces which give us a sense of the debate within the family, but the sense that I have is that Pat Nixon was much less interested in a return to the White House than her husband was. Her husband was plotting a return, not for '64, necessarily, but for later. He was traveling abroad; he was meeting with foreign leaders in an effort to keep his name out there. Most importantly, in 1966, he takes advantage of a midterm election to go out and collect chits. He starts campaigning for people around the country, and they win, and they remember the fact that Richard Nixon campaigned on their behalf. He is preparing for 1968. The extent to which Pat Nixon was looking forward to 1968, I have my doubts, but he certainly was. This is where the partnership may have changed.

BRENNAN: She was not a stupid woman. Pat knows that he's planning to go back to the White House. She knows what he's planning, but she's lost in terms of trying to figure out what to do. This is a woman whose children are growing up, and she is somebody who's always had work to do, so she goes back and works in his office. There are times when she goes back and answers phones as "Miss Ryan," because, "It makes the time go by." She doesn't have something else to do. So, there is a sense of her trying to figure out what she's going to do at this point.

NAFTALI: [After Richard Nixon's second, successful bid for the White House in 1968,] Pat didn't want to have to choose an issue. In fact, it bothered her when, in the first few months of the administration, she kept being asked, "What is your focus?" She said, "People." She didn't want there to be one issue. Volunteerism would be what she'd be best known for in that first year. She'd made trips around the country to show her support for [a program called]...Vest Pockets of Altruism. But the thing about it was that she didn't want to be programmed. Lady Bird Johnson was known for the beautification program. Pat Nixon did not like the fact that it was assumed that she would be programmed to do one thing.

BRENNAN: Volunteerism worked for her, in the sense that...she had, in a way, volunteered her whole life. So that worked. It worked with the Nixon Administration, in terms of what they wanted to do, [but] she didn't want to pick one topic. She would rather go out and see people and see what they were doing. She tells [White House organizers], "I don't want local officials; I don't want the CEOs and the heads of these corporations coming. I want to go see the volunteers, and I want to see the people they're helping, and I want to talk to them." She was very much involved with the people, not with the big shots....

That first term, she's really trying to find herself as first lady, and she doesn't have some of the tools yet to stand up to the West Wing.

NAFTALI: The tensions between the East Wing and the West Wing are really important. As President Nixon begins to separate more and more his personal life from his political life, Pat Nixon is actually seeing the effect, because H.R. Haldeman, chief of staff to President Nixon, doesn't particularly enjoy working with Pat Nixon and does not take advantage of her many skills.

In fact, when she goes to Africa and does such a wonderful job of representing our country in January of 1972, and gets rave reviews, there's a note that the president gets about how well Pat did, and it was [shown] to Pat Nixon. Pat writes to her friend, Helene Drown, "Well, they finally figured out what I can do."

BRENNAN: Mrs. Nixon loved traveling. It's important that when she traveled as first lady, that was when she felt the most useful. It got her away from the control of the West Wing, and it reconnected her to the days when they were the second couple, when she and Dick were a team, and they could go out and do things....

NAFTALI: Her first foreign trip, which is to Peru, happens at the request of President Nixon. It's not that President Nixon is forcing her out of the White House. [Their daughter] Julie writes about this.

The demonstrations following the 1970 Kent State massacre traumatized the Nixon family, and Pat decided to bring the family back from Camp David so that Richard Nixon wouldn't be alone in the White House. It's clear that this period, from early May through June of 1970, was very difficult for the Nixon family, and especially for Pat Nixon. She was concerned [because] she had heard about the earthquake in Peru; fifty thousand died, eight hundred thousand people were left homeless. She was watching what was happening, and I suspect that the president realized that to restart her, he needed to give her something where she felt she was doing something good. Peru was a very interesting choice, because the United States was not close to Peru. There was a revolutionary government there, which had criticized the United States. To send Pat to Peru, of all places, involved a little bit of a political risk. But, she did it. This was Richard Nixon's choice. She said yes, and it proved to be wonderful for her and very good for U.S.-Peruvian relations. She ended up getting an award from the government of Peru, and the Peruvian government, which had not had much say that was very good about the United States, actually thanked the United States for what Pat Nixon helped to do.

The trip to Peru was her first solo trip. She did accompany the president in 1969, and that's when she went to South Vietnam. She actually spent time in a hospital meeting with wounded soldiers, and that was her choice.

BRENNAN: She's the first first lady to travel into a combat zone [Vietnam]. She insisted on visiting soldiers in the hospital, on visiting the troops. She was not someone who wanted generals to give her an update. She wanted to go and talk to the soldiers. It didn't matter that it was a combat zone. She needed to go and talk to the boys themselves, and to be able to calm them down, because both of her sons-in-law had been in the military. She felt very close to all of these young men.

[On Nixon's historic 1972 trip to China,] since the press was allowed to go [along], and the Chinese government allowed the press to follow them, and since the president was in closed-door meetings, what the American public saw of China was what they saw through Pat. She was the one taking them around. To the Chinese public that she met, she was the representative of the Americans, and she introduced America to China…. For her, this was an amazing trip. She got to meet people. They would come up and try to quote Mao to her. She would say, "Oh, yes, I've read that book," and then she would go on to something else, because that wasn't what she wanted to do. She would talk to the people as much as she could.

NAFTALI: …There's a little bit of controversy over whether, in fact, she had asked for the pandas [gifted to the United States by the Chinese government]. One of President Nixon's aides told me that it was a misunderstanding. Pat Nixon smoked, [and] she didn't like to show people that she smoked, but she smoked a lot. Olivia Anastasiadis, the supervisory curator at the Nixon Library, said there were pandas on the Chinese cigarette packs. It's not clear whether Mrs. Nixon was just motioning towards the panda because she wanted a cigarette or because she really liked pandas and wanted them for the United States. It's not clear whether Chinese Premier Zhou Enlai actually knew what she was asking for, but the outcome was wonderful for the United States and for the National Zoo [when China gave the U.S. two pandas].

When Pat Nixon came to the White House, one-third of the furnishings were antiques. When she left the White House, two-thirds of them were antiques. Dolley Madison is famous for saving the canvas of George Washington in 1814. She actually saved two canvasses. The other one was a portrait of herself, and Pat Nixon brought it back to the White House.

BRENNAN: She actually worked very hard behind the scenes [on the White House]. She worked with Clem Conger as a curator, and they worked very hard to restore the White House, to pick up where Jackie Kennedy had left off and continue to get period pieces. She could be very persuasive in convincing various institutions and museums to return pieces and to loan pieces to the White House. They went out and sought out people to donate the money to be able to get the proper pieces to fill the rooms.

She had always been very interested in decorating. She had decorated a number of their homes. So, this was something that was very important to her and not something that was widely known. They didn't publicize this. She was doing it for a while before anybody realized that she was doing it…. Pat really tried to give the credit to other people, rather than taking it herself.

NAFTALI: The Nixon Administration made a big effort with regard to hiring more women into the federal service. Barbara Franklin was made the point person for this. Did this come from Pat Nixon? We don't know. We know that Julie Nixon played a role, working with Barbara Franklin. There's no doubt that Pat Nixon was supportive, [and]…we do know that she was very disappointed in October of 1971 when President Nixon had two open seats on the Supreme Court. She really hoped that one of them would go to a woman. When that didn't happen, she let President Nixon know at a private family dinner that she was not happy.

BRENNAN: She didn't speak to him for a while, which was her way of letting him stew on things and getting back at him. She thought she had a promise from him that he was going to appoint a woman. She was very upset about that.

NAFTALI: Part of the story of Pat Nixon in the White House is a story of the pressures on the family because of the country's reaction to the president's Vietnam policy. Whatever you think about the president's Vietnam policy, it's hard to dispute the fact that the country's reaction had a very strong effect on the Nixon family, and Pat, in particular, was affected by it. One of the reasons why the president encouraged her to leave on these solo trips was to pick up her morale.

[The wedding of her daughter Tricia to Ed Cox] was probably Pat Nixon's happiest day in the White House. I don't think there's any doubt. It's an inflexion point, because right after that, you have the Pentagon Papers controversy and the Watergate plumbers [scandal] and things start to get out of hand. So, that moment in the summer of 1971 is a very sweet moment for the family.

After the successful conclusion of the negotiations which resulted in an agreement in January of 1973 to end the American participation in the war in Southeast Asia, the White House very much wanted to celebrate this achievement. They wanted to put a positive final note to what had been such a difficult war for this country. [The largest event ever thrown at the White House, to this day, was President Nixon's May 24, 1973, tribute to the Vietnam prisoners of war] because the president had made the argument that he had been thinking always about getting the POWs out. Their coming to the White House was a symbol of his achievement....

The fact is that, for Pat Nixon, as for the other members of the family, seeing the POWs was a source of pride and happiness and accomplishment. I don't doubt that that evening was very special for all of them.

BRENNAN: [Watergate and Nixon's ultimate resignation from the presidency in August of 1974] was a very trying time. It's important to remember that the president didn't discuss policy with her, so when Mrs. Nixon told people that she only knew what she read in the papers, that was all she knew. She was also someone who trusted her husband and who didn't trust [Nixon senior aides] H.R. Haldeman and John Ehrlichman and the men surrounding Richard, so it was very easy for her to believe that these men were setting him up. But she kept getting all these questions, and the questions became increasingly hostile and increasingly persistent so that she couldn't avoid them. Here she is, at the height of finally figuring out what she wants to do as first lady, and now she can't avoid these questions about Watergate.

She became, in many ways, the rock. She continued to do her [public] schedule. They'd go and visit people, go out to teas, go to meetings, because she has to. Was she drinking more [because of the pressures of Watergate]? She was someone who liked to have a drink after dinner. Almost everyone of that generation did. People knew she drank Jack Daniels; it was common knowledge. Did she drink more? Probably. Who wouldn't? Was there any evidence that she was an alcoholic? No....

NAFTALI: It's clear that the president lied to Pat about a number of things. This is an important part of the story, because she was absolutely loyal to Richard Nixon. She was suffering for him. He tells her that he had nothing to do with the [so-called Nixon] enemies list, when it was his idea. He tells her that Lyndon Johnson had bugged his campaign plane in the '68 campaign. That wasn't true, and he knew it wasn't true.

He filled her mind with things that made what she was reading in the newspaper make no sense at all to her. In the end, Richard Nixon didn't even have the courage to tell her he was going to resign. The first time he thought he would resign, August 2, 1974, he had Julie tell his wife. Then the whole family persuaded him not to resign. When he finally made the decision to resign, he had [his secretary] Rose Mary Woods tell Mrs. Nixon. His secretary! He didn't even tell her.

The one regret she had from that period, and this is, again, evidence that she was affected by Watergate, but had no role whatsoever in managing it, was that the president didn't tell her that there was a White House taping system. The president also didn't involve her in the decision of what to do about his tapes when it became clear that it was going to be a major issue when the taping system was revealed to the public.

She felt that he had made a huge error and that he should have destroyed the tapes. By the way, he could have destroyed them, because at that time in United States law, those tapes were private property that belonged to the president. Once they were subpoenaed, it would be a different issue, but they hadn't been subpoenaed yet. She wanted to get

As the Nixons leave the White House following President Nixon's August 9, 1974, resignation from office, President and Mrs. Ford say their farewells.

rid of them, but he never asked her. She was not part of this at all; she just suffered from it.

She was a rock during the last few months of the administration; at least that's how she's been described. She continued to be very strong when the president nearly died...a few months after leaving office. He got phlebitis, which is an inflammation of the veins. He actually went into cardiac arrest because of the reaction to an infection. This happened in Long Beach, California. [The former president was hospitalized for twenty-three days.] He nearly died, and she was very strong for the family.

What's important here, though, is that she found the resources within herself, despite this national tragedy, to pull her and the family together during his health crisis. The real tragedy is that she then has her own health crisis.

BRENNAN: [Mrs. Nixon had a very serious stroke in 1976.] She couldn't move her left side, her speech was slurred. She worked very hard to regain her strength and to be able to move her left arm…. She was determined to come back, that she was not going to let this get her. It was very serious.

NAFTALI: The original Nixon Library, the only private presidential library at that point, was opened in 1991. Mrs. Nixon was alive to see it open. She died in 1993, the year before he does, and she's buried at the library. I never found any evidence that she participated in shaping the museum, but I do believe that the rose garden that the library has reflects her interests…. She was very interested in opening the gardens of the White House to the public. She was the first to do that, so it makes a lot of sense that visitor to the Nixon Library sees Pat's rose garden.

BRENNAN: [She died after she had] another stroke, and she had emphysema and lung cancer from years of smoking.

[Richard Nixon was videotaped at her funeral service weeping over her grave.] What you have is a man who loves his wife and who perhaps in some ways did not realize how central she was to holding him up, to propping him up. She was that way for her daughters, but certainly for him. It goes back to their original relationship and the love that we saw there in the beginning. She was a woman of tremendous strength who could not have been plastic. She had to be steel.

Pat Nixon's legacy:

NAFTALI: [Her greatest contribution to the role of first lady was] dignity under strain. She was dignified and proud throughout her period in office.

BRENNAN: [One of her legacies was] making sure that people understood that the White House was their house, and that everyone should have a voice, and that everyone should be able to come, and everyone was welcome.

Elizabeth (Betty) Bloomer Ford

"Being ladylike does not require silence. Why should my husband's job or yours prevent us from being ourselves? I do not believe that being first lady should prevent me from expressing my ideas."

Betty Ford, 1974

Born: April 8, 1918, Chicago, Illinois
Married: April 23, 1942–47, to William Warren (divorced); October 15, 1948, to Gerald R. Ford (1913–2006)
Children: Michael Gerald (1950–present); John Gardner (Jack) (1952–present); Steven Meigs (1956–present); Susan Elizabeth (1957–present)
Died: July 8, 2011, Rancho Mirage, California

Contributor:

RICHARD NORTON SMITH, presidential historian; executive director at five presidential libraries; author of several books, including *Patriarch*; history consultant for C-SPAN; and academic advisor for C-SPAN's *First Ladies* series

RICHARD NORTON SMITH: Betty Bloomer was born in Chicago. Her parents are a fascinating contrast. Her mother clearly was the dominating, defining figure in her life, Hortense Bloomer, who I've often thought was a character straight out of Tennessee Williams. She came from a very prosperous family; status meant a lot to Mrs. Bloomer. She insisted, for example, that Betty wear white gloves when she went shopping. She was a perfectionist to end all perfectionists.

Betty, as a child, was prone to overeat, at least as far as Hortense was concerned, who responded by hanging a sign over her daughter's neck saying, "Please, don't feed this child." Hortense was a formidable figure. Talk about patterns: Betty's father was a traveling salesman and an alcoholic who died amidst mysterious circumstances when she was sixteen. It was one of those deaths that was never quite fully discussed. In fact, it was only then that Betty learned that her father was an alcoholic, and that those trips that her mother had made from time to time to be with him on the road, were a consequence of his illness. It was a house where secrets flourished. She had two brothers, one of whom was an alcoholic. So, in many ways, she was genetically or culturally programmed for the disease that she would have later on.

Hortense Bloomer was a larger-than-life figure.... She wanted Betty to join the Junior League at a very early age and rise up the ladder. She had problems with a daughter who had a mind of her own, who, for example, wanted to pursue a career as a Martha Graham dancer.

Betty spent a couple of years in Bennington, Vermont, associated with the dance program there. Then she joined the Martha Graham Company. She never made the first ranks. She was very modest in the later years, but it is a key to her personality. She was a natural performer. She was perfectly comfortable being on the stage. In some ways, that came back to her to aid her when she became first lady.

She came back to Grand Rapids, and she taught dance. She worked as a fashion coordinator at a local department store. She, by her own acknowledgement, was a party girl who met a party boy—actually, she'd known him since she was twelve years old—Bill Warren, who was himself a traveling salesman and an alcoholic, and they were married. She was twenty-four. She had almost overnight embraced a whole different set of values. She was ready to settle down and be a wife and have children. That was not necessarily the same agenda that he had.

The interesting thing is she made the decision after about three years to divorce him. Then, he went into a diabetic coma, and she spent the next two years nursing him back to health. Then, she filed for a divorce. She called it her five-year misunderstanding.

[When Gerald Ford and Betty first started dating, she didn't know she was getting a politician.] That's what she says. It's hard for me to believe that she was totally naive. Jerry Ford was a big man on campus, a local hero from his high school days playing football. It's not terribly surprising that he should decide to go into public life. But there is no doubt, she was surprised. They were married in October 1948.

West Michigan then, considerably more than now, was a very culturally conservative place, a place where the Dutch Reformed Church held sway. Ford, who was certainly always a fiscal conservative, nevertheless was running [for Congress] against an entrenched Republican incumbent, a mossback isolationist who opposed the Marshall Plan. Ford was one of those World War II returning veterans who had seen the consequences of American isolationism, and went into politics with an idea that America would have to play a continuing, significant leadership role in the world.

Mrs. Ford was a divorcée. He told her when he proposed that he wanted to get married, but he couldn't tell her when, and he couldn't tell her why he couldn't tell her. But the fact of the matter was his political advisers were very concerned that in West Michigan he was already facing an uphill campaign, and that having a divorcée in the family might lengthen those odds even more.

They were married on October 15, about three weeks before the election. He showed up late. Actually, he showed up at the rehearsal dinner late—in time for dessert. He was late for the wedding. He showed up in brown shoes and a dark suit. The shoes were muddy because he'd been out campaigning.

Their glamorous honeymoon consisted of an overnight in Owosso, Michigan, sitting outdoors listening to [Republican presidential candidate] Thomas E. Dewey, the favorite son of Owosso, and then a football game in Ann Arbor, his beloved University of Michigan. She stayed in the hotel in Ann Arbor while he went to the game, then they went back to Grand Rapids on Monday. He said he had to campaign that evening, and could she make him a sandwich. He said, later on, she never let him hear the end of it. They took a number of second honeymoons to compensate.

[When Jerry Ford, then House minority leader, was appointed in 1973 to serve as Nixon's vice president,] Betty Ford was back at their house in Alexandria, Virginia, but she said she realized for the first time in her life, she had to be on time. That was a lifelong issue. She was not the most punctual of people. There are those who think that it was passive-aggressive. It was one of the few things in their marriage that she could control. But, in any event, all that changed once she became the vice president's wife. She also had causes that she was involved with. She had been involved, from an early age, with disabled children. The Washington Children's Hospital was something she was involved with. In addition to that, she also now had a vice presidential residence that had never been occupied before that had to be decorated. In August 1974, a few days before Richard Nixon resigned, the vice president agreed to accompany his wife to the house that he, by then, knew they were never going to live in. If he didn't [tour the new vice president's house], the press would have sensed that we were in the end game [of the Nixon presidency]. He didn't want to give that away.

That night, somehow, they went to a dinner party and he kept all of this [quiet]. On August 1, 1974, he had been told by General Al Haig, the White House chief of staff, about what became known as the "smoking gun" [among the Nixon White House] tapes. It was pretty clear what the consequences of that would be. After midnight that night, he said, "Betty, we're never going to live in that house."

Every other American household, in the summer of 1974, at some point, sat around the dinner table discussing what was happening [with Watergate] and what might happen in the White House. The only dinner table in America where that discussion apparently never took place was the Fords'. For Mrs. Ford, it really was a case of denial in a lot of ways.

She said that August 9, 1974, [when Richard Nixon resigned the presidency] was the saddest day of her life. In part, she felt badly for the country, but even more, she felt badly for Pat Nixon and the Nixon family, who were good friends of the Fords'. And finally, Jerry Ford had never aspired to the presidency. She was even more reluctant with the idea of going to the White House, and she really didn't find out until about a week before it happened.

Everyone remembers those famous pictures of Richard Nixon at the helicopter giving the "V" sign [as he and Mrs. Nixon left the White House for the final time]. What they don't know is what soon-to-be President Ford said to his wife on the way back into the White House. Jerry Ford realized his job was to reassure the country, and if he couldn't reassure his wife, he couldn't reassure the country. He leaned over and whispered in her ear, "We can do it." It was just the right thing to say. He said a lot of right things that day.

There were a lot of problems and controversies that ensued. There was a sense that it was as if the country had been building up to this thunderstorm, and the storm raged for a while and then, suddenly, the clouds parted and it was normal again....

[Living in the White House] was like going to live on another planet for the Ford family. The first days Betty actually lived in the White House, she didn't understand [the protocol]. She would walk through the halls and say hello to people when she saw them—Secret Service agents, household personnel, whatever—that was her nature. And no one spoke back to her.

She finally went to Rex Scouten, the legendary White House usher, and said, "Am I doing something wrong? Do they dislike us for being here?" And he explained, no, the Nixons were somewhat more formal, and had established that practice. So word went out to the White House staff that it was okay to talk to the first family. Before long, stories [came out] about President Ford and the butler comparing football scores....

[A few months after they came into office, Mrs. Ford discovered she had breast cancer.] This was, in some ways, the indelible moment when she first impressed herself on the American people. The whole Ford family did. It is really hard, forty years later, to conceive of the degree to which people didn't talk about this disease. Euphemisms were employed. Even in obituaries, people didn't die of breast cancer. They died of a "wasting illness." What Mrs. Ford did was to bring this out in the open and, overnight, transform the way women, in particular, looked at this disease.

For her, it was also a lesson. It was her first and most important lesson in the influence that a first lady could have just by being herself, by shining the light on a dark corner, by educating the public. It initiated a national conversation, a conversation among women, a conversation between women and their doctors. When it comes to women's health issues, literally, history is divided into two periods: there's before Betty, and after Betty.

[During this very brief presidency, they hosted thirty-three state visits.] The reason it was so concentrated was it was the bicentennial year. In addition to 1976 being the year for this very hotly contested Republican race for the nomination, and then the fall campaign, played out against the backdrop of the American Bicentennial. Betty Ford was a woman who was accustomed to being on the stage. As first lady, she was back on the stage. She really enjoyed the entertaining part of the job. Their entertainments were really personalized.

[The Ford White House] differed in a number of ways [from previous administrations], and some of them are purely social. For example, she restored the round tables at dinner. She thought it was much more informal and led to conversation. She did not do a lot of decorating. But there is on the second floor a private family dining room, and Mrs. Kennedy had located some spectacular and historically invaluable French wallpaper portraying the American Revolution in very graphic military terms. Mrs. Ford, who had the utmost respect for Mrs. Kennedy's taste, nevertheless said, "I can't sit there and watch these people shooting each other on battlefields," and she had the paper removed. Rosalynn Carter had it put back.

A number of things [made Betty Ford controversial as first lady]. First of all, she spoke her mind…. Quite frankly, you can understand a lot of the criticisms by people who were accustomed to, for lack of a better word, a more traditional approach to the job. First ladies were not overtly political. First ladies did not wade into intensely debated moral issues like abortion, for example. First ladies certainly did not discuss whether their children had used marijuana or whether their daughter might have an affair.

Part of what was different was, for the first time, she was being asked questions that no one would have put to a Pat Nixon or a Lady Bird Johnson. The difference is she was willing to respond. She connected with millions of women. She was candid about her personal struggles. A lot of people didn't realize when she became first lady that she had been married before. Bonnie Angelo, a magazine correspondent, asked her about that and why people didn't know about it. She said no one had bothered to ask her before…. A lot of people looked at Betty Ford, this Cub Scout den mother, this Sunday school teacher from West Michigan, and they labeled her. They wrote her off, in effect. Then, they discovered, "No, actually, this is a woman with views of her own. This is a woman who has had a lot of challenges in her life," and a lot of those challenges bonded her with millions of other women who entertain similar doubts and uncertainties.

[An interview on the television program *60 Minutes*] defined her for millions and millions of people. First of all, it was the first time they'd seen Betty Ford in that kind of setting.... People were not accustomed to a first lady answering these kinds of questions. Her view was, look, people are talking about these issues around their dinner tables all over America. Why shouldn't the first family have the same privilege?

[She was asked about issues such as divorce, use of marijuana, her daughter's dating, and sex before marriage.] She also talked about her use of pillow talk to get a woman in the cabinet. She also mentioned she was working on getting a woman on the Supreme Court. John Paul Stevens [President Ford's 1975 Supreme Court appointment], it's safe to say, would probably not have been her first choice, but then, she wasn't doing the choosing.

Publicly, Betty Ford was arguably the most political first lady since Eleanor Roosevelt. She was the most outspoken advocate for the Equal Rights Amendment. She publicly disagreed with her husband during the presidency on the *Roe v. Wade* [abortion] case, which she famously discussed on the *60 Minutes* interview and [in] other venues. She was very much an independent force. Initially, that terrified people in the White House. After the *60 Minutes* interview, the president said jokingly, "You've lost me ten—no, twenty million votes."

It was only a few days later when the first polls came in and the people in the White House were astonished that, in fact, an overwhelming 70 percent of those who were polled sympathized with the first lady's candor, if not necessarily her specific views.

There's no doubt Betty Ford was a polarizing figure. When I said 70 percent voiced approval, that meant 30 percent disapproved. You can be sure that that 30 percent was disproportionately the Republican base, certainly conservative Republicans, traditionalists, if you will.

There was a legitimate debate [about her impact on her husband's political career]. John Robert Greene wrote a book on...Mrs. Ford.... He makes the case probably stronger than I would that she was, on balance, detrimental to her husband's reelection prospects, particularly within, but not exclusively within, the Republican Party.

There's some controversy about [how Betty Ford was used in the 1976 election]. There are people who think that she was misused, overused,

President and Mrs. Ford celebrate winning the 1976 Republican nomination at the party's national convention in Kansas City, Missouri, besting challenger Ronald Reagan.

that she was a rather fragile, delicate figure. She was certainly very active in the primary campaign in the Ford-Reagan race. There are people who remember that the 1976 convention had dueling candidates' wives, the entrance of Mrs. Reagan to the convention hall, and the entrance of Mrs. Ford who, by the way, had the great good fortune, in her mind, to be introduced by Cary Grant.

In the fall campaign, again, there's a school of thought that she wasn't used as well as she might have been.

Of course, Betty Ford felt badly [when President Ford lost the '76 election]. There are people who still remember that Jerry Ford lost his voice at the very end of the campaign, so it was left to the first lady—this is another first—to read his concession statement and the telegram of congratulations that had been sent to President-elect Carter.

At the same time, Betty wouldn't miss life in politics. Jerry had promised her, long before Watergate, that they were going to retire in 1976. Once he concluded that he was never going to be speaker of the House, she had exacted a promise that, after 1976, they would leave Washington, go back to Grand Rapids, and he would practice law....

Of course, intervening events played havoc with that plan, but they still left Washington. They just went to a different destination.

[Betty Ford's drug and alcohol use first] became a real problem in the sixties. First of all, there were a number of contributing factors. There was actually a physical [component]—she had developed arthritis and she had a pinched nerve, which may or may not have been the result of reaching up to raise up a window. It was excruciatingly painful. She had pills prescribed for her and the pills made her feel better, and the alcohol made her feel better still.

There is anecdotal evidence to suggest she's what I call a circumstantial alcoholic, if there is such a thing. As far as the pills are concerned, we mentioned thirty-three state dinners. She was, in all of them and by all accounts, a very vital hostess. The problem really erupted when they left Washington. There was a significant problem before the presidency, and it was an almost lethal problem after the presidency. But ironically, [for] those two and a half years in the White House, it was much less of a problem than we read.

One thing that might surprise people...until the end of her life, she had butterflies before she went on stage.... She was terrified. A part of that is the perfectionism that was bred in her by her mother. We talked about her genetic disposition to alcohol. There was, in a way, an emotional disposition, as well. She writes particularly in her memoir, *A Glad Awakening*, about her emptiness and low self-esteem. She was very sensitive about the fact she didn't have a college degree, for example. Earlier in her life, her husband's career was taking off. By the time they came back to Southern California, he was out on the road almost as often as he had been before, and now the kids were gone. So that emptiness, in effect, became everything. It was easier for her to slip back into the old habits.

After an intervention in April of 1978, she was checked into Long Beach Hospital. It shouldn't be sentimentalized or romanticized; it was a very gritty, very demanding, somewhat risky period. She didn't want to be there. She made it very clear, for example, that she didn't want to share a room with three other patients.

She read the statement that said that she was there because she was overmedicated, which was true, but far from the whole truth, and they had to push her and push her to, in effect, reveal a full truth that she had an alcohol problem. She was detoxified there and that was not pleasant. But within a week, she was toasting the future in fruit juice. It was the beginning of a whole new life in a lot of ways.

Her neighbor in Rancho Mirage was a man named Leonard Firestone, a successful businessman. He'd been ambassador to Belgium. He was an alcoholic as well. About a year after her successful intervention, the Fords and their friends staged one with the Firestones. To make a long story short, Leonard Firestone and Betty Ford decided together to go to the Eisenhower Medical Center with the idea for what became the Betty Ford Center, [which treats people with alcohol and drug dependencies. Founded in 1982, she served as its chair until] 2005.

[She was a] very active, very hands-on [chairperson]. She said her friends hated to see her coming because they knew she was going to put the touch on them for fundraising. She was a phenomenally successful fundraiser. Every year they would have an alumni event [at the Betty Ford Center]. The president was so proud of her. At the alumni event, you could find Betty holding court, while President Ford was cooking hot dogs for the alumni. He also said that…when the history books are written, her contribution to America would be considered greater than his own.

Betty said very little about [President Ford's decision to issue] the Nixon pardon. She thought it was necessary. She thought it was an act of courage…. Toward the end of his life when the John F. Kennedy Library chose to give President Ford their Profiles in Courage Award specifically for the Nixon pardon, he was initially reluctant to go. To go all the way across the country at his age, he didn't see the emotional significance of this. It was Mrs. Ford who convinced him, "Jerry, this is the greatest honor that's been bestowed on you since leaving office." He said, after that, for twenty years, everywhere he went people asked him about the pardon, and after the Profiles in Courage Award, people stopped asking.

[Gerald Ford died on December 26, 2006, at the age of 93.] Mrs. Ford was very much a part of [planning President Ford's funeral]. She said the one thing he was adamant about was he did not want a horse-drawn caisson through the streets of Washington. She kept saying,

"Keep it simple and think of [our] kids," because, to her, this was only partly a national or public event. This was first and foremost a family event.

She died on July 8, 2011, which is about four and a half years [after President Ford died]. She died of being ninety-three.

Betty Ford's legacy:

She broke the mold more than she started traditions.

[In 1999, the Fords were awarded the Congressional Gold Medal. In presenting it, President Bill Clinton said of Mrs. Ford, "Perhaps no first lady in our history, with the possible exception of Eleanor Roosevelt, has touched so many of us in such a personal way…because she showed [us] it was not wrong for a good person and a strong person to be imperfect and ask for help. You gave us a gift and we thank you."]

Rosalynn Smith Carter

"Before Jimmy's inauguration, the press had painted us as country farm people who would bring gingham and square dances to the White House. We did. Sometimes. But we also brought a parade of America's greatest classical talent and some of the most elegant events ever held to the White House."

Rosalynn Carter, February 1977

Born: August 18, 1927, Plains, Georgia

Married: July 7, 1946, to Jimmy Carter (1924–present)

Children: John William (Jack) (1947–present); James Earl (Chip) (1950–present); Donnel Jeffrey (Jeff) (1952–present); Amy Lynn (1967–present)

Contributors:

JAY HAKES, former director, Carter Presidential Library and Museum; Special Assistant, Executive Office of the President, Carter Administration

GRACE HALE, history professor and director of American studies, University of Virginia, focusing on the history of the U.S. South

GRACE HALE: A lot of things are intersecting in interesting ways to help Jimmy Carter and [future] first lady Rosalynn in their rise in national politics in 1976.... [Democratic officials] want a candidate that's not going to, in their minds, be able to be pigeonholed as representing a certain kind of liberal or left part of the Democratic Party. Carter, with his Southern roots, his small-town background, they think he's going to appeal to people who wouldn't vote for McGovern.... He's a really interesting candidate because he is from the South, and yet he is publicly speaking out in support of integration, in support of the gains of the civil rights movement up until to that point, and that also really helps to create a momentum behind them. He's seen as a candidate who can bridge a lot of different divides, draw in a lot of different people.

JAY HAKES: The Carter "Peanut Brigade" were mainly friends of the Carters from Georgia who went to other states to campaign.... The advantage the Peanut Brigade had is they personally knew the Carters, so when you're going up to a voter and saying, "I'm asking you to vote for somebody that I personally know," that carries a lot of weight.... With the Nixon scandals surrounding Watergate, the idea of running as an outsider worked in 1976 in a way that it might not have worked in other years. It was the right campaign for the right time.

HALE: Jimmy and Rosalynn Carter were always churchgoers, growing up in Plains, and in their married life, attending different churches depending on where they lived, but his and her faith became really important when he was campaigning for the presidency.

That was a really interesting moment, a pivotal moment, just like for women's rights. It was a moment when more theologically conservative Christians were really embracing the public sphere; they were coming out of self-imposed isolation and taking up a public life. Carter spoke to them, a lot of people that would later find themselves as part of what we would call the Christian Right. Many of those people voted for Carter, and that was, for some of them, the first time they ever voted in a national campaign.

HAKES: [Plains, Georgia's population is] about six hundred people; a small town. When Rosalynn was growing up there, it was dirt roads.... It doesn't look that much different today than it did back then. They are probably surprised they ended up back in Plains, because when they were young, their goal was to get out of that small town.

[As young people, Jimmy and Rosalynn] probably saw each other from a distance because Rosalynn was a friend of Jimmy Carter's sister, Ruth.... As they got older, and it became known he was going to go into the Navy and travel around the world, she started to focus on him. After the first date they had, which was probably when she was about seventeen and he was about twenty, he went home and told his mother that he was going to marry Rosalynn.

It took him a while to convince her to marry him because she felt she was too young even though she was quite smitten with him....

Jimmy Carter was very active in the Navy's submarine program. In fact, he helped develop nuclear reactors for the U.S. Navy. He was at sea a lot, and they had three sons who were born while he was in the Navy. Jack was born in Portsmouth, Chip was born in Hawaii, and Jeff was born in Connecticut.

Rosalynn had a lot of jobs while raising their sons, because Jimmy was not around a lot of the time. She would run the family finances, which is a task she took on at their farm as well. She was very busy, but she also enjoyed the opportunity to travel to all of these great places. They really enjoyed living in Hawaii, for instance. It was a very special experience for them.

Jimmy's father, Earl, passed away in 1953, and son Billy was too young to take over the farm. It was a question of whether the farm might be lost to the family if Jimmy didn't go back. When he went back for his father's funeral, he found out that his father had been more active in the community, helping poor people and giving loans to people that needed help. Jimmy had never realized that as a child. He thought, "Well, I could do more good back here."

The thing is, he didn't consult with Rosalynn on that question, and she actually refused to talk to him on the trip [back] to Plains. He said, after that, he learned his lesson, and he would never again make a major decision without consulting with her.

[Jimmy's mother, Miss Lillian,] was a major force through the whole town of Plains because she was a nurse. Whereas the prevailing attitude was that African Americans had to come through the back door and the schools were separate, as far as Miss Lillian was concerned, everybody was equal and she had to carry out her nursing responsibilities that way. Everybody saw that. One of Rosalynn's sisters was named after Miss Lillian, so there was a respect for her.

Even at this time, although the prevailing culture was of a segregated society, both Jimmy and Rosalynn grew up with a basic sense of fairness that said, this isn't the way things ought to be. Then, of course, as they traveled around the world, they also broadened their perspective.

HALE: However, neither of them were amongst the white southerners that stood up against the segregationist way of life. They may well have had their personal views that these things aren't fair, but they were very quiet about those personal views. That's what is really interesting about his governorship; that's when you start to see that change in the Carters.

They started off by getting involved in local politics. It's a well-worn path. Jimmy Carter became involved with the school board in Plains, and used that as a jumping-off point to the Georgia state legislature. From there, eventually, he launched two campaigns for governor. The first wasn't successful, and the second was. They really used their rootedness in Plains and their experience of the broader world coming together to help them to get into national politics.

HAKES: Both of the Carters really believe in "doing your homework." He read Gary Hart's book on his 1972 [presidential] campaign to find out what went right, what went wrong. She took meticulous notes. When they ran for election in 1979 and '80, she pulled out all of these notes from the 1975 and '76 campaigns of the names and the phone numbers of everybody. They started off knowing that they didn't know how to do this; they'd never run for president before, but they did their homework. They came home on Sundays so that...the family members wouldn't all be off saying different things. They'd come back and compare notes on Sunday, and then they'd head back out to the field, and it was a very powerful combination.

I can't believe the work schedule that Rosalynn had during that campaign: very little sleep and visiting multiple towns in a day. Growing up on a farm, you learn how to put in long days, but she was willing to make that kind of commitment.

One of my favorite stories from Mrs. Carter was [that] she and her friend Edna Langford would go around the states—Rosalynn spent seventy-five days in Florida—and they would go into a small town, and they'd look for the tallest antenna in town, because they figured that was probably a radio station. Then they'd drive up and say, "Would you like to interview us?" They would actually bring a sheet of questions that the interviewers could ask. It was a very low-budget cam-

Rosalynn Smith, age 18, weds Navy Ensign Jimmy Carter on July 7, 1946. Both had grown up in the tiny town of Plains, Georgia. *Courtesy Jimmy Carter Presidential Library*

paign, but in that particular year, under the finance laws of that time, that was the way to do it.

[Jimmy Carter won the 1976 election against incumbent President Gerald Ford.] In some ways, the transition for Rosalynn Carter from Plains to the governor's mansion in Atlanta was a big transition. But there, she did get a chance to host parties, to take on issues, and do the kind of things that first ladies do at the White House, albeit at a smaller level. In one sense, they were the Washington outsiders coming into a town where they had not spent much time. But also, they had that experience as governor that she used as a foundation for what she expected to do as first lady.

HALE: [The Carters walked up Pennsylvania Avenue to the White House after the inauguration. This] was important in a lot of different ways.... It became a symbol of their desire to connect with people, to not present themselves as elite, above the people, to really be in touch with ordinary Americans.... Mrs. Carter has spoken about people along the way weeping as they walked by and shook hands, and spoke to people. It clearly was meaningful to people who were there.

HAKES: They had decided they wanted a less imperial presidency, and walking Pennsylvania Avenue was an impressive thing because it was a surprise. The Secret Service only allowed this to happen because it was kept secret.

They, to some extent, disagreed about certain aspects of the imperial presidency. Jimmy didn't want "Hail to the Chief" to be played at all, and Rosalynn thought he'd overdone that too much; she thought it maybe ought to be played a little bit more. So he was very adamant about reducing the imperial nature of the presidency; she thought maybe they should do some of that, but maybe not quite go so far.

The Carters were relatively young occupants of the White House, and then Amy was very much the young daughter. It's not unique, but it's unusual for presidents to have a daughter that young, so it was exciting for the whole country.

HALE: The decision to send Amy to public school [in Washington] was a decision that many people commented on, and it became very politicized. It was, in many ways, an example to the nation, and, in some ways, a rebuke of a lot of white Southerners, who were sending their kids to segregated private schools at the time.

Rosalynn became the first lady at a time of great change in women's roles, and that made her job challenging, but it also gave her some really wonderful opportunities which she really worked hard to seize.... People were surprised that she was such an outspoken person coming from a background in the small-town South, and that she really tackled issues in a serious way. She really made a mark in that way. Rosalynn Carter wanted to be a serious player on the issues. She wanted the president to take her seriously. They had a close partnership. They communicated back and forth very openly, very candidly. She was not afraid to criticize him in private. It was a strong [entry into] the modern era, as first ladies got involved in the big, substantive issues where they could make a difference.

When the Carters took office, there were only four states that still needed to ratify [the Equal Rights Amendment], and Rosalynn really got out there and campaigned, and it really looked like it would make it. But [at the National] Women's Conference in Houston, in 1977, that was really a moment when the organization of the fight against the

ERA really became public. Conservative women across the country had organized to get themselves elected as delegates to that women's conference. They really began fighting back against what they saw as changes that they were not welcoming, and began to systematically campaign for the ERA to be stopped....

In many ways, if you said that a woman from a small town in Georgia, somebody like Rosalynn Carter, with her background, would be a champion of the ERA, and it wouldn't pass, you would have been surprised by that. She really gave it her all. She has also said that was a very disappointing loss for her, that it was not ratified.

HAKES: The Carters today are still involved to some extent in this fight [for women's equality] because some parts of the Baptist Church don't allow women to be pastors or deacons, and the Carters have withdrawn their memberships from those churches.... The Carters appointed a lot of women to the judiciary. Ruth Bader Ginsburg was appointed to the appeals court by President Carter, elevated to the Supreme Court by President Clinton. Rosalynn recognizes there's been a lot of progress made, and they were able to be part of that progress.

[Rosalynn Carter was publicly involved in a number of substantive policy issues. Her 1977 trip to Latin America as an official envoy of the U.S.] was somewhat misunderstood, both in this country and abroad. That was a very substantive trip, because President Carter was trying to send a message: "It's a new day for human rights. Just because you're an ally doesn't mean you can lock up political prisoners." You can't deliver that message publicly, because people react against it. So, by having Rosalynn deliver it, it was more effective.

[She also served as the host for the Camp David summit between Egypt and Israel.] President Carter had gotten the CIA to develop these very fine profiles of the participants, and he knew what made them tick. He felt like they would all perform a lot better if their wives were there. Mrs. Sadat couldn't come, but she was in frequent phone contact with Anwar Sadat, and Mrs. Begin was there, and Mrs. Carter was there for the vast majority at the time. Their being there had a very specific purpose.... They were talking about things that would affect their grandchildren and their families, and having the spouses there would be a positive....

HALE: [Rosalynn Carter was named chair of the Mental Health Commission and the appointment became controversial.] It was a challenge. It was particularly challenging during the years when Rosalynn was trying to navigate those roles, because women's position in society as a whole was changing so rapidly across the '70s.

   She not only had to negotiate the difficulties of being the first lady and being in the media all the time, but also it's at a time when women themselves are very much disagreeing about what the proper role for women in society was. It was not just the time of feminism, after all, it was the rise of conservative women's backlash against feminism, and critique of it. Rosalynn had a difficult job there.

HAKES: She wasn't going to let a legal opinion [that a close relative of the president could not chair the Mental Health Commission] close her down. She [decided she] was able to do it [as honorary chair, instead], and had a great impact. She was so committed to reducing stigma for mental illness, to getting it treated as a medical condition. In her own sweet way, she was running that commission.

The Mental Health Commission issued reports in 1977 and 1978, and then in 1980. Fairly late in the Carter presidency, they passed the mental health bill, which was basically requiring that mental illnesses be treated like other illnesses.... You have to have a lot of patience in the public sector, and she has been frustrated that more has not happened at a faster pace. She has been ahead of her time on a lot of these issues and now, some of them are coming to fruition.

HALE: The pivotal point for her [originally getting involved in mental health issues] was when Jimmy Carter was running for governor of Georgia. So many of the people that came up to her on the campaign trail with things they want her to work on mentioned problems that they had in their family, and particularly the stigma that was attached to mental health issues. That was the beginning of it. She developed a very strong mental health program in Georgia, and then she had one at the White House.

HAKES: The Carters had some pretty great events at the White House in 1980...a poetry conference which they had in January; then they had all the jazz greats come in for a long concert with Eubie Blake, and that was another stunning event. So, as much as she was the modern first lady in adopting these big issues like mental health and the ERA, she also knew that that didn't mean that she gave up the other part of [the role which] was to make all of this function smoothly.

HALE: [When they lost the 1980 election to Ronald Reagan,] they were devastated. I don't really know what to add to that.

HAKES: The election was not close, but until the last week or so, the polls showed it was an open race. Both of the Carters realized before Election Day itself that [the loss] was coming, and it was hard.

Rosalynn is very candid. If you read her memoirs, she doesn't really try to cover up how she feels about things, and she said, "Everybody pretended like they weren't bitter, but I sure was."

Obviously, for anybody, after what you put in to run for the office, and you put in to do that job, it's tough when you get a verdict like that from the voters, but they've come to peace with it and have been able to make a great use of the rest of their lives.

[In 1981,] they moved back to Plains to plan the rest of their lives. They were pretty young to be out of the White House. Eventually, they came up with the idea of the Carter Center, still a part of Emory University. From there, they were able to launch whole new careers working on some of the same issues, and to continue to have a very big impact both in this country and around the world.

These [post-White House Carter] lives are pretty epic stories when you look at them closely, because when the Carters started working on the Guinea Worm epidemic in the 1980s, there were 3.5 million cases around the globe…. It's just now in four countries: Mali, Chad, Ethiopia, and Sudan. This is a remarkable achievement. It's going to be the second disease after smallpox to be eliminated from the face of the Earth.

…They've now monitored elections in thirty-seven countries, many of those countries more than once. In countries like Indonesia and Liberia, they've helped nurture them as they've gone through several election cycles. Liberia is a perfect example. They've not only moved to democracy, where they elected the first woman president in an African country, but they had no mental health care. So the Carter Center organized a program where they train mental health nurses….

I'm just scratching the surface, but you start to see all of these different things going on around the world, because they can open that door as ex-president and ex-first lady, and it's still going on. It hasn't stopped.

Rosalynn Carter's legacy:

HALE: ...It's been a very successful post-presidency. In many ways, the Carters have reinvented that job, and it doesn't seem like it's going to stop here in their later years.

Perhaps the jury's still out [on the public perception of the Carter White House]. It's not seen as the most successful presidency of the postwar era, but, at the same time, trying to change some of the directions of events, promote some of the issues that he was promoting like energy conservation, energy independence, the spread of democracy in various parts of the world—those are important issues still today.

HAKES: Rosalynn Carter generally has ranked in the top five or the top ten first ladies, depending on which poll you use. The jury is still out. Papers are still being declassified; people are still getting the broader perspective. And hopefully, people will keep having these kinds of discussions [about her legacy].

Nancy Davis Reagan

"However the first lady fits in, she has a unique and important role to play in looking after her husband. And it's only natural that she'll let him know what she thinks. I always did that for Ronnie, and I always will."

Nancy Reagan, December 1988
Courtesy Ronald Reagan Library

Born: July 6, 1921, Flushing, Queens, New York
Married: March 6, 1952, to Ronald Reagan (1911–2004)
Children: Patricia Ann (1952–present); Ronald Prescott (1958–present); stepchildren: Maureen Elizabeth (1941–2001), Michael Edward (1945–present)
Died: March 6, 2016, Los Angeles, California

Contributors:

CARL CANNON, Washington bureau chief, *Real Clear Politics;* lecturer on the press and the presidency; author of several books, including *The Pursuit of Happiness in Times of War*

JUDY WOODRUFF, co-anchor and managing editor, PBS *Newshour;* interviewer for PBS documentary, *Nancy Reagan: The Role of a Lifetime*

JUDY WOODRUFF: It was a remarkable partnership. It was a strong marriage. Ronald and Nancy Reagan loved each other deeply. But theirs was also very much a working partnership, once it was clear that Ronald Reagan was interested in politics. And it all started with being the spokesman for General Electric, traveling around the country in... 1954–55. From that moment on, and once the friends they made in Los Angeles decided Ronald Reagan would be a great candidate for

California governor, and when he went on to be elected governor in 1966, Nancy was the person who…made sure that the people around her husband were people who always had his best interests at heart. That was one of the principal things she brought to the relationship, always having his back.

CARL CANNON: …Nancy was the "personnel director." Stu Spencer called her that. [He was] the political consultant who ran Reagan's first campaign for governor in 1966. In September of 1980, when things start to hit a rocky road, and the [presidential] campaign is in a little bit of trouble, it's Nancy who says, "Where's Stu Spencer?" Mike Deaver called him. Deaver was only back in the campaign because Nancy had helped bring him back. There was just one person Stuart Spencer asked Deaver whether it was okay [for him to join the campaign], and that was Nancy.…

WOODRUFF: Hers was not the smoothest childhood. Nancy's mother was an actress, Edith Luckett. Her father, Kenneth Robbins, had been a salesman. She was born in New York City. The marriage between Edith and Kenneth did not last very long. Nancy was around two when they divorced.

Her mother really wanted her acting career, and she wanted a safe life for Nancy, so she had Nancy live from the time she was two until she was eight, when Mrs. Luckett remarried, with Nancy's aunt, her mother's sister, in Bethesda, Maryland, right outside of Washington. Nancy lived in what was then a suburban neighborhood with the woman who was described as very different from her mother. Her mother was very outgoing, somebody who was the life of the party and was in the middle of every conversation. Her aunt was much quieter. The rules were fairly strict.

It was a tough time. Nancy herself talked in the interview we did for the documentary [*Nancy Reagan: The Role of a Lifetime*] about how she missed her mother, and she would be thrilled when her mother came to visit. It was rocky for a few years.

CANNON: [Life changed for Nancy when her mother married a Chicago physician,] Loyal Davis. Then things picked up. There was money. He was successful. She went to boarding school. She went to Smith College. He was the doting parent she had lacked. Through her life, that's the man she called her father, and it gave her an idea of what a family could be. From that moment forward, she had an idea of what she wanted to be, and what she wanted out of life, and she wanted to build a family. That was the family she didn't have, and it's something that she and Reagan had in common.

After Smith College, she went to the theater, and then she moved out to Hollywood, but she was typecast...as the steady woman, and that's what she was.

WOODRUFF: [Nancy Davis and Ronald Reagan met in] Hollywood in the late '40s, when there was the communist scare. It was after the end of World War II. There was the blacklist, where people were named for being somehow associated with the Communist Party.

"Nancy Davis" showed up on a blacklist as someone in the Hollywood community who had had something to do with the Communist Party. She knew that that was not she, and she wanted to get her name off. She asked her good friend, a producer, Mervyn LeRoy, "How can I get this done?" He said, "I know Ronald Reagan, who's the president of the Screen Actors Guild, and I think I can talk to him." She said, "As soon as I heard that, and I knew who Ronald Reagan was, I was very interested...." So Mervyn LeRoy called Ronald Reagan. He said he'd be glad to talk to her about this.

One thing led to another. There was a meeting, and then it became a dinner. She really tells a funny story about how they both agreed to go to dinner, but insisted it had to be an early evening because they both had an early call, which neither one of them actually did....

CANNON: It's an old Hollywood ruse. If the date doesn't work out, you can end it in a civil way by saying you have to get up early. But they didn't end it early, and it was a good thing, because they didn't have anywhere to be the next morning.

WOODRUFF: That was 1949. They married in 1952. Actually, their daughter, Patti, was born in 1952. Nancy pretty much gave up her movie career. She had been getting some roles fairly steadily, and his career was actually the one that was stalling out at that point, and then the GE offer [for Ronald Reagan to be their spokesman] came along.

She became the homemaker. She did do a few television roles over that first decade of their marriage, but mainly she devoted herself to being his wife, the mother of Patti, and then, about six years later, Ron, Jr., was born. Her family was her life, and she devoted all her time to that.... Eventually, as he came closer to thinking about politics, she became much closer to the wives of some of the men who would be influential in that regard.

CANNON: [Nancy learned to like politics because she loved Ronald Reagan.] She didn't love politics, and she wasn't built for politics. It was on-the-job training, and it wasn't always easy. She came to Sacramento in 1967, she didn't like the town, and the town reciprocated those feelings.

She was asked to move into this governor's mansion, which was a dilapidated Victorian structure downtown on a one-way street.... Nancy properly called it a firetrap, which offended some of the city fathers.... Nancy decided they weren't going to live there, and they moved to East Sacramento, and that started an uneasy relationship with the Sacramento press corps and the Democrats in the legislature.

WOODRUFF: Nancy developed a thick skin during that period. She didn't like the criticism. She especially didn't like the criticism of her husband. She talked about how, when they came to Sacramento, she knew it was not going to be easy, but she underestimated how much the press, as it is everywhere, is critical of politicians.

CANNON: She shopped in Beverly Hills, and Sacramento didn't have any stores like that. She was used to the cool breezes of Pacific Palisades, and Sacramento gets very hot in the summer. Mostly, she hated the *Sacramento Bee*, which was the dominant newspaper and a very Democratic newspaper. They were relentless in their criticism of Reagan. She canceled the subscription and told people about this. Reagan would pull people aside and say, "It's okay, I get it at the office."

I think of the Sacramento years, in a way, as the time Reagan took care of her, the same way she took care of him in Washington. In those years, she was a little bit brittle....

She felt picked on, and Reagan protected her in this time.... She treated the staff like servants, was one of the complaints. In all of these things, in those years, she had rough edges, and Reagan had to smooth them off.

WOODRUFF: That was a period when she really learned how to be a political spouse. She learned that... there are the great moments when you feel terrific and you feel appreciated, and then there are the really tough moments. That's what helped prepare her for the presidency.

CANNON: She also had these causes.... [As California first lady, she was] interested in drug abuse and in youth as early as 1967. She was the one who helped get Reagan interested in the Vietnam POWs.... The other thing about Sacramento that you notice is [that] all these causes that came up later in Washington were present there.

WOODRUFF: There was a group of influential, wealthy Republican men, mostly men, and Nancy was very close friends with their wives.... [They] had their eye on Ronald Reagan. There were people around the country who thought he had been such an effective spokesperson for the conservative cause as the GE spokesman. When Barry Goldwater ran for president, Ronald Reagan gave a much-commented-on speech. You can argue that it was the coming-out speech for Ronald Reagan. All of those disparate forces came together while he was still in the governor's office, and they jelled, more or less, in that year. So, when Gerald Ford was running for election in 1976, Ronald Reagan popped on the public consciousness as a very appealing, conservative potential challenger for Gerald Ford.

...After '76, when Ronald Reagan showed that he had substantial support in the Republican Party, from then on, it was an all-out effort to win the nomination in 1980 and to go on to win the White House.

That doesn't mean that he was a shoo-in. There were other Republicans running. There were still people arguing that he was too conservative, that he was a "warmonger"; he was known to have very strong anti-Soviet views.

I covered the Carter White House during those years, and Reagan's name would come up, and the critics would say, "He's the one who's got his finger on the bomb." There was a lot of this rhetoric flying around. This [candidacy] was by no means a walk-in for him, but when the time came, he had the people and he had the money.

CANNON: The Reagans were living out in California [in 1976], and it was like he was the nominee-in-waiting for four years. It was a very interesting time.... He had the money, he had the support. The Republican Party was in transition, and it was going to be Ronald Reagan's party. There were people in the East who didn't realize that, but that's how it proved. Nancy sure thought it was true, and she turned out to be right.

WOODRUFF: [Inauguration Day 1981] was an extraordinary time. I tell this from the perspective of the Carter White House. They had had a very painful final year of his presidency, for all the world to see, with the hostages that had been taken at the U.S. embassy in Tehran. They were being held by Iranian extremists.... The hostages were being released [as Ronald Reagan's inauguration occurred], and this was being done deliberately by the Iranians to spite Jimmy Carter.

...Ronald Reagan was shot [just sixty-nine days into his presidency]. I was a part of the press pool that day. It made Nancy much more protective. She was already completely focused on him and his safety, but after this, you could argue it was her sole focus. At one point she said something like, "When he left to go somewhere, I wasn't even able to breathe deeply until he came back."

CANNON: Reagan's line [to Nancy after he was shot was] "Honey, I forgot to duck...." For Americans of their generation, that was a famous line. It's the line that Jack Dempsey used after he lost to Gene Tunney, the heavyweight championship of the world....That line was reported in the press here, and Americans really admired Reagan for it because they realized what he was trying to do, which was reassure his wife.

WOODRUFF: As in California, where she found a governor's mansion that she felt was unsafe and not up to the standards of what a governor's home should be, she felt the White House was practically in disrepair. She felt that not only repairs needed to be done, but she felt the furnishings were shabby, and she wanted a complete renovation and refurbishing of the White House with new drapes, new upholstery on the furniture.

She raised private money to get this done. She often said, "I loved entertaining. I thought that was an important part of being in the

White House. It's a way to connect with people," but, "we didn't even have a full set of china for a state dinner." So she raised the money to buy a new set of china.

She also was very interested in style and fashion. She'd always been a woman who cared about her appearance. Combined with the efforts to redecorate the White House, the new set of china, and then the publicity about her interest in clothes, you put it all together, and it was the image of a woman who cared more about things that really didn't matter. It did not go over well with the Washington press corps. They jumped, and there's no question that contributed to the public's perception of her.

CANNON: For Nancy, she came here and she thought it would be a fresh start, and [instead], it is déjà vu all over again. It was [just like] Sacramento. She expected Washington to be a little more sophisticated. It wasn't, in her mind. Designer dresses, they're criticizing her. They criticize her for going shopping at Bloomingdale's. Her friend was Betsy Bloomingdale. Of course they're going to shop at Bloomingdale's....

WOODRUFF: The Reagan presidency was a different time. It was twenty years [after the Kennedys and Camelot]. The country was probably getting a little cynical. They'd been through Watergate and certainly been through Vietnam. The American people, and certainly the press corps, were not as willing to just swallow and accept whatever it was that the president and the first lady were doing.

[Nancy performed a skit poking fun at herself at the Washington press corps' Gridiron Club dinner in 1982 to try to rehabilitate her image.] Her instincts were exactly right-on. She had self-deprecating humor. She made fun of herself and the press ate it up, the city ate it up. It turned an important corner for her.

CANNON: Everybody talks about how Reagan was an actor, but she was an actor, too. She was on the stage. She had twelve feature films. The comfort level of these two before the camera [is] the envy of every political couple, and they used it as easily as you and I would just pick up a telephone and call a friend. That's what they showed. Even the little things...they understood the lighting, they understood the message, how the message should go with the pictures. They really got it all, and it was almost second nature to them both.

[She chose an anti-drug campaign as her] signature issue, and this was something she actually cared about and she knew about. There was a phrase that was [used] in the anti-drug movement among the psychologists, "Just Say No." They're always thinking of some way to approach young people. It's not easy. Nancy seized on it, and popularized it. Some people criticized her for being maybe simplistic, but her answer to that was disarming. She said, "If it saves one child's life, it's worth it."

WOODRUFF: The Reagans used state dinners at the White House strategically. Number one, they liked entertaining. Having come from Hollywood, social life was important to them. Nancy Reagan herself talks about this…. She said this is an opportunity to play host to a visiting head of state. She said anybody will come; whoever the Hollywood stars of the time were—Frank Sinatra, Elizabeth Taylor, you name it. If you're invited to a White House state dinner, you come. That's true today for any president. The Reagans were very conscious of that and conscious that they could make a splash and impress their guests. She also said you can get business done on these occasions. Yes, they were social, but they were also about business.

Her second term was different. She was burned by the experience of the first year or so, and she came out of that and really was always very careful in her dealings with the press, and was very sparing in the interviews she gave. She had a presence about her, a poise, and she was able to communicate in a way that was helpful to the White House. The second term was very different from the first term in that way. By then, they both had learned a lot, but it was also rough, as we know; presidents' second terms can be rough. And the problems came…

CANNON: [There were not any issues on which the Reagans didn't see eye-to-eye,] not that I know of, but with the staff, absolutely. There was open warfare on many issues. The most important issue was Iran-Contra and dealing with the Soviet Union. Nancy had a point of view, and she would push on the Soviet Union. She believed strongly in negotiating with [Soviet leader] Mikhail Gorbachev, and she didn't push Reagan, because they saw eye-to-eye, but she pushed back against staffers who she thought didn't have his agenda at heart.

Reagan thought he could do business with Gorbachev. That's the phrase he used to his aides. The speeches kept getting changed in the White House speechwriting shop. Allida Black, a first ladies historian, credits Nancy with helping Reagan push back…. Reagan kept saying to anybody who would listen on his staff, "I can do business with this guy. I don't want to be calling him names." He took Nancy there as an ally to show the world that the two couples could get along, and maybe the two countries could get along.

WOODRUFF: Nancy was a moderating influence on him. She wanted him to be the best president he could be, and to have the best legacy. She felt the best legacy was a legacy of moderation.

In some ways, they didn't disagree. She wanted no daylight between the two of them, certainly in public, but there's no question that she worked very hard behind the scenes, especially with George Shultz, who had been secretary of state, and others, to make sure that President Reagan was listening to those who argued "we need détente," rather than the opposite.

Nancy did two things [about the Iran-Contra scandal, which broke in 1986]. She didn't think Reagan had done anything wrong, but she recognized it as a threat to his presidency, and she doubled down on getting Reagan to negotiate with Gorbachev. She encouraged that because she thought that would be a better way to change the conversation. But the other thing she did, according to my father, Lou Cannon, who is really Reagan's preeminent biographer, that he thought was the most important contribution Nancy made as first lady, was pushing Reagan to make the apology on Iran-Contra. It may have saved his presidency.

[In 1987, the next-to-last year of the Reagan Administration, Nancy Reagan was diagnosed with breast cancer and had a mastectomy. She decided to go public with this.] She talked about it and handled it with grace. This was another event that drew the public to her because she was able to talk about it. She had a mastectomy, and by no means was this something that was easy to go through, but she could talk about it at a time when it still was kind of hush-hush. Betty Ford had been through her own episodes, but for Nancy Reagan to do this made a big difference.

CANNON: On AIDS, there were people in the White House who thought Reagan should speak out about it early on. There were people who didn't want him speaking out. Nancy was on the side of the people who wanted Reagan to talk about it.

It's not true that he never mentioned AIDS until 1987. He talked about in '85 and in '86. But in 1987, he gave a speech, and Nancy didn't really trust that the White House domestic policy shop would say what she wanted Reagan to say, so she sent for Landon Parvin. He had been a speechwriter in the White House, and he came back. He was writing these speeches, and Parvin got some pushback. Finally, he said, "This is how she wants it." "She" meant Nancy Reagan, and that was the end of the conversation.

[To raise money for the Reagan Library,] they went to their friends, many of whom gave a lot of money, but also through other foundations. They worked very hard. To Mrs. Reagan, and initially to the president before he became ill, this was the way of not only telling Ronald Reagan's story, but it's seen as a way of maintaining Ronald Reagan's legacy. We know that in the Republican Party today, Ronald Reagan is still very much a revered figure, as is Nancy Reagan.

In 1991, at the eightieth birthday for Reagan, British Prime Minister Margaret Thatcher came, and they held it at this library. Reagan got up and spoke, and he spoke glowingly about Thatcher. Then he turned to Nancy, and he said, "Put simply, my life really began when I met Nancy and has been rich and full ever since." So there was a time there after they left the White House where it was really magical for them.

WOODRUFF: They left the White House in January 1989, and it was just five years later, in 1994, that he announced that he had Alzheimer's. That's five years, and you could add maybe a few years after that when he was communicating and recognizing her. But the point came in the late '90s where she was telling people he didn't recognize her. She was open about that. Ronald Reagan died in 2004.

She called it "the longest goodbye." Maybe they weren't her words, but people around them called it the longest goodbye, because it was 1994

President and Mrs. Reagan in August 1983 at Rancho del Cielo in Santa Barbara, California, their vacation home throughout his presidency. *Courtesy Ronald Reagan Library*

when Ronald Reagan wrote that letter and announced to the world that he had Alzheimer's.

Of course, no one knew then what it meant. That was at a time when people knew of Alzheimer's, but it wasn't nearly as familiar to us as it is today. There was no way of knowing how long he would live. He would live another ten years, out of public view, but she was with him. They were in their home in Bel Air, in Los Angeles, and their closeness was with them right up until the end.

CANNON: It was [a particularly special political partnership between Ronald and Nancy Reagan] from the very beginning, from the Sacramento days, from the Hollywood days. But the partnership that we see on display as Nancy pats his coffin [at Ronald Reagan's funeral] is heart-breaking. It's like she lost him twice. As she pats that coffin, you imagine her patting his shoulder every night for ten years, as she said goodnight to him. And every night, it was like losing him again.

Nancy got a rough start in this town, and she got a rough start in Sacramento, but she won everyone over in the ten years that Ronald Reagan had Alzheimer's and she took care of him.

WOODRUFF: [After the president's death, she would occasionally get involved in public policy debates.] It was all about pushing and preserving her husband's legacy. It was all about Ronald Reagan, the man who was at the center of her life for fifty-five years until his death. Her interest in stem cell research, even when it was not a popular thing in the Republican Party, was all about the connection to Alzheimer's.... She lobbied President George W. Bush in the early 2000s, when this was an issue, and again, she went against the party. She called members of Congress. She was a fierce advocate. She made speeches for it. You could trace almost everything she's done since then to something that either has to do with what her husband did, or Alzheimer's.

Nancy Reagan's legacy:

WOODRUFF: First ladies, certainly in the modern era, have been close to their husbands and have paid close attention to policy. Nancy Reagan took that to a new level because it wasn't so much that she wanted to be sitting in cabinet meetings or policy-making meetings. She didn't do that, but she was very aware of her husband, wanted him to be successful, and was ready to act to make sure that the people around him were serving his best interests and letting him be, as she put it, the best person that he could be. In that way, she exerted enormous influence, because she would move a mountain to make sure that her husband was protected.

CANNON: Stu Spencer says she was really the personnel chief. Okay, but no White House personnel chief has actually ever slept with the president, and this one did, and so she has more influence. She has the old kind of influence and a new kind of influence. She's a very modern first lady in that sense.

Nancy once said that Reagan preferred heights to valleys, so she would make sure that he could go up to Rancho del Cielo up in the mountains [outside Santa Barbara]. There was nothing for her to do up there, but she made sure he could be there as often as she could, and she went with him. And she did it metaphorically, too. She was a height, not a valley, in his life. By doing that, she lightened his mood and she helped him make a mark on a country that needed bucking up.

Barbara Pierce Bush

> "I hope that if I have a legacy other than being 'The Enforcer,' that it will be that I raised, along with George, a great family."

Barbara Bush, January 1990
Courtesy George Bush
Presidential Library and Museum

Born: June 8, 1925, New York, New York
Married: January 6, 1945, to George Herbert Walker Bush (1925–present)
Children: George Walker (1946–present); Pauline Robinson "Robin" (1949–53); John Ellis "Jeb" (1953–present); Neil Mallon (1955–present); Marvin Pierce (1956–present); Dorothy "Doro" (1959–present)

Contributors:

JEFFREY ENGEL, director, Center for Presidential History, Southern Methodist University; author of several books, including *The China Diary of George H.W. Bush*

MYRA GUTIN, professor of communication, Rider University; first ladies scholar; author, *Barbara Bush: Presidential Matriarch*

MYRA GUTIN: Barbara Pierce was born in New York [in 1925]. At the time of her birth, her father, Marvin Pierce, was on the staff of the president at the McCall's publishing company. Her mother, Pauline, was a descendant of an Ohio Supreme Court justice, and the Pierce family was distantly related to President Franklin Pierce.

The family moved to Rye, New York, where Barbara and her siblings—an older sister and two younger brothers—grew up. It was a comfortable upbringing. They went to private schools. When Barbara was old enough for high school, she was sent away to Ashley Hall, a boarding school in South Carolina. Home for Christmas break of her junior year, she went to a country club dance, and that's when she met George H.W. Bush.

JEFFREY ENGEL: According to both of them, they were attracted from the start. Because of the distance, they developed a real intimate correspondence, which was typical for the times, especially a correspondence that continues as George Bush decides to join the Navy and pushes forward and actually becomes the youngest aviator in the Pacific theater. Their correspondence throughout that entire period is emotional; it's intimate; it's something that drew them both together when they couldn't be together in the same spot. Then, the times when they were together, were electric for them. They really knew from the very start that they were for each other.

GUTIN: [She began studying at Smith College.] She was there for a year, and admitted that she really wasn't the most dedicated of students. She was more interested in her boyfriend, George Bush. I believe she was rather active in athletics in her time at Smith. She went back for the first semester of her sophomore year, and then left school to marry George Bush.

ENGEL: It's a truly harrowing story [of how George Bush was shot down in the Pacific during World War II]. He was on a bombing run over an island called Chichi-jima, and he went in on the run, started the dive down with his bomber, and was immediately hit by enemy flak.... He actually spent about four and a half hours bobbing up and down in the Pacific before he was rescued by the USS *Finback*, a submarine, and spent another several weeks continuing with the submarine on their patrol mission. During that time, it was very unclear for the Bushes, his parents, what had happened to him. He was officially listed as missing in action. They made a conscious decision not to tell Barbara at that time what was going on until they knew for certain that he was going to be fine.

GUTIN: They missed their first wedding date because he still wasn't back. Finally...on January 6, 1945, about two weeks after the original date, they were married. He served in the military until 1945, until the peace treaties were signed. He had flown so many sorties during the war that he had many points accumulated, so he was able to take an early out. Then he and Barbara left for New Haven and Yale and the beginning of his long-delayed college career.

George Walker Bush was born during that time. It was also at that point that George H.W. Bush was playing varsity baseball at Yale, and Barbara was the official scorer for the team. It was a happy time for them at Yale.

[The Bushes had six children.] When Robin [their second child] was a little over two years old—and at this point, the Bushes were living in Texas—woke up one morning, she said to Barbara, "I think today I'm just going to stay in bed, or maybe I'll go out on the lawn and look at the clouds going by." That raised a red flag for Barbara right away, because her daughter was very active.

She took her daughter to the pediatrician. The pediatrician asked Barbara and George to come back a little bit later that day, and she said to them, "Your daughter has leukemia." George Bush said, "What does that mean?" At that point in time, who knew what it was? The doctor said, "It means that she's not going to live very long."

The doctor's recommendation was that Robin be allowed to go home and enjoy things, be around her family, but one of George Bush's relatives was a doctor at Sloan Kettering hospital in New York. Robin was taken there to try some different treatment modalities to try to deal with the leukemia. They prolonged her life a little bit. She even returned to Texas once, but she passed away.

ENGEL: President Bush spent his entire life writing letters. That's one of the things he's known for and famous for. Perhaps the most painful letters that we have in the archive are from him writing about his daughter, writing to his mother years later, talking about the pain in his heart: the thing that's missing, the fact that "we really do need a little girl in our lives running around," that life was not the same since.

[I believe it is true that Barbara's hair turned white after Robin's death,] and not surprisingly, given the devastating nature of losing a child. She took the death very, very deeply. This is a time where we would say today that she went through a period of depression. It was only after she was so sad for so many months that she heard [her son] George outside saying to a young friend, "I'm sorry, I can't come out and play today because I have to take care of my mother," that she realized this was too much burden to put on a little boy....

To understand Barbara Bush, you need to appreciate that she was really a product of her times. The passion that she passed on to her children was the fact that she had devoted her entire life to them, to raising a family, and to being a good and loyal wife to her husband over the course of his varied careers. In many senses, he was an active [but] absentee father for many years because he was on the road as a salesman, then he was on the road as a politician, then he was on the road as a government official. She was the one who was there every night. So, for George W. Bush, in particular, that helped form a real bond between [him and his mother], especially after Robin's unfortunate death.

GUTIN: The Bushes came back to Midland, Texas, and they had a great deal of success there. After that, they moved to Houston, and it was then that George Bush was asked to consider running for Harris County Republican chairman [in 1963]. That was his first campaign. It was Barbara's first campaign. She really enjoyed it. She felt very competitive, and they won that race. I believe there were 189 precincts, and they visited every one, and it was on from there.

ENGEL: When he ran [for the Senate in Texas] in 1964, he was hopeful of winning, but frankly, no Republican was going to win in 1964 when Lyndon Johnson had the longest coattails in American history and the biggest landslide for any president in American history.

Consequently, he became a congressman. Then, Richard Nixon, one of his mentors, encouraged him in 1970 to run again [for the Senate, but he lost once more]. Richard Nixon then...told him, "I'll take care of you. You can go and become United Nations ambassador up in [New York]."

George Bush didn't have any [foreign policy experience], and he'd be the first one to admit it. He said, "I know nothing about foreign policy, but I'm going to learn." This is actually one of the reasons that Nixon chose him, because ultimately what Nixon and his secretary of state and national security advisor, Henry Kissinger, wanted was somebody who was going to be loyal, not somebody who was going to pursue their own mind.... As an ambassador, he went to all the different nations in the offices around the U.N., something an American ambassador had never done before, and he really relished the personal sense of learning about diplomacy on the ground level.

GUTIN: Hard for us to believe now, but when they went to the U.N., Barbara Bush had not yet gone outside the country. Her first time leaving the country was when they were in China. She loved their time in New York. They had a suite in the Waldorf Towers where they entertained constantly.... For both Bushes, there was an understanding, a comprehension of the importance of personal diplomacy, and it worked very well for both of them.

ENGEL: [After the U.N. position, George Bush was then made head of the Republican National Committee, which,] unfortunately for President Nixon, was during Watergate. Of course, Watergate doesn't show up until after George Bush was already in the position, and he had the unenviable job of going out every day and defending the president. He felt it was his duty as Republican chair to defend the president no matter what his own sinking suspicions were about the president's guilt. He refers to this period as being in the eye of the storm, that this is the worst part of his life.

GUTIN: Watergate was a difficult [time for Barbara and their family, also]. She really wondered how he was soldiering on. There came a point where Mr. Bush had to go to President Nixon and say to him, "It looks like most hope is lost. We hadn't hoped that things were going to come to this, but it looks like they will."

ENGEL: [The new president, Gerald Ford,] turned to Bush, and essentially said, "You've been a loyal soldier for the Republican Party for all these years, and, quietly, I'd like to get all of the people who were involved in Watergate, even publicly, out of the city, out of the limelight. What would you like to do? I know you like diplomacy after having been in the U.N. Where would you like to go? I can offer you Paris; I can offer you London...." George Bush looked at him and said, "I'd like to go to China.... China is going to be the future. China is growing. China is an exciting place." Also, and this is really key and came up in his personal correspondence at the time, China is a lot cheaper than London or Paris....

After all these years in public service, George Bush…wanted to go someplace that was a little bit more affordable. His diary throughout his time in China is filled with references to how not only exciting it was, how vibrant it was, but how wonderful it was to live in a place that was so inexpensive.

GUTIN: Barbara Bush said it was probably her favorite place to be. The kids were not there…. She had George Bush to herself. The two of them took advantage of the many possibilities that China offered. They learned to speak some Chinese. They were able to enjoy going out into the countryside. We didn't have a full consulate there; it was the U.S. Liaison Office, so there was also a little more freedom that came with that, that might not have been there otherwise. She was very unhappy when they had to leave after a year.

Barbara Bush wrote some columns for newspapers which were sent home. She found so many things to be unique about the experience.

[After China, the Bushes went back to Washington, where George Bush ran the CIA.] They certainly were [more challenging years]. She was not happy to return to Washington, particularly not for her husband to become the director of the CIA. It meant, among other things, that he could not tell her anything that was going on in his workplace. This has been a relationship where the two of them had really discussed everything. The kids were gone, and the beginning of the women's liberation movement was starting, and Barbara Bush plunged into depression. Those were some difficult times for her.

Her husband suggested that she get professional help, but perhaps with a Yankee self-reliance, she felt that she could handle it. I've heard her say that today, if someone says to her, "I'm depressed," she says, "I'm sorry to hear that. Get help." She's come full circle on that. Those were tough years.

ENGEL: I don't think it was much of a decision [for George Bush to run for president in 1980] at all. It was a *fait accompli* that he was going to run for the White House. As early as the time that he's in China, he's actually telling visitors that he intends to run for the White House.

…He had actually wanted to stay on at the CIA after President Carter took over, but Carter put his own man in. George Bush goes back [to Texas], does a few years of business, but really is laying the ground-work for his ultimate campaign, and actually does surprisingly well against Ronald Reagan.... Unfortunately for him, at that point, the Reagan steamroll begins and Reagan winds up winning the nomination handily. George Bush goes to the Republican convention really thinking that was it. He was going to release his delegates. He had played his part.... Reagan then turned to George Bush, the man who had finished second, and offered him the spot on the ticket, and George Bush took it in a heartbeat.

...The Bushes were very adamant that they wanted to be friends with the Reagans. That was how they lived their entire lives, making friends and social connections and moving up through political circles by melding politics and friendship. The Reagans were a very isolated couple, self-isolated. They liked each others' company and, frankly, not a lot of other people. Consequently, they really never reciprocated the overtures and the friendship and the warmth that the Bushes put towards them, especially Nancy and Mrs. Bush.

GUTIN: The Bushes were only invited to the family quarters [in the White House] a few times. They were certainly at the White House many times for ceremonial occasions, but there was a level of tension between the two [women].

They worked pretty well together. They had the sense that they were working towards the same goal. Of course, they also had very divergent interests. Nancy Reagan was talking about anti-drug measures, and Barbara Bush was focusing on literacy. So their paths diverged.

When [the Bushes] came to the White House, [after George Bush's election in 1988,] Barbara told her press secretary, Anna Perez, that there were three areas where the critics better keep hands off: her fella, her family, and her dogs. And that pretty much followed through. She was very concerned, and reacted sometimes very quickly, if there was criticism of George Bush or their children.

[Some family members have referred to her as "The Enforcer," but] her husband always called her "Miss Frank," and, indeed, she is. She has had his back and the backs of all of her family members all of these many years. If someone was critical of them, she was going to respond.

Barbara and George H.W. Bush, August 1988, in Kennebunkport, Maine, their longtime vacation home. *Courtesy George Bush Presidential Library and Museum*

There was a story that a reporter once told me that if you wrote something negative about Bill Clinton during the Clinton Administration, maybe the Clintons would forgive you and let you write another story. If you said something negative about George H.W. Bush, you were done until the next administration.

[During the Bush Administration, domestically there was] a lot of social upheaval, [such as] the changes in society over the role of women.

Barbara Bush stayed away from the abortion issue. Many years later, in a televised interview, she came forth and pretty much came out and said that she'd been pro-choice all along, but certainly, she stayed away from it. When George Bush had become Ronald Reagan's vice presidential candidate, both Barbara and George had had to take a few steps back from their positions with regard to family planning, and she didn't speak about it.

She felt that, certainly, gays should have rights. She was sympathetic to what was happening with the AIDS holocaust, but she wasn't particularly verbal about it. She was there, she was talking about it, but her participation was somewhat muted.

ENGEL: I don't think that we should let her role in the AIDS crisis go unmentioned, because she did a dramatic thing when she was only in her first weeks of being first lady. She went to an AIDS orphanage and held up an AIDS baby, who subsequently died several weeks later. The picture of a first lady holding an infant with AIDS was really quite shocking to people at the time, back at the time when people thought that people with AIDS should be shunned or should be put away.... It was really a remarkably important cultural moment.

She was always very good at making solid political statements quietly, holding a baby, putting a candle in a window. Her rationale, for example, of ultimately explaining that she was pro-choice was that she was not in favor of abortions, but she thought this is something that should be between a mother and a father and a doctor, and the government didn't have a role in this.

She was very, very keen to set boundaries for where the government should intervene. She wanted to take moral stands, but without interfering with her husband's political career, so she would make them through very subtle, but strong statements.

Barbara Bush had been invited to be the commencement speaker in June of 1990 [at Wellesley College]. A few weeks after she accepted, one hundred fifty of the six hundred Wellesley seniors who were graduating sent a petition saying they felt that she was an inappropriate speaker, because anything that she had achieved in life was because of whom she was married to. There was a short period where perhaps Mrs. Bush thought, "This speech isn't a great idea." Instead, she finessed it, and she said, "You know what? I was twenty-one once myself, and I questioned things, and I think that I have things to tell them."

She let them know that she was going to give the speech. She invited Raisa Gorbachev, the wife of Russian Premier Gorbachev, who would be visiting at the same time, and the two of them went up to Wellesley together.

Over time, she became more popular, in terms of public perception, than the president, so her political role increased as her popularity did, as well.

People could relate to her. People looked at her and said, "Boy, that looks like somebody whom I know." There is a wonderful advertisement that comes out for a furniture sale at this time, where on the side of a bus, the advertisement says: "Get Nancy Reagan furniture at Barbara Bush prices." Now, Barbara Bush was a rich woman. She could afford a lot, but she had this image of being somebody who would live just down the street from you.

GUTIN: People said they felt like they could sit down and have a cup of coffee with her, and this was either an innate political sense or an innate sense of self. Leading into the campaign, advisers were saying, you need to lose weight, you need to dye your hair, and she said, "We can do anything but you can't make me lose weight, and you can't make me dye my hair."

Hers was very much an everywoman kind of persona. People really could relate to her because she wasn't a size two, as [was] Nancy Reagan. She dressed nicely, but maybe not in the same high style. She just seemed like someone you could talk to. It worked politically. She also had the kind of demeanor where she seemed to be someone who would listen....

ENGEL: [During the White House years, Mrs. Bush, the president and their dog, Millie, were diagnosed with Graves' disease, affecting the thyroid.] It's very unusual [for so many to develop this type of autoimmune disease at the same time]. In fact, President Bush joked that "we wouldn't have this problem if we would just stop drinking out of the dog's bowl."

They went back and tested everything. They tried to figure out why this could possibly be, and no one has ever been able to determine any particular environmental link for why this happened. This did significantly affect the president in his last year in office, because he lost weight, he lost a lot of energy and had a lot of trouble with his handwriting during this period.

GUTIN: Barbara Bush was annoyed [in 1992, when Texas businessman Ross Perot entered the presidential race]. She felt that, again, her husband had been a superb president, and she had already started to focus on Bill Clinton [as their Democratic opponent], and then Perot said he was going to enter the race because he didn't think that either candidate was particularly good. Then, with Perot's success, that annoyance really moved to concern.

ENGEL: Mrs. Bush...is a person who did not directly involve herself in policy. But there's an important distinction to be made there. She cared a lot about politics. She knew what was going on in Washington. She knew all the players. She knew all the actors. She made sure that she knew the gossip, but she wasn't interested in changing the policy. That was the president's job.

[She was less about being involved in] campaign strategy than being out in front for the campaign, because, especially as the president moved into campaigning for his second term in 1992, she was really much more popular than he was, in terms of polls throughout the country. There were many times when the president not only would send her out on the campaign trail, but really would begin to answer questions with, "Well, Barbara and I think," and that was a way of saying that he was with her, she was the popular one.

[Barbara's personal popularity] didn't [translate into enough additional votes for her husband in 1992], and largely because both Perot and Clinton had a singular line of attack against President Bush, and that was that he was more concerned with foreign affairs than domestic.... By the end of his administration, the president was primarily concerned with foreign affairs, and with good reason. There was the fall of the Berlin Wall, the fall of the Soviet Union, Tiananmen Square, the Gulf War, all kinds of things that would attract a president's attention. President Bush even writes in his diary at this time, "I really do like foreign affairs more than domestic."

With the economy beginning to slip a little bit, the public perceived this. Bill Clinton said we're going to focus on the economy, "It's the economy, stupid." Ross Perot said we're going to focus on the budget. Both of these essentially opened up a vulnerable flank for the president's reelection bid, and ultimately, it did him in.

GUTIN: Barbara Bush had trouble understanding how anyone could elect Bill Clinton. She felt that her husband had done a superb job as president and deserved reelection. Along came the governor of Arkansas, and there were disclosures about his having had an affair. She just could not understand how people would go ahead and elect him. As far as Hillary Clinton went, she thought she was bright, she thought she was sharp, but Barbara Bush did not entirely know how to deal with her, because she was someone different. So there was a certain level of discomfort with both of them.

ENGEL: This difference is really quite crucial, because there is a real cultural shift, even a generational shift going on in America at this time. Barbara Bush was from a generation where a traditional woman's role was to stay home and raise the kids and support her husband's career. Hillary Clinton did not come from that model…. Being confronted with a woman who clearly had taken other choices really left the two of them, Hillary and Barbara, at odds, not so much with each other personally, but ideologically. They were from two different worlds.

GUTIN: They are friendly [with the Clintons now], particularly Bill Clinton and George H.W. Bush. They're good buddies. They've partnered on a number of important projects, but certainly the relationship between Barbara Bush and Hillary Clinton has seemed to be cordial. They've shown up at some of the same meetings together. It's a polar opposite of 1992.

Part of Barbara was really relieved [that her husband wasn't reelected]. She slipped into [post–White House life] very gracefully. She wrote her autobiography, her first. She was enjoying seeing her family and the children. They were back in Texas. She was back with friends and on more familiar ground. Then, son George W. Bush decided he was going to run for governor, so they were back into politics again.

ENGEL: Most presidential administrations essentially like to work on [their presidential library] during the second term, but this one, of course, was without a second term. They began working on the Bush Presidential Library almost immediately after losing their reelection bid. This really became one of the focal points for the post-presidency, working down at Texas A&M, a place that the Bushes really felt comfortable.

ENGEL: The Bushes spend half the year in Houston and half the year in Kennebunkport, their home up in Maine, and attending every social and athletic function that they possibly can. To see them is to see people who really enjoy their life. It's a good job to be an ex-president, and I think that they know it.

Barbara Bush's legacy:

GUTIN: Barbara Bush is an American classic. She's someone who is still tremendously popular, and she's wise, and she's smart, and she brought that commonsense approach to the White House. She has also, as have many of us, been through a great deal, the death of a child and the races for the many offices, and living all over the country. What we would learn from her is the importance of flexibility. She is someone to be admired.

ENGEL: ...More happens during Bush's four years in office on the international scene, and he was confronted with more difficult decisions than any other president during four years, with the possible exception of Franklin Roosevelt during the height of World War II.... Behind the scenes the entire time was Barbara Bush, who in a period of great tumult and a period of great turmoil, with President Bush out front every day trying to calm international tensions, she essentially was behind the scenes, helping him keep calm. That's an important legacy.

She solidified [the role of first lady]. She did a marvelous job of establishing that the presidency was about more than just the man, it was about the family, and she really allowed the American people to see her family without simultaneously appearing too much behind the curtain, having a respectful distance, if you will.

Hillary Rodham Clinton

Hillary Clinton, 1992

"Soon my staff became known around the White House as 'Hillaryland.' We were fully immersed in the daily operations of the West Wing, but we were also our own little subculture within the White House. My staff prided themselves on discretion, loyalty, and camaraderie, and we had our own special ethos. While the West Wing had a tendency to leak, Hillaryland never did."

Born: October 26, 1947, Chicago, Illinois
Married: October 11, 1975, to William Jefferson Clinton (1946–present)
Children: Chelsea Victoria (1980–present)

Contributors:

DAVID MARANISS, associate editor, *Washington Post;* presidential biographer and author of several books including *First in His Class: A Biography of Bill Clinton*

GAIL SHEEHY, contributing editor, *Vanity Fair;* author of several books, including *Hillary's Choice*

DAVID MARANISS: Hillary Clinton is the best-known woman in the world. She's an incredible story, whether you like her or dislike her, and everyone has an opinion pretty strongly one way or the other about her. She's a pioneer. She blazed a path for every woman to follow, in terms of her political career and activism. And she's a survivor, as is her husband. For all of the incredible ups and downs of their lives together and moving forward, she keeps going. She once quoted Woody Allen saying that "Ninety percent of life is just showing up," and she keeps showing up.

GAIL SHEEHY: The most significant thing about Hillary's childhood was the way she saw herself, which was, from the age of eight or ten, a star. Her fantasy was—and she wrote about this—that she would get out on her lawn and dance and spin under the sun, and imagine that God was beaming the sun down on her, only her, and that heavenly cameras were filming her every move. She made that a reality. For many years now, maybe not heavenly, maybe satanic cameras, but cameras, nonetheless, are following her every move. She made it happen.

MARANISS: I wouldn't quite call her mother [Dorothy Rodham] a traditional housewife. She was a housewife, but she was very strong and independent, and infused that into Hillary. Her father [Hugh Rodham] was a rock-ribbed Republican. Park Ridge, Illinois, was 99.5 percent white. It was in the deep part of the Midwest middle class. It was very sheltered in that sense that children were the chosen ones, and Hillary thought of herself as the chosen of the chosen ones.

   She also had her father's politics, but the politics were incidental to who she thought she was. She was very strongly a Methodist throughout her life, but it started in her early teenage years. Her youth minister, Don Jones, was a very progressive person who was challenging Hillary and many of the other kids to think about the world outside of Park Ridge, so that was going on in her mind even before she blossomed or changed her politics.

SHEEHY: Her mother told me one of the significant stories about her childhood. When they moved to Park Ridge, the vicious social hierarchy of four-year-olds didn't admit her, and a little girl named Suzy used to beat her up every day, and she came back crying. One day her mother said, "This house is no place for cowards. You go back out there and you knock that girl off her pins." And that's what Hillary did. The boys were watching, their mouths agape, and Hillary came back home and said, "Now I can play with the boys."

Two other ways in which her mother had an important influence on her were [first,] that she wanted her to have equilibrium. She used a carpenter's level as a visual to say, "Keep the bubble in the middle." And then, she also wanted to warn her never [to] get divorced, because Dorothy Rodham's parents had been divorced, and they abandoned her, and it blighted her life. So Hillary never agreed to give Bill Clinton a divorce, even though at one point, he wanted it.

The other amazing thing about Hillary was, when she met Martin Luther King, introduced by [the Methodist minister] Don Jones, she was really taken. She heard him in Chicago, and she realized that there were no black people that she saw in her class or in Park Ridge, and she read up on it. She realized that the Emancipation Proclamation hadn't really been carried out, and she wanted to do something [about it].

MARANISS: She was a very smart student, and she was the president of her high school class. Wellesley College was an all-girls school near suburban Boston. Her parents drove her out in Hugh Rodham's Cadillac.

SHEEHY: It made her father furious when he realized that it was a snobby Eastern liberal girls' school. He never visited her there until her graduation....

Her "a-ha" moment was at Wellesley the day that Martin Luther King was shot. She heard about it, and she came in sobbing and saying, "This cannot go on." That was when she really turned off from being a little Goldwater girl to being a real progressive, a real liberal.

MARANISS: That was 1968, and she would graduate the next year. That was a moment where she turned into an activist, but you could see her politics changing as soon as she got to Wellesley, as did [the politics of] hundreds of thousands of that generation of kids when they got to college.

SHEEHY: [She was student body president at Wellesley and was asked to give a speech at her 1969 commencement.] Her generation did not want to hear from a moderate Republican [Senator Ed Brooke of Massachusetts], even though he was a black man, about entering the workforce and going on to be competitive and so on. So she got up, and said, "We don't believe in just materialism and competitiveness. We are looking for ecstatic experiences."

Her student body ... gave a roar of applause. The faculty was mortified. Hugh Rodham got out of town as fast as he could, but it got her into *Life* magazine, and she was already a star.

MARANISS: [Going to Yale Law School was] what somebody who wanted to have an active life, effecting change, would do in that period. She got to Yale Law School in 1969, a year before Bill Clinton, and took a five-year program to get through Yale Law School.... She wanted to be a lawyer more than he ever did, but they both saw it as a way to the life that they wanted in politics and in effecting social change. Yale Law School was a very socially active place during that period. The classes were the opposite of Harvard Law. It wasn't like everything was rigid; it was very loose.

SHEEHY: When I asked Hillary Clinton, "What was the most ecstatic experience of your twenties?" she said, "Falling in love with Bill Clinton." I said, "What attracted you to him?" And she said, "He wasn't afraid of me."

In the case of Hillary, she had not been popular with boys, in a boy-girl sense. She liked big, handsome hunks, and Bill Clinton was this big, handsome, red-haired guy with Elvis sideburns and, yeah, he was rough around the edges, and he had this Southern charm. He was walking after her out of class, kind of like a lovesick hound dog panting behind her, and it really made her feel like a woman. That was a new experience for her.

Then she realized how brilliant he was, and how they clicked, and how she could really do something with this guy. She could really bring him up. When she left [her position with] the Watergate impeachment committee to go out to Fayetteville, Arkansas, [to be with Bill Clinton,] her best friend was saying, "You're crazy, Hillary. What are you doing? You're leaving this fabulous career in Washington, where you're in line to be in political life." And she said, "Bill Clinton is going to be president someday, and I'm going to marry him." Her friend said, "Does he know that?" And she said, "Not yet."

MARANISS: From Bill Clinton's perspective, obviously, there were a lot of women that were interested in him, and he in them, but Hillary was different. During that period, his roommates at Yale would say that he would prepare and prep them for times when Hillary was coming over because he wanted to impress her so much. The reason was that she wouldn't put up what she called his "Arkansas palaver." She was the one girl who had the guts to say, "Oh, come off it, Bill."

But also, beyond that, they understood that they actually did have a lot in common. They were completely different personalities, but they had the same ambitions. They saw they could get places together that they couldn't get to apart. They shared a love of politics and of movies and of books and of intellectual things, and there was a spark there. Hillary, from the very beginning, was head over heels for him. Bill saw her as someone different and someone who could really help him and be a partner.

They met in 1970, and they got married in 1975. She came out to Arkansas when he was running for Congress, and…they also were law professors together at the University of Arkansas. It set the tone for the differences between them. Bill Clinton was an easy professor who gave everybody B-pluses at the worst, and mostly A's. The feeling was that they were all going to be voters in Arkansas someday, [so] he didn't want to upset them. He also was known for…being on a plane and leaving the exams somewhere. Hillary was completely organized, and her classes were tough. The dean of the law school said that if he was going to hire one of the Clintons to be a law professor, it would have been Hillary.

SHEEHY: When Bill was running for his first congressional race, and his campaign was chaotic, and he was losing, Hillary dropped everything, flew out there, and came into the little campaign [office]. They shooed the college girl that he was having a romance with out the side door. Hillary came in, and said, "What's going on? This is a mess."

She took over, and that night, the night before the vote—they knew they were going to lose—she and the campaign manager and his wife all got locked in a room together to find out what was really going wrong, and Hillary was giving them the third degree.

The campaign manager's wife said, "I even had to take Bill Clinton's girlfriend as my babysitter to get her out of the way." Hillary turned on the campaign manager, and said, "You got Bill Clinton a girl while I was away? You SOB." She started swearing and cursing and throwing things. The next thing, a window was broken. It was a melee. And who sat through the whole thing—nobody ever mentioned him—with the passivity of a Buddha, was Bill Clinton. That set the mold for the way she dealt with all of those eruptions. It was never his fault; it was always somebody else's fault.

MARANISS: She came into the [role of] first lady of Arkansas as Hillary Rodham. Two years into their governorship, he was defeated. He was rendered the youngest ex-governor in American history. Part of the campaign against her, and against Bill, was this woman who wouldn't even take her husband's last name, and that was so un-Arkansan.

Although Bill Clinton was always called the protean character who could adapt to any setting, Hillary was also adaptable. She's the one who came from Illinois and the East Coast to Arkansas. After those first two years, she really figured out how to work in Arkansas. Over the rest of his governorship, she was very much part of that whole social and political and cultural milieu.

SHEEHY: A lot of it had to do with image. She hadn't given any thought to her appearance, buying dresses off the rack. She dressed like a hippie. She didn't wear makeup; her hair wasn't fixed. She really spruced up. She pulled herself together and began to look more like an acceptable Southern lady and give teas and do more of the first lady duties. She was also supporting them [financially]. The big thing that she gave Bill Clinton was money. She was the breadwinner while he was making a very paltry salary [as governor] for many years. She was made partner at Rose Law Firm three years after she was hired, once he was back in the governor's office, because that was now a very big connection.

[Her activities in Arkansas that led to the Whitewater investigation during their White House years were that] she was trying to make money. She was investing. She had a hotshot investor who got her into cattle futures, and she made a big profit.

MARANISS: Jim Blair was a friend of theirs. Diane Blair was in Fayetteville at the university when the Clintons were there, and her husband was very sharp with trading, and that's how they got into this. Put in $1,000 and make $100,000 on cattle futures. The connection to other people in Little Rock is when she got in trouble with the Rose

Law Firm records and actions involving Jim McDougal, who was actually Bill Clinton's friend. It's all in the morass of Arkansas politics that they got trapped in.

SHEEHY: It was 1989 when Bill Clinton...fell in love with another woman, really fell in love with her. This was not a bimbo. This was not a black-rooted lounge singer. This was actually a woman of quality, a professional whose family was in Arkansas and in politics. He asked Hillary for a divorce. She consulted with her minister and herself, and came back and said, "Nothing doing. That's not going to happen. This affair is going to end." That was the end of it. He never brought it up again. They found their own arrangement [for their marriage] much later....

Early in '92, the day after she and Bill had appeared on *60 Minutes* to address the Gennifer Flowers [affair allegations], I flew with Hillary in a tiny little plane to Pierre, South Dakota, where she was going to appear before the pork rib feeders roast. As soon as we'd landed and got into a motel, there on this television screen was Gennifer Flowers, playing her tapes with Governor Clinton.

I was right next to Hillary, and I watched her expression. Not one iota of surprise. Just a lizard eye blink, and then directing her press secretary, "Get Bill on the phone. Get our surrogates on the phone. Get [aide George] Stephanopoulos on the phone." Boom, right into battle mode. She then swept into the pork rib feeders roast and charmed the whiskers off the farmers. Then she was told all three TV networks led with Gennifer. She went to the phone again and came back boiling mad.

We got on the plane, and for the next half hour, she staked out what would become their battle plan for the rest of their time in the White House. She said, "We've got to run against the Republican attack machine because they're now doing paid character assassination, and [we've got to] run against the press."

The second one was a really big mistake. She did shut off their access to reporters, which really alienated them a great deal. She stumbled all the time, and she lied much of the time. The press very early on stopped giving them glass-half-full [treatment] and started giving them glass-half-empty.

She had decided that she'd made a choice. The name of my book was *Hillary's Choice*. She was either going to rise with Bill Clinton or

The Clinton family—Chelsea, President Clinton, and First Lady Hillary Clinton—walk down Pennsylvania Avenue on Inauguration Day, January 20, 1997.

fall with him. They were symbiotic; they were joined at the hip. She knew what she was getting. They had an unspoken agreement. She didn't ask him for any details about the women, and he didn't ask her about Whitewater or Morgan Guaranty or her cattle futures or her investments.

They made a lot of mistakes in the beginning [of the 1992 presidential campaign]. The public was not prepared for a "two-for-one presidency"; I don't know if they ever will be. But it was stunning to suddenly see this really intelligent, outspoken, totally confident woman who had been given the role of co-president. If we had a co-presidency, that might be a really cool thing, because partners in power are happening more and more.... Actually, it took a Hillary to raise this president. She did have to keep Bill in the channel, because he was brilliant, but all over the place, and reckless.

To swallow all of that was really quite [a lot] for the American public. It took her almost six years to really figure out how to do it....

[Hillary's appointment to lead the Clinton health care reform initiative created] a long hangover for the Clintons.... She never showed any deference to the people on this committee, one of the oldest and most important committees in Washington, to say, "I look forward to your expertise to educate me." What she said was, "I know. I've studied. I've talked to thousands of Americans, and this is what we need to do." She got off on the wrong foot…with members of Congress. Everything was in secret; many, many meetings, then this giant, thousands-of-pages thing was dropped on the table. Then [came the] same complaints, the same opposition from Republicans on every single score…that Obama faced. The Clintons just were way ahead of their time. The key was… when she said, "I don't understand why I couldn't make policy just like any other public official." She wasn't a public official.

MARANISS: You could see when they got to the White House that they were protecting Chelsea. She wasn't part of the story until there were certain times when they needed to present an image of family, and then, all of a sudden Chelsea would appear in *People* magazine.

There's nothing negative to say about their parenting, and there shouldn't be. They were excellent parents. They showered her with knowledge and books and love. She became very much like parts of both of them, the better parts of each of them.

SHEEHY: Chelsea was devoted to her mother. Her father used to come home and have dinner with her, oftentimes when Hillary was traveling, and so he'd have his Saturday night date with Chelsea. One of the things that was the most heartbreaking for him, when he had really gone over the line with Monica Lewinsky, was that he lost Chelsea for a while.

…Hillary did not know, or did not allow herself to know, that Monica Lewinsky was really a sexual relationship until Bill Clinton actually had to sit her down and tell her. She threw things at him and exploded, and we saw how the family split apart. It was a very tragic thing to watch.

But for most of that year [of the scandal and investigation], she was right in there fighting for him. The attorney who was working with them on damage control [said], "They were always holding hands. Their arms were around each other. They were totally affectionate. They were in this together." What you saw was that when crisis engulfed them, they would be like they were at war. They were in the foxhole together. The bombs were exploding all around and it's your battle buddy; it's you two against the world, and it made them closer.

MARANISS: That's exactly right. There was this cycle to their relationship, where one was up and the other was down, then one would be up and the other would be down. They'd keep going back and forth. That actually had an effect of keeping them together through all of this…. In '99, of course, things fractured [over the Lewinsky investigation], but the thing to remember from that is that they stayed together. One of the great ironies of modern politics is that the Clintons have stayed together when [political] families like [Clinton's Vice President Al] Gore, who everybody thought had a perfect family, split apart.

[By 1999,] Hillary Clinton had already had her eye on [the Senate]. Because of Bill Clinton's troubles, she was frustrated in those last few years in the White House and was looking to go out on her own. They had risen together as far as they could for twenty-five years, and now it was her turn, and that's the way she felt.

SHEEHY: She was fifty-three years old. With the current generation of women, it's not going to take that long to speak with their own voice, but she had to wait that long and still had to wait a little bit longer after that. She did start her campaign before she left the White House, moved to New York, and started a whole new life. She began to be seen socially and began to move away and develop a separate channel. They never got divorced, but they found a way to cohabit in the universe and still help each other.

MARANISS: She was actually very well liked in the Senate. I don't think that you could point to any specific legislation that came through during that period that she was related to, although very early in her first term, 9/11 happened, and she was the senator from New York where that took place.

The key issue and vote that ironically hurt her [in her 2008 presidential bid] was the vote in 2003 on invading Iraq. She supported it. One can see the connection between being the senator from New York where the Twin Towers were and her war vote a couple of years later. One can easily make the case that this vote cost her the 2008 Democratic nomination, because Barack Obama—who had not been in the Senate, but gave a strong speech opposing the Iraq war—won the progressive vote in Iowa and took off from there.

[Her 2008 presidential campaign failed because it] was a mess. As tight as her White House operation was in what they called "Hillaryland," the campaign itself had all these different factions of Hillary people and Bill people and a lot of disagreements and tactical errors.... In the end, it always comes down to the candidates themselves.... At a point where Barack Obama was winning the emotion vote—his speeches, the energy that he had, the youth, and all that—Hillary was considered too much of a machine, an automaton candidate. [At a campaign stop in New Hampshire in 2008, she tried] to show, "I'm human, too," but it was a little bit too late.

SHEEHY: She had just lost [the Iowa caucuses]. She was in third place in Iowa, a terrible shock to her. She came to New Hampshire [and met with] a small group of women, and an older woman asked her, "How do you do it day after day?" That kind of got to her. It was Hillary unplugged for once, where you saw a little bit of her being a human, of being a woman. Then she got slammed for crying. She didn't cry. She just choked up a little bit. There were men crying all over the place in politics in that period, and getting away with it.

It certainly was [a momentous decision for Hillary Clinton to serve as Barack Obama's secretary of state]. She came into that discussion with a strong negotiating position. She didn't accept right away. She said, "I have my own agenda. I want to bring my Vital Voices," which was her program in the White House to empower women and work for gender equality in countries all around the world. She wanted to bring that into the State Department as an official U.S. policy. She said to Barack Obama, "If you can accept that, fine. Otherwise, you can find somebody else." He agreed [to her request]. This may be her greatest legacy, to have made progress for women and girls around the world.

MARANISS: [Her congressional testimony after the attack on the U.S. consulate in Benghazi, Libya, where an ambassador and three other Americans were killed] also was Hillary unplugged in a very different way. That was a Hillary that a lot of people have seen in campaign meetings behind the scenes. She was angry [at the congressional questioning]. I don't think [her performance there] was staged at all. That was the way she was feeling at the time. There are some legitimate points she was making. She has said that Benghazi was her main regret as secretary of state, the fact that four people were killed on her watch.

...In the course of history, people could say, what did she do as secretary of state? In terms of international diplomacy, you can't point to that many accomplishments. You can point to something that has been part of her [legacy] from when she went to Beijing as the first lady and spoke about women's rights. The larger impact that Hillary Clinton has had on the world has to do with her speaking out so strongly about women's issues.

SHEEHY: She cannot not run [for president in 2016]. She now has the former Obama machine backing her... She has Ready for Hillary, which is a grassroots operation.... She can't disappoint all these people. Plus the fact she's always wanted it. She's had so much scrutiny, and here we are scrutinizing her all over again, and everybody else will be doing the same. She's in many ways bulletproof on a lot of what's gone on in the past.

MARANISS: I would never say bulletproof, but I think that there were a lot of people who voted in the primaries for Barack Obama, who, a couple of years after that, were thinking, "Well, maybe Hillary would have been a good president or had more experience even than he." Everything seems totally greased for her, and that always sends off alarm bells in my mind. Everything seems inevitable. History is never inevitable. . . . I'm counterintuitive enough to think that something else might occur.

Hillary Clinton's legacy:

SHEEHY: Hillary Clinton, from the very beginning, wanted to be helpful in advancing the lives, the security, the opportunity, and the impact of women and the protection of girls. You see that through time in every framework that she has operated in, right to this day, and that that has been her greatest impact on the world.

MARANISS: I would say she was almost one of a kind [as first lady]. The role model that she modeled herself after was Eleanor Roosevelt, but there was a great difference between the two. Bill Clinton and Hillary Clinton, from the very beginning, saw that they could get places together that they couldn't apart, whereas Eleanor was very active as a first lady, but she was really on her own track, separate from President Roosevelt. Bill Clinton relied on Hillary for much of his policy from the very beginning, going all the way back to Arkansas. That "two-for-one" comment which she made...was a reality to them.

Laura Welch Bush

> "For a first lady, there are moments of maximum political controversy, and they often strike without warning."

Laura Bush, October 2005

Born: November 4, 1946, Midland, Texas
Married: November 5, 1977, to George Walker Bush (1946–present)
Children: Barbara Pierce and Jenna Welch (1981–present)

Contributors:

ANN GERHART, senior editor-at-large, *Washington Post;* author, *The Perfect Wife: The Life and Choices of Laura Bush*

MARK UPDEGROVE, presidential historian; director, LBJ Presidential Library; author of several books, including *Baptism by Fire: Eight Presidents Who Took Office in Times of Crisis*

MARK UPDEGROVE: George W. and Laura Bush had transitioned into White House life relatively easily. Right before 9/11 occurred, Laura Bush started hitting her stride as first lady. She just had a first state dinner for the president of Mexico. She had just done the first National Book Festival using the Texas Book Festival as a template. She was really starting to hit her groove in that role.

And then, 9/11 occurred. She talked about a friend of hers who had called her and said, "When you first took on this role, I thought, 'Oh man, I don't envy her at all,' but now I envy you because you have a role to play; a very important role to play as our nation picks itself back up in the wake of this tragedy." And she did an admirable job of it.

ANN GERHART: I was with [Laura Bush on 9/11] because I was covering her as first lady for the *Washington Post*. There was some confusion initially as to whether anyone was going to appear or speak, anything, and then the [Senate committee hearing she was attending] was suspended. She and Senator [Ted] Kennedy made a brief statement to the press who were there.... Mrs. Bush twists her fingers at her side when she's struggling with something, [and this] was clearly very dramatic. I remember thinking, she is wise enough. Her mother-in-law was in the White House. She knows her life has changed in this moment.

She said...what she came to say over and over again, "I think we just have to make sure we tell our children that we love them and that America is a strong country, and we will get through this." It was spontaneous and sincere, very much in keeping with her [role] as a librarian and teacher. She dedicated herself to that, but things were very different immediately.

Laura Welch was born in Midland, Texas, which is West Texas; it is boom and bust oil country. It is the kind of place that you can see from miles away; it kind of shimmers like Oz from thirty miles around the horizon because it's very wide and very flat and very much big sky.

Laura's father was a builder and her mother was a homemaker. Her mother came from Texas's strong female stock. Her mother had managed a dairy farm when her grandfather was away. It was very much a [piece] of who she was, and gave her a sense of strength about the land and the prairie and doing for yourself....Laura's friend, [Jan O'Neil,] who wound up introducing her to George W. Bush, said she remembers coming home from the supermarket one day with two little kids, and there was a tumbleweed the size of a Volkswagen Beetle in front of her door; she had no idea how to get into her house. So, it is in some ways very harsh and forbidding, and you have to have a special appreciation. I think it made Laura tough.

UPDEGROVE: Laura Bush's book [*Spoken from the Heart*] is really a love letter to Midland, Texas, in a way. It's so much a part of her. She talks about the sky, and how her mother and she used to look up at the sky for hours on end, and how important that is to that part of the country. George W. Bush mentioned to me one time that this kind of country broadens your horizon. You see people for who they are. There are no trees and the sky is the limit.

GERHART: Laura was the only child, so that is also always insulating in a way. It can sometimes be a lonely existence, and there weren't a lot of folks who came in from the outside.... People had their own hide-bound ways of being and their own divides as to where you were in the social stratosphere....

They used to say that you raised hell in Odessa and that you raised your kids in Midland, so there was a certain way of behaving and a propriety for that. You went to the Methodist church; you went to the Episcopal church, in some of the ways of small-town America every-where. People had to be dependent on each other because it could be kind of harsh.

...There were three different high schools [in Midland], and they all got together for a reunion when the Bushes were in the White House. Nobody even really remembered about the black high school and in-vited any kids from that. I don't think that it was a matter of overt separation as much as within a certain class of people, there was al-most obliviousness....

When Laura went off to Southern Methodist University, she had said, and some of her friends had said, they necessarily didn't have a remem-brance of Martin Luther King and some of the race riots that were going on around the rest of the world. There were the sock hops, and there were the sodas at the drive-in, and in that way, it was isolating.

[Right after turning seventeen, Laura Welch was in a car crash in Mid-land, Texas, and it resulted in the death of a schoolmate and very close friend of hers, Michael Douglas.] What she has said about it...was that when you are young, you expect that the world is going to be a certain way. She would have attained that maturity anyway, but, [because of this accident, it] came to her pretty quickly. She is an empathetic person by nature, and it probably made her less judgmental about other peo-ple, in a way that we don't often see in Washington. She is more given to thinking people may have interior backgrounds and things that shaped them that we don't know.

That has certainly made her the kind of person who worried more about her own daughters. She worried about her husband because she had seen at a very early age how an instant and a miscalculation can change everything.

UPDEGROVE: She said...that she grew up out of that experience, and there were things that happen in your life that you can't change and you have to find a way to move on. That experience, while very formative for a young girl in Midland, Texas, was very helpful to her in the days after 9/11. She had seen the role that fate can play in this world and realized that you have to move on; you have to be strong. Faith plays a great role in both of the Bushes' lives.

GERHART: People frequently overlook [the fact that she is the second first lady in history to have a postgraduate degree], because they make the mistake of thinking that she is a conventional woman, which she is not at all. She is quite interior and has a certain modesty, if that word really means much anymore. She didn't ever really boast about it a lot, but she certainly was very self-directed. When she came back from SMU and teaching, she said she wanted to go on to the University of Texas [to] get a library science degree. Her father said, "Now, I will never get her a husband." [She went on to] get her master's degree when many people thought if you went to college at all, it was for an "MRS." degree. Then she very purposefully moved into a part of Austin which is still the barrio, on the east side, and taught at an almost entirely Spanish-speaking school. In a very dedicated fashion, she deliberately chose this school where she thought she could have an impact helping kids learn to read, and she felt as if they were being exposed to other parts of life they weren't getting....

[Laura Welch and George Bush were both growing up in Midland, Texas, at the same time but] they did not actually [meet then]. They attended the same schools, but she says that she doesn't recall him, and then she knew who he was after a time. He was a roustabout from a good family, and a well-known family, the Bushes, in Midland. At one point, they lived in the same building...in Houston. I think she thought he was a bit too carousing, so she had other pursuits. Then her friends from Midland fixed them up [when] she was thirty and he was about the same age. He was ready to settle down, and they got engaged and married very quickly, in three months.

Laura…famously "stepped to" with Barbara Bush, who has a large personality, when she first came to [meet the Bush family in] Kennebunkport. Barbara Bush was said to say somewhat tartly to Laura, "And you do what?" when the Bush boys were all running around competing against each other. Laura Bush said, "I read, I smoke, and I admire." That was her way of saying, "This is who I am. This is what I'm going to be doing and I may not fit some mold." She respects very much her mother-in-law's life, and Barbara Bush, for her part, has been very grateful to her for settling down her boy. She once said Laura was the one with the first lady potential.

UPDEGROVE: Laura Welch had had a lot of suitors in her life, but none of them quite clicked, and in Texas at the time, she talks about feeling like an old maid. By Texas standards, [at 30], she probably was. Then, here comes this guy, George Bush, who was so different from her in so many respects and yet so complementary. They really clicked, and so it was somewhat uncharacteristic that she would be swept up in this romance.

GERHART: Laura always said that he made her laugh, and she wanted somebody who would make her laugh…. She had really longed to have a sibling and she really liked his boisterous, cut-up nature. He wanted someone who was steady; Laura, steady as she goes, would settle him down. I see that in them still. You can never know what's in someone else's marriage, but I was struck when I saw them on the *Tonight Show*. He said something, and she tossed her head back and laughed. They still have that bond that he is funny.

UPDEGROVE: …They went out on the campaign trail right after they got married. George Bush campaigned unsuccessfully for a seat in congress in West Texas, and they got to know each other so well on the campaign trail. They'd have these endless hours of driving around the plains of West Texas talking about their lives, and that really helped their marriage begin on the right footing.

She supported Eugene McCarthy. She was a card-carrying Democrat for many years. She married into a Republican family and loves her husband, has great faith in him, in his judgment, and supported his platform, but she is not a natural Republican.

[After his unsuccessful congressional campaign,] he had to figure out what he wanted to do, and he went into the oil business in Midland. They were there for the first ten years of their marriage. It's where their daughters were born and where they raised them in their toddler and childhood years. It was a pretty middle class existence for a long time until he decided to do other things later in his life.

GERHART: They did both have a certain modesty about them in that way that continues today.... I think he felt a strong need to make it on his own... As you find with a lot of sons [of successful parents], he didn't want to feel as if he was born with a silver spoon in his mouth....

UPDEGROVE: The other thing is that Midland is both a boom town, which it is right now, and a bust town, depending on the oil industry. When he was coming up in the oil industry, it was really in bust mode. That was not a very prosperous business to be in at that time. So, he struggled in that business before finding great success as the owner of the Texas Rangers [baseball team].

GERHART: He always had his father's friends, who were there to bail them out. So, certainly, they were not uncomfortable by any stretch of the imagination.

Laura very much wanted to have children. She always knew she wanted to have children, and she always imagined herself as having a family. They described that as being a very idyllic time. She really loved reading to these darling little girls, and raising them, and being very immersed in caring for them. Your children find a way to challenge your preconceptions of what it's going to be like, and they had a set of twins, one who probably has her daddy's personality a bit more, and one who has her mother's. They delighted in that and the years that they spent in Austin [during George W. Bush's tenure as governor,] where they were all together, and what is in some ways a very close and a very easy town to be in. They describe those years as being idyllic years, too.

As first lady, Laura Bush continued her advocacy of reading programs, here reading to children at Florida's West Palm Beach Public Library, October 2006.

UPDEGROVE: [Regarding George W. becoming sober,] Laura said to him, famously, "It's either me or Jim Beam." She realized that he was drinking too much; he realized that at a certain point, [too]. There was a conversation that George W. Bush had with Reverend Billy Graham, who was a guest of his father's at their compound, Walkers Point, in Kennebunkport, Maine. As he began talking to Billy Graham, [he began] embracing God in a way that he hadn't before in his life. That was the threshold of middle age. He turned forty when he gave up drinking, and when he took God into his heart. Laura Bush was extremely supportive of all the decisions that her husband made, including his embracing Christianity in the way he did.

GERHART: Laura Bush was embraced pretty easily [by the public as first lady of Texas], and, in many ways, it is a very low-key position. She would talk about how she liked ducking out the back door and going around the corner to the drugstore, or going to the post office to buy a postage stamp. It's hard to imagine with everything that's happened after September 11 that she could live like that today. She really enjoyed it. She had a rich life. She started the Texas Book Festival.

UPDEGROVE: She was supportive of his intention [to run for president]. There's no question about it. I think she was confident he'd win. When he had his mind set on the statehouse in Texas, when everyone thought he was going to lose to Ann Richards, she knew he was going to win. She knew that he was tenacious in his drive for things, and she had that same faith when he tossed his hat in the [presidential] ring in 2000.

GERHART: ...They had been [in the White House] before in a way, because George Bush's father was the president of United States. They'd spent plenty of time there. They had some guidance as to what that felt like, and what that looked like, what the contours of that are like. Running for president is a marathon, and if you get there or you don't, you're in for a surprise either way. That's a very steep learning curve. They had some exposure to that, so that transition was somewhat eased for them.

[The 2000 election pitted George Bush versus Al Gore in]... a famously bitter recount. Laura Bush spent most of the time in Austin, as did George Bush. She talked about how she tried to keep herself busy. There was just this time to wait, and you couldn't really get too much started because you couldn't really be sure of what's going to happen.

Once they were sworn in, she spent many months not being in Washington. She had two daughters who were going up to college, so she wanted to make sure she got them settled. She saw that as her first responsibility. She was only beginning to figure out what she was going to do and how she was going to focus her attention when September 11, 2001, came along.

Everyone...knows about the many challenges this country faced during the eight years of the Bush Administration. It was a difficult time for the country, not only the 9/11 attacks, but after that, the decision to pursue the wars in Iraq and Afghanistan. Also during that time period, there was Hurricane Katrina, and ultimately, the 2008 financial crisis. On the domestic policy side the big initiative was No Child Left Behind, the administration's major education initiative.

Laura Bush continued to pursue her own interests even as the country responded to the various Bush Administration policies. We've seen this throughout [history, with] first ladies standing beside their husbands as the public opinion of their work changes. How challenging is that for a spouse, to see the increased criticism that the person that you're married to is receiving in the public eye?

UPDEGROVE: It's very difficult for them to see the scrutiny exacted at their husbands because they know the man. They know the real person. Very often, we can get caught up in the heat of the moment when we scrutinize our presidents, and they have always become caricatures in a way. For Laura Bush, who is so deeply in love with her husband, to see the way he was treated must have hurt deeply. She continued to stand by him. She traveled far more in his second term than she did in the first term. She had found a voice on so many issues particularly relating to women, and tried to further that cause by hitting the road, trying to better explain his policies to our nation and to the world.

GERHART: Laura Bush loves her husband, and she's very loyal to her husband, and one of the things that I have come to admire and appreciate about her is that she has navigated this bizarre volunteer job [of first lady, and found] areas of commonality with people with whom she might find differences. She would campaign for Republicans, for instance, but I saw her once change a speech script because...she was not going to attack a Texas Democrat this person was running against in that specific way.

She has things that are very interesting to her and her friends. They care about literature, care about the book festival; she's very much of an avid conservationist and environmentalist. She's pretty active in women's rights and taking those things on.

[In terms of her personal view of the world,] she is not a judgmental and harsh person, but also certainly has never felt that it was her role to crusade on behalf of causes such as reproductive rights, or benefits for same sex couples. She has tried to have her impact in areas which we might consider safe subjects that everyone can get behind. But what she would feel and I would argue correctly can have an impact, [is that] her foundation gives a million dollars away to libraries across the country every year which are woefully, inadequately funded.

The National Book Festival remains a persistent legacy of hers; two hundred thousand people [attend]. She admired Lady Bird Johnson because, all these years later, after what was considered flimsy initiatives to put wildflowers on the nation's highways, they bloom year after year and bring a sense of beauty. So, she's trying to make her impact where she could and let her deeds speak for herself....

UPDEGROVE: ...What she saw with Lady Bird Johnson is that a first lady.... had their own bully pulpit, in a sense. They could take on a cause and make a real difference without world events coming across their desk and their having to react. Then 9/11 occurred, and instead of getting deeply involved in education or literacy, as she would have liked, she had to do other things.

She did find her voice in that issue [of how women and children were treated by the Taliban in Afghanistan]. She talks about going to Austin to visit her daughter at the University of Texas, where Jenna was attending college at that time. [She went] with Jenna to a department store, and there were a couple of Middle Eastern women behind the counter who thanked her for making [a national radio] speech raising awareness about the brutal treatment of women under the Taliban in Afghanistan. She realized at that moment what a profound difference that she could make. When you're in a studio making a radio address, you don't see the people that it affects, but it was that moment that told her that she was making a difference.

GERHART: ...One of the things we had never really talked much about with first ladies is their qualities of leadership. We talked about leadership in terms of chief executives and people who we elected to put in charge. We think of leadership as also being really specific and targeted and focused about how much time you have and what you can accomplish with that time you have.

In the case of Laura Bush, particularly in that second term when she realizes that it's her last chance to have an impact, there are many, many things that she may be concerned about, that she may discuss privately with her husband that she's certainly not going to relate to the rest of us. She may have issues that she disagrees with him on. The idea of trying to remain focused on the areas where she would like to have an impact, and knowing that she can fritter her time away if she doesn't remain what we would call "on message"…is something that we see her do then.

I think what drove a lot of those decisions [to get involved in international issues like African AIDS relief and malaria eradication efforts] was, again, the issue of women's rights and their full participation in the societies in which they [lived]. An extension of that was she felt women wanted to know that they could raise their children to have lives that were sustaining and successful as best they could, and the human rights flowed out of that. The teachings of the Dalai Lama have been of interest to her philosophically….

[After they left the White House in 2009,] the Bushes went very comfortably back into their private lives. I don't think that they missed the grandeur of the White House. They've gone back to their lives in Dallas. Mrs. Bush continues to be very much involved with the Bush Center that includes the Bush Institute and the Bush Library. She was instrumental in the planning of the Bush Library. Her touch can particularly be seen in the grounds surrounding it, with its native grasses and native plants, something she has a great passion for. She continues to lead a very full life and continues to pursue some of the causes that were dear to her as first lady through the Bush Institute.

One of the nice things about being first lady is that you think you'll have just the brief period of time, but your impact does continue. She actually has more room to continue to be involved in these policy initiatives than, certainly, the former president does, or would, or has suggested he wants to. He doesn't think it's right for a president to be criticizing another one. But she and Mrs. Obama, for instance, have both been together in Africa, have had a summit for first ladies of Africa, they've worked together on a number of things. Mrs. Clinton and she have carried on those things, and she has been surprisingly and happily engaged in a way she thought she might not be.

Laura Bush's legacy:

GERHART: With all of these first ladies, it's really hard to judge them in almost the contemporary times in which we are in now…. I think it's too soon for us to know exactly what kind of impact Laura Bush has had in terms of women's rights.

She has been a representative for rights in a way that is not as expected...with what some people see as her more traditional mien, to speak from that position on behalf of women who do not have opportunities. In some ways, this makes her more effective because it's not quite expected, almost as if she's championing it in a place that we wouldn't expect to hear it, perhaps.

UPDEGROVE: Both the Bushes take the long view of history. Actually, Laura Bush talks about the fact that she admired her husband for taking a long view of history, and making difficult decisions during the course of his presidency that wouldn't necessarily manifest themselves in popularity. His presidency and how it's reflected is very much in the balance; we'll see what happens, he knows that, and I think most historians know that. Her contributions as first lady will be revealed as we begin to see the forest for the trees in the tenures of both of them in the White House.

Michelle Robinson Obama

"I think it's an evolutionary process. You grow into this role. You never get comfortable if you are always pushing for change and growth, not just in yourself, but in the issues you care about."

Michelle Obama, February 2013

Born: January 17, 1964, Chicago, Illinois
Married: October 3, 1992, to Barack Hussein Obama, Jr. (1961–present)
Children: Malia Ann (1998–present); Natasha (Sasha) (2001–present)

Contributors:

LIZA MUNDY, journalist and author, *Michelle: A Biography*

KRISSAH THOMPSON, staff writer, *The Washington Post*, who covers Michelle Obama

KRISSAH THOMPSON: [On 2008 election night, the Obamas were victorious in their campaign against Republican John McCain.] They were going to be in history books regardless, because they were the first [black first couple]. So there comes the moment when the history is made and you see in the photos of the Grant Park celebration this sense of jubilation amongst their supporters there. It is still a very divided electorate, but you heard afterwards that many people on both sides of the aisle felt a pride in the country for having at least eclipsed that racial barrier. As the president himself said, he thinks people were excited about that for about five minutes, and then they want to know what you're going to do.

They both faced pretty quickly this idea that they did not only want to be history-making for having achieved this really remarkable feat of being the first, but then to leave a legacy that's greater than that.

LIZA MUNDY: Michelle Robinson was born in Chicago in 1964. It was a very segregated city still. She grew up on the South Side of Chicago, where there were a lot of different neighborhoods, and a lot of immigrants, different ethnic neighborhoods. There was a lot of racial redlining. The city was just opening up a little bit so that her family, when she was still pretty small, was able to move into a neighborhood that had been a white neighborhood. [Her brother,] Craig, has said, and neighbors have said, that they remember the white families started moving away when families like the Robinsons were moving in. They would have been aware that opportunities were opening up for better neighborhoods and better schools, but at the same time, there was a white flight going on....

THOMPSON: Her father, [Frasier Robinson,] was a central figure in her life,...as were both of her parents. Her brother describes their childhood as being kind of a Shangri-La of Chicago, where their parents spent lots of time with them; they weren't leaving the kids with babysitters. Often, when they went out for entertainment, they did it together. They built the kids' self-esteem and made it seem like they were wonderful people to be around, and that confidence infused their lives.

The Robinsons played board games, took family trips. There was a much broader Robinson clan in town, and so they knew all their relatives and went to visit, and they describe a really warm, family-centered childhood, and their dad was at the heart of that.

MUNDY: Her dad was a precinct captain. In some ways, he was a community organizer like Barack Obama, getting people out to vote. Neighbors said that he was a joking man and he had a very good sense of humor, and that he was an extrovert. It may be that he genuinely enjoyed being a precinct captain; it may also be that it was necessary to be a precinct captain in order to get his job as a pump operator, because that was the way back then with the city machine when you would get a job with the city through your political help.

Having a good city job meant for them that Michelle Obama's mom could stay home with the children in a way that many women in their community were not able to do. African American women have a much longer tradition of having to go out to work. When Michelle had children, she asked herself, "Should I be home with my daughters the way that my mother was home with me? It probably made her father's job seem all the more valuable to have.

THOMPSON: [Michelle Obama's emphasis on education came from] her parents. They were really clear that this was the road to get ahead. Her brother writes about his mom teaching them to read at home and doing math tables and that kind of thing. When they got to school, even as early as first and second grades, they were already steps ahead of everyone else, and that continued along with their own hard work through high school. They were excelling really early on.

MUNDY: When Michelle Obama got into a magnet school that was in a completely different part of Chicago, at a pretty early age, she had to take several modes of transportation to get to her high school, and leave really early in the morning in the Chicago winters.

THOMPSON: [Michelle Obama's family can be traced back to a slave in Georgetown, South Carolina.] When you look back to 2008, there were some questions early on about, "Is Barack Obama black enough?" but you never heard that sort of thing about Michelle Obama. Part of that is rooted in the more traditional African American experience [of her family], so, in that way, she serves as a validator for him when you talk about questions of race.

MUNDY: Her family's history is quintessential in that some of her family stayed in Georgetown, and she has relatives who are still there. There was a train depot very close to town, and at least one of her male ancestors would have traveled to Chicago because that's where the trains went. He was able to settle in the South Side, where there were the meatpacking plants, and the stockyards, and all of that industrial labor. There was still a lot of racism, there were still different wage scales for black men and white men, but it was better than the South.

Then the Robinson family was able to establish a very broad and rooted family in Chicago, so that when she and Barack Obama were first going out, that was a real epiphany for him. It was an experience to be in such a rooted family, where your uncles were coming around and people were visiting with each other, a different family life than he had experienced.

Michelle Obama was on the Princeton campus at a really interesting time. The campus had opened up to women, to African American students, to a more diverse student body, but there was definitely resistance and backlash against that. It was a time where a lot of students on campus didn't have a lot of experience or hadn't traveled a lot, and so they were coming to campus and made aware of their difference in a way that they had never been made aware before.

Everybody around campus [thought] if you weren't quite sure what you were going to do, you went to law school. At that point, the Civil Rights Act was not that old, and you thought, "I'll change the world; that'll be what I do if I go to law school." There was a pretty strong conformist push to law school at that time. An administrator at Princeton who knew Michelle very well, tried to talk her out of going to law school. She said Michelle did call her when she was at Harvard Law, saying, "You were probably right."

Michelle did [go back to Chicago after law school, and got a job at a corporate law firm that specialized in telecommunications law] for a while.... Barack Obama was a summer associate [at this Chicago law firm, Sidley Austin], and she was his boss; she was assigned as his supervisor. Probably modern workplace laws would not permit this relationship to develop. He was taken with her. Her colleagues who became aware said that in the late afternoons they'd walk by her office and he'd be perched on her desk, and they could tell that something was developing. I don't think it took too long, actually, before they were going out and were both smitten with each other.

[They didn't marry for four years, because] he had to go back to law school. She was in Chicago; he was going back to Harvard Law. There were several years where they were not necessarily living in the same town. She tells a funny story on herself, where she began to pressure him, and they were going out to dinner in Chicago, and she started in on the "When are we going to get married?" conversation. For a while, he would say, "Oh, marriage is just a word," etc. So she started in, and then, with the dessert, a ring was delivered. She says, "That did shut me up."

THOMPSON: [They were married in 1992 at Michelle Obama's church, which was the Trinity United Church of Christ in Chicago, whose pastor was Reverend Jeremiah Wright.] Reverend Wright becomes an important part of the 2008 campaign, and it really speaks to this latent question that was always out there: Is America ready for African Americans in the White House? Is America ready for a black president? So, in some ways, Jeremiah Wright stands in as a charge point for that question; he comes out of a strain of African American pastors in black liberation theology and there were many radical sermons which were excerpted and lines taken from them that became a huge political problem for the Obamas. But he was also a man who, for a time, had quite a bit of influence on them. President Obama, when he was in the U.S. Senate, took the title of his second book, *Audacity of Hope*, from one of Reverend Wright's sermons. In that sermon, Reverend Wright is talking about this idea of not having very much hope, but hoping anyway, and holding on to hope. These are some of the ideas that connect the Obamas to him and the church. When this [controversy about Reverend Wright's preaching] breaks open in the campaign...there's really a large national conversation about race that begins.

MUNDY: [Their first daughter, Malia, wasn't born until 1998. In those six years,] they were working very hard. Barack Obama helped persuade Michelle Obama that she could leave corporate law...and she could do something less conventional and more interesting; that she didn't have to follow a predictable path. That's one thing he did for her at the same time that she gave him a very rooted family, and the sense of belonging in Chicago. He gave her a sense of what was possible for her.

She took a job in the city government, then she took a job with a nonprofit called Public Allies; he was teaching at the law school and getting started in politics. They were both really working very hard and very intensely—two very intense people.

THOMPSON: [When Barack Obama starts to move from community organizing into elective politics,] Michelle would often say, "You only think about yourself. I never thought I'd have to raise a family alone." This was a classic marital argument that happened in their household repeatedly during this time because she was shouldering so much of the weight of raising a family. This is a difficult point for them in their marriage, and about what he's going to do with his life.

He had to convince her [to let him run for office,] according to the way her brother tells the story. First, Barack Obama went to Michelle's brother, Craig Robinson, and had a conversation with him: "I think this is the opportunity and I think I should do this." Craig says, "Have you talked to your wife?" Barack Obama says, "I thought you could help me with that." Craig Robinson floats the idea [of Barack running for office] with both his mother and his sister, and he describes paving the way. As a family, they made the decision that this is something that they would do with counselors and strategists.

MUNDY: Michelle came from Chicago, which was a city of machine politics, a city that had not been politically just or fair to its African American residents. She had a lot of reason to be skeptical of politics when she was growing up. Her family was famously skeptical of politics to the point where Barack Obama, when he confessed to Craig Robinson that he wanted to be a politician, Craig said, "Well, don't tell [our] Aunt Gracie; keep that under your hat."

Michelle even described herself in 2007 as having been the last one to accept or know that Barack Obama was really going to run for president, so [her transformation into her husband's trusted political adviser] must have come during the presidential campaign.

THOMPSON: There is this idea that she was a reluctant campaigner. She was reluctant to sign on, in part because they had two young daughters at the time, and she was thinking about the sort of sacrifices that would have to be made. She had already been through a campaign for Senate that took them all across the state, and her mom had to step up in many ways and help with the daughters. So when you think about taking that to the nation, there was a lot to consider and she counted the cost. Once she signed on, she was all in....

...The role of the first lady in the modern campaign has been to humanize, if that's the right word, the candidate [in order] to help people connect with who he is as a person and what he's about, what he's like at home. In her campaign stump speech when she traveled around, Michelle would talk about how he leaves his socks out sometimes, and he snores, and that kind of thing. [In other words,] he's a real guy. [She was] talking about him as a man.

MUNDY: In her case, it was even more important, because she was also Americanizing him. She was confirming, "Okay, this guy has a funny name; I thought he had a funny name, too, when I first heard of him when I was at Sidley Austin. But then, when I met him I realized he was just as American as you and me; he has a Midwestern family." She walked the audience through that process [that she went through herself].

THOMPSON: People enjoyed hearing her [speak on the campaign trail in 2008,] in part because, unlike the candidate, she wasn't so strictly on message, she just spoke from her heart without a lot of notes. At that time, the Democratic grassroots found that refreshing. And then comes this moment where this one line is [extrapolated] from her speech [in Wisconsin, when she said, "For the first time in my adult lifetime, I'm really proud of my country,"] and it begins to define her. The campaign gear has to immediately snap into action and begin to create a different story around her because one emerges that is not favorable.

MUNDY: ...[The quote was] used as alleged evidence that she was unhappy with America. She was talking a lot at that time. [For example,] she would talk about racial division if she was on a college campus talking to students, and she'd say, "Look, there are white students sitting here; there are black students sitting there. I know what that's like. You guys need to come together."

She would talk about America being isolated...a sense that there was a coming together that still needed to happen. That was where that concept was coming from. The campaign definitely kicked into gear after that [backlash], and there was not another episode like that.

THOMPSON: During the 2008 primary campaign, it really becomes a dogfight [between Obama and Hillary Clinton] towards the end.

They're grasping, and it got ugly at some points, and you had two really defined camps within the Democratic Party, the Clintonites and the Obamas. There were some questions as to whether everyone was going to be able to come together in a very natural way. This idea that Hillary Clinton would serve as secretary of state did a lot in terms of mending those bridges. Early on in Obama's term, Michelle Obama goes over to the State Department, and they have some interaction and are very warm to each other publicly. That was another moment of coming together.

Michelle Obama has been a very different kind of first lady than Hillary Clinton was. So, in many ways, she relied on Laura Bush's team early on to give her staff guidance about how things would operate in the East Wing. Hillary Clinton had had an office in the West Wing, which was different than the way Michelle planned to set things up.

Michelle Obama...leaned on some of that staff knowledge [from Mrs. Bush's team] about how things work in the house. It's a significant institution, and Michelle Obama, unlike some other first ladies, had not been a governor's wife, so she did not have the experience of really setting up shop and home in that way.... Nancy Reagan came in, and they had lunch, and I'm told some of Nancy Reagan's advice was, "Have lots of state dinners."

MUNDY: ...One thing also that struck me about Michelle Obama, particularly compared to Hillary Clinton, is Michelle did define herself as "mom-in-chief." That had a big effect on changing her image. One thing that you saw is that before the 2008 election, she still polled [well], her favorables were high with Democratic women and Democratic men, but what you saw after the election and the inauguration was that her favorables really rose with conservative women.

Presenting herself as a mother first and foremost did a lot to change her image and to soften her image. It's also something that women of Hillary Clinton's generation could not say of themselves. Hillary Clinton was in the generation where you couldn't even have a photo of your children on your desk if you wanted to be seen as a credible working woman. [You would be seen as] too soft, and you would remind people that you had children, and you weren't supposed to do that in the 1980s. You were supposed to be all there at the workplace. That was a generational difference between the two women.

The Obama family in the White House Green Room, September 2009. Bringing two young daughters into the White House, first lady Michelle Obama often described herself as "mom-in-chief."

In part because of reality television, we are so intimately involved with people that we don't know well, and, in some ways, people feel like they know the Obamas and their relationship because it's on public display in something of the same way.... We catch wind of when they're on a date night.... Even his campaign, at one point, sent out a photo of them together embracing one another, and that went viral. There were pieces in newspapers about what it means to see a modern marriage in the White House.

It's a very conscious [effort by the Obamas to serve as a role model marriage for African American couples]. It's not just for young people who've been a focus of both the president and first lady, but also for families. There is so much talk now about how you do family well in this country. How do you raise well-adjusted teenagers? And you have a woman doing that in the White House giving parenting tips? People want that kind of information. It also provides some of that personal connection that this White House has done really well in helping people to feel like the White House is the people's house, and this is a family that could be the family-next-door that you can relate to.

[In the years that she's been at the White House,] Michelle has become more optimistic and positive. [In one speech, she] articulated something almost like "imposter syndrome," when people feel like they aren't supposed to be where they are. It takes her a while to get over that feeling to realize, "Wow, I'm just as good as everybody else," because maybe she came from a background where she wasn't expected to be in this place. If she felt any of that, she's certainly gotten over it. She seems very comfortable in where she is.

THOMPSON: Michelle Obama has clearly made Washington, D.C., home. It was the [visits to] nonprofits, it was visiting the [cabinet] agencies, but also going out to restaurants with girlfriends, and her daughters being in school here, so she's at soccer games, and catching shows at local theaters, and that sort of thing. She was getting to know the city as a place outside of federal Washington.

That's become not only rare for first families, but for political families in Washington, in general, where you have folks who are jetting back to their home states every weekend. The idea of spending time in Washington is almost bad for your political life. But she has made a concerted effort to get to know this city. As I was putting a list together of all the places in D.C. where she's been, I had colleagues saying, "She's been to more restaurants in town than I have."

Michelle Obama has not allowed the White House to be, as Martha Washington said, "something like a prison," the idea that you can't get outside this bubble. She has found ways to do that.

There was an intense interest [in Michelle Obama] from the beginning, and a willingness on the part of her staff to engage the public outside of the traditional press corps. The many magazine covers [featuring her] are one example of that. It meant everything from *Vogue* to *Better Homes and Gardens* to *Amtrak* magazine, *Prevention*, *Essence*. It was such a broad spectrum, and you were speaking to those audiences of those magazines in a very personal way.

In the same way, she's on Univision, and she's on urban radio talking to people directly. In some ways, it is like social media that removes some filters, and she's able to connect.

MUNDY: Part of that is [a strategy of] actually bypassing the traditional media and going to soft outlets, which, of course, are very eager to cover her. When I was writing my book, [she was] not accessible, and they were being very, very careful about her public image. It was after the "does she like her country?" episode, so they were…really not making her accessible. I had to find other ways to report the story, and I think that's really still the case.

[Michelle Obama's approval rating has remained high and consistent, while President Obama's has been lower and come down over time, because of] the management and tending of her public image; their very strategic approach to print media; the mom-in-chief image; the fact that their family does seem to be flourishing and remains a very appealing family tableau; and the issues that she's chosen. They're not hard issues, they're not mold-breaking issues, such as the "Let's Move" campaign. I think they're in line with literacy and other traditional first lady programs like that.

THOMPSON: There's a lot of money tied up in the food industry [and Mrs. Obama has taken on the issue of healthy eating]. And so, there's also some strategy in how you address these issues. Food politics, for those who are involved in it, are very contentious. You see some of this in the debate, this idea that she's a part of the nanny state and telling kids what they can't eat…. She talked about not needing to pass legislation to get some of these things to happen, but she was very supportive of the legislation that changed school lunches, which, in some corners, has been a bit controversial.

Michelle Obama also got involved with the issue of military families really early on. During the campaign, she talks about having met, in many cases, women who were raising their families without their husbands who were away at war, and being really moved by their sacrifices. She wanted to do something for not only the veterans, but their families who were left behind, realizing that, like herself, most Americans don't have relatives who are serving in the military.

…Especially on social issues, she's pretty progressive, and their family talked about same-sex marriage before [the president] came out in support of gay marriage. She was for it and it was a family conversation. Even in her 2012 stump speech, before Vice President Biden came out for same-sex marriage, before the president came out for same-sex marriage, she was talking about not discriminating against people because of who they love. That line was in her speech. It didn't generate a lot of headlines, but she made clear where she stood on that issue.

Similarly, earlier in her time in the White House, there was this moment where she was with the first lady of Mexico in a school in the Washington, D.C., suburbs. There was a young girl who was in the audience...and she raised her hand and said to the two first ladies who were there, "What should do I do? My mom doesn't have [immigration] papers." That was a really gripping moment. It's hard to imagine that there weren't conversations back at the White House about this encounter on immigration.

I was there when she gave a speech [at Maryland's Bowie State University about the importance of education]; it was very well received. In holding those meetings, and thinking about what she would spend her time doing in addition to the healthy eating and military families, the connectivity that you could see that she had with these audiences where she was talking about issues around education became clear to her staff. They plan to develop this issue of education as one that she will be focused most closely on. She'll be working with the Department of Education to reinforce to high school students, particularly those who are still early in their high school years, that they really need to be preparing themselves for college.

MUNDY: She's also going to be sending her daughter to college [before their term ends], which is a really significant transition as a family. I don't know that we'll see much of that, but that is a significant transition.

Michelle Obama's legacy:

MUNDY: [When they leave the White House], Michelle will stay in public life somehow.... She does have a forceful and charismatic personality. What you also don't see, interestingly, [is that] when she was in high school she was terrified of public speaking. She had to work up the courage to give a public speech when Barack was running for office. She has really grown into a role of being so comfortable, having fun in giving speeches. She's [now] found the spotlight and is very comfortable in it.

She gets compared to Hillary Clinton, [but] I don't think she's like Hillary Clinton. She gets compared to Jackie Onassis, and, in some ways, because of the glamour and the arts and the harnessing of the culture, I would make more of a comparison there, actually.

THOMPSON: You could take pieces of first ladies and compare them, because there is some of the Jackie O. with the cultivation of the image and the family. Then you can see a little bit of Laura Bush [in terms of] being very popular with the base. She was also a popular fundraiser within her party. Hillary Clinton is a more difficult comparison, but I think that Michelle Obama is ambitious in her own way just as Hillary Clinton clearly is.

APPENDIX

Further Information:
www.c-span.org/FirstLadies

First Ladies' home on the Internet, where you can view each program in C-SPAN's yearlong television series, *First Ladies: Influence and Image.* The site also provides additional biographical information about each first lady, quotations, video clips from the programs, information about first ladies' historic sites, and classroom resources for teachers.

ACKNOWLEDGMENTS

First Ladies and the yearlong C-SPAN television series from which it was drawn are unique in their gathering of the contemporary historic, scholarly, and journalistic communities who are engaged in the study and preservation of the history of these interesting and important women. As such, we have many contributions to acknowledge, with apologies that no list can be inclusive of all who had roles to play in such a large undertaking.

Our academic advisors, present at the series' creation, particularly Richard Norton Smith, who first suggested the *First Ladies* series to C-SPAN. Historians Edith Mayo, William Seale, and Rosalyn Terborg-Penn also helped guide us throughout the process.

The series' editorial team, led by executive producer Mark Farkas, our programming vice president Terry Murphy, co-host Peter Slen, Andy Och, Andrew Nason, Rick Stoddard, Chellie Zou, and Shannon Rice.

The series' technical team, led by Greg Czzowitz, directed by Garrette Moore, and assisted by Yetta Myrick, Jamie Statler, Patrick Clyburn, Rick Gross, Ken Buck, and Johnny St. John, with oversight from vice president Kathy Cahill, and Dan Morton and Paul Orgel.

Our series partners at the White House Historical Association, including president Stewart McLaurin, retired president Neil Horstman, John Reilly, Leslie Jones, Bill Bushong, and Alexandra Lane.

First Ladies web site designed by C-SPAN's Yi-Pei Hseih-Easton, with guidance from Stephen Harkness.

Art work designed by Ellen Vest and Leslie Rhodes with direction from vice president Marty Dominguez and help from Ed Aymar and Rachel Katz.

In reality, all 280 C-SPAN staff members in our various departments contributed to the success of *First Ladies,* and we acknowledge their many contributions to this project.

First Ladies is our latest publishing endeavor with our friends at PublicAffairs. Thanks to Peter Osnos, founder and editor-at-large, our editor Benjamin Adams, and publisher Clive Priddle.

The First Ladies writing and editing team: Like the television series, this book has been a collaborative project. Major thanks to Molly Murchie, who was an editorial partner for initial drafts of this book, along with Peggy Keegan, Zelda Wallace, Laura Stassi, and our intern Emma Lingan. And a big cheer for project editor Marco Pavia.

Finally, with great appreciation to my longtime C-SPAN executive colleagues and friends, founder Brian Lamb, co-CEO Rob Kennedy, and counsel Bruce Collins for their support throughout the production of this book, and to our partners at the nation's cable and satellite companies, particularly our board of cable CEOs, whose ongoing support makes C-SPAN possible.

INDEX

C-SPAN's Susan Swain (center), joined by the *First Ladies* editorial team: (from left) Peggy Keegan, Zelda Wallace, Molly Murchie, and Emma Lingan.

Susan Swain was the moderator for C-SPAN's special yearlong history series, *First Ladies: Influence and Image.* Swain is C-SPAN's co-CEO and, in addition to her senior management role at the network, has been an on-camera moderator for C-SPAN for over thirty years, interviewing public officials, historians, and journalists for the public affairs network. This is her ninth book project with C-SPAN and PublicAffairs. She lives in the Washington, D.C., suburbs.

PublicAffairs is a publishing house founded in 1997. It is a tribute to the standards, values, and flair of three persons who have served as mentors to countless reporters, writers, editors, and book people of all kinds, including me.

I. F. STONE, proprietor of *I. F. Stone's Weekly*, combined a commitment to the First Amendment with entrepreneurial zeal and reporting skill and became one of the great independent journalists in American history. At the age of eighty, Izzy published *The Trial of Socrates*, which was a national bestseller. He wrote the book after he taught himself ancient Greek.

BENJAMIN C. BRADLEE was for nearly thirty years the charismatic editorial leader of *The Washington Post*. It was Ben who gave the *Post* the range and courage to pursue such historic issues as Watergate. He supported his reporters with a tenacity that made them fearless and it is no accident that so many became authors of influential, best-selling books.

ROBERT L. BERNSTEIN, the chief executive of Random House for more than a quarter century, guided one of the nation's premier publishing houses. Bob was personally responsible for many books of political dissent and argument that challenged tyranny around the globe. He is also the founder and longtime chair of Human Rights Watch, one of the most respected human rights organizations in the world.

•　　•　　•

For fifty years, the banner of Public Affairs Press was carried by its owner Morris B. Schnapper, who published Gandhi, Nasser, Toynbee, Truman, and about 1,500 other authors. In 1983, Schnapper was described by *The Washington Post* as "a redoubtable gadfly." His legacy will endure in the books to come.

Peter Osnos, *Founder and Editor-at-Large*